Basic Writing
A First Course

Basic Writing
A First Course

Peter Carino
Indiana State University

HarperCollins*Publishers*

Sponsoring Editor: Jane Kinney
Development Editor: Patricia Rossi
Project Coordination, Text and Cover Design: Carlisle Publishers Services
Cover Illustration: Interface Studio
Production: Michael Weinstein
Compositor: Carlisle Communications, Ltd.
Printer and Binder: R. R. Donnelley & Sons Company
Cover Printer: New England Book Components

Basic Writing: A First Course

Acknowledgments

"What's Wrong With Black English?" by Rachel L. Jones, NEWSWEEK, 12/27/82. Copyright © 1982 Rachel L. Jones. Reprinted by permission of the author.

Paul Roberts, UNDERSTANDING ENGLISH. NY: Harper & Row, Publishers, Inc., 1958, pp. 315–317.

"The Maker's Eye: Revising Your Own Manuscripts" by Donald M. Murray, THE WRITER. Copyright © 1973 Donald M. Murray. Reprinted by permission of the author and Roberta Pryor, Inc.

ISBN 0-673-46232-3
ISBN 0-673-53586-X

Library of Congress Cataloging-in-Publication Data

Carino, Peter.
    Basic writing: a first course / Peter Carino.
        p.   cm.
    Includes index.
    ISBN 0–673–46232–3
    1. English language—Rhetoric.   2. English language—
Grammar—1950-   I. Title.
PE1408.C29567   1990
808'.042—dc20

90-5082
CIP

91 92 93 9 8 7 6 5 4 3 2

Contents

Preface xvii

chapter four
The Process of Writing Essays 75

unit three
Writing Paragraphs and Sentences 145

chapter seven
Writing Body Paragraphs 147

chapter eight
Writing Introductions and Conclusions 169

chapter nine
Sentence Structure 185

chapter ten
Writing Good Sentences 221

chapter fifteen
Editing Verb Forms 339

chapter sixteen
Editing Pronoun Problems 367

chapter seventeen
Editing Misused Words 385

Preface

As the title indicates, *Basic Writing: A First Course* is designed for basic writers who have come to college underprepared: traditional students who had inadequate high school training or nontraditional students whose skills have become rusty in the years since high school. Many texts for such students have drilled them in grammatical principles before taking them through a series of exercises, perhaps leading to the writing of short paragraphs. Scholarship in composition and rhetorical theory, however, has repeatedly argued that accomplished writers do not learn to write in incremental steps aiming toward an abstract notion of an essay. A central principle of the now entrenched process approach is that students learn to write by writing. *Basic Writing* subscribes to this premise. Thus, without overwhelming beginning writers, it launches them immediately into writing whole pieces of discourse as they gradually learn to polish and refine them.

The text is organized in five units designed to develop students' abilities to manage global and local matters. Unit I, The Writing Process, provides a brief overview of the process, offers several strategies for invention, defines writing situations, and instructs students in managing general and specific language. Unit II, Writing Essays, focuses on the writing of short essays using the writing process and provides instruction in applying the process to timed writings, such as impromptu essays and examination questions. In Unit III, Writing Paragraphs and Sentences, students learn to refine the parts that form the whole. Unit IV, Revision, synthesizes and expands upon the discussions of revision throughout the earlier units before concluding with examples of two students' revisions. Unit V, Editing, serves as a handbook that students can refer to throughout the semester and from which teachers at any point can develop mini-lessons to address a grammatical problem that may be troubling most of the class.

In addition to its global-to-surface, large-to-small organization, *Basic Writing* contains several features to help beginners acquire the knowledge and experience they will need as they enter the standard composition course:

> **Discussion of the writing process** that breaks it into manageable parts while recognizing its recursiveness and respecting the idiosyncrasies of individual writers.

Manageable but challenging writing assignments that place students in rhetorical situations and ask them to write in response to their own experiences and observations.

Student essays at the end of each unit that serve to reinforce principles taught in the unit, stimulate class discussion, and provide models for writing.

Treatment of the modes as strategies for invention rather than formulas to be followed.

Numerous exercises using both models and the students' own writing, many of which lead students to a completed piece of writing.

Discussion of dialect variation that provides a context for the treatment of errors as deviations from standard English rather than as the mistakes of the underprepared.

Glossaries of key terms following each chapter to enable students to talk about their writing and review the material under consideration.

A friendly style that acknowledges the reading abilities of basic writers without condescending to them.

It is impossible to identify all the people who have contributed to this book: my many colleagues in the field whose work has influenced my own directly or indirectly and my colleagues at Indiana State University who have used materials that became part of this text or who have engaged me in discussions of it. I am further indebted to the many others whose influence was more direct and identifiable. I would especially like to thank Ann Smith and Tisha Rossi for their work during the initial stages of the project, Ben Jordan for his support once the project was underway, Sue Baugh for her guidance and good sense during the reviewing process, and Stephen Calvert for the careful polishing of the manuscript in the final stages of the project. I must also thank the reviewers whose careful attention to and astute comments on the manuscript in various stages often challenged me to rethink and revise my assumptions and approaches: Jan Barshis, Helen Gilbart, Kate Kiefer, Ellen Andrews Knodt, Judith Olson-Fallon, and Mary Sue Ply.

Finally, I must thank those who are perhaps most deserving of my gratitude: the many students whose questions, comments, and suggestions put much of the material here to the test when it was still in the form of classroom handouts. I must thank particularly those students whose writing appears in the pages of this book.

Peter Carino

unit one
The Writing Process

Writing can be thought of in two ways: as a thing, a finished **product** on paper, or as an activity, a **process** that a person goes through. When students say their writing is good or that it is bad, usually they are talking about their written products—completed pieces of writing—instead of the process it took to produce the writing. It's obvious that this is so because in order to know their writing is good or bad, they have to have finished it and received comments from others. The finished piece of writing—the product—is important because it must communicate the writer's purpose and message clearly to the reader.

Unlike the finished product, which can be read and evaluated, the writing process is the activity, from start to finish, that results in the product. Without the process, there could not be a product, but students who say their writing is good or bad rarely are referring to their writing process. They do not realize that the quality of the product—the completed piece of writing—depends a great deal on the quality of the process. If the writer's process is bad, the product will likely be bad, too.

Most of the time, beginning writers feel that they cannot learn to write well because they think that experienced writers just write ideas down, and by some miracle of talent the finished paper is organized, clear, and correct. When beginners write, they try to do what they think good writers do: just sit down and write. They begin by staring at a blank page and thinking. Then they write a sentence or two, crumple up the paper, and start over. They do this three, four, five, *ten* times and break out in a sweat. Then they try again. But this time, they are so frustrated and angry that they don't care how the writing sounds or whether they are getting their ideas down clearly; they just want to get finished. Their minds are on the product rather than on the process needed to make it. So they keep writing, maybe crossing out a word or a sentence here and there. Then they copy the paper over neatly, and that's the final product. Some students call this the crumple-and-sweat method of writing. Other students, however, have learned better ways to go about the writing process and have saved a lot of sweat and paper.

The Writing Process

Experienced writers write well because they have mastered a process for planning, drafting, revising, and editing their writing. Your instructor probably will refer to the writing process very often. Actually, each writer has his or her own process because there are different ways to make the product. There are good processes and bad ones, like the crumple-and-sweat approach. Though experienced writers' processes may differ somewhat, the process usually contains four parts: **invention, drafting, revising,** and **editing.** Later chapters will say a great deal about the writing process; for now, let's get a general idea of each.

Invention

Invention is the part of the process when the writer is planning the paper and coming up with ideas. Most invention is usually done *before* the writer begins writing. Thus, invention is sometimes called *prewriting*. Invention involves everything from thinking about the paper to be written as you are driving a car to jotting down brief lists of ideas to adding ideas that occur to you as you write the first draft. We will look at a number of strategies for invention in Chapter 1. For now, remember that without some type of planning—without invention—you will be left staring at a blank piece of paper trying to come up with ideas, and that is too difficult for even the best writers.

Drafting

Drafting involves your first efforts to write the sentences and paragraphs that will make up the paper. When you draft a paper, you are usually working alone, but there are several tips you can follow to make drafting easier.

When you draft a paper in fact, any time you write—you should create a comfortable writing environment. If you like silence when you write, find a quiet place such as the library. Or you may like to write with a certain amount of background sound—for example, music from a radio or the sound of a TV program. This is fine if it helps you write, but make sure it does not distract you.

Choose your tools as carefully as you choose your environment. Some writers prefer to draft in pencil, some in pen. Other writers prefer to draft on a typewriter or a word processor. By discovering what tools you write best with, you make writing more of a routine, thus reducing some of the difficulty of producing a draft. Of course, your teacher sometimes will specify the kind of paper, ink, or type for the final copy of a paper or for writing done in class. But when you draft, use whatever tools make you most comfortable.

While drafting, stop every so often to read your writing. Studies show that experienced writers read and reread their drafts much more often than beginners. Reading and rereading a draft helps you know what you have said and what you have left to say, where you have been and where you are going. You do not have to read every paragraph after you write it, but it is wise to read each page as you finish it and occasionally read the entire draft from the beginning.

When you have completed a draft, have others read it. Don't be shy. Ask a friend or family member. Even if this person is not a writing expert, his or her reaction as a reader can help you learn whether the draft needs to be clearer or better organized. In a writing class, some teachers may collect and comment on all the students' drafts before the final copies are written. Some writing teachers also set aside days when the students read and comment on one another's drafts. Whatever the case, get as many readers and as much feedback as you can before you revise your draft.

You will also need to plan your time, so get familiar with your writing habits. Given a paper that will require two hours of drafting, some people can work a half hour a day over four days. Another writer might not be able to keep a train of thought on this schedule and would do better by setting aside two hours to work continuously. Also, some people simply write faster than others and are able to set aside less time. As you gain experience in writing, you will learn how much time you need to complete a particular paper. But plan on a little more time than you think you need so that you will have enough time to deal with unexpected problems. When you plan your time, consider that you will probably take breaks from drafting. These breaks may include pacing around the room trying to think of words or ideas or having a cup of coffee and forgetting about the paper in order to come back to it fresh. If you use breaks wisely, they can help make the writing easier.

Because you will want to make changes in your draft, leave plenty of room on the paper. Some writers like to write on every other line so they can make changes on the blank lines in between. Other writers leave wide margins where they can make notes and changes. If you are typing or writing on a computer, use double-spacing. Whatever you do, avoid crowding the page. You will need room for changes, and a crowded page is also more difficult to read when you revise and edit.

Revision

You may have heard the word revision applied to writing. Notice that it contains the word *vision*. In its most exact sense, the word *revision* means *reseeing*. When writers revise, they resee their draft and make changes. These changes are often major ones: adding a whole paragraph or more, taking out one or more paragraphs, changing the order of the paragraphs, adding or taking out whole sentences, rewriting sentences to make them smoother, changing words, and so on. Writers revise, in other words, to improve the content (what is being said) and the style (how it's being said) of their writing.

Although you may do a little revising as you are drafting, revision usually follows drafting. And unless you are facing an immediate deadline, you should let some time pass between when you finish the draft and when you begin to revise—at least two hours, preferably a whole day, so that you can "resee" the paper. Setting aside time between drafting and revising will enable you to see the paper as it really is, not as you *think* it is.

As you revise your draft, think about the purpose and main idea of your paper. If you find that your draft does not follow what you planned to say during invention, you may have to add or cut material to get the paper back on track. On the other hand, if you find that what you said in the draft—though different from your original plan—is what you want to say, stick with the ideas you discovered while drafting, cut material that does not fit, and add material to support the ideas you want the reader to understand.

As you gain experience, you will develop your ability to revise your papers. Unit IV will provide you with many strategies for revision. For now, remember that writing experts say that "good writing is rewriting."

Editing

Beginning writers sometimes confuse editing with revision or lump the two together. Editing is the point in the process when the writer looks for and corrects misspelled words and errors in grammar and punctuation, whereas revision involves changes—sometimes major ones—in the content and style of the writing. If you remember this important difference, you will write better papers.

It may come as a surprise to you, but good grammar is not the most important thing in writing. One piece of writing may have no errors but be poorly organized, unclear, and lacking in ideas and examples. Another paper, with a half-dozen errors in it, might be better because it is well organized, clear, thoughtful, and developed fully with examples. Nevertheless, it is important to edit out as many errors as you can, not because errors are sins against your English teacher, but because errors distract readers.

While you draft and revise, you will do some minor editing of errors as you find them. But once you have finished your final draft, edit it once again, concentrating only on finding mistakes. You should also edit the final copy that you present to your instructor. Most instructors will not object to a *few* corrections made neatly on a final copy.

You may already know that one difficulty in writing is that there are many possible errors you can make. Unit V of this book covers those errors and shows you ways to correct them. Although the unit on editing comes last in the book, refer to it whenever you have trouble with a point of grammar. You might not become a grammar expert, but you can reduce distracting errors.

You may feel that you make a lot of errors, but most beginners actually make only a few—they just keep making them over and over. Reducing errors takes time, but an **error log** can help. An error log is a notebook in which you record your errors so that you can try to avoid them in future writing. When your teacher returns a graded essay to you, read and think about his or her comments on its content, form, and style and then reread the paper. Then write down in your error log the kinds of errors you made. Next to each error you record, rewrite the sentence correctly with the help of the discussion of the error in Unit V. Before you edit your next paper, review the error log carefully for the errors you made on the previous paper. After you have written a few papers and recorded your errors in the log, you will begin to see which points of grammar you need to study. Eliminating all errors takes time and experience, but if you use the error log, you will reduce your errors greatly.

Overlap in the Process

We have been discussing the writing process as a series of steps that a writer performs. In general, the process works this way: You start with invention (coming up with ideas to write about), draft your paper, revise it, and edit it before you type a final copy. In this way, the process does go along step by step. On the other hand, the parts of the process often overlap, and you may find yourself involved in more than one at the same time.

Suppose you are drafting a paper and you find you have misspelled a word or made a punctuation error. When you stop to correct this error, you are editing. Or suppose you have jotted down a list of points before writing and you think you have them all, but as you are drafting the paper, you discover other important points that you feel should be made. Coming up with these points is part of invention, but here you have come up with them after you have started drafting. Similarly, even though you revise *after* completing a draft, you might make some major changes in sentences and paragraphs *as* you are drafting. So as you can see, the writing process does not always proceed step by step. In fact, it can get quite messy.

If you do not have much writing experience, the messiness of the process may disturb you. Some students write well but think they are not good writers because they have to go through so many steps. They become discouraged because their notes and drafts contain scratched-out words and sentences or words and sentences added between the lines. These students see all the changes as errors, when in fact these marks are necessary to make the writing clear. These students are using the writing process as they should. Yet they see themselves as poor writers because they do not know that—except for a few extremely talented people—most good writers have to go through these steps, too. The writing process may be messy, but in the end it makes you a better writer. And the best thing about the process is that it can be learned.

Computers and the Writing Process

Computers have affected almost everything in our society. They have also influenced the way many people write. Writing on computers is commonly called **word processing.** If your school has computers available for writing, your instructor may require you to use one and provide instruction for doing so. Even if you are not required to use a computer to write, you should learn how to use one if you can. There are many different word-processing programs, as well as programs specially designed to help you with the writing process. Your school may have one or more of these that you can use.

When you write on a computer, the words you type on the keyboard appear on the screen of a monitor. After you have finished a draft, you can then have the computer print out the draft in typed copy. Once you have the typed copy, you can read through it and think about possible revisions. You can then put the writing back up on the screen and make the necessary changes. For instance, using the computer, you can add, cut, or move words, sentences, and even full paragraphs—all with a few strokes on the keyboard. You can then print out your revised writing a second time, and you can revise again and again if needed, all in a very short time. In this way, computers can make writing much easier and faster.

Some words of warning, though. As you type a draft on a computer, you will do some editing and revision as you go along, just as you do when you write a draft by hand. But before you revise and edit your paper, it is wise to print a copy first and make changes on it before you make the changes on the screen. Be careful, however. Because the printout of your draft is neat and clean and has a finished look—unlike a messy hand-written draft—you may think you are done when you are only getting started. Though computers cannot do our writing *for* us, they can make writing easier.

chapter one
Invention Strategies

When you think of the word invention, you usually think of such things as the telephone, the electric light, the automobile, or any other technological advance. In grade school, you probably learned about how Bell invented the telephone and Edison invented the electric light. These people were inventors in the most common sense of the word. But the word also can have a broader meaning, one that applies to the writing process. If you look up the word *invention* in any dictionary, at least one of the definitions will say something like "to think up, to conceive, or to produce in the mind." This definition fits the writing process because writers, before actually putting pen to paper, must think up, conceive, or produce in their minds what they want to say.

Sometimes writers know exactly what they want to say about a topic before writing a single word. For example, a reporter covering a fire makes notes about the location of the fire, the time it occurred, the amount of time it took firefighters to put it out, the number of fire companies responding to the alarm, the extent of property damage, and the number, identities, and ages of any people killed or injured. The reporter, as a result of careful observation, has "produced in the mind" what he or she needs to write the story about the fire.

Other times, writers may not be so sure of what they want to say, and here invention strategies help. As a beginning writer, you may be assigned to write about something that will require you to be a careful and thoughtful observer. Although many people may witness a fire, the reporter, as a trained observer, is the one who can come up with the material necessary for a good newspaper story. Sometimes, as a beginning writer, you may be asked to write on a subject that requires you to be a careful observer, and although you may not be a trained observer like the reporter, you can use your powers of observation as you "invent" what you want to say.

Let's assume your teacher has assigned you to write about water pollution in a local river. At first, you may think you know very little about this subject and will have a hard time writing anything about it. However, upon going to the river in question, you see beer cans and old tires floating downstream, dead fish along the shoreline, a chemical slick on the surface, and a murky brown color to the water. With these observations, you have been engaging in invention—you have been finding things to write about.

Careful observation is one activity that contributes to invention. But sometimes you cannot completely observe the subject you want to write about. A fire or a polluted river is something **concrete.** When we say something is concrete, we mean that we can experience it through the senses: see it, hear it, smell it, touch it, or taste it. At other times, a subject may be **abstract,** meaning that you experience it mostly as an idea in your mind. Take the word *democracy.* On the one hand, you can experience democracy concretely in actions and events that you associate with it: voting, reading what you want, saying what you please about elected officials, choosing your own religion—or choosing not to be religious at all. On the other hand, you have an abstract idea about democracy that is broader than your experiences living in a country that claims to be a democracy. When you write about an abstract subject, you can use your experiences and observations, but you will also have to develop ideas beyond your experiences.

Whether the subject you are writing about is concrete, abstract, or somewhere in between, you will need to use some kind of invention strategy to develop what you want to write before you write. **Invention strategies** are methods writers use for developing ideas to write about and for coming up with details to support the ideas. Invention strategies will not always work the same way or lead to the same idea. But they are more efficient than trial and error. Invention strategies are used before you write a first draft and sometimes while you draft. We will look at a few types of invention strategies. As you gain practice using them, you can decide which one is the best for you.

Brainstorming Lists

You may have heard the word *brainstorm* before. In a broad sense, it refers to a sudden idea. In using **brainstorming lists** in the writing process, the writer thinks of the topic to be written about and then quickly lists in single words or short phrases all the facts or ideas that suddenly come to mind. When you choose a subject yourself, you often know quite a bit about it or you would not have chosen it. In this case, you brainstorm to get down what you know. But suppose you are assigned a subject that you believe you do not know much about. In this case, brainstorming lists can help you find out what you do know. For instance, suppose in a psychology class the instructor asks you to write a personal-experience paper on some aspect of family relations. You may feel you know little about the subject, but as a member of your own family and as someone who has observed other families, you can begin to make a list of what you do know. Your list might look something like this one:

> father–son relationships
> brother–sister relationships
> fights among family members
> sharing of chores
> single-parent families
> father–daughter relationships
> mother–son relationships
> financial responsibilities
> brother–brother relationships
> rivalries among siblings
> family traditions
> age differences in children
> parents' rules for children
> family meals
> family recreation
> loyalty to family vs. loyalty to peers
> domestic violence
> effect of family size on relationships
> sister–sister relationships
> mother–daughter relationships
> large vs. small families
> spanking
> change in family relationships as members age

This list saves the writer from the helpless feeling that he or she does not know anything about the topic. In fact, there is so much on the list that the writer—given time and more information—could probably write a book on family relationships. The writer will have to sort out the items on the list and decide exactly what he or she wants to say on the subject.

Exercise 1.1

Choose one of the subject areas below and make a brainstorming list.

1. air pollution
2. Compact Disks
3. television game shows
4. quitting smoking
5. gun control
6. traffic
7. starting college
8. infants
9. managing money
10. crime

Once you have created a brainstorming list, sort it out by grouping similar items together. The list on family relations might be grouped like this:

> Relationships among parents and children
>> father–son relationships
>> father–daughter relationships
>> mother–son relationships
>> mother–daughter relationships
>> parents' rules for children
> Relationships among siblings
>> brother–sister relationships
>> brother–brother relationships
>> sister–sister relationships
>> rivalries
>> age differences in children
> Family sharing
>> sharing of chores
>> financial responsibilities
>> family meals
>> family traditions
>> family recreation

Other
  loyalty to family vs. loyalty to peers
  domestic violence
  effect of family size on relationships
  spanking
  change in family relationships as members age

Exercise 1.2

Group the list you made in exercise 1.1 into related categories.

Once you have grouped lists, you can begin to narrow the subject of family relationships down to a topic for an essay. First, ask yourself which group seems most interesting to you. About which do you feel you have the most important things to say? Let's say the writer of this paper chooses to focus on relationships among brothers and sisters. She could now make another brainstorming list. As she makes this second list, she would be wise to look at the items on the total list. Do any of them also relate to her topic? For instance, "age differences" is under the category "other," but could it affect sibling relationships? Also, could parental treatment of siblings affect the way they relate to one another? Once the writer has considered such questions, she can make a second list, which might look something like this:

  have to babysit younger brother
  older brothers are protective
  compete with brothers in school
  compete with them in sports
  tough being a middle child and the only girl
  older brother's friends can be attractive or annoying
  age is a big factor
  brother a lot younger is like kid to be taken care of
  little brother fun to play with
  fun to help little brother with schoolwork
  can boss little brother around
  older brother acts like parent
  little brother gets most attention from parents

older brother's ''breaking rules'' makes it easier for me
older brother helps with problems

Exercise 1.3

Choose a narrow topic from your grouped list and make another brainstorming list.

If you look at the last list on family relationships, you can begin to see a purpose emerging. That is, the young woman's list begins to show the advantages and disadvantages of being the middle sibling between two brothers. Also, you can begin to see how she uses her concrete experiences and observations in this position to narrow the topic and find something to write about the abstract subject of family relations. She is not yet ready to write, however. Just as the first list was sorted into categories, this one needs to be sorted the same way. For example:

Advantages of having a little brother
little brother fun to play with
fun to help him with schoolwork
can boss him around
Disadvantages of having a little brother
have to babysit him
brother a lot younger is like kid to be taken care of
little brother is parents' favorite
Advantages of having an older brother
older brother is protective
older brother's friends can be attractive
older brother's ''breaking rules'' makes it easier for me
older brother helps with problems
Disadvantages of having an older brother
his protectiveness is sometimes unwanted
some of his friends are annoying
Other
compete with brothers in school

compete with them in sports

tough being a middle child and the only girl

age is a big factor

Exercise 1.4

Grouping related items, sort the list you made in exercise 1.3.

This last list on family relationships divides the young woman's points into categories that can become part of her paper. She could organize the paper by first writing about the advantages and disadvantages of having a little brother and then about the advantages and disadvantages of having an older brother. That leaves the category marked "other."

Sometimes information in such a category can be left out, but here it can be worked into the other categories. For example, age is a big factor when she discusses the attractiveness of her older brother's friends because if he is a lot older than her, his friends would not be interested in her at all. Also, if she is only a year or two older than her little brother, it is unlikely that she would have to babysit him much. Likewise, the points on competing in school and in sports with her brothers could be worked in. For example, if playing basketball with her brothers helped her become a better player, the competition would be an advantage. But if trying to compete in sports was a means to compete for her parents' attention, then the competition could be a disadvantage. The point that it is tough being a middle daughter between two brothers relates generally to both categories on the disadvantages, so if the writer decided she wanted to stress disadvantages, this point could serve as the main idea of the whole essay. Thus, she might place it at the beginning of the essay to show the reader her purpose in writing.

Given these brainstorming lists, this young woman could begin drafting her essay. However, she could also brainstorm further, making lists of details on each point to ensure that her essay would be developed enough to achieve her purpose. For example, on the point of her older brother's friends being annoying, she could make the following list:

friends teased me when I was young

called me tomboy in sports

didn't always want to let me play with them

friends I did not like tried to date me when I was older

friends tried to find out things about my girlfriends

If this writer were to make such a list for every point, her paper would be nearly written. Of course, she would need to write out her points in sentences and paragraphs, but because of her thorough brainstorming, she would not be staring at a blank page and wondering what to say about family relationships. She would have a topic, a purpose, and plenty of information to write a well-developed paper.

Exercise 1.5

Choose one point from your last list and brainstorm further to add details on that point.

Making all these lists and sorting them may seem difficult and time-consuming. But think of the alternative: staring at a blank page and writing by trial and error, which takes even more time and is not likely to result in a good product when you are done.

Of course, the more you know about a topic, the easier it is to brainstorm. However, even when you think you know nothing about a topic, brainstorming helps you recall what you really do know—and often you know a lot more than you think you do. Brainstorming is also helpful when the topic is very broad and general, as the topic on family relationships was. The lists can help you narrow the topic, decide on your purpose, and put your information in an order that your reader can follow and use.

Clustering

Clustering is another strategy for invention. It is similar to brainstorming in that you begin with a broad topic and write down whatever you think of regarding that topic. But when you use clustering, you create diagrams. These diagrams are helpful for people who like to see things in images. When you cluster, you write the topic in the middle of the page and draw a circle around it. Then you draw spokes coming out from the circle, and at the end of each spoke, you put one of the things that comes to mind as you are thinking about the topic. Here is an example of a cluster on the broad subject of rock music:

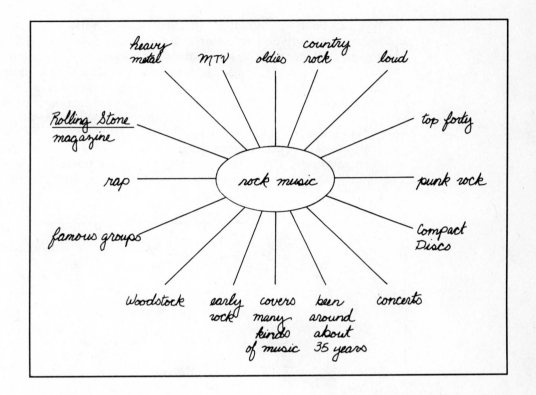

Exercise 1.6

Choose one of the subjects below and explore it with a cluster diagram.

1. high school teachers
2. college teachers
3. fast food restaurants
4. mass transit
5. films
6. shopping malls
7. automobiles
8. baseball
9. T-shirts
10. July 4th

You may have noticed on the diagram on rock music or on the one you did in the exercise that you could think of even more points to add to the cluster. Some writers do not like clustering diagrams because they can't hold as much as a brainstorming list. That may be true in some cases, but writers who prefer diagrams to lists just use bigger sheets of paper. These writers prefer clustering because they believe you can usually see and sort your points more easily than you can with a list. Depending on your purpose, you can then take a point and expand on it again using the cluster.

Suppose you looked over the diagram on rock music and decided to write on heavy metal music. You now have narrowed down the subject and can make a cluster diagram to explore heavy metal music as a topic:

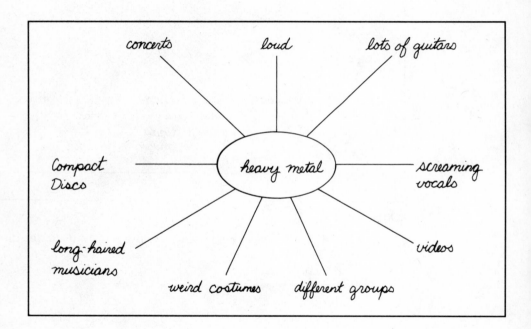

Exercise 1.7

Pick one item from your first cluster, place it at the center, and start a second cluster.

With the second cluster on heavy metal, you have a narrower topic, but there is still too much to cover in an essay. So you should pick the item that interests you most and make a third cluster. For example:

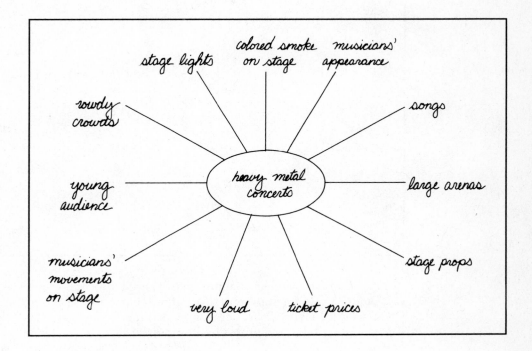

Exercise 1.8

Pick one item from the cluster you made for exercise 1.7 and cluster it further.

The cluster focused on heavy metal concerts brings you close to the point where you can begin writing, but first you need to decide on a purpose and a main idea. Looking over this diagram, you could decide that heavy metal concerts are a very exciting experience for young people or that they might be quite shocking to some adults. Once you have a main idea for your essay, cluster each item further. For example, if you are trying to show how heavy metal concerts can be shocking, you might come up with the following cluster on their appearance:

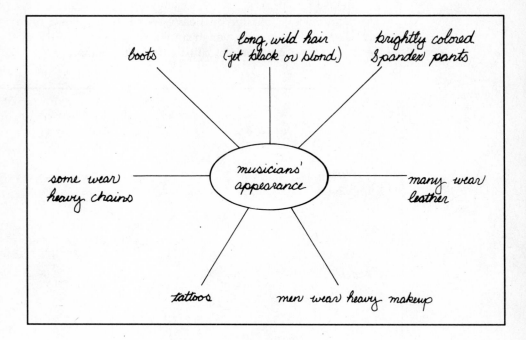

If you made a cluster diagram like this one for each section of your paper, you would have much of your work done before facing that blank page. Clustering works well if you are someone who likes to think in images rather than in straight lines. Whether clustering or brainstorming is the better invention strategy depends on what you as a writer find easier and more effective.

Exercise 1.9

From your earlier clusters, come up with a main idea about your topic. With this idea in mind, cluster each item further.

Freewriting

Both brainstorming and clustering require you to jot down notes, either in lists or in diagrams. Freewriting, in contrast, is an invention strategy in which you take the broad topic and begin writing whatever comes into your head as quickly as you can, preferably without stopping. Don't worry about spelling, grammar, sentence structure, or the order of your ideas; just get the ink flowing and the ideas down. Don't ignore any idea that comes into your head. Of course, you will have to worry about spelling, sentence structure, and so on later, but when you freewrite, the emphasis is on the word *free*—freeing your mind for invention. A piece of freewriting on the subject of T-shirts might look like this:

> Almost everybody wears t-shirts. I see even senior citizens wearing them. An older woman in Atlantic City had one on that said, "I beat the slots at Bally's Casino." It seemed a little funny, but she seemed to be having fun with it. A lot of t-shirts are fun. They have crazy sayings on them or funny pictures, like Garfield or Farside comics. Also there's the ones with places, so people can show where they have been. Vacation souvenirs. It's funny that t-shirts used to be just for underwear—and just plain white. But there were the old colored ones with a pocket, mostly for work. I wonder when people started to wear t-shirts with things on them, like the funny sayings and pictures. I think it started with school shirts. Students are big on t-shirts. They wear all kinds with school names and logos, and they wear the ones with rock groups on. In my high school, it was against the rules to wear any t-shirt with an alcohol advertisement on it. There are alot of them, especially Budweiser or the black Jack Daniels shirts. It's funny people become like billboards for products or with the ones with the funny sayings, it's like they are trying to tell everybody about themselves. It's an identity thing, showing where you go to school, where you have visited, what products you like, or what kind of attitude you have with the sayings. They also have t-shirts with sports teams, so you can show who you are for. I have also seen pictures of the tie-dyed t-shirts that the hippies used to wear. They seem to be getting popular again, very colorful. Maybe that's when people started wear t-shirts other than underwear and work shirts. T-shirts are really comfortable and easy to wash—no ironing. It's hard to imagine back years ago when nobody wore them except men for underwear. They would have to wear regular shirts in the summer. You can't where t-shirts everywhere but they sure come in handy in the warm months for casual wear. They are comfortble and not that expensive, but some are.

If you read this paragraph carefully, you will find some spelling and grammar errors. Reading even quickly, you will see that the ideas are not in any logical order. The writer repeats himself about the comfort of T-shirts; the different kinds are mentioned as they come to the writer; and more than once he wonders when people started wearing T-shirts other than as underwear. In short, the points are put down just as the writer thought of them. That's fine. That's the way to use freewriting—to get started, to overcome that blank page.

Exercise 1.10

Choose one of the subjects from the previous list, and freewrite on it for at least ten minutes. Try to write nonstop, and do not worry about the order of ideas or the correctness and quality of your sentences.

Freewriting is a good start, but then the writer needs to figure out his or her purpose and audience and pick out the ideas that are most interesting and important. The writer can then pick out a main idea for the paper and look for other information in the freewriting to support it.

Let's return to the freewriting on T-shirts. Suppose the writer picked out all the different kinds of T-shirts people wear. He might come up with a list like this one:

> People wear sports team shirts to show which teams they root for.
>
> People wear school shirts to show which school they attend or identify with.
>
> T-shirts with sayings reflect an attitude.
>
> People identify with products printed on t-shirts.

From this list, the writer could begin to form a main idea. Obviously one idea suggested by this list is that people wear all kinds of T-shirts. But this idea is too obvious to be interesting. It does not tell readers anything they do not already know. But if you look back over the freewriting, you can also find an idea that relates to why people wear all kinds of t-shirts: The writer says, "It's an identity thing." This might work better as a main idea because it explores why people wear different shirts. Once the writer has a main idea in mind, he can freewrite on each of the individual points. Freewriting on why people wear shirts with sayings on them might look like this:

> Many people wear T-shirts with sayings on them that show a certain attitude. I remember seeing a biker with a shirt reading "I had to come back from the dead because God wouldn't let me in heaven, and the devil was afraid I'd take over hell." He was not someone I would mess with. I wouldn't want him to date my sister either. Other T-shirts are more cheerful—like the guy who wore one with a funny-looking clown face on it that said "Crazy world, ain't it." He seemed like he would be a real joker. I

saw this woman with one on that simply said "foxy and expensive" in glitter writing. I guess she was really into herself. Another woman had one on that said, "When God created man, She laughed." Feminist humor.

Even though the writer needs to revise this paragraph, he has a section of the paper moving toward completion.

Compared to brainstorming and clustering, freewriting has both advantages and disadvantages. Some of the advantages are that the act of writing, as opposed to listing, tends to generate more ideas and occasionally produces details that develop the ideas more than a list does. On the other hand, some writers feel that writing sentences slows down their thoughts, whereas listing speeds them up. Of course, you can combine strategies. You might freewrite on a topic, pick out an important idea from the freewriting, and then make a brainstorming list or cluster diagram for that idea. Or you might start with a cluster diagram or brainstorming list and then freewrite on one of the items from the diagram or list. Once again, the choice is yours. As you gain experience, you will find the best strategy to fit your personality and habits.

Exercise 1.11

Pick out three or four related items from the freewriting you did in the last exercise. Try to come up with a main idea that these items could support. With your main idea in mind, freewrite on one of the items.

The Journalist's Questions: Five W's + H

The journalist's questions are another invention strategy that newspaper reporters have been using for many years. These questions can enable you to explore and limit a topic and to come up with the ideas and details needed for writing. To use this strategy, simply ask:

> Who?
> What?
> When?
> Where?
> Why?
> How?

Below is the opening paragraph of a magazine article. Notice how the answers to the journalist's questions—the five *W*'s + *H*—are evident even in the short space of a few lines:

---

when →   At about sunset on a cold wintry day in early

December 1958, a black <u>woman named Rosa</u>   *who*

how   <u>Parks</u> <u>wearily</u> <u>boarded a Montgomery city bus</u> on   *what*

where   <u>her way home</u> <u>after a hard day's work.</u>   <u>Her feet</u>   *when*

what   <u>ached</u> <u>from standing and walking</u> on the job for   *why*

who   eight hours.   <u>As Rosa Parks</u> <u>boarded the bus,</u> she   *what*

how   <u>instinctively</u> <u>went for the first empty seat.</u>   *what*

Robert L. Satcher, Sr., *"Reflections on the Montgomery Bus Boycott"*

The rest of the article went on to discuss Rosa Parks's arrest for not sitting in the back of the bus, how her arrest resulted in blacks boycotting Montgomery buses, and how Martin Luther King, Jr. played a major role in the boycott.

Exercise 1.12

Label information in the paragraph below according to how it answers the questions about who, what, when, where, why, and how.

Bangkok, Thailand. Six U.S. military experts returned to Bangkok on Sunday after working with Vietnamese officials to resolve the fates of missing American soldiers, a U.S. Embassy spokesman said.

Associated Press, May 1, 1989

You may not be planning to become a reporter, but the journalist's questions can help you generate and organize ideas for almost any kind of writing you do.

You can use the journalist's questions, like other invention strategies, to explore broad topics and then continue using them to narrow the topic and develop parts of your paper.

Let's start with the broad subject of intramural sports:

Who?	College students
What?	Can join and play various intramural sports
When?	During the various sports seasons: football in the fall, basketball in winter, softball in the spring
Where?	At college facilities
Why?	To get exercise, have fun, and meet people
How?	By forming a team with friends and registering with the school's intramural office

If you put these notes together, you can come up with a pretty good main idea for an essay: College students can get exercise, have fun, and meet new people by playing intramural sports any time of the year. With this sentence, you have a good start. Your purpose would also be clear: informing other students of the advantages of playing intramural sports.

In using the journalist's questions, you probably noticed that there was less thinking and sorting out. That's true because you started with a fairly limited topic. The questions did not lead you to the topic, but they did help you put an idea down clearly and completely. Of course, next you have to generate details that expand on the advantages of intramural sports. Here again, you could pose the questions, either as a group or one at a time. Suppose you need details on finding out how to get involved in intramurals. You might try the *how* question:

How? If you live in a dorm, check the bulletin boards for notices of teams forming.

How? If you are a commuter, ask classmates what they know about intramurals.

How? Call the physical education department at your school for information.

How? Once you are on a team, attend practices and games.

By posing the question most important to each section of your essay, you could continue to come up with the details you need to make your explanations clear. For instance, under *why* in your first set of questions, you said intramural sports are a good way to get exercise. Using *why* as your question, you could then come up with reasons why the sports provide exercise. For example, playing basketball is a good aerobic exercise.

As an invention strategy, the journalist's questions are a more structured method of ordering ideas. Their disadvantage is that usually you have to limit the topic somewhat before the questions can help you. Their advantage, however, is that—unlike clustering, brainstorming, or freewriting—they help you see relationships between ideas. For instance, if you are writing a paper in which you need to keep asking *why* questions to develop it, you are more likely to dig into the causes of *what* you are writing about. Also the questions are the same questions readers ask. Just as with the other invention strategies, you can use the journalist's questions in combination with another strategy. You might freewrite or cluster to narrow down a topic and then use the journalist's questions to explore it. Once again, the choice is yours.

Exercise 1.13

Use the journalist's questions to explore one of the topics from the previous exercises.

Invention Strategies and Drafting

We have been discussing invention strategies as the part of the writing process that you do first. As stated in the introduction to this unit, because writers usually do some invention before writing, invention is sometimes called *prewriting*. You may have heard this term in high school or in your college writing class. And although invention *usually* comes first, it can occur *during* drafting or revising. Remember also that while the parts of the writing process can be seen as steps, these steps sometimes overlap.

Let's return to the paper on being a middle sibling. As you probably remember, the writer ended up with the main idea that it was difficult being a girl with two brothers, one older and one younger. One of the disadvantages she cited was having to babysit for her younger brother. But suppose that in writing about babysitting she began to find that it also had many advantages: earning money, taking responsibility, and learning how to care for children. She would then have to change her original plan for this part of the paper. If the same thing happened with other parts of the paper—she discovered that what she thought were disadvantages were actually advantages—then she might even have to change the main idea of the paper to show that generally it was a *good* experience being the middle child with two brothers.

Remember that invention is not a formula. Sometimes you will follow your invention notes straight through a draft and revisions. But at other times you might find that you are changing your mind as you write because the act of writing itself generates ideas. When this happens, do not feel that you are getting off track or doing something wrong. Just change your plans and follow the new ideas through.

Invention Strategies and Studying

As a college student, you will be taking many examinations. While invention strategies are primarily used for writing, they can be a helpful tool for preparing for exams. Suppose you are facing an exam in a marketing class and the professor tells you the test will cover different methods for determining prices: demand-based pricing, cost-based pricing, competition-based pricing, and so on. You could use an invention strategy to study each method of pricing. For example, you could create a brainstorming list for demand-based pricing or apply the journalist's questions to examine cost-based pricing. Because the invention strategies enable you to explore a topic in detail, you would be reviewing all your knowledge of each method. If this exam consisted of essay questions (see Chapter 6), you would be involved in the writing process before even entering the classroom. Even if the exam consisted of objective questions, you would be likely to have better recall, having gone through an invention strategy.

Writing Assignment

Throughout this chapter, you have been working with topics in the exercises. Write an essay of 300–400 words from your invention notes.

Key Terms

Invention strategies: Any means that a writer uses to come up with ideas for writing. Invention strategies are generally used before writing but can be returned to during drafting or revising.

Abstract: A word, subject, or topic is abstract when you experience it as an idea rather than through the senses. Abstractions can be expressed through concrete examples, however.

Concrete: A word, subject, or topic is concrete when you can experience it through the senses. For example, speed is an abstract term, but a racing car is something concrete because you can see and hear it.

Brainstorming: An invention strategy in which a writer quickly lists anything that comes to mind about a topic.

Clustering: An invention strategy in which a writer circles the topic in the middle of a page and then draws spokes leading out to different points about the topic.

Freewriting: An invention strategy in which the writer writes anything that comes to mind about a topic as quickly as possible. When freewriting, the writer does not worry about the order of ideas, grammar, spelling, or any other feature of writing.

Journalist's questions: An invention strategy in which the writer asks of the topic: who? what? when? where? why? how?

— speaking vs. writing
— the writing situation/purpose
— writers' role

chapter two
Writing for Different Audiences

Most writing is written to be read by others. There are exceptions, of course. Someone keeping a diary or a personal journal, for example, may not want others to read his or her writing. If you freewrite during the writing process, you use the freewriting as a means of invention, not with the intention of others reading it. Except for these and similar situations, writers usually intend that someone else will read what they have written. Thus writers—whether professionals writing for publication, workers writing on the job, or students writing for school—must keep in mind that they are writing for an audience: the person or people who will read their work.

You may think of the term *audience* only in the sense that it is commonly used: to define a group of people watching a play, movie, or some other event. But the term also is used to describe communication situations. If you write a letter to a friend, your friend is the audience. If someone is speaking to you, you are the audience for that speaker. Whether you are speaking or writing, you always intend that the audience will get your point. In this sense, writing is a means of social interaction: One person writes something; others read it and react.

As you know, social interactions almost always have rules. You do not wear a tuxedo or a formal gown to a barbecue. You take a gift when you attend a wedding. In short, people expect others to behave in certain ways in social interactions. The same is true of audiences. They have expectations. By viewing writing as social interaction, you will become more aware of the needs of your audience and the requirements of the situation in which you are writing.

Speaking vs. Writing

"What did you say?" "What do you mean by that?" "Huh?" In everyday conversations, you have probably had all these questions addressed to you. When people do not understand you, the social interaction of conversation breaks down because you are not meeting your listener's needs and expectations. When we speak to people, we have the luxury of their presence. If they do not understand us, they can ask questions, and we can answer them to make ourselves clear. In writing, we do not have this luxury, unless we are present while our audience is reading our work. Except for peer-editing situations, this is rare. Thus, when writing, we have to be sure to present all that the reader needs to know and avoid the fits and starts common to speech.

When we speak, we have to think at the same time. We do not have the time for the invention or revision that makes writing clear and organized. We might speak in incomplete or run-on sentences, pause briefly to remember what we want to say, interject words that are not part of our message (uh, like, ya know). This kind of speech is common, even among the most educated people.

Examine this example of speech written down:

I was . . . uh . . . watching the news the other day. They had on a thing about the stress of education in Japan. How . . . uh . . . seriously parents and kids take it. Like . . . uh . . . little kids take these tests to get into the best kindergartens. And high school's the same. People taking . . . uh . . . these real hard tests to get in the best ones. Not like here where you go by where you live. They said . . . uh . . . that kids get all kinds of stress. Like some of them burn out on school or end up with bad nerves, ya know. College, though, is easier there. I guess cause if ya make it through high school you deserve a break. It's just the opposite of here, really.

This spoken paragraph gives us quite a bit of information, and if the listener needed more, he or she could ask the speaker. For example, who are "they" who reported the information on the news? In written form, this paragraph would have to supply any missing information as well as cut all the pauses, unnecessary words, and incomplete sentences because an audience would not expect to see such things in a piece of writing. In other words, language that is acceptable in the social interaction of conversation may not be acceptable in the social interaction of writing.

Compare the written paragraph below with the spoken paragraph, assuming that the writer is now using the information in a paper for an education class:

On March 18th, on the "Today" show, Maria Shriver reported on education in Japan. Shriver's report focussed on the stressful conditions children face as a result of the competition in the Japanese schools. Children at three and four years of age are tutored rigorously to pass entrance exams that will enable them to enter the more prestigious kindergartens. If they excel in the elementary grades, they then face another set of difficult exams if they want to enter the best high schools, unlike in the United States where students generally attend the high school nearest home. Parents pressure children to excel at all grade levels so that the kids can advance to the next level in a good school. Upon graduation from high school, Japanese students again compete for placement in colleges and universities. For some children, this competition creates extremely stressful conditions; some develop nervous disorders or even burn out on education altogether. However, if students survive their elementary and high school years, they find that the college curriculum is much more relaxed, unlike in the United States, where post-secondary education tends to be the most difficult.

The difference between this paragraph and the first should be obvious. There are no pauses, the sentence structure is smoother, and conversational vocabulary—such as the words *thing* and *really*—has been eliminated. The paragraph now reads like writing. There is also some new information: who reported on Japanese schools, when the report was presented, and on what program it appeared. In conversation, a listener could ask for this information if he or she wanted it. Here the writer gives it because she knows the professor will want to know where she got her information.

Although some material is added to the written version, there is not much other new information. In terms of presenting information, the conversational paragraph does a pretty good job. As *conversation,* it works. It would be difficult to speak the way the second paragraph is written, but through invention, revision, and editing, the writer has composed a paragraph that meets the expectations of its audience—a professor—because of the organized and specific content, the smoother sentences, and the more formal vocabulary.

Exercise 2.1

Below are two paragraphs: one is conversational, the other written. Make a list of the differences you notice. Consider the sentences, the word choice, and the general and specific language.

Abraham Lincoln's home is in Springfield, Illinois. You can visit there. It's got like all the old furniture from when he was there . . . uh . . . there's even wooden sidewalks out front. The house is pretty big, and everything is just like it was back then. Most of the furniture is from the times, but . . . uh . . . some of it really belonged to his family. It's really pretty neat.

The Lincoln home in Springfield, Illinois, is open to the public for tours conducted by the National Park Service. This two-story frame house, common for a man of Lincoln's class in the nineteenth century, has been authentically restored from the wooden sidewalks out front to the picket fence surrounding the backyard. Inside, the furniture reflects the period in every detail. Some pieces actually belonged to the Lincolns, but most are period pieces like those the family would have owned. Paint, wallpaper, and draperies all simulate the decor of the times when the Lincoln family called the place home. Touring the Lincoln home is educational and entertaining for old and young alike.

Exercise 2.2

Rewrite one of the conversational paragraphs below so that it would be more appropriate for a college-level audience of readers.

Taking the bus can be a hassle. You hafta like wait for it in cold weather. Or if it's hot . . . uh, it's really bad if it ain't like air conditioned. It's really crowded going to school in the morning with like everybody going to work. Then . . . uh . . . you might have to stand up, ya know. I uh wanna get a car as soon as I can. Really, it's a hassle everyday.

Property on the east and west coasts is like real expensive. Over a hundred thousand bucks for even just a small house, like nothing fancy. There's . . . uh . . . so many people in places like L.A. or New York and Boston, so like if you wanna buy a house, there's not many for sale and lots of people wanting to buy em. Uh . . . if you move to the south or midwest, you can buy like a really neat house for about a third less money.

The Writing Situation

Writing is produced as the result of situations. For instance, a lawyer writes a brief for the judge before a trial. A sales representative writes a monthly report to the sales manager. A marketing executive writes a market analysis for a new product. A college student writes a term paper for a sociology course. In each case, writing is produced as the result of a situation that requires writing. In each situation, social interaction takes place because the writer has a particular audience. In relation to that audience, the writer also has a **role** and a **purpose.** The writer's role and purpose, along with the **audience,** make up the **writing situation.** These parts sometimes overlap. For example, a writer may write in a particular way because all three influence the way he or she wants to sound on paper. But you can understand the parts of the writing situation better if you analyze each one separately.

Analyzing Your Role: Who Are You?

When you hear the word *role*, you may first think of actors and actresses playing roles in plays or movies. In this situation, people are being someone they are not. In your life, you play various social roles, but you are playing a role that you are. You are a student, perhaps a wife or husband, maybe a boyfriend or girl-friend, a worker, a son or daughter, or whatever. When we use the term *role* this way, we are not talking about anything phony. You can't have a role that you are not, like the actor *creating* a role in a movie. For instance, if you are not in school, you do not have the role of student. If you are not married, you do not have the role of wife or husband.

In your daily behavior, you use whatever roles you have. You act one way with friends, perhaps a slightly different way around your employer, and a still different way around children. The same is true when you find yourself in a writing situation. You have a role, and it affects the way you write. If you write a paper for a biology class, you do not use slang words because in your role as student, you know that using slang will not get you a good grade. When you write a letter to a friend, you write casually, avoiding formal language, because in your role as friend, you know that your reader expects you to be casual and familiar. If you write a letter to a senator complaining about wasted government funds, you will probably be forceful, but you will not curse because as a citizen you know that you should not use curse words when you discuss civic matters, even if you are angry.

Whenever you have a writing situation, you should take a moment to analyze your role. If you are not used to a particular role, this may be difficult. For instance, as a beginning college student, you may wonder how you should sound in that role. Sometimes students think they should use all the big words they know and write long, fancy-sounding sentences. It is fine to draw on your vocabulary, but don't use big words unless you are sure what they mean. And don't use them if a less fancy word will get the point across more clearly. As for your sentences, don't go out of your way to make them long, but combine them when you find they are so short that the writing sounds choppy or childish. And, of course, try to correct as many grammar problems as you can because in the role of college student, you will be expected to write as correctly as you can.

Exercise 2.3

Briefly describe how your role would affect your writing in each of these writing situations:

1. A letter to a company about a product you are dissatisfied with.
2. An answer to an examination question in college.
3. An advertisement for a church bake sale, to be published in your local newspaper.
4. A recipe for a friend.
5. A letter complaining to the police chief about crime in your neighborhood.

Analyzing Your Purpose: Why Are You Writing?

When students first hear the idea of **purpose** in writing, they sometimes like to joke that their purpose is to fulfill the assignment and earn a good grade. Whether the reader is a teacher in school or a boss on the job, satisfying someone who asks you to write can certainly be part of your purpose. But that's not the most important purpose.

As a writer, you should consider what effect you want your writing to have on the reader. Do you want to tell a story to entertain someone? Do you want the reader to solve a problem for you? Do you want to persuade the reader that he or she should do something you want? Do you want to tell someone how to do something? Do you want to explain how something works? Do you want to show someone what you know about a subject?

You should keep your purpose clearly in mind throughout the writing process because it, like your role, will influence the way you write. Remember the example above on writing to your senator about wasteful government spending. What is your purpose? You will be trying to persuade the senator to think about wasteful spending and do something to reduce it. Keeping this purpose in mind, you know that you will have to give examples of how the government is spending money wastefully. Do you mean money for defense? Education? Transportation? In other words, you have to provide several examples of wasteful spending or you will not achieve your purpose: to point out a problem to your representative.

Your purpose also will determine your language, much like your role does. Though you might be very angry about the government wasting your tax dollars, you do not want to be sarcastic because sarcasm can anger the representative—and as you know, people who are angry usually won't do things for you.

Good writers always keep their purpose clearly in mind. Examine the paragraph below. Written by Dawn Bryan for a magazine for business travelers, it comes from an essay explaining how Japanese gifts are wrapped:

> Gifts are usually wrapped in lovely rice paper. For formal occasions heavy white paper is used, then decorated appropriately. Packages are always crisp and clean, wrinkling is avoided, and folding is precise. There are even different folds for happy and unhappy occasions. Each gift situation requires certain colors, knots, and superscriptions. Red or gold and white cords are for happy events; black or blue and white for unhappy. After the gift is superscribed according to the occasion, the sender's name is written at the center bottom, the recipient's name in the upper left. Japanese shops will wrap the gifts suitably for the occasion and usually deliver them.

As you can tell from this paragraph, the Japanese take gift wrapping more seriously than Americans do. In Japan, it is common for business people to give each other gifts when they start and finish a business deal. The article is written for American business people who are going to Japan, and the writer's purpose is to tell them how to give gifts properly: Because wrapping gifts is so complicated, it is probably best to have it done at a shop. Perhaps, as you read the paragraph, you found it interesting, or maybe you got bored because you thought it told you more about Japanese gift wrapping than you wanted to know. Dawn Bryan wrote the article with the purpose of teaching American business people about Japanese gifts. Because gift giving in Japan is complicated, she needed to include all the details. Thus, her purpose influenced how detailed her article had to be to show Americans how the Japanese exchange gifts.

Writers can have many purposes: to inform, to teach, to persuade, to criticize, to point out a problem, to entertain, to scare, to encourage—the list could go on. Sometimes these purposes can overlap. For example, someone pointing out a crime problem in a letter to a newspaper might also criticize the police. Stephen King, a writer of horror novels, wants to entertain his readers at the same time he scares the daylights out of them. Whatever the case, if you keep your purpose, or purposes, in mind during the writing process, you will produce better writing.

Exercise 2.4

Identify the purpose(s) of the writers of the following items and briefly tell how the writer's purpose(s) might affect what he or she writes.

1. a cookbook
2. an essay against abortion
3. a newspaper story about a football game
4. a textbook
5. a comic book
6. a police report
7. a letter of application for college
8. an advertisement in a magazine
9. a newspaper story about a plane crash
10. an essay supporting abortion

Analyzing Your Audience: Who Is Reading Your Writing?

We previously defined *audience* as the reader or readers of your paper. But in a writing class, this is not always true. Sometimes your instructor may ask you to write the paper for an audience of fellow students. Although your instructor will read the paper, he or she may evaluate it in terms of how well it communicates to other students.

There are three questions you need to ask about your audience: (1) Who are the members of the audience? (2) What are the audience's attitudes toward what I am writing? and (3) How is the audience going to use my writing? These questions seem simple enough, but they raise other questions. If we analyze each question separately, we can see that it leads to other questions:

Who is the audience? In all writing situations, you know something about your audience. In some situations, you will know your audience better than you do in others. In a letter to a friend or relative, you know the audience intimately. In a paper for sociology class, you know the professor, but not in the same way you know a friend or relative. If in a college writing class you are assigned to write for fellow students, you know some things about students as a group, though what you know may not be true of every student. Even if you write a letter to a company or a government agency and you begin it with "To Whom It May Concern," you assume that someone who reads it will be able to take care of the matter covered in the letter.

You can't know everything about your audience, but as much as you can, you should try to estimate how much the audience knows about the topic of your writing. For example, if a heart surgeon wrote an article about a transplant operation to another heart surgeon, he or she could write in complex language full of medical terms and the other surgeon would understand. But if the heart surgeon wrote about the same operation in a book for a high school biology class, he or she would have to define all the terms and try to explain things in everyday language that the students can understand.

When writers forget about their audience, they usually write as if they are writing to someone exactly like themselves. And because no two people are exactly alike, the writer may fail to communicate. For example, Indiana State University is located in east-central Indiana, so it attracts students from both the northern and southern areas of the state. When students there are assigned to write papers on campus life for an audience of their fellow students, the students from the north refer to Indiana State as "down here"—"I'm glad I came down here." In contrast, the students from south of the university might write, "I am glad I came up here." We always joke that students from the north must think the university is hell and those from the south must think it is heaven. In both cases, these students are writing as if everyone is like them. The lesson to be learned is that writing won't communicate if we don't say something in a way that means the same thing to our reader as it does to us. For these students, a simple remedy would be to write "Indiana State" because all of them know what that means.

For many writers, even experienced ones, it is difficult to remember that readers are not like them. In addition to using terms the audience might not know, we often assume wrongly that the audience knows as much as we do about what we are writing about. For instance, students majoring in a particular subject sometimes write about it as if all their readers knew as much about it as they do. If you're sure that your readers do not know as much about a subject as you do, then you certainly need to explain yourself in more detail and in simpler terms. For instance, an essay written for teenagers about rock'n'roll in the Fifties would have to explain how the music, clothing, hairstyles, and instruments were different from those of modern rock bands. But if the essay were written for people who lived during the Fifties, the explanation of differences would not be necessary.

What is my audience's attitude about what I am writing?

There is always a relationship between writer and audience. Part of this relationship comes from the reader's attitudes toward what the writer is saying. Because these attitudes can vary, you, as a writer, need to raise questions about them. Will the audience be friendly and receptive toward what you are saying and inclined to agree? Will the audience be hostile and inclined to disagree? Will the audience be neutral? Given your purpose, these can be important questions.

For example, when writing to persuade your senator to look into wasteful spending, if you know he or she is in favor of spending a lot of money for defense, you will have to provide clear examples of money that was truly wasted on defense spending. On the other hand, if you know the senator has a record of opposing defense spending, your letter might not have to be as convincing.

You already are familiar with this feature of audience from your daily encounters with others. If you need to borrow some money and you have one friend who is generous with money and another who is careful, you probably will use different approaches when asking each friend for a loan. With the careful friend, you might go into more detail about how, and how soon, you would pay back the loan.

How is my audience going to use my writing?

Just as writers write for a purpose, readers read for a purpose. The reader's purpose may be general, as is the case when someone reads the newspaper to be informed. Or the reader's purpose may be very specific, as is the case when someone reads a recipe for a chicken casserole or directions for fixing a carburetor. In both cases, readers *use* the writing. If you read a book of jokes, you are using it to entertain yourself. An economics professor reading an examination will use the writing to evaluate the student's knowledge of economics.

As a writer, you need to consider what the audience needs to know to use the writing the way you want it used. With the letter about wasteful government spending, the senator—before deciding to look into the matter—needs to know exactly where the money is being wasted, who is wasting it, and how the waste could be prevented. To learn whether a student knows about a particular principle of economics, the professor needs a clear explanation of the theory and examples of how it functions in the world of finance.

The way you want your audience to use your writing is directly related to your purpose. Let's say the editor of your college newspaper is planning to write an editorial against rising tuition costs. Her purpose is to point out to the administration that higher tuition is making it more difficult for students to attend school. She has no solution to the problem, but she hopes the administration will use what she has written to study the problem and perhaps come up with a solution. In this case, she will have to show why students are having difficulty paying tuition, how many students are affected, and what the consequences of higher tuition are: students working more hours after school, taking large loans, transferring to other schools, or leaving school altogether.

In discussing audience, we raised three major questions about the writer's audience. Now we can break these questions down into further questions. Use this list to analyze your audience when you write. The list can get you started, but if you think of other questions that can help you learn about your audience, consider them, too.

1. Who is my audience?
   a. What do they know about the topic?
   b. What references can I assume they will know?
   c. What references must be explained?
2. What is my audience's attitude about what I am writing?
   a. Are they likely to agree?
   b. Are they likely to disagree?
   c. Are they neutral?
3. How is my audience going to use my writing?
   a. To inform themselves?
   b. To entertain themselves?
   c. To make a decision?
   d. To examine or solve a problem?
   e. To change their behavior?

As you can see, the writing situation can affect what you write and how you write it. As you approach a writing situation, always consider, your role, purpose, and audience. To get a further grasp on how these elements work in the writing situation, try the following exercises.

Exercise 2.5

Below are some writing situations. Identify the writer's role, purpose, and audience. Then briefly discuss how the writing situation would affect what is written and how it is written. Study the example before completing the exercise.

Example: a stock broker's report to a client about some new bonds.
Role: an expert counseling someone who is not an expert.

Purpose: to inform the client so that he or she can decide whether the bonds are worth buying.

Audience: a client who is uninformed about the bonds and not a financial expert.

Analysis: The writer would have to be sure to include an explanation of the type of bonds. Cost, interest rate, and time of maturity would also need to be discussed. Since the writer is trying to help the client, not just sell the bonds, he or she would have to explain the risks as well as the benefits of the bonds. Not being an expert, the client, as audience, would want careful explanations and complete information. But the writer could assume the audience knows some basic terms, such as *interest rate*.

1. A recipe for lemon chicken written for inexperienced cooks.
2. A recipe for lasagna written for experienced cooks.
3. A newspaper editorial arguing that automobile insurance rates are too high. The audience is the general public.
4. A pamphlet on football written for some visiting French dignitaries who will be attending a National Football League game.
5. A paper on eating disorders written as a requirement for a nutrition class.
6. A letter asking a company to refund your money for a defective product.
7. A two-page essay introducing you to your writing teacher.
8. A letter to a friend telling about your first experiences as a college student.

Exercise 2.6

This exercise provides you with writing situations followed by information that could go into the writing. Given the situation, mark whether the information is appropriate or inappropriate and tell why. Consider both what the information says and the way it is written. If the information is inappropriate, tell what should be done to make it appropriate.

Situation: Term paper on Albert Einstein written for the professor of a class on great scientists.

Information: Einstein was an awesome dude.

Answer: Inappropriate. Slang would not be used in a term paper. The student should substitute the words *brilliant scientist* or *exceptional intellect* for *awesome dude*.

1. **Situation:** letter to a friend about your first day of college.
 Information: "I am pleased to inform you that having completed my first day at an institution of higher education, all my faculties remain intact."
2. **Situation:** lasagna recipe for experienced cooks.
 Information: "Mozzarella is a white cheese available in most supermarkets."
3. **Situation:** college handbook for new freshman.
 Information: "If you drop a class, you will receive a full refund of tuition only if you drop during the first two weeks of the semester. A 50% refund will be granted to students who drop before the sixth week of the semester. After the sixth week, no refund will be granted."
4. **Situation:** a business textbook for beginning students.
 Information: "Increases in the GNP often result in fiscal drag and in a reduction of aggregate expenditures."
5. **Situation:** a letter asking a company to repair a defective microwave oven.
 Information: "I purchased an Electroline Microwave, model 87541, on July 2, at Alexis Appliances in Greensboro, North Carolina. While still under warranty, the timer on the microwave stopped working."
6. **Situation:** an informal, comic description of someone you know written with the purpose of entertaining the teacher and other students in your writing class.
 Information: "At family picnics, Aunt Lil would tell stories about her five husbands, ending each one with a chorus of 'Hit the Road, Jack' and a shrill cackle."

The Writing Process, the Writing Situation, and Your Audience

When experienced writers write, they are aware of the writing situation and their audiences as they use the writing process. As you write more, you will notice that the elements of the writing situation affect the writing process. Depending on the situation and audience, you may have to put more effort into one part of the process than another. The best way to see how the situation affects the process is to look at a few cases.

Note to the teacher. Suppose you have a child who misses three days of school because of illness. Writing a note to your child's teacher would require very little invention because you do not have to come up with ideas about the illness. You know what the illness is, and the note will be short. In this sense, your purpose—to tell the teacher why your child was absent—does not require much effort for invention. However, if you are like most people, you would probably pay close attention to editing because you would expect the teacher to notice mistakes. In this sense, your audience influences your process.

Letter to a friend. Let's say you have a close friend or relative who has moved far enough away that telephone calls would be a very expensive way to keep in touch. Now suppose you haven't been in touch for three months. You decide to write a letter. Since you have not been in contact for three months, this letter will require some invention. You will have to think about every-thing that has happened to you, and you might even jot down a few notes. As you draft the letter, writing about some of the things that have happened to you will probably remind you of others. However, in your role as friend, you probably will not spend much time editing because you know that a good friend, unlike an audience you do not know, will most likely forgive you any misspellings and comma errors.

Psychology paper. Suppose you are taking a class in psychology and the pro-fessor asks you to interview ten people on their feelings about smoking and write up your findings. For this paper, you will need to use all the parts of the writing process carefully. Your interviews will be part of invention. So will any comparisons you draw from the ten people's answers. If you find that half of the ten people you interview are strongly against smoking, three are against it but not strongly, and two are smokers, you will have to come up with conclusions about the meaning of the data. You will also have to figure out in what order you are going to present the data. Therefore, the paper will require a lot of invention.

Drafting the paper will be a big job because you will have a lot of information to present. As you write, you might find you have to revise the order in which you present the results of your survey to make them clear to your audience. Also, you will revise and edit the completed draft very carefully because your teacher—the audience—will be using the paper to see how well you can collect and present data from a survey.

As you write more and more, you will develop a sense of the writing situ-ations you encounter and your relationship to your audience in each. Remember that writing is social interaction and that not all social situations are the same. Be aware of your role, purpose, and audience through every step of the writing process, and you will learn to include the information you need and to use language appropriate to the needs of the situation and the expectations of your audience.

Writing Assignments

1. Writing to audiences unfamiliar with a topic provides good experience. Below are topics directed to audiences who would know little about them. Choose one and write a short essay directed to the audience specified.

    a. Argue the merits of heavy metal music or some other type of popular music to an audience of senior citizens.

    b. Explain one of the subjects you are taking in college to a class of fourth-grade students.

    c. Persuade someone of another ethnic group to try a dish particular to your ethnic group.

2. Advertisers are highly aware of their audiences. Choose a print or television advertisement, and explain the values, personality, and behavior of the group the advertisement is trying to reach.

3. If you wrote an essay in response to one of the assignments in Chapter 1, rewrite that essay for a different audience. For instance, if your audience was your peers, write the paper for an audience of small children or senior citizens.

Key Terms

Writing situation: A situation where the writer has a purpose for communicating with an audience and a role in relation to the audience. A writing situation is a form of social interaction.

Role: When writing, a person has a role in relation to the audience. Depending on the writer's purpose, the role can range from friend, to teacher, to student, to citizen, to consumer, and so on.

Purpose: A writer always has a purpose for writing: to provide information, to display knowledge, to entertain, to instruct an audience, to ask for something, to persuade an audience, and so on.

Audience: The readers of a piece of writing are its audience. Audiences have values and needs that the writer must consider if the audience is to be able to use the writing in the way the writer intends.

chapter three
Generalizing and Specifying

Suppose you were looking for an apartment near campus and came across this advertisement in the newspaper:

Nice three rm. apt., close to campus, ideal for student, low rent.

This apartment sounds like just what you are looking for. You figure that "nice" means the apartment is clean and recently redecorated. You assume "close to campus" means you can walk to your classes, and the "low rent" fits your budget exactly. But when you go to see the apartment, you find that the ad did not describe it accurately. The walls are a faded yellow that looks as if it were once white but has been stained by years of people smoking in the apartment. The carpet is a dirty green, the bathroom sink is chipped in several spots, two of the burners on the stove are broken, and the bedroom is so small that you know you cannot fit both a bed and a desk in it. The apartment is two miles from campus, "close" by car (you don't own one), but a long walk.

But needing an apartment badly and having a tight budget, you figure that you can paint it, shampoo the carpet, have the landlord fix the stove, and put up with the chipped sink. You decide that the two-mile walk will help you keep fit and that in bad weather you can take the bus. So you inquire about the "low rent," only to find that it is $100 a month more than you can afford.

You leave disappointed, feeling that the ad lied to you and that the landlord wasted your time. But let's look at the ad. You might think it lied to you, but actually the problem with the ad is that it described the apartment poorly—so poorly that you were misled. The word *nice* says very little. What is nice to one person may not be to someone else. To someone with a car, a distance of two miles is close to campus; to someone without one, it isn't. Finally, whether a rent is low depends on one's budget. The problem with all these words, and others like them, is that they are too general, and general language leaves too much of the meaning vague.

Defining General and Specific Language

Before we discuss the ad further, let's define the terms **general** and **specific** as they are used to describe language:

> General language refers to a whole category of things, people, activities, or ideas. For example, the word *person* is general. It covers millions and could refer to anyone from a five-year-old boy in a third-world country to a sixty-year-old senator. Similarly, the word *fun* is a general reference to a positive activity in life. It can refer to anything from playing softball to going to a party to taking a vacation or to any other activity that some people find pleasurable.
>
> Specific language refers to a particular thing, person, or activity that belongs to a larger category. For example, a Frenchwoman is a specific member of the general category of French people, and French people are a general group belonging to the still more general category of people. Parisians are a specific group of French people, but a general group in relation to individuals living in Paris. One particular Parisian, a woman named Simone, is a specific example of the general group.

Now that you know the difference between general and specific language, you need to consider the degrees of generality and specificity. For instance, some words are general, some are less general, some are specific, and some are more specific. The linguist S. I. Hayakawa showed the degrees of generality and specificity with a diagram of a ladder. If you think of these degrees as steps on a ladder, you will understand them more easily. Note in the diagram how each step leads down from a general word to a specific word (or up from a specific word to a general word).

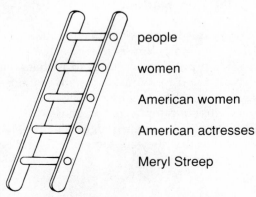

people

women

American women

American actresses

Meryl Streep

Exercise 3.1

Following the example, arrange each group of words below into a ladder diagram. Put the most general word at the top rung and the most specific at the bottom.

Example   eggs, the Western omelet Jake had for breakfast, food, Western omelets, omelets.

> food
> eggs
> omelets
> Western omelets
> the Western omelet Jake had for breakfast

1. meat, food, a Big Mac, burgers
2. Hurricane George, problems, natural disasters, hurricanes
3. painting, art, the "Mona Lisa," paintings by Leonardo
4. Fairbanks Elementary School, education, schools, elementary schools
5. Empire State Building, buildings, structures, skyscrapers
6. teachers, professionals, workers, my fourth-grade teacher, educators, elementary-school teachers
7. engaging in physical activity, Magic Johnson sinking a game-winning jump shot, playing sports, shooting a basketball, Magic Johnson shooting a basketball, playing basketball
8. animals, Siamese cats, bluepoint Siamese cats, cats, pets
9. Madonna's video of "Like a Prayer," television, media, music videos
10. Steven Spielberg movies, fun, *Indiana Jones and the Last Crusade*, entertainment, movies

Choosing Between General and Specific Language

As you draft and revise, you may wonder when to use . . . more general language and when to use . . . more specific language. Usually specific language tells the reader more, but at times you need general language to present an overview. For example, in writing an essay on rising costs of tuition, you might tell the reader that tuition costs are rising across the nation. That statement would be very general because it covers many schools and many different raises in tuition. But the statement would be necessary to explain a main idea of your paper. You would then have to provide specific examples of the amount tuition has gone up at particular schools.

Good writers are able to mix general and specific language, depending on their purpose and on their audience. Examine the sentences below and the discussions that follow:

This week I had to spend about *$150* on *books*, so already I have only *$25* left of the money I saved before coming *here*.

If a college student living away from home wrote this sentence in a letter to her parents, the language would be fine. There are two very general words—*books* and *here*—and they need not be specific. The student's parents (her audience) will assume she means college textbooks. She does not need to name the books because her purpose in writing the sentence is to show how she has had to spend most of the money she saved. If her purpose were to tell her parents that she is learning many new subjects, she might name the books specifically to give her parents an idea of the variety of her studies. Similarly, she can refer to her school generally as *here* because her parents already know where she is.

In contrast, notice how she refers to money in specific amounts. She tells her parents exactly how much she has spent and exactly how much she has left. If you guessed that in her next sentence she asked her parents for more money, you guessed right—and she probably got it. But would her parents have sent her money if she had written, "I spent a lot of money and don't have much left." Perhaps they would have sent *some* money, but because they would not know how much "a lot" is and how little "much left" is, they might not have realized how badly their daughter needed money. Also, without the specific reference to textbooks, the parents would not have known that the student used the money for something important. So by using specific details, this student makes sure her parents know that she had not wasted her money and needs and deserves more.

Now we will examine another sentence. This one comes from an essay telling about a disappointing experience the student had on a blind date:

On Saturday night, July 22, 1989, I went on my first blind date.

While the mention of the day, month, and year is very specific, do the readers really need to know exactly when the date took place? Probably not, since the purpose of the essay is to entertain the audience with the story of the date.

Suppose the specific reference to the day was cut, leaving: "On Saturday night, I went on my first blind date." Now there is a new problem: The sentence is too general. It sounds as if the date took place on the Saturday evening before the student wrote the essay, but that cannot be true because he wrote it during the third week of the fall semester, but he went on the date the previous summer. Below are some groups of words. Which group would fit best at the start of this sentence?

1. One time
2. One Saturday night last summer
3. One night last summer
4. One night

If you picked number 2 or 3, you are catching on. Numbers 1 and 4 are too general. Though the essay will focus on dating, not time, the words *one time* and *one night* do not give the reader any idea of when the date took place or how old the student was at the time. Number 3 is good because it locates the date on a summer night, and we often associate summer nights with romance. Number 2 is even better. It does everything number 3 does but also adds to the focus on romance and dating because Saturday night is the most popular night for dating.

Exercise 3.2

In the following sentences, the underlined words are either too general or too specific. Cross them out and then write a more fitting word in the blank. Following each sentence is a reference to the kind of writing in which the sentence occurs. When you make each change, ask yourself the purpose of the writing and the needs of its reader.

1. *A president* _____ freed the slaves. (elementary school history book)
2. Simmer the vegetables for a *few* _____ minutes. (cookbook)
3. Congress passed a law that would lower federal funding for *elementary schools, middle schools, high schools, community colleges, state universities, building maintenance for all of these, and teachers salaries* _____.
   (newspaper article on lower funding for education)
4. When you get off the *bridge* _____ take a left *down the road for a few blocks* _____. (directions in a hotel brochure)
5. *Hamburgers, tacos, pizza, fries, milkshakes, colas at low prices* _____ are not good to eat all the time. (pamphlet on nutrition)

Showing vs. Telling

By now you should have a fairly clear understanding of general and specific language. You know that language can get too specific if it shows us something we already know or something we do not need to know. (Remember the student's reference to the exact day of his date?) If you completed the exercises, you also know that specific language shows us more than general language.

Sometimes there are exceptions, but most of the time when you write, you should prefer specific language because it shows what you are writing about, while general language merely tells. Suppose, for instance, the advertisement for the apartment had read:

> Three-room apartment in need of paint; stove has only two burners working; bathroom sink is chipped; and bedroom is small. Two miles from campus. $500 a month.

The landlord would never write such an ad because no one would come to see the apartment. In other words, he can't *show* the apartment in writing and expect anyone to come see it. It is not in his interest to be too specific. But unless you are trying to rent out a shabby little apartment, it is best to be specific in your writing because specific language shows that you have knowledge of a subject.

When you consider your need to show or tell, you are considering your audience. As we said in Chapter 2, you have to consider what the audience wants to know and how much information it needs to use the writing, as well as what you the writer want to show the audience.

The following two paragraphs are on the same subject: the movie *Batman*. The writer's purpose is not only to convey the atmosphere of the film but also to put the audience in his place. Read them and compare the use of language according to the writer's purpose:

Paragraph 1
> Batman was a real strange movie. Gotham City was made to look like a comic book city. The streets were weird looking, and the buildings were real strange. The people dressed funny too for the kind of city they were in. The Batcave was a real spooky place, but it had all Batman's equipment for catching the bad guys.

Paragraph 2
> *Batman* was a movie with strange atmosphere. The sets for Gotham City made it seem like a place in a comic book. Close-up shots showed dark, dirty

alleys and garishly lit streets. Longer shots, many of which were animated, showed buildings that looked like a combination of old castles and futuristic skyscrapers. Adding to the strangeness, most of the characters dressed as if they lived in the 1930s, but the cars were contemporary with the 1980s. The Batcave, Batman's secret headquarters, had black rock walls and ledges fogged in a continuous mist. On one of the larger ledges was a control board with the high-tech computer and video equipment that Batman used to figure out the Joker's moves.

As you can see, the second paragraph is much longer because it includes specific details to *show* us what the atmosphere of the movie was like, while the first paragraph merely *tells* us about the weird atmosphere generally. Compare the paragraphs on the following points:

> the buildings in Gotham City
> the streets
> the people
> the batcave
> the crime-fighting equipment

As you probably noticed, the second paragraph brings the atmosphere of the movie to life—that is, it does not just tell us it was strange, it shows the strangeness. We can get a strong sense of the movie if we have not seen it or identify with the writer's examples if we have. Thus, the paragraph achieves the writer's purpose by using specific language that shows rather than general language that only tells.

Exercise 3.3

Below are pairs of sentences. Read them carefully, and on a separate sheet of paper, write down which one you think is better and the reasons for your choice.

1.a. My parents did not understand my brother when he went punk.
1.b. My parents threatened to send my brother to a psychiatrist when he dyed his hair blue, got a Mohawk haircut, and started listening to bands with names like Dead Kennedys.
2.a. Ellen has to work all day as a paralegal, tidy up around the house, care for her child, attend law school at night, do her homework, and get enough sleep each night.

2.b. Ellen is very busy and has many responsibilities.

3.a. In Los Angeles, we had a good time.

3.b. In Los Angeles, we visited Disneyland, ate in several fine restaurants, toured Universal Studios, and danced in trendy nightclubs.

4.a. When I was younger, my parents always set strict curfews for me.

4.b. When I was a teenager, my parents always made me stay home on school nights and punished me if I violated my 11 o'clock curfew on weekends.

5.a. Good writing should be lively.

5.b. Good writing uses specific details that show the reader your experience or opinions.

Exercise 3.4

Rewrite the sentences below so that they show rather than tell—that is, make the language more specific.

1. My next-door neighbor is a funny lady.
2. I get mad when it is noisy while I'm trying to sleep.
3. The boy found some money.
4. The Fourth of July is an important holiday.
5. I hope my favorite team will be the best in baseball this year.
6. The movie was lousy today.
7. A new car costs a lot.
8. Ellen was wearing a nice suit.
9. The meal was not very good.
10. Cigarette smoking can be bad for you.

Exercise 3.5

Rewrite one of the paragraphs below so that it has more specific details. If you have trouble, go back to the ladder diagram that explains general and specific language. (Do not feel that you need to change every word.)

1. Driving on a highway in heavy traffic requires a lot of attention. You have to watch out how you handle the car. You also need to notice what other drivers are doing. You have to make sure you know where you are going, or you can get lost.

2. Hobbies are a good way for people to get their minds off things. There are many hobbies people can take up. Some of these are time consuming, requiring the hobbyist to be dedicated. Other hobbies take little time but can provide rewards and amusement.

Making Your Writing Specific

So far, you have learned about the difference between specific and general language and you have had some practice changing language from general to specific so that it shows rather than tells. Sometimes you may have had trouble thinking of more specific words to replace the words in the exercise, especially if you did not know much about the topic the sentences in the exercises talked about.

For instance, if you do not know a lot about professional baseball, you might have trouble making the following sentence more specific: "Throughout the 1950s, the New York Yankees were the best team in baseball." Someone who followed baseball in the Fifties, or has read about it, might write: "During the 1950s, the New York Yankees won eight of ten American League Championships and six World Series." This change improves the sentence because it specifies the team's accomplishments. From this example, we can see that the writer's knowledge of a subject helps him or her to be more specific.

For essays or paragraphs assigned to be written out of class, you should always take the time to use some kind of invention strategy to help get your thoughts flowing. The invention strategy will not only help you think of ideas and remember details, but it will help you to be specific, to show rather than tell. Here is an example of how one writer focused a topic and developed specific details by using one of the invention strategies: the journalist's questions:

Who?	People visiting Chicago
What?	Art Institute, Museum of Science and Industry, Field Museum of Natural History, Shedd Aquarium
When?	Open all year, weekdays less crowded, takes a whole day to see
Why?	To enjoy themselves and to learn
Where?	Art Institute on Michigan Avenue at Grant Park Others on the south end of Lake Shore Drive
How?	Easy to reach by car or bus

Drawing on these notes, the writer has enough to begin writing a paragraph, and here is a possible first draft:

> Chicago has many excellent museums that visitors can enjoy and learn from. The Art Institute, on Michigan Avenue at Grant Park, houses paintings and sculpture from around the world and regularly has special exhibits. The Field Museum of Natural History contains artifacts from various cultures of the past. The Museum of Science and Industry offers exhibits on the development of technology and the progress of the human race. At Shedd Aquarium, visitors can see hundreds of different kinds of fish in the museum's many tanks. All of these museums are easy to reach by mass transit, and, except, for the art museum, each offers access to free or inexpensive parking.

This paragraph sticks to the topic, offers several examples of museums, and discusses ways to get to them. But despite these virtues, the paragraph remains rather weak because it never gets very specific. Other than naming the museums and stating generally what each offers, the paragraph does not give us enough specific information to make us want to visit one. Although the writer has used the journalist's questions, the topic is not *limited* enough to allow for specific discussion in the space of a paragraph. In fact, the paragraph raises more questions than it answers. What paintings by famous artists are in the Art Institute? What specific cultures are represented in the Field Museum and what type of exhibits represent them? What marvels of technology and progress will we see in the Museum of Science and Industry? What are the major attractions in Shedd Aquarium?

Answering these questions could help a great deal in fulfilling the writer's purpose: to convince the reader to visit one or more of the museums. But the writer could not specifically develop the answers to the questions above in the small space of only one paragraph. In fact, if each museum treated each reason specifically, you could probably write a whole essay on the topic or a whole paragraph on just one of the museums. But first you need to use an invention strategy to develop specific details for each museum. Note the journalist's questions applied to just one of the city's major museums:

Who?	People visiting the Museum of Science and Industry
What?	Over 2,000 exhibits; major exhibits are a full-size space shuttle model, an underground coal mine, and a World War II German submarine, other small exhibits
When?	Open every day of the year 9:30 to 4:00 except from 9:00 to 5:30 weekends and holidays and every day from Memorial Day to Labor Day

Why?	The museum is exciting and educational
Where?	Located at 57th St. and Lake Shore Drive
How?	Spend a whole day there, get there by city bus or car

The questions again provide plenty of details to write a paragraph, but now the topic is limited enough to generate specificity. When you read the paragraph below, notice also that listing these details generated even more:

The Museum of Science and Industry, at 57th Street and Lake Shore Drive in Chicago, is an interesting and educational place to spend a day. The museum offers over 2,000 exhibits tracing progress in science and technology. Among the most popular of the larger exhibits are a life-size model of the space shuttle, a real World War II German submarine, and a coal mine far below the fifteen-acre building. Museum visitors can tour the shuttle or the submarine or take an elevator down to the depths of the small but authentic mine, where they ride in mining cars. The smaller exhibits are equally interesting, illustrating various scientific and biological principles. One has baby chicks hatching continuously; another allows the viewer to look into or place a hand in front of a camera that magnifies the skin 500 times on a video screen. On weekends and holidays and daily from Memorial Day to Labor Day, the museum is open from 9:00 to 5:30; the remaining days of the year, from 9:30 to 4:00. It is easily reached by city bus, and for those driving, there is a large parking lot.

This paragraph has approximately 175 words. The writer does not have to worry about having enough to write about because the invention strategy has helped to develop the topic, which, unlike the first one, has been limited enough to make the invention strategy work. As a result, the paragraph describes one museum and will convince most readers that it is certainly worth visiting. Why is this paragraph better than the first one? It is better because it helps us envision what the museum is like. We may want to know more about the exhibits, but we have been shown enough to lead us to find out for ourselves by visiting the museum. In short, the paragraph has achieved the writer's purpose.

Writing Assignments

When you write the following two paragraphs, first use one of the invention strategies. Then go over the paragraph you've written to see if any of the sentences are general enough to develop into another, more specific paragraph.

1. Write a paragraph that *shows* one reason you like someone you knew in your past. Assume this person is up for a community award for helping others and that your paragraph will serve as a testimonial to be read by the judges. The following sentence can serve as a pattern for stating your main idea:

(Name) was my favorite person because (*give one general reason*).

Even though the reason you fill in will be more general than the specific examples that support it, don't make the reason too general.

Don't say this: "When I was playing basketball in high school, Coach Dawson was my favorite person because he was a great guy."
Say this: "When I was playing basketball in high school, Coach Dawson was my favorite person because he taught me the value of discipline."

The problem with the first sentence is that it is so general that to develop the idea of greatness would take many examples. You would have to mention just about everything from Coach Dawson's sense of humor and knowledge to the generosity he showed in having the whole team over to his house for pizza.

In other words, to cover all the specifics that make for greatness, you would have to write hundreds, maybe even thousands, of words. You don't have time (and probably don't want to) write so much. And even if you did have the time and desire, a paragraph is only a small piece of writing and doesn't have room for everything that made Coach Dawson great. If you did write about his greatness in a normal-size paragraph, you would have to be very general, and you would end up with a weak paragraph, similar to the first one on Chicago's museums.

The second sentence on Coach Dawson could work well for one paragraph full of specific details because all you would have to cover was how Coach Dawson taught discipline. You might have specific examples of how his studies of game films long after practice influenced you to put extra time into your own work. You might show how he would bench even star players in big games if they were late for practice or cut class.

In short, you would only have to cover the points about Coach Dawson that taught discipline and then end the paragraph with a general statement on how learning discipline benefited you. Also, if you limit the paragraph to discipline, you will not have to worry about the specifics of his humor, intelligence, and generosity.

Of course, writing a limited paragraph requires that you think about your memories thoroughly to come up with specifics. The invention strategies can help. Use them—and then use them again after you have written the first draft of the paragraph. If you have trouble getting started, try some freewriting. As you remember from Chapter 1, when you freewrite, you just put pen to paper and write anything that comes into your head about the subject (in this case, the person). Once you have some thoughts written down, read over the paragraph, pick out one idea that is important to you, and then develop it with any of the invention strategies. The trick is not to confuse the freewriting with the finished paragraph you are asked to write. The freewriting is just a warmup, like the stretching exercises a ballerina does before dancing or a football player does before a game.

2. Write a paragraph that shows some aspect of a place. Use the paragraphs on Chicago's museums as models of what to do and what not to do. The purpose of the paragraph is to make someone want (or not want) to go there. Make sure to limit the topic. A whole town or city cannot be presented specifically in one paragraph, although a park probably can.

Key Terms

General: General language refers to a whole class of things or people. Example: bodies of water.

Specific: Specific language refers to a particular thing or person in a group. Example: Lake Tahoe

Telling: Writing tells when it gives us only a general idea. Example: "The landscaping is pretty on the campus quadrangle."

Showing: Writing shows when it uses detail to give us a specific idea of something. Example: "On the campus quadrangle, the flower beds circling the flagpole contrast brightly with the green of the neatly trimmed lawn and the whiteness of the concrete paths."

unit one

Essays for Reading

The four essays that follow were all written by college students. Brian Bolinger's "Battle" discusses how one student engages in the writing process. Perhaps you will recognize similar traits in your own approach to writing or pick up some pointers from Brian's approach. Lynette Schaefer's essay, "Through the Years with the Piano," relates how she discovered and developed musical ability for her own enjoyment. John Trevarthan's essay, "Moving Out," shows a young man maturing through living on his own, and Karla Kern, in "My Grandfather," pays tribute to her grandfather by focussing on the one day a week they always enjoyed together. As you read each essay, try to imagine the process the writers went through in composing their essays and note how their use of specifics enabled them to communicate their experiences to others.

Battle
Brian Bolinger (freshman)

Everyone has a different writing process in one way or another. My writing process is easier to talk about than to actually do, but I have developed a process which enables me to write successful essays. I believe that if you keep your writing process simple and basic, you can use most of your energy developing good content for your paper. When I receive a writing assignment, I know that from that moment until I turn in the final copy I am not going to be the most rational guy in the world. In other words, I do not like the thought of fighting the assignment because in my case I think the process of writing a paper is a war, me against the assignment. Even though writing seems to be a struggle for me, I have developed a process within my first three months of college that helps me win the dreaded battle.

When I receive the writing assignment, I start by rounding up all of the needed equipment to fight the battle. I look at this part of the process as if I were gathering up the troops. I write down the assignment on a blank piece of paper with about twelve additional blank sheets stacked underneath. The paper is just the ordinary white paper with blue lines on it; in addition to the paper I lay out my favorite black Uni-ball pen, my handy Webster's dictionary, and occasionally my grammar handbook.

Even though I get out all my equipment, I do not always start right away. I procrastinate the actual writing but use the extra time to my advantage—I think over and over about the topic. I cannot start putting my ideas on paper until everything is just right. That is another reason I look at writing as a war because before a country invades another country everything has to be perfect. And everything is perfect for me only when I have at least four hours of free time, my thoughts are focused on the assignment, I am not tired or hungry, and there is no other alternative activity going on.

Once I am ready to dive into the battle, I grab my writing equipment and head to the stairwell in my dorm. I go down two flights of stairs to get to the study room on the quiet floor of the building. The closer I get, with every step I become more nervous. I finally reach the quiet floor door, I grab the door knob, I feel a force pushing me away, I fight it by pulling the door open, and then I feel as if I am being pulled into a wind tunnel. Once I am in the room, I feel the heat from the heat ducts, am blinded by the glare of the lights, and numbed from the ticking of my watch. I place my equipment on my favorite desk, and at the same time I imbed my carcass in the chair.

When I am writing, there has to be complete silence in the room. My ears will pick up the softest sounds, so if I hear anything, my train of thought completely blows up. I envy people like my roommate, who has to write in a room with a blaring stereo or television. And at times he will even be talking at the same time he is writing. But I need quiet.

To begin with, I start getting some ideas on the paper by making a brainstorming list. This list usually consists of short phrases, words, and sometimes sentences. I take the ideas from the brainstorming list and try out a couple of good thesis sentences. Once I have chosen a thesis that best expresses my opinion on the topic, I rearrange my ideas into the order that I will try to follow throughout the process, but in most cases I will end up with a different order than I originally planned. This changing and rearranging does not cause a problem because I keep my ideas on track with the thesis, or change the thesis if I discover new ideas while writing.

As you can see, I am the kind of writer who likes to invent and revise a lot while I am drafting, instead of writing a draft straight through and then revising. The revising I do while drafting helps me discover what I know and want to say on the topic. I guess for me the writing process goes on all at once, rather than in steps, though I am aware of the invention, drafting, and revising as I am doing them.

Finally, I edit the paper, looking particularly for errors rather than worrying about content and organization because by this point they should be the way I want. I look at editing as dressing the wounds after the battle. Usually I read the paper three or four times when I edit. When I am satisfied that I have edited my paper as best as I can, I put it away until the next day. Then I type it, perhaps making minor changes. At last, I proofread the typed copy and make minor corrections, if needed, neatly with my black pen.

In this battle called writing I am not alone. Knowing that other students struggle with the act of writing gives me comfort. I believe that there is not a perfect writer in this world, so if you can't perfect writing, all you can do is develop ways to make it easier to win the battle. And winning feels pretty good!

Questions for Study and Discussion

1. Bolinger does many things to prepare before he puts anything on paper. Which of these seem to be helpful? Are there any that would make the process easier and more effective if he eliminated them?

2. What in Bolinger's preparation indicates that he takes his writing very seriously?

3. What type of invention strategy does Bolinger use? How is it similar to the way brainstorming is discussed in Chapter 1?

4. Bolinger compares the writing process to a battle. Cite specific instances where the comparison seems true. Are there other instances where it seems exaggerated?

5. Bolinger says everyone has his or her own writing process. How is his writing process different from the process as described in the introduction to Unit I. How is it similar?

6. To what extent is the writing process a series of steps for Bolinger? To what extent do the steps overlap?

7. Bolinger talks about finding a thesis —the main idea of the paper. Does this main idea stay the same throughout the process? What can change it?

8. What is Bolinger's role in writing this paper, and who is his audience? What evidence is there that he has a specific audience in mind?

9. What is the main point Bolinger is trying to get across to his audience?

10. Many writers say they hate writing but love having written. Bolinger compares writing to a "dreaded battle." But is there evidence that he also likes to write?

11. Compare your approach to writing to Bolinger's.

12. Using a brainstorming list, jot down some ideas that you have about the way you write.

Through the Years with the Piano
Lynnette Schaefer (freshman)

Playing the piano has been a hobby which I have enjoyed ever since I started taking lessons when I was eight years old. As I grew older, I realized I was serious about the piano. I feel I have a natural talent for playing the piano, and it has provided me with a great deal of enjoyment and confidence all my life.

I was an excited little girl when I had my first piano lesson. I absolutely could not wait to learn how to play the piano just like my older sister. When I was a very young child, my sister would play the piano for the family on Sunday afternoons, or she would play carols at Christmas when all of my family was together. So I was very eager when my chance for piano lessons finally came.

As I progressed through the years, my piano teachers always considered me to be one of their best students, one who could sight-read well, and who advanced a little more every day. To be a good pianist, I had to practice every single day for at least half an hour. At eight years old, making myself practice required quite a bit of self-discipline, which was difficult to have at such a young age. My mom would always tell me how I needed to practice because of the large sum of money my parents put into my piano lessons, whether she was driving me twenty miles to town to buy the books I needed or paying for my lessons. Therefore, I wanted to practice for my parents' sake as well as for mine so that I could be the pianist I wanted to be.

Shortly after I started my lessons, my sister stopped taking lessons. I had always been envious of her because she could play so well, but I gradually began to play better than she could. I realized I was the one with the natural "built-in" talent because I had advanced more quickly in a shorter period of time.

Playing the piano built up my self-esteem. I knew I was successful because at this point I could play almost anything. My ability gave me confidence to play for anyone, whether I was playing a hymn at my church, playing on keyboards for the Marshallaires (a local band), accompanying soloists for my junior and senior proms, or playing slow pop songs such as "Faithfully" for my own enjoyment.

Playing the piano can be uplifting or relaxing for me. It all depends on the type of piece I play. For example, if I play for relaxation, I play a slow piece or a classical piece, but when I play a faster song or a pop song, it lifts me up and puts me in a happy mood. But whatever I play, the piano helps clear my mind and give me time to myself.

My piano lessons have not continued since I turned eighteen and entered college. My piano teacher, Mrs. Lee, felt I had learned everything there was to learn from her. Although I will not be majoring in music or pursuing a career as a pianist, I will always enjoy playing. When I focus back ten years ago to my first piano lesson as a young girl, walking into the room, scared, clueless but extremely excited, I know that I couldn't realize how much I would get out of piano playing, but now I know the benefits are immeasurable. Now I can play anything from Mozart to the latest songs on the pop chart. Piano playing is my favorite pastime, and even though my piano lessons have not continued, my talent and interest for the piano will always remain.

Questions for Study and Discussion

1. How and why did Schaefer start playing the piano?

2. Schaefer says she became a good piano player. What examples and details support her claim?

3. How would the paper differ if Schaefer did not tell us about the kinds of music she can play?

4. What benefits has Schaefer gained from playing the piano?

5. If this paper started with a brainstorming list, what items would be on the list?

6. Cite instances in the paper in which Schaefer's examples and details "show" rather than just "tell."

7. How would you describe Schaefer's purpose in this essay?

8. What is the main idea of the essay? Is it stated in any one sentence? Is it restated elsewhere?

9. Whom do you think Schaefer had in mind as an audience for this essay?

10. Suppose Schaefer is assuming an audience of classmates. How appropriate are her language and use of details for this audience?

11. Have you enjoyed a long-term hobby or activity that makes you feel the way Schaefer feels about playing the piano?

12. Freewrite for about five minutes on something you enjoy doing. Using a brainstorming list or a cluster diagram, generate additional specifics that you would need if you were expanding your freewriting into a paragraph or short essay.

Moving Out: Everything That It's Cracked Up to Be?
John Trevarthan (sophomore)

Living on your own definitely has its ups and downs. You have all the freedom that you could possibly want or need, you have the opportunity to meet new and interesting people, and you are finally allowed to make your own decisions without your parents' interference. In other words, you are independent. However, it has been my experience that the negative aspects of leaving home outweigh the positive, by far.

One of my main problems living on my own is making and managing money. Since I am a student, classes and studies take up a great deal of my time, leaving me less time to work. It seems as if there is always some bill that needs to be paid, which makes it impossible to get caught up financially. On one occasion, when one of my bills was due immediately, I was forced to desperate measures to come up with the cash. My water was dangerously close to being shut off, so I decided to donate blood plasma at the Blood Products Center. The entire experience was humiliating. Some of the people in the clinic were talking about how they were going out to buy beer after they received their fifteen dollars for donating. Judging by the smell they gave off and the several layers of dirt and grime on their bodies, they may well have decided better to buy a few bars of soap. The two and a half hours that I spent in the clinic were painful and extremely awkward. It was like driving through a bad neighborhood late at night and almost being out of gas with no service stations around. Fortunately, I was able to shower as soon as I got home.

Living on a limited income also forces me to cut down on a few luxuries, such as food. I'm not saying that I have ever really starved, but I can recall several times when I lived on macaroni and cheese and dry cereal for a few days. Eating out and ordering pizzas, which I thought would be the norm before I moved out of my parents' home, are rare occasions.

Not having much money also puts a damper on my so-called social life. I would almost rather give up eating than to have no social life. However, it seems as if I always have to pass up nights out with my friends because I lack funds. Also, as this year's spring break approached, like every other red-blooded college student in America, I had aspirations of journeying to Florida to tan, play, and get drunk. But my finances were depleted, forcing me to stay home and enjoy my break "here-in-town" style. Ugh!

Another problem of living on my own is that people take advantage of the situation. Many a time I have found people that I hardly know dropping in and then helping themselves to the contents of my refrigerator, or making a mess in my bathroom for me to clean up later. These people seem to think that they have these rights since they are not at home and won't have to clean up after they throw up in my closet. Believe me, I speak from experience. Even the people I call my friends come over to my house at all hours of the night looking for a place to sleep or watch TV. They think that because I don't live with my parents, they don't have to worry about waking anyone up. I guess they forget that I, too, need my rest and cannot operate on only one or two hours of sleep a night. I can't wait until they have apartments of their own, so I can have a little revenge for all those sleepless nights.

My neighborhood is another headache. I live right down the street from Simrell's Tavern, a favorite college bar, and my other neighbors are the Phi Delta Thetas. With the combination of the two, what do I get to look forward to when I get home late from work on a Friday or Saturday night? Drunk fraternity guys relieving themselves on my front lawn! Not to mention the lushes who want to borrow my phone, car, bathroom, or money to go a couple of more rounds at the bar.

Because I have had problems living away from home, you may think that I would be anxious to go back to my old home. But the answer is a resounding "No!" I choose to live out on my own because I feel that it will make the transition from college to life much smoother. I think that I would be facing quite a culture shock after graduation if I spent my college years home with my parents. Living on my own has given me the opportunity to gradually develop from a naive kid into a mature young adult, but it was the naive kid in me who thought having my own place would be continuous fun; the mature young adult now knows better.

Questions for Study and Discussion

1. What is the main idea of Trevarthan's essay? How does he keep that idea in focus throughout the paper?

2. Money is a major concern for Trevarthan. What are three aspects of his life that it affects?

3. In Trevarthan's first paragraph, he talks about having "all the freedom that you could possibly want." How does the evidence of the essay show that he has freedom? How does it show he does not?

4. List at least five items that might be on a brainstorming list or a cluster diagram in preparation for writing this paper.

5. Give at least four examples of Trevarthan's use of specific details to support his points. Why does he tell us specifically about what he eats?

6. At the end of the essay, Trevarthan says he has matured. Cite evidence that supports his claim. Does anything in the essay indicate that though becoming more mature, he still has some maturing left to do?

7. Trevarthan also says in the last paragraph that living on his own will prepare him better for life after college. To what extent is this claim true? To what extent is it not?

8. Who is the intended audience for this essay? Who else might enjoy reading it?

9. If you have never lived on your own, how typical do you think Trevarthan's experience is?

10. If you have lived or are now living on your own, how is his experience similar to and different from your own?

11. Make a brainstorming list to explore a topic on some experience that did not turn out as you planned.

12. Choose one of the items on your brainstorming list and cite specific details that would bring it to life for an audience.

My Grandfather
Karla Kern (freshman)

My grandfather was one of the most unforgettable people in my life. He was a man who loved the outdoors, and some of my most vivid childhood memories are of him cultivating his garden or mowing the wide expanse of yard behind the house where he and my grandmother lived. Even though he is no longer alive, I will never forget the time we spent together or the stories and laughter he shared with me.

The garden where my grandfather spent so much time during the sunny summer months was situated behind his house on a small rise, which was surrounded by a neighboring hay field. In this huge garden, my grandpa would grow a wide variety of fruits and vegetables, ranging from strawberries and raspberries to potatoes and tomatoes. I was always amazed at how he could spend hours and hours out in the blazing summer heat with all the pesky insects and still love his work. I remember helping Grandpa pick raspberries one cool summer evening and his telling my grandmother that I had "canned" (eaten) more out in the garden than I had brought up to her. I still cannot help laughing each time I think of that day.

When it was time to mow the yard, Grandpa always enjoyed doing it himself. Each Saturday morning, while I would be cleaning the house, he would go out and climb on the lawn tractor and work until he had trimmed the enormous yard, with its numerous apple, cherry, and white maple trees, to his satisfaction. I can still remember many a Saturday morning, after I finished cleaning, going outside and standing on the patio watching Grandpa make pass after pass on the little tractor. He would always be wearing a baseball cap and, if it was cool, an ancient, blue quilted jacket, as he stared intently at the task before him. Grandpa always liked the yard to look "just so."

The winter months were fun with Grandpa, too, because winter meant it was basketball season, and when March rolled around it was time for the high school state championship games on television. So on Saturday mornings when Grandma was at the beauty shop, I would finish early with the house cleaning so Grandpa and I could watch the games together. While we were riveted to the TV, we would munch on creamy peanut butter and homemade raspberry jelly sandwiches that Grandpa had made, and we would cheer the opposite teams just so we could tease each other. When Grandma would come home, she would find us both yelling incoherently at the television or making some more sandwiches. We shared many worthwhile times together. Sometimes it's hard to believe that we will never be able to do those things together again.

When there were no chores to do or basketball games to watch, Grandpa would fill a Saturday afternoon showing me old, yellowed photographs of himself when he was in the army during World War II. Grandpa would then describe to me life in the army and how those days were some of the best in his life. Next, he would tell me how he met and married my grandmother while stationed in England. One of my favorite stories told how when he first brought Grandma to the U.S., she washed his high school letterman's jacket, which had leather sleeves, in the washing machine. I can still sometimes hear the ringing merriment of his laughter in my ears after he told that story.

My grandfather was a very special man whom I loved very much. When I think that some people never know their grandparents or are born after they have died, I am so glad we were able to spend many Saturdays together before he died. I will never forget him.

Questions for Study and Discussion

1. What is the main idea of Kern's essay? What do you think was her purpose in writing it?

2. Where is the main idea stated? Is it stated more than once?

3. We see only the finished product of Kern's essay. What details do you think appeared in her invention notes?

4. How has Kern limited her topic in this essay?

5. How does information in Kern's first and last paragraphs relate to information in the middle paragraphs?

6. Why isn't Kern's grandmother mentioned very much in this essay?

7. Pick out specifics that bring Kern's experiences to life.

8. Some people might argue that Kern's essay is too sentimental. Do you agree or disagree?

9. What do Kern's references to her grandfather's gardening and mowing grass tell us about him?

10. Kern is obviously from a rural area. Does this rural background affect how her readers perceive both her and her grandfather?

11. If you have completed assignment 1 at the end of Chapter 3, how does your paragraph compare to Kern's essay in terms of specific detail?

12. If you have not completed assignment 1 at the end of Chapter 3, list ways Kern's essay could help you develop your paragraph.

A Town Untouched by Time
Julia A. Lee (freshman)

Nestled in Central Illinois, surrounded by coal mines, is a small town named St. David. It is a tiny community of approximately 400 citizens, maybe less, of Croatian and Italian ancestry. My grandfather emigrated here at the age of 16 when he left his native Yugoslavia, and here he and my grandmother, also from Yugoslavia, started their lives in this country and raised their family. Though America seems to change every day, St. David always seems to remain the St. David of my grandparents.

The town has a gray nature to it. If you can picture a town with fences and gardens and flowers but no color to it, you can understand what St. David looks like. Although it is not like towns in old Western movies, barren and dust-blown, St. David seems shaded, sort of bland, as if years of coal dust have settled on the buildings and their inhabitants.

What the town lacks in physical color, it makes up for in the personalities of the inhabitants. The barely paved streets of the town are dotted with time-worn men playing bocci in threadbare clothes. They're always ready to converse, and the main question asked is "What family are you from?" Then they speak with enmity or fondness towards situations that happened in yesteryear. Their feuds are protracted and bitter, just as their love is stalwart and vigorous. There is no middle ground. Everything is done and felt in extremes, the mark of a Slavic or Latin nature. The old women still hang up clothes in their backyards and converse with neighbors over the fence in languages I could never understand. I have never noticed many children in the town, probably because the generation of children that was raised there moved away, leaving a breed of elders.

The town has an old-time atmosphere. Everyone has a clothesline, wooden lawn chairs, a picket fence, and a large garden. The pungent smell of onions and garlic still reminds me of warm afternoons playing in my grandparents' back-yard. There are many garages but few cars. The people walk to where they need to go. Garages are used for repair rooms and storage of the fruits of the harvest. There are no doctors' offices, no gas stations, no restaurants, one grocery store, but numerous taverns. There are also two churches, one Italian and one Slavic, and the Optimists Club. This building is the pride and joy of the town. Home-comings, church functions, weddings, and wakes are held there.

The town loves a good gala. Being of Slavic ancestry, the people love danc-ing, gatherings, feuds, and drinking as shown by the many taverns. The St. David Homecoming, held under the canopy of the Optimists Club, draws more people than any other social function in the area, running ahead of the second place Dunfermline Polka Dance/Chicken Fry. Even now my grandmother, par-ents, aunts, uncles, and cousins attend these events.

My memories of St. David are affectionate ones of noisy family gatherings, Grandma's Croatian cooking, the numbed silence of the nights, and the placid-ity of the whole town, a town seemingly unaffected by the motion of the rest of the world.

Questions for Study and Discussion

1. What is the purpose of this essay?

2. Who is Lee's audience? What details show that Lee assumes an audi-ence of people who have never been to St. David?

3. What is the main idea of this essay? Where does Lee state it? Is it stated more than once?

4. Cite effective use of specific details. How do the details support the main idea?

5. What items would probably appear on a brainstorming list for this essay?

6. How has Lee divided these items to organize her essay into paragraphs?

7. Do you think St. David would be an interesting place to visit?

8. Is it similar to or different from your idea of small towns?

9. Why do you think Lee finds St. David a subject interesting enough to write about?

10. Lee characterizes the town as being "untouched by time." In a short phrase, how would you characterize the town or neighborhood where you live?

unit two
Writing Essays

The first three chapters have asked you to do some writing, and along the way we have mentioned many different types of writing products: letters, reports, examination questions, paragraphs, and essays. This last type—the essay—is one of the most common writing products of the college writer, in English and in other classes. This unit will show you the process of writing essays, provide strategies for organizing them, and show you how to write them under the pressure of time so that you can produce the finished product. Before this discussion, let's define the product. After all, to make a pizza you have to know what a pizza is.

What Is an Essay?

You may already have your own definition of an essay. You may have written one of the essays assigned in previous chapters or read one of the student essays at the end of Unit I. You also may remember reading essays in magazines or writing them in high school. If you are familiar with what an essay is, this section will review and clarify your definition. If you do not have a definition of the essay clearly in mind, this section will help you to form one.

   An essay is a short piece of writing in which the writer purposefully presents ideas and information to influence an audience on a single topic. What does this definition mean? Let's break it down.

Length

When we say an essay is short, what do we mean? An essay can be as short as 250 words—about one typed page or two–four handwritten pages, depending on the size of the handwriting—or run to thousands of words and dozens of typed pages. Essays written for college classes will run anywhere from one to twenty pages. Don't worry about that twenty-pager—such essays are usually assigned only in upper-level courses in your major. So by the time you have to write one, you will have plenty of experience as a college writer and also a solid knowledge of the subject area. In a beginning writing class, your essays will probably range from 200 to 1,000 words.

Essays vs. Paragraphs

An essay is usually thought of as a short piece of writing, but it is almost always longer than one paragraph. In the next chapter, we will discuss ways to improve the paragraphs in your essays. For now, we need to know that essays are divided into paragraphs to help the reader.

When you read newspapers or magazines, it's easy to see the ways paragraphs help readers. They show when the writer is moving to a new point and allow readers to rest their eyes a bit as they read. To grasp this point, imagine if this book were written without any breaks for paragraphs. Readers would have to go through line after line after line without a break for their eyes. As a result, they could tire and lose interest or miss the point. So unless your teacher asks you to write a one-paragraph essay like the one assigned in Chapter 2, be sure to divide your essay into paragraphs.

Essays and the Writer's Purpose

Part of our definition of an essay states that a writer purposefully presents ideas. This means, as we discussed in Chapter 1, that the writer has a purpose for writing. As you remember, the purpose can be as simple as wanting to inform the reader how to change a flat tire, or it can be as complicated as wanting to change the audience's views on a political issue. Whatever the purpose, the essay presents the writer's ideas on some aspect of real experience.

If an essay is well written, you should be able to tell what the writer's purpose is. For instance, in writing the one-paragraph essay assigned in Chapter 2, your purpose was to show how the person you chose to write about was significant to you, so you probably chose examples that would make the reader see the person's significance.

Essays vs. Stories

Sometimes beginning students will talk about the *stories* they are reading in their textbook or about the *stories* they are writing. They are confused about what an essay is. An essay is not a story, although sometimes an essay tells a true story.

There are basically two types of writing that we refer to as stories: newspaper articles and works of fiction. A newspaper story deals with real events that the reporter writes about—a law passed in congress or a natural disaster, for example. But newspaper stories present the events themselves, not the writer's ideas about the events. Thus, a newspaper story is not an essay. In a fictional story, the writer may make up all or some of the events. Fictional stories may present ideas, but they are not essays because the events, though possibly based on real life, are changed and shaped by the writer's imagination. You probably will read fictional stories in some of your college English classes. These stories can teach you a lot about life and can be fun to read. But when you talk about essays, use the word *essay*, not *story*, because there is an important difference. Knowing the difference will help you be a better reader and writer.

There are, however, other words used sometimes to refer to an essay. When written in a college course, an essay is sometimes called a theme, a composition, or simply a paper. So if your teachers or classmates use these terms, know that they are talking about essays.

Identifying the Audience

An essay, like most pieces of writing, is written for an audience. As we discussed in Chapters 1 and 2, the audience will influence the writer's choice of content and language, what is written and how it is written. If you were to write an essay telling working parents how to choose a day-care center, the financial status of the audience would be important for you to consider. If this essay were written for low-income parents, you would have to offer information abut free or low-cost centers provided by public and private agencies. If your audience were high-income parents, you probably would spend more time discussing expensive private centers. If your audience included both high- and low-income parents, information on all types of centers would have to be included. After you have had some practice reading essays, you will be able to tell whom the writer has in mind as an audience. If we read the essay on day-care centers and found it covered only expensive centers, we could assume it was written for wealthy people. In other words, when an essay is well written, the reader can easily identify the audience it is written for.

The Essay Topic

In our original definition of an essay, we said an essay is written on a single **topic.** Simply defined, a topic is part of a larger **subject.** For example, the theories of Sigmund Freud would be one topic in the subject area of psychology. Hockey would be a topic in the larger subject area of sports, and playing goalie would be a topic within the larger subject area of hockey. A subject is general; a topic is more specific.

The topic of an essay, then, emphasizes a single part of a larger subject. As a result, the topic often determines the length of the essay. The bigger the topic, the longer the essay. When a topic is too big for the length of the essay, writers say the topic is too broad. When a topic is too broad, the essay usually ends up being too general to say very much. If you wrote the paragraph assigned at the end of Chapter 2, you should remember how the example in the directions limited the topic to how Coach Dawson taught self-discipline. This is one topic in the larger subject of Coach Dawson.

Suppose that you were assigned to write an essay of about 500 words with the purpose of explaining something about your college experience to friends who are not in college. If you tried to cover the all of your experience in 500 words, you would have to be very general. You might end up with 100 words on the classes and another 100 words each on teachers, campus activities, social life, and so on. This essay would be so general that your experience in college would not sound any different than what most people generally assume about college even if they have not gone there. Thus, readers would gain little from reading the essay, and there would be little purpose in your writing.

But let's say the assignment was narrowed down to require you to pick one part of your college experience and write an essay with the purpose of showing why this part is significant to you and other students. Now you would be beginning with your college experience as a subject, but the one part you picked to write about would be your topic. For example, suppose you picked the topic that college students can have difficulty coming to terms with new ideas that sometimes conflict with the beliefs they have learned at home. Because there is not as much to say about this idea as there is to say about all of college experience, you could probably write a pretty specific essay in 500 words.

The Thesis

Simply defined, the thesis is the main idea of an essay. Many times this idea is stated in one sentence, called the thesis sentence. A thesis is not the same as a topic. A topic is what you are writing about; a thesis is the point you make about that topic. For instance, college students dealing with conflicting ideas is a topic. But before you have a thesis, you need to ask, "What *about* college students dealing with conflicting ideas?" When you answer this question by saying that students have difficulty coming to terms with conflicting ideas, you have a point—and thus a thesis—on the topic.

For beginning writers, finding a thesis can be difficult. When you have a topic, you tend to want to write everything you know about it. When you do this, you end up with a paper that either has no point or has so many different points that the audience cannot tell what the essay is trying to say.

As a written product, an essay should have a topic that can be covered within the length of the essay and a clear thesis that says something about the topic. To ensure that it has both, the writer must give careful consideration to both the topic and thesis during the process of writing.

chapter four
The Process of Writing Essays

Unit I took you through the writing process. In this chapter, we apply the writing process to the writing of an essay.

Finding a Topic

From time to time teachers will assign you topics to write about. For example, in a class on the environment, the teacher might assign an essay asking you to show why the survival of a certain species is essential to the balance of nature. When a teacher assigns such a specific topic, your job is easier because you do not have to start with a broad subject and narrow it to a limited topic.

Other times, a teacher might give you a broad subject area to write about, and you have to limit the subject to a topic. For example, in a class on twentieth-century American history, a couple of weeks might be spent studying the Vietnam War. At the end of the unit, the teacher might assign an essay on some aspect of the war. Given that you learned much about the war in the unit, you could not cover all of it. So from the subject area of the Vietnam War, you would have to come up with a limited topic, such as drug abuse in Vietnam, military strategy, or the financial cost of the war.

In some cases, the teacher will just tell you that you have to write a paper on something covered in the course. In this case, you have to start with a very broad subject area—the whole course—limit yourself to a smaller subject area that interests you, and then further limit the subject area to a topic. A former student of mine once came into my office with such an assignment. She was taking the course Black American History and was told to write a five-page essay on any aspect of the course. Beginning with the subject of black history, she limited herself to the life of W. E. B. DuBois, the famous black sociologist. But she complained that since DuBois did so much in his life, she could never cover it in five pages. She was right, and after thinking about the subject of DuBois's life, she finally limited her topic to how DuBois overcame extreme prejudice to become the first black person to earn a degree from Harvard University.

Learning how to limit a topic takes practice and experience. But the more you write, the easier it becomes. First, keep in mind that a topic is much more specific than a subject area. However, you also have to be careful not to limit your topic so much that you do not have enough to say to produce an essay as long as you want. Working through the following exercise will begin to show you what writers have to consider in moving from a subject to a limited topic. As you do the exercise, remember the ladder diagram in Chapter 3. Subjects are more general and are higher on the ladder; topics are more specific and are lower.

Exercise 4.1

The following items are either subjects or topics. After each item is a specified number of typed pages. On a sheet of paper, identify the item as a subject or a topic and briefly explain why the item would or would not make a good topic for an essay of the length specified. Before doing the exercise, read the examples carefully.

Example 1: How to pitch a pup tent (ten pages). This is a topic, but it is probably too limited for a ten-page essay because even though there are certain steps to follow in pitching a pup tent, the writer would run out of things to say unless he or she went into details that the reader would not need to do the job.

Example 2: The Space Shuttle (four pages). This is a subject because it is too broad for a four-page essay. Because there were many shuttle missions, four pages would not allow the writer to be specific about any of them.

Example 3: Reasons for dropping a class (three pages). This is a good topic for an essay of this length. The writer could go into how students sometimes get bad advice, how teachers might make poor first impressions, and how the class might not be what the student expected. The writer could provide specific examples for each reason.

1. Rhythm and blues (four pages)
2. Urban street gangs (four pages)
3. John F. Kennedy (ten pages)
4. Deciding to go to college (one page)

5. The quality of a particular restaurant (three pages)
6. Changing a flat tire (ten pages)
7. A music video (two pages)
8. College classes (three pages)
9. The exterior appearance of a campus building (three pages)
10. The nutritional value of a slice of pizza (two pages)

Using Invention Strategies to Find a Topic

In Chapter 1, as you were introduced to invention strategies, we went through the process of finding a topic. Although our focus was on how to use the strategies rather than on how to find a topic, we began with the broad subject area of rock music and eventually limited ourselves to a topic on heavy metal concerts. Below you will see how invention strategies can be used as a way to limit a subject area to a topic that you could cover in an essay of about 600 words.

Suppose you were taking a class on mass media and were asked to write a paper on some aspect of it. You could start with the broad subject area of media and, using the brainstorming strategy, limit it to one topic. You probably remember that brainstorming involves making lists. The following is a list on media:

television
news
radio
all around us
magazines
newspapers
relation to politics
shapes public opinion
books
comic books
records
protected by First Amendment, on free speech
sometimes unfair
very powerful

This list gives you a lot to think about. Some of the items are types of media; others are facts or points about media. Some are more general, such as television; others are more specific, such as the fact that the First Amendment protects the media in the United States. If you sorted all of these items and grouped related items together, you could probably write an essay on media. However, because you have only 600 words to work with, this essay would not be very good because it would be so general that it could not say anything about the media that is not obvious. So you would need to pick one item on the list and brainstorm further. Let's try newspapers.

local newspapers
big-city papers
school newspapers
supermarket tabloids
newspaper comics
home delivery
reporters
news stories
photos
foreign-language newspapers
interesting to read
millions daily readers
history of newspapers

This list still provides too much information to cover in a 600-word essay. The topic of newspapers is too broad, so again your essay would be too general. Some of the items on the brainstorming list are limited enough themselves, so if you choose one and make another brainstorming list, you would have a topic and be on your way to developing it. Suppose you decided to pick supermarket tabloids, thinking that it is less obvious than some other aspects of newspapers and thus perhaps more interesting:

National Enquirer	*National Star*
politicians	*The Globe*
Weekly World News	sold at supermarket checkouts
millions of readers	Elvis's "ghost"
supernatural stories	celebrity gossip

UFOs

disease stories

crime stories

advertisements

exaggeration and untruth

horoscopes

weird people and occurrences

With this list, you are beginning to see specific material that would help you form a thesis and come up with a paper, but the items are in random order, and you would need first to group related items together:

Different tabloids
  National Enquirer
  The Globe
  Weekly World News
  National Star
Stories
  celebrity gossip
  crime stories
  disease stories
  supernatural stories
  weird people and occurrences
Other
  advertisements
  horoscopes
  exaggeration and untruth
  millions of readers
  sold at supermarket checkouts

If you look over this list, you will notice that a couple of items have been cut—for example, the stories on UFOs and Elvis's "ghost." These do not appear on the second list because they are covered under supernatural stories. You would probably mention them when you wrote the paper, but in organizing your list, you should consolidate related categories. With this list, you could begin to think about what you want to say about tabloids and begin formulating a thesis.

Although we have used the brainstorming strategy to limit a general subject to a specific topic, you could reach this topic using any of the other invention strategies. Rather than work through each strategy completely, we will present one step in each:

Clustering

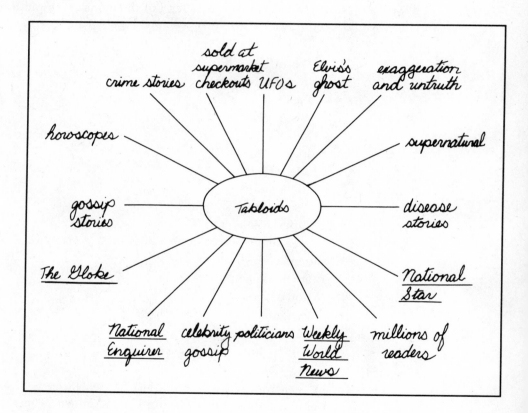

The Journalist's Questions

Who? Millions of people read tabloids.

What? Gossip about celebrities; stories about weird crimes, diseases, UFOs, Elvis's "ghost," odd people and occurrences; also horoscopes and advertisements.

When? It doesn't matter, but tabloids appear weekly.

Where? Doesn't matter where they're read; sold at supermarket checkouts.

Why? Not sure, to find out about celebrities and strange things not in regular newspapers, to amuse themselves, to not be bored.

How? Does not apply to this topic.

Freewriting

I like to look at the covers of the tabloid papers when I am at the supermarket checkout. One says Big Foot had been spotted in the Catskills, another one tells about a woman claiming she is pregnant by an alien. You wonder why people buy them. They probably like to read about all the celebrities, like who Cher is dating now or who is getting a divorce or on drugs. I buy them once in a while for a laugh. The stories are exaggerated or untrue, but they are funny. There's some gruesome crimes, though, like in the *Weekly World News,* and real weird stuff in *The Globe.* The *National Enquirer* and *National Star* are mostly celebrities, but they have some weird stories too. All of them have horoscopes and ads for diets, ways to get rich, and the kind of products you see also advertised on TV late at night.

Any of the invention strategies, of course, can help you explore the topic. You may have noticed that the journalist's questions and the freewriting bring up additional points, such as why people read tabloids. Also, near the end of the freewriting, the writer begins to compare tabloids containing mostly weird stories to tabloids containing mostly stories on celebrities. Either of these points might lead the writer toward a thesis. With the brainstorming list and clustering diagram, you obtain information on the topic but you would then have to decide on a purpose and a thesis.

Exercise 4.2

Choose as a subject something you are good at: a sport, a hobby, a job, a leisure activity, a school subject. Don't overlook your skill in any area; students have written this essay on everything from physics to rearing children. Once you have made your choice, try each invention strategy to come up with a topic and notes that are limited enough to be covered in an essay of about 500 words.

Writing the Thesis Sentence

Earlier in this chapter, we made two key points in defining a thesis sentence: a thesis sentence states the main idea of the essay, and a thesis is what the writer says about the topic. Once you have chosen a topic, you need to say something about it in a complete sentence. But as you write the thesis sentence, you need to make sure you have a point to make and a purpose in writing. For example, suppose you wrote the following thesis:

Tabloid newspapers are very strange.

Although this sentence is true, it is too general and obvious to be of interest. Most people have seen the covers of tabloids while in line at the supermarket, so they would probably agree with this thesis and not be motivated to read further. Therefore, there would be no purpose to a paper with a thesis stating something most people already know. Also, the word *strange* is rather vague.

A good thesis requires us to think about what we feel. Here are three possible thesis sentences for the paper on tabloids:

Tabloid newspapers are trash read by people who must have boring lives.

Tabloid newspapers are harmless entertainment.

Tabloid newspapers are popular because they involve readers with extraordinary events and people, unlike those usually encountered in everyday life.

Each thesis could come from the writer thinking hard about the brainstorming list and discovering a purpose for writing according to his or her opinions. The first writer decides that the tabloids are trash; her purpose would be to make readers of tabloids reconsider why they read them. The second writer sees no harm in tabloids; his purpose is to show people who look down on them that they are really not so bad. The third writer does not take a stand for or against tabloids but has the purpose of showing why people read tabloids. In each case, the thesis makes a point about tabloids.

A thesis must be a sentence that needs to be argued or demonstrated. The first two writers would have to argue their positions on tabloids; the third would have to demonstrate that people do indeed read tabloids for the reasons stated in the thesis. The following summary of the qualities of a good thesis sentence can help you to test any thesis sentence you come up with for an essay.

A Thesis Is Limited

A thesis is limited according to the topic and the length of the essay. For instance, an essay of around 500 words needs a very limited thesis:

Too broad:	There is a serious crime problem in the U.S.
Limited by place:	There is a serious crime problem in Washington, D.C.
Limited by number (one problem):	Muggings are a serious problem in Washington, D.C.
Limited by time:	In the last two years, muggings have become a serious crime problem in Washington, D.C.

Exercise 4.3

The following thesis sentences are too broad and need to be limited. Limit them by place, number, or time.

1. Exercise is a great way to stay fit.
2. Teenagers need to be more careful about safety.
3. The media are sometimes biased in reporting the news.
4. The University of Notre Dame has a great athletic history.
5. Political conventions to nominate the President are dull and needless exercises.
6. Playing cards is fun.
7. Skateboarding has become controversial in some places.
8. American students know very little about history.
9. Mass transit fares are too high for the service provided.
10. Bicycles are a great way to get around.

A Thesis Is Neither Too General nor Too Specific

A thesis sentence should be general enough to cover all aspects of the topic but specific enough to let the reader know exactly what point the writer wants to make. When a thesis is too general, the reader does not quite know what the paper will say about the topic. When a thesis sentence is too specific, it usually contains details that should come later in the essay or that have nothing to do with the writer's purpose and should be cut. Compare these thesis sentences:

Too general:	Many students are too concerned with grades.
Too specific:	Many students at _____ just cram for tests and don't care what they learn. (Cramming would probably be only one point used to support your thesis.)
Just right:	Many students at _____ College value grades more than learning.

To make sure your thesis is not too general, try to avoid using such vague words as *interesting, bad, neat, unique, great,* and so on. To make sure your thesis is not too specific, save your details for the body of the paper.

Exercise 4.4

Some of the following thesis sentences are too general and some are too specific. Rewrite them to make them more effective.

1. Nikons are great cameras.
2. Seven of ten police officers in _____ believe they are underpaid.
3. My high school geometry teacher, Mr. Majewski—who was very large and had a booming voice—could strike fear into the hearts of any student from a timid freshman to a cocky senior.
4. In the 1960s, people tended to be idealistic.
5. Badminton can be fun.
6. In the 1960s, young people favored tie-dyed T-shirts and bell-bottom jeans.
7. Middle Eastern food is very hot because it contains lots of ginger and curry powder.
8. Mexican food is tasty.

9. Richard Hatcher, Tom Bradley, Andrew Young, Kenneth Gibson, and Harold Washington, black mayors of large cities, have shown that blacks can excel in high political office.
10. Blacks have been very effective as mayors of large cities.

A Thesis Should Be Argumentative or Demonstrable

A thesis should not be an obvious fact that your audience will accept without argument. A thesis can be a controversial argument, such as a claim that gun control is right or wrong, or it can be a sentence that just needs to be demonstrated for the reader to accept it.

Fact:	Los Angeles has a smog problem.
Thesis:	Smog makes Los Angeles an unpleasant place to live.
Fact:	My paper will explain the Battle of Bull Run.
Thesis:	The Battle of Bull Run showed the North that the South was prepared to fight the Civil War.
Fact:	A Kraco car stereo costs less than an Alpine.
Thesis	A Kraco car stereo sounds just as good as an Alpine.

Exercise 4.5

Below are some possible thesis sentences. If a sentence is an arguable or demonstratable thesis, put a *T* next to it. If it is a fact, write a sentence that could be argued or demonstrated about the same topic.

1. Rodney enjoys wind surfing.
2. The Macintosh computer has a simple but powerful word processing program.
3. The Eiffel Tower is in Paris, France.
4. Admission to Disneyworld costs over $20, but once people are inside, all attractions are free.
5. Stripping and refinishing furniture is a time-consuming but worthwhile hobby.
6. The red star is a symbol of communism.

7. Arizona is in the Southwest.
8. Mickey Mantle and Willie Mays were both center fielders, and both were elected to baseball's Hall of Fame.
9. The number of business majors today could lead to a poor job market in business in the future.
10. My paper is about the British Navy in World War II.

Exercise 4.6

In the space following each sentence, tell why the sentence would or would not make a good thesis sentence for a paper of about 500 words.

1. *Batman* was a very popular movie.

   _____

2. International relations can be very complex.

   _____

3. Word processing is the easiest method of writing.

   _____

4. Faulty wiring is the major cause of house fires.

   _____

5. Pool is a game deserving of a better reputation than it has.

   _____

6. The proper grip is the key to an effective golf swing.

   _____

7. Ronald Reagan was President from 1980 to 1988.

   _____

8. My paper is about bass fishing.

   _____

9. Senior citizens can benefit more from exercise than most people think.

   _____

10. Snowmobiling is fun.

   _____

Exercise 4.7

In exercise 4.2, you formulated a topic for an essay on something you are good at. Now write two possible thesis sentences for your essay—one bad one and one that you could use to write the essay. Be ready to explain why one is bad and the other is good.

"There are many fish in all the lakes so you can always count on catching some."

"With no sign of civilization in sight, the sun took a shot peak through blackish-grey clouds, it seems as almost we were in a dream."

$$\frac{15}{15} - \frac{5}{5}$$

$$\frac{13}{15} - \frac{14}{15} - \frac{4}{5}$$

$$\frac{10}{15} - \frac{12}{15} - \frac{3}{5}$$

$$\frac{9}{15} - \frac{2}{5}$$

$$\frac{5}{15} \qquad \frac{2}{5}$$

$$\frac{4}{15} \qquad \frac{1}{5}$$

$$\frac{1}{15} - \qquad \frac{0}{5}$$

$$0$$

$$\frac{50}{50} \to \frac{15}{15} \qquad\qquad \frac{50}{50} \to \frac{15}{15}$$

$$\frac{45-49}{50} \longrightarrow \frac{14}{15} \qquad \frac{47-49}{50} \to \frac{14}{89}$$

$$\frac{40-45}{50} \to \frac{13}{15} \qquad \frac{44-44}{50} \to \frac{13}{15}$$

$$\frac{36-40}{50} - \frac{12}{15} \qquad \frac{41-43}{50} \to \frac{12}{15}$$

$$32-35 - \frac{11}{15} \qquad \frac{38-40}{50} - \frac{11}{15}$$

$$\frac{32-37}{50} - \frac{10}{15}$$

$$\frac{25-31}{50} - \frac{9}{15}$$

$$\frac{20-24}{50} - \frac{8}{15}$$

$$\frac{16-19}{50} - \frac{7}{15}$$

$$\frac{200}{3}$$
$$\frac{}{100}$$

$$28 \quad \frac{8}{6}$$
$$\frac{9}{14} \quad \frac{4}{2}$$
$$\frac{}{68}$$

550
776
1326
200
1526
500
1026

Fred **KERR**

FOR GOVERNOR '94

REPUBLICAN

"Straight Talk"

Keeping Your Audience in Mind

In the process of planning your essay—as you use invention strategies, find a topic, and write a thesis—you need to remember your audience at all times. If you look back over previous discussions, you will notice that the audience is often referred to. While you think of your audience throughout the process, you should also spend some time analyzing it directly.

In Chapter 3, you saw a series of questions for audience analysis. When planning and writing an essay, you should refer to those questions. You may remember the three major questions:

1. Who is my audience?
2. What is my audience's attitude about the topic?
3. How is my audience going to use my writing?

If you apply these questions to the topic on tabloid newspapers, they can help you to consider it more fully. Because the essay was assigned in a college class, you can assume an audience of classmates. Toward which ones is your essay directed? Those who read tabloids, or those who do not? What is their attitude toward the topic? Suppose you were using the thesis that tabloids are harmless entertainment. Those who read them would probably agree and use the essay to confirm ideas they already hold. Some might not read tabloids and have no opinion one way or the other. Your purpose then would be to persuade them to accept the thesis you put forth. Others might consider tabloids trash and be hostile, so your purpose would be to change their minds.

Throughout the paper, you would need to give examples that stress the harmlessness of tabloids, but because of the hostile segment of your audience, you would also have to admit that there is a large amount of exaggeration, even some untruth, in the tabloids. You would also have to be careful to use language that would not anger the hostile segment even more. For example, you would not want to call people who dislike tabloids snobs, even though you may suspect they are. On the other hand, if you were writing with the thesis that tabloids are trash read by people with boring lives, you would have to be careful not to insult those members of your audience who read tabloids. People do not want to be told their lives are boring.

Whatever the case, do not lose sight of your audience as you write. Spending some time analyzing the audience will help you to keep it in mind, and you will write a better essay.

Exercise 4.8

Using the full set of audience analysis questions in Chapter 3, analyze the possible audience for your essay on something you do well.

Organizing Your Invention Notes

Once you have come up with a set of invention notes, formed a topic, written a thesis, and analyzed your audience, you are ready to begin organizing your draft. At this point, you should return to your notes and think about the order in which you want to present the material and then group related information together. For instance, our third brainstorming lists looked like this:

> Different tabloids
> > *National Enquirer*
> > *The Globe*
> > *Weekly World News*
> > *National Star*
> Stories
> > celebrity gossip
> > crime stories
> > disease stories
> > supernatural stories
> > weird people and occurrences
> Other
> > advertisements
> > exaggeration and untruth
> > horoscopes
> > millions of readers
> > sold at supermarket checkouts

With this list, you can begin to plan a rough draft. You have to consider in what order you want to put the information, which items will become full paragraphs, which items can be combined in single paragraphs, and how all items will relate to your thesis. Assuming you are working with the thesis that tabloids are harmless entertainment, you would probably need full paragraphs to show how each type of story is entertaining, giving examples of each. As you look at the rest of the material, you might decide that the names of the tabloids, the size of their audience, and the places where they are sold should appear in the first paragraph so that the reader knows immediately what the topic is. That leaves the point on exaggeration and untruth and the items on advertisements. You could develop a paragraph on advertisements but the point on exaggeration and untruth should probably be worked into each paragraph because it is the reason why some readers find tabloids harmless amusement. The fact that the stories are so exaggerated makes them unbelievable and funny. With these considerations in mind, you could set up an informal outline to guide your draft:

> Introduction (one paragraph)
>   Millions read tabloids
>   Everyone sees them at supermarket checkouts
>   Names of tabloids and a little about each
>   Thesis: Reading tabloid newspapers provides harmless entertainment.
> Body (at least a paragraph for each item)
>   celebrity gossip
>   crime stories
>   supernatural stories
>   disease stories
>   weird people and occurrences
>   advertisements
>   exaggeration and untruth
>   create entertainment
> Conclusion (one paragraph)
>   Reassert idea that tabloids are harmless amusement

Exercise 4.9

Organize the notes you have been making into an informal outline for your essay on something you do well.

Drafting the Essay

When you finish invention and planning, you must draft the essay. If you have planned well, drafting the essay should not be too much trouble. However, remember that your plans could change as you draft, so remain flexible. Assemble your tools and set aside a couple of hours to work on the draft.

Keeping the Draft Organized

As you write the draft of an essay, stay aware of the way you are organizing it. The informal outline gives you a map. For instance, while writing an essay on tabloids, if you're covering weird crime stories, you would not want to stray into a discussion of supernatural stories. On the other hand, you might have an item that *seems* to fit in one paragraph, but really belongs in another. For example, tabloids often run stories claiming the ghost of Elvis Presley has done this or that. You might start by discussing Elvis stories in the paragraph on celebrities because Elvis was a major celebrity. However, ghost stories are supernatural, so you would want to reserve the paragraph on gossip to discuss only live celebrities.

While considering what should go into each paragraph, you should also consider the order of the paragraphs. The informal outline provides an order, but you might find that another order would work better. Suppose in writing about crime stories you discover that they appeal to the darker rather than the humorous side of people. Also, you might begin to wonder if reading them is really harmless. This discovery would make the crime stories different from your other examples. Thus, you might want to put them first or last in the body rather than in the middle of the other examples.

Developing the Draft

Developing the draft means including enough information to meet the needs of your audience and supporting the claim made in your thesis sentence. The invention notes and informal outline give you a start, but you have to develop each point in your notes more fully in your draft. You cannot simply say that tabloids have weird stories; you have to be more specific and detailed if you expect the audience to accept your thesis. You need to give examples of specific stories. You might brainstorm again to remember stories that struck you as particularly amusing. You might even buy a couple of tabloids to find fresh examples if you can't remember enough.

If you have enough examples, you still must be sure to bring them to life. For instance, it would be pretty dull if you wrote, "One story told of a body disappearing in front of people at a funeral." The reader would grasp the sense of exaggeration better if you wrote, "One story reported that a body glowed and vaporized into thin air before the eyes of a stunned priest and funeral congregation." Writing lively sentences is difficult because you have to call forth colorful language. However, you should try as much as possible as you draft, and later when you revise, to write sentences that are as specific and as lively as possible.

Exercise 4.10

Take one of the points from the notes on your topic and jot down additional information and details that you would use to develop that point to meet the needs of your audience.

Changing Your Thesis in Midstream

You may have heard the old saying, "the best laid plans of mice and men often go astray." Sometimes in writing, as in most everything else, no matter how much you plan, things change in the doing. Suppose while drafting a paper with the thesis that tabloids are harmless entertainment, you discover that many of the stories are not harmless—for example, that the stories on strange diseases make fun of the victims, or the stories on bizarre crimes appeal to the cruelty in humans. Now you have material that does not fit your thesis, so you have to change it. If you still feel that supernatural stories and celebrity gossip are fun, you might devise a thesis like one of these, depending on what you want to stress:

Tabloids contain much that is harmless entertainment, but they also print stories that are cruel and insensitive.

Tabloids contain much that is cruel and insensitive, but they also print stories that are harmless fun.

These thesis sentences argue that tabloids combine desirable and undesirable elements, whereas the original thesis was wholly favorable to the tabloids. In fact, your thesis could change even further. If you begin to think of celebrity gossip as a tasteless invasion of privacy and supernatural stories as ridiculous insults to one's intelligence, your thesis could become wholly negative toward tabloids.

Changing your thesis during drafting is fairly common. Although you should try to plan your essay with as much invention as possible, if, when drafting, you discover that you are thinking differently than you first did, do not worry. That is one of the benefits of writing: It helps you discover what you think.

Revising the Essay

Once you have completed the draft, you will need to revise it. The same considerations apply when you revise as when you draft: thesis, audience, organization, development. Unit III will cover revision in depth, but for now, consider the following strategies.

Revising the Thesis

Sometimes when you have completed a draft—even if you haven't changed your opinions—you may find that your thesis no longer fits exactly what you have written. Suppose you are arguing that tabloids are harmless and you discover that nearly all the paper focuses on how the articles are humorous if read with a light-hearted attitude. You might want to add the idea of humor to your thesis to focus it more directly. You might need to make only small adjustments in your thesis, but always reconsider the thesis after you have completed the draft.

Revising for Better Organization

If you organize your invention notes well, you should have a good idea of the way the parts of your draft will fit together. However, upon completing the draft, you might find that paragraphs could be put in a different order, combined, or separated.

In the informal outline for the tabloid paper, we placed the advertisements last in the body paragraphs. Having completed a draft you might find that this paragraph does not illustrate your thesis as strongly as some of the others. Because it is wise to put the strongest examples last so that readers remember them, you could move the paragraph on the ads to the beginning of the body.

Also, we listed quite a bit of material that would go into the introduction, but not much for the conclusion. Suppose you find upon completing the paper that the introduction is very long, with discussion of each tabloid, reference to the number of readers, and mention that tabloids are sold largely at supermarket checkouts. Suppose, too, that the conclusion is very short, with little more than a restating of the thesis. In this case, you might decide to move the information on the readers and the supermarket checkouts to the conclusion to flesh it out. This change would work as long as the discussion of the types of tabloids worked as an introduction.

These changes involve moving fairly large chunks of the essay. Remember that such moves are always an option, and read your draft carefully to see if choosing such options will improve your essay.

Revising for Development

When you revise the way your essay is developed, you either add information and details or cut them according to your purpose. Your purpose in one version of the tabloid essay is to argue that they are harmless entertainment. If, after completing the draft, you remember a funny article about a man who claims his wife is an alien, you certainly would want to add such an example.

On the other hand, suppose in discussing celebrity gossip four of the six examples are on Madonna. You would probably need to cut some of the examples on her and add some on other celebrities to create more variety. You would also have to be sure that you did not go into so much detail on any of the stories that the audience would forget the purpose of the essay.

A student of mine once wrote an essay with a thesis stating how a trip to Florida with friends showed him he was not as mature as he thought. He had notes on points to support this thesis, such as how he did not have enough sense to get tanned gradually and was severely burned and how he mismanaged his money, among other things. But he spent the first three pages of the paper writing about how he and his friends prepared for the trip and made the drive. His details on these points were fine, but they had nothing to do with his thesis.

As a beginning writer, you may hate to cut anything because you fear that you cannot get enough down to develop an essay. However, if you fully develop the points you should to support your thesis and meet your audience's needs, you will have no problem cutting unneeded material.

We have worked through much of the writing process for an essay. Of course, when you revise a draft, you might write a second or even a third draft. When you are satisfied with the content and organization of the paper, you should begin editing for errors and misspellings. Unit IV focuses on revision and can give ideas tips if you need them. Unit V can help you edit various errors. When you are finally satisfied with an essay, you type or neatly write the final copy and proofread it once more before turning it over to your audience.

Writing Assignment

Throughout this chapter, you have been working in the exercises on a topic about something you do well. Write a 400–500-word essay on that topic. Be sure to limit the topic and thesis sufficiently. Assume that your audience is a group of students unfamiliar with the topic and your relationship to it. Considering your purpose and role, assume that you will need to show what the activity is, why it is worthwhile, and why you are good at it.

Key Terms

Essay: A relatively short piece of writing in which the writer purposefully presents ideas and information to affect an audience on a single topic.

Story: Unlike an essay, a fictional story does not present real events, though it will present the writer's ideas and opinions. A newspaper story describes true events, but, unlike an essay, it does not present the writer's opinions and ideas.

Subject: A general area that usually cannot be covered in a short piece of writing, but the writer can start with a subject and then limit the essay to one topic within that subject.

Topic: Simply, a topic is what an essay is about. A topic can also be a limited area that can be fully developed within an essay.

Thesis; thesis sentence: A thesis is the main point the essay makes about the topic. The thesis sentence states the main point. A thesis needs to be argumentative or demonstrable.

Organization: The part of the writing process when the writer decides how to arrange the information in the essay. Organization can take place during invention, drafting, and/or revision.

chapter five
Strategies for Organizing Essays

In the previous chapter, you organized your invention notes for the essay on tabloids once you had a thesis sentence. When you have a thesis sentence, it often suggests a strategy for organizing the rest of the essay. For example, suppose you wanted to argue that the United States needs a national health care program sponsored by the federal government. This thesis suggests that there is a problem—some citizens need health care. It also suggests that there is a solution—a government program. Looking at this thesis, you could then organize your paper into sections, the first discussing the problem, the second proposing a solution. Thus, your thesis would supply a strategy for organizing your essay.

There are many strategies for organizing an essay. Sometimes these strategies are identified as patterns of organization in completed essays. You may have heard someone say an essay is an example of narration, process analysis, comparison-contrast, problem-solution, classification, definition, or argument. When you read an essay, you can identify its pattern of organization and understand the essay more clearly.

You need to think of these patterns as strategies that you can use for writing essays. You do not start out thinking, I am going to write a classification essay or a comparison-contrast essay. Rather, these patterns result from your thoughts about your topic, as the problem-solution pattern emerged from your thoughts on health care. Likewise, if the essay on tabloids had separate sections for each type of article, the essay would be considered an example of classification because you would have divided the large category of articles into different classes of articles. In other words, the topic and the way you thought about it during the writing process would have resulted in a classification essay, a pattern you could identify in the finished product of the essay. However, had you chosen the thesis that some articles in tabloids are harmless while others are cruel, you would be comparing and contrasting the types of articles, so you would end up with a comparison-contrast essay. But again, this pattern would develop from the way you thought about the topic—from your purpose and thesis.

In short, the strategies for organization are ways of thinking that become ways of writing when you put your thoughts on the page. We have discussed how these strategies develop from a thesis. But sometimes they can help you find a thesis and thus are a useful part of invention. When you have a topic and invention notes but do not know what you want to say, the strategies can help you think toward a purpose and thesis. For instance, suppose you began with the topic of home videos. You could think about videos using various strategies:

Comparison-contrast: How is viewing a movie on home video different from seeing it in a theater?

Problem-solution: Is there a problem with home videos? If so, how could it be solved?

Causal Analysis: Why are home video rentals increasing everyday, and what effect, if any, will they have on movie theater attendance?

These are just three of several strategies for organization. Any one of them could lead you to a thesis and provide you with a way to think about your topic so that what you write about it is organized clearly. If you are not sure what comparison-contrast, problem solution, or causal analysis are, don't worry. You have been thinking with these strategies most of your life, and we will discuss how these and others apply to writing.

Narrating

Even though we said earlier that an essay is not a story, when you are narrating, you are telling a story. But in a narrative essay, the story is based on true events and contains your feelings and opinions about those events, unlike fictional stories, which are imaginative, or newspaper stories, which contain true events but usually not the reporter's opinions. Therefore, a narration can be an essay. You have been narrating since you were a small child, for narrating is a common human impulse for organizing and relating experience. When you were a child, if your parents ever asked you what you did in school on a particular day, your answer would be a narration because you would tell what happened and what you thought about it.

In narrating, you present the material in your essay in chronological order. **Chronological** means according to the order of time. If a returning student were to use narration to develop an essay on going back to college, he or she would tell of the events from the time of the decision to apply to the arrival in the first class. For this essay, a brainstorming list might look like this:

> disliked working in textile mill
>
> thought for a while about applying to college
>
> discussed idea with family
>
> picked up brochures and application from local community college
>
> wrote for brochures and application to a state university within commuting distance
>
> considered courses of study
>
> decided on nursing major
>
> filled out applications
>
> was accepted unconditionally to the community college
>
> accepted into a conditional program for returning adults at state university
>
> decided on the community college
>
> discussed decision with family
>
> quit textile warehouse job and found a part-time job
>
> visited the campus to enroll, pay tuition, and meet with advisor to fill out a schedule
>
> went through registration
>
> attended first classes

Given this list, the student has plenty to write about, but she would have to over the list and decide how she felt about the events leading to college. For example, she might see much of the process as frightening if the job in the textile mill was secure and contributed largely to her family's income. However, she might also feel confident and satisfied now that she is in college. Such feelings would generate a thesis such as this:

> Applying to college was a frightening experience, but now I know I made the right decision.

On the other hand, she may have felt confident and enthusiastic about applying to college but was disappointed once she got there, resulting in a different thesis:

> I was eager to attend college, but now that I am in school, I feel higher education is not for me.

Obviously, the thesis depends on what the writer feels about the events narrated. The point is that a narration should have a purpose and thesis—to express how a person feels about a particular experience or event.

As the student drafted her essay, she would follow the chronological list but would add details to support the thesis and liven up the essay. For instance, were the applications difficult to fill out or surprisingly simple? What kind of person was her advisor? Kind and friendly? Stern and intimidating? Before writing a draft, the student could make additional brainstorming lists on each point to provide the details that would answer such questions. Such details would make the essay show rather than tell, making the writer's experience real and important to the reader.

Many topics lend themselves to narrating. For example, suppose an art history professor asked you to write a report on a tour you were assigned to take at a local museum. Your purpose would be to show what you saw and what you thought about it. In this case, you could use narration to take your audience (the professor) through each part of the tour.

When you are narrating on a topic, you have to decide where the coverage begins and ends, according to your purpose. For example, the brainstorming list above starts with the writer's dissatisfaction with her job because that is the first thing that prompted her to consider college. Avoid starting too far back in time from the topic. For instance, in reporting on the museum tour, do not spend time writing about how you got to the museum; after stating your thesis, start at the point the tour started.

Narrating can be an effective strategy for organizing essays on some topics, but sometimes other strategies are more effective. For instance, in the essay on tabloids, it probably would not be effective to narrate your experience of reading a tabloid. If you did, you would be discussing the articles and advertisements in the order your read them, and this could be confusing because you would be jumping back and forth among all the different kinds of articles. Also, your purpose in that paper was to discuss the tabloid itself, not your experience of reading it. This is not to say that there is anything wrong with narrating, but, like all strategies for organization, it works better for some topics than for others.

Exercise 5.1

Choose an experience in which you learned that things are not always the way they seem, and make a brainstorming list in which you organize your material chronologically in preparation for a narrative essay. Then write a thesis sentence to fit the essay.

Analyzing a Process

Analyzing a process is another strategy for organization. Like narration, it uses chronological order. In analyzing a process, you organize your topic step by step. There are two methods of analyzing a process. In one type, commonly called the *how-to essay*, a writer tells a reader how to perform some task, such as tuning a car, building a doghouse, choosing a college, swinging a golf club, and so on. In this type you assume your audience is going to perform the task you are writing about. For example, the writer of the narration on her experience of returning to college could analyze the process for an audience of students like herself. Her analysis of the process would differ from a narration because she would be telling others how to go to college rather than how she did it herself. She probably would not mention working in the textile mill because that is her particular experience, not the audience's. She could, however, include a section on how potential returning students should consider how they feel about *their* jobs before considering college.

A second method of analyzing a process is to tell how something is, or was, done. In this type, you assume the audience is not going to perform the task but wants to know how something works. This method could help you in certain college papers. For instance, in a finance course, the professor might ask you to write a paper showing how higher interest rates affect the stock market. In a political science course, you might be asked to show how a certain system of government works. In an automotive engineering course, you might have to write a paper showing the workings of something as simple as a turn signal or as complicated as a fuel injection system. The list could go on and on. Analyzing processes is a widely used method of writing because audiences will often be interested in how something is done or how something works.

When you analyze a process, you have to consider these questions:

1. What is/was needed for the process to occur?
2. What are/were the steps in the process?
3. Are/were there smaller processes in the larger process?
4. In what order do/did the steps occur?
5. How does/did one step affect other steps?
6. What is/was the result of the process?

In previous chapters, you have learned much about the writing process. We will apply each question to a discussion of the writing process and compare it to an essay analyzing how a blow drier works.

What is needed? In our initial discussion of the writing process, we wrote that for writing to occur there first has to be a writing situation in which the writer has a purpose, role, and audience. If you were writing about the blow drier, you would have to show how it relies on household current and how it must contain a switch to regulate the current, a small electric motor to power a plastic fan, a fan to blow air over a heating coil, and a casing to hold all the parts in place and to serve as a nozzle for the air flow.

What are the steps? By now you probably know quite well that the writing process consists of invention, drafting, revising, and editing. In writing about a blow drier, you would have to trace the flow of electricity from the electrical outlet through the wires to the switch, fan motor, and heating element. You would also have to trace how the fan creates a flow of air that is warmed as it passes over the heating element before being directed through the nozzle onto the hair.

In what order do the steps occur? In the chapter on the writing process, although we showed how the steps could overlap, we ordered them chronologically to show how most invention comes first, drafting second, revision third, and editing last. In a hair drier, electricity must first power the motor to turn the fan before an air flow can be created, and the element must first be heated before it can heat the air passing over it.

Are there small processes within the larger process? Certainly there are small processes within the *writing* process. Each invention strategy, for instance, is itself a process with steps to be followed. Similarly, the blow drier switch performs a process in regulating electricity to the fan motor and heating element to control the speed and temperature of the air flow.

How does one step affect another? In discussing writing, we talked about how good invention strategies can make drafting easier. We also stressed how one step in the process could overlap (happen at the same time as) another. Writing about the blow drier, you would have to show how the fan-turning and the element-heating have to occur at the same time because both are necessary to make the warm flow that leaves the nozzle to dry the hair.

What is the result of the process? Even though the result is the last part of the process, in organizing the essay you put the result first. That way the audience does not have to guess what the process is leading up to. For instance, did you ever see a recipe that does not tell you what you are making before giving directions on how to make it? Similarly, our chapter on the writing process began by discussing writing as a product—the results of the process. And if you were writing an essay on a blow drier, you would want the reader to know right away that it is a device that provides a warm, concentrated flow of air to dry and style wet hair.

Exercise 5.2

Choose one of the following assignments and make a brainstorming list for an essay on analyzing a process. Then write a thesis sentence to fit the essay.

How-to. Former Boston Red Sox star Ted Williams once wrote a whole book on how to hit a baseball. Choose something you enjoy doing—say, baking bread, shooting a jump shot, shopping for clothes, riding a jet-ski—and make invention notes for a short essay telling someone else how to do it.

How it is done, how it works, how it happens.   Make invention notes for an essay on some process that your audience will not perform themselves. Tell how some process you know is done, how some device you are familiar with works, or how some natural phenomenon comes about.

Analyzing Causes

In analyzing processes, you show how to do something or how something is done; in analyzing *causes*, you show *why* something happened. If you think about it, analyzing causes is a very common strategy in thinking as well as in writing. Humans are naturally curious—we like to know why things happen. Also, if something bad happens, knowing the cause can perhaps help us prevent it from happening again. If something good occurs, knowing the cause may help us make it happen again. But whether you can prevent an undesirable event or promote a desirable one, seeing causes and effects enables you to understand why something occurs. You often see writing that analyzes causes. For example, an editorial in a newspaper may analyze why the government cut money from a particular program or why a particular law will be bad for the country.

When you analyze causes, you start with the result of a chain of events. This result is called the effect. You then work backwards, looking for the reasons—causes—for this effect. Or you can analyze causes to predict an effect that you think will take place in the future.

With either type of causal analysis, a brainstorming list can be helpful. Suppose you were analyzing why teen marriages have a higher divorce rate than marriages of older couples. Your list might look like this:

> financial problems
>
> divorces are easy to get
>
> few career opportunities
>
> not used to household responsibilities
>
> not psychologically ready to settle down
>
> mistake sex for love

No matter what your topic, you would then have to analyze your causes and divide them into major causes and minor causes. Here is where your judgment would come in. While you might believe that financial problems are the major cause of teenage divorce, someone else might argue that the difficulty in handling household responsibilities is the major cause. You would also need to explore how one cause might have led to others—for example, are the financial problems the result of having few career possibilities?

In analyzing causes, you must always take care not to simplify your analysis. While you may see financial problems as the major cause of teenage divorce, you would have to admit that other causes contribute as well. How would you organize the causes?

> Minor causes
> > divorces are easy to get
> >
> > mistake sex for love
> >
> > not used to household responsibilities
>
> Major causes
> > not psychologically ready to settle down
> >
> > few career opportunities
> >
> > financial problems

In drafting the essay, you would cover the minor causes first. Next, you would admit that even with these problems some teen marriages survive. You would then move to your major causes and show how very few marriages can survive these. Usually the causes would be arranged with the most important ones last. Each cause, of course, would have to be developed in detail and related to other causes. For instance, if a couple is not psychologically ready to settle down, they may spend money foolishly entertaining themselves. This behavior, in turn, could contribute to financial problems. While having few career opportunities also contributes to financial problems, the reverse is also true: Without financial stability, it is more difficult to change jobs or pursue education leading to career opportunities.

One way to grasp the way causes are analyzed is to remember that an essay that analyzes causes will usually have a thesis that presents an argument: This happens because of this. In contrast, an essay analyzing processes will usually have a thesis that needs only to be demonstrated: Here is how this happens.

Exercise 5.3

Make a brainstorming list that shows the causes of some problem you are facing. Then organize this list into major and minor causes and write a thesis sentence that covers all the causes.

Posing and Solving a Problem

Sometimes an essay will merely pose a problem without offering a solution. Other times the essay will also offer a solution. At the beginning of this chapter, you saw the thesis that the United States needs a national health care program. This essay would define the problem and then provide the solution, which is the common way to organize an essay of this type.

In using the invention strategies, you would apply them to both the problem and the solution. You have bee using brainstorming lists quite a bit, so we will try the journalist's questions applied to the problem of campus crime:

Who? Students and nonstudents are committing crimes.

What? Mugging, rape, burglary.

Where? Muggings on paths from the library and in poorly lit parking lots; rapes in dorms and in parking lots; burglaries of dorm rooms.

When? Mostly late in the evening.

Why? A college campus, like a city or town, is a community, and all communities have crime or the potential for it.

How? Muggings and rapes often involve weapons or more than one criminal against the victim; dorm locks are easily slipped by burglars; or other students enter a room when one leaves briefly without locking the door.

The journalist's questions allow us to compile quite a few details on the problem of campus crime. You could then think about these details and apply the questions again to come up with possible solutions to the problem:

Who? Campus security and students must work together; administration and legislature must give support and funding to crime prevention.

What? Student organizations should form escort services for the paths and parking lots and floor-watch groups in the dorms; campus security should be more vigilant and should check to see if people on campus are really students; the administration and legislature should fund the hiring of more security officers and increased parking-lot lighting and should impose stiff penalties on campus criminals.

When? As soon as possible.

Where? Here at Tech.

Why? Because law-abiding students should be safe on campus and because students will not want to apply to this school if it has a reputation for crime.

How? By the combined and conscientious efforts of all involved.

With this much information, you would be ready to begin formulating a thesis and writing a draft.

When considering solutions to problems, you should always make sure that the solutions are possible. For instance, part of the solution for the campus crime problem requires that more money be allocated for security officers and parking-lot lights. These seem reasonable, but if your state and university are short of funds, these solutions might not be possible, in which case you would need to stress other measures that could be implemented until funds are available.

Exercise 5.4

Using any of the invention strategies, make notes for an essay posing and solving a problem on your campus or in your town or neighborhood. When you have completed the notes, write a thesis sentence.

Comparing and Contrasting

Comparing and contrasting is a strategy you use all the time in your thinking. In comparing and contrasting things, you come to know them and thus can make judgments and form opinions about them. If you were buying a car, you might find two that you like and compare them at the same price while contrasting the features of each. We constantly compare and contrast people, places, books, classes, TV shows—the list is endless.

Because comparing and contrasting is so basic to the way we think, it is also a very common type of writing, both in college and in the workplace: An executive writes a report comparing a new product to a competitor's product; a student of political science writes a research essay comparing the campaigns of two presidential candidates.

Like all strategies for organization, comparing and contrasting is the result of the writer's thought and purpose. If you think about two similar objects or ideas, you will naturally compare and contrast them. As a result, you may decide that one is better than the other or that both are equal, and your purpose would be to show the findings of your thoughts.

If you have a topic that requires you to compare and contrast, you can organize your draft two different ways. For instance, suppose that in a class on urban development you are studying park systems and are asked to compare and contrast two parks: Golden Gate Park in San Francisco and Central Park in New York. You would have two ways to organize this essay: successive coverage and alternate coverage.

Successive Coverage

If we say one thing succeeds another, we mean it follows another. Using successive coverage to compare and contrast, you would make all your points about one thing and then all the same points about the other. For example, notes for an essay comparing and contrasting the two parks might look like this:

Central Park
    size
    terrain
    sports facilities
    family facilities
    natural beauty
    safety
Golden Gate Park
    size
    terrain
    sports facilities
    family facilities
    natural beauty
    safety

As you drafted this essay, you would first cover each of these points on Central Park before covering the same points in the same order on Golden Gate Park. Successive coverage works well when you do not have many points of comparison and contrast and your essay will be relatively short.

If you have a lot of points to compare and contrast, successive coverage will not work well because the reader will have to remember everything about the first item in the essay while reading all about the second. When you have a lot of points, alternating coverage works better.

Alternating Coverage

When you use this technique, as the name implies, you alternate between the items you are comparing and contrasting. Rather than present all the information about one and then all about the other, you list your points of comparison and contrast and then alternately discuss each item. Your notes for an essay on the parks might look like this:

Size
    Central Park
    Golden Gate Park

Terrain
    Central Park
    Golden Gate Park
Sports Facilities
    Central Park
    Golden Gate Park
Family Facilities
    Central Park
    Golden Gate Park
Natural Beauty
    Central Park
    Golden Gate Park
Safety
    Central Park
    Golden Gate Park

Using alternating coverage, you could cover as many points as you wanted without worrying that the reader has forgotten what you said about one of the items being compared and contrasted. Therefore, in writing longer essays, you can use alternating coverage rather than successive coverage.

Exercise 5.5

Choose one of the pairs below, and make two sets of notes—one using successive coverage, the other using alternating coverage. Then write a thesis sentence for the essay.

1. Two movie actors
2. Two campus buildings
3. Two opinions on a controversial issue (e.g., abortion, gun control)
4. Two coaches
5. Two teachers
6. Two styles of dress
7. Two campus organizations
8. Two politicians

Classifying

As you worked through the essay on tabloids in the last chapter, you got some experience in classifying. As you remember, one version of that essay classified the types of articles according to what they were about: celebrities, crime, the supernatural, and so on. To set up a system of classification, you need at least three groups. The items in each group should share some quality that places them in that group, but they do not have to be exactly the same. For instance, if you have a dresser with socks in one drawer, underwear in another, and sweaters in another, you have a classification system. But within one class—say, the sock drawer—the items can have differences.

As you have probably realized, human beings classify constantly. Like comparing and contrasting, classifying is a way of thinking that you do all the time. It is a way of putting things in order and of seeing differences between one group and others.

Because people often think in terms of classification, they frequently write the same way. In classifying, the writer usually wants the reader to see the differences between classes for some purpose. For example, by classifying the types of articles in the tabloids, you would be showing a variety that could appeal to different readers.

There are two ways to classify: by built-in qualities and by imposed qualities. When you classify by built-in qualities, the differences in the groups are already there. For instance, if you group teachers according to the courses they teach, you will have the built-in classes of math teachers, English teachers, history teachers, science teachers, and so on. But if you group teachers as good teachers, average teachers, and poor teachers, you will be imposing the qualities on each class. In other words, your judgments will form the classes.

Sometimes an essay can use both systems. For instance, if you classify automobiles according to the country where they are produced, you might come up with the following classes: American cars, Japanese cars, German cars, Italian cars, and British cars. Once you have these classes, you can divide each class by imposing qualities on the cars in it. For each class, your divisions might then look like this: American cars you like, American cars you consider average, and American cars you do not like.

You might have noticed that you have ended up with classes within a class. That can happen, too. Think of the drawer full of socks. It forms one class of your clothes. Then suppose you put white athletic socks on the left side of the drawer, dress socks in the middle, and heavy woolen socks on the right. You would again be classifying items that are part of the larger class: socks.

When you set up classes, make sure that each class truly constitutes one and is not a member of another class. Examine this list of classes of television programs. See if you can find items that are represented as classes but that are actually members of another class:

> situation comedies
> news programs
> sports programs
> "The Cosby Show"
> specials
> music video programs
> miniseries
> "Eyewitness News"

"The Cosby Show" belongs in the class of situation comedies, and "Eyewitness News" belongs in the class of news programs. Neither one is a class by itself, and thus it should not be listed with other classes.

Similarly, you should not have a class that could contain items that are also in other classes. For example, what is wrong with this list of classes of crimes?

> burglary
> violent crimes
> murder
> rape
> armed robbery
> extortion
> embezzlement

You have violent crimes listed as a class by itself. However, many of the other classes—such as murder, rape, or armed robbery—involve violence. Thus, the class violent crimes does not fit this system.

Exercise 5.6

Using built-in qualities, classify one of the items below into at least three groups. Then, using imposed qualities, divide each group into at least three more classes and write a thesis sentence for the essay.

1. professional baseball teams
2. students
3. department stores
4. men's hairstyles
5. pets
6. exercise

Defining

Sometimes the purpose of an essay is to provide the audience with a definition. A few years back, for instance, when AIDS burst into the news media, you would see magazine articles defining the disease. But more commonly, defining is used as part of an essay. For instance, analyzing a process, you might have to define a term so the audience can follow your analysis. If you were analyzing how a computer disk drive works for an audience unfamiliar with computers, you would have to define the parts of the disk drive or your analysis would mean little to the audience.

In defining, your first step is to place a thing in its proper class. For example, oak is a type of wood. Your second step is to show how the thing differs from other members of that class: Oak is a type of wood lighter in color and harder than most common woods. You can also add the function of the thing: Oak is a type of hardwood often used for furniture, floors, and moldings. You can also define by comparison: Oak is nearly as hard as mahogany. Or by contrast: Oak is much harder than pine.

As you can see in this sentence, the strategies overlap. Our purpose was to define oak, but in defining it we compared and contrasted it with other woods. Definitions can be as short as one sentence, as we saw above, or they can be extended, as in the paragraph below:

Table hockey is a game played on a small table-sized rink 36″–48″ long and 18″–24″ wide. The rink is made of a molded plastic or pressboard sheet mounted on a rectangular frame of plastic, metal, or wood. At each end of the frame are metal rods that can be turned, pushed forward, or pulled back to control the direction and action of the players. These rods are connected to gears or springs beneath the rink surface. Approximately 3″ tall, the molded plastic players are mounted on pivots extending through slots cut in the surface. The players slide up and down these slots and can be manipulated to turn, pass, or shoot. Like real hockey teams, table-hockey teams consist of six players: a center, two guards, two forwards, and a goal tender who protects a goal slot 3″–4″ wide. The game is played with a plastic puck about the size of a nickel but about 1/4″ thick. Using the rod controls, skilled players can make several passes to set up a shot or move the team into defensive positions. Although the game is fast and exciting, it does not enjoy widespread popularity in the United States.

The primary purpose of this paragraph is to define. As you can see, the paragraph starts by placing table hockey in the class of games and then tells how the game is constructed and played.

In college, you may have some occasions when you will be asked to write fully developed definitions—for example, in essay examinations. But rarely would you write a whole essay that is only definition. If you do, you will need other strategies for organization. While the other strategies enable you to define, remember also that short definitions may be necessary when you write essays using the other strategies.

Exercise 5.7

Pick three of the items below and write a short definition (one or two sentences) that places the item in a class, shows how it differs from other members of the class, and identifies its function. Then pick one of these items and write a paragraph-length definition (50–75 words).

1. Compact Disc
2. olive oil
3. any one of the strategies for organization
4. toothpick
5. stopwatch
6. backpack

Arguing

When you think about arguing in writing, you should not confuse it with the typical way we think of the word. It usually calls to mind two people engaged in a hostile shouting match. Arguing in writing, though it can be hostile, is more like debating. The writer addresses some issue with reasonable appeals in an attempt to win the agreement of the audience.

Arguing overlaps with the other strategies. (As we will see later in this chapter, essays often mix strategies.) For example, if you were comparing and contrasting a Toyota Corolla and a Nissan Sentra and concluded that the Toyota was the better car, you would be using comparison-contrast to advance an argument. Some readers would disagree, but you would be trying to change their minds with your comparison-contrast. Similarly, our previous example of a problem-solution essay was an argument. In pointing to the crime problem, we had to argue that there was indeed a problem before we could propose a solution.

As you can see, argument in writing is more of a purpose than a strategy for organization. However, there are certain strategies for thinking about arguing that can help you to write arguments more convincingly.

Strategies for Arguing

Ethical Appeal.   When you use ethical appeal in arguing, you appeal to the audience's sense of morality and fair play. Suppose you were writing an essay arguing against a proposed raise for congressional representatives. Assume this raise calls for a 15% increase and that the average American worker receives only an 8% raise. You might write a sentence like this:

> While the average American worker has to be satisfied with an 8% raise this year, it is unfair for congressional representatives to raise their salary 15%, nearly twice as much.

As in all strategies for arguing, the facts must be accurate in an ethical appeal. You must also consider extenuating circumstances before making your claim. For example, if representatives had not had a raise in five years but in that period the average worker received a 6% raise each year, then this claim would be a faulty use of the ethical appeal.

Logical Appeal.   When you use logical appeal, as its name suggests, you appeal to the reader's sense of logic. You present facts that lead to a reasonable conclusion. For example:

> In the *Morning Herald*, City Road Commissioner Stefanie Michaels said that the city had a surplus of $50,000 in its budget. Thus, the county can afford to fix the potholes on Kirkwood Avenue between 7th and 9th Street.

This claim relates the possibility of solving a problem to the problem itself. If the potholes can be fixed for $50,000, then they should be because the money is available and the job of the road commission is to keep city streets safe. As with ethical appeal, the assertions must be accurate to make the audience accept your point. If the road commissioner had also said the surplus money would be used to install needed traffic signals on the city's busiest street, or if the potholes on Kirkwood were not hazardous, then the above claim would not be convincing.

Emotional Appeal.   In ethical and logical appeals, your claims are supported by facts, thus appealing to the reader's thoughts. In an emotional appeal, you direct yourself to the reader's feelings. All advertisements are, in one sense, arguments: They argue that we should buy a product. Advertisers often use emotional appeals, implying that driving a certain car will make us more exciting or wearing a certain perfume will make us more desirable. Emotional appeal is the least effective type of argument because it is not based on logic or fact, yet it can be very effective when combined with facts or when facts are unavailable. For example:

> The potholes on Kirkwood Avenue have reached the point where they are dangerous to the public. Drivers swerving to avoid them could cause accidents, resulting in injury and even death.

Here there are no facts. The writer is merely projecting possibilities, but the reference to injury and death serves to frighten the audience into accepting the seriousness of the problem. Of course, for the appeal to be effective and ethical, the problem of potholes should be as serious as the writer claims.

Conceding and Rebutting.   When you concede in an argument, you give in on a point. For example, if you were arguing about a campus crime problem, your opponents might point out that the crime rate on campus is far below that of the surrounding area. If this were true, you would have to admit its truth. However, you could then rebut this argument. Simply put, *to rebut* means to counterattack. Your concession and rebuttal might look like one of these sentences:

> Some people argue that crime on campus is not as bad as in the surrounding area; however, Tech has the highest crime rate of any campus in the state.

> Although the crime rate in the surrounding area is higher, the crime rate on the Tech campus is the highest of any campus in the state.

Conceding a point to your opponent does not weaken your argument; it strengthens it because the concession shows that you have considered both sides before choosing your position. Conceding and rebutting usually require sentences like those above, in which you state the opposing argument in one sentence and then connect your argument to it using *but* or *however.* Or you start the sentence with *although* and then join your argument with a comma. Writing these kinds of sentences will keep you from sounding as if you are arguing both sides equally.

Avoiding Faulty Arguments

All of the strategies above need to be used carefully. In an ethical or logical appeal, you should not twist the facts or exaggerate your claims. In an emotional appeal, your claims should be possible—unlike in advertisements, where we are promised that buying a particular soft drink or brand of gum will make us attractive to the opposite sex. Along with keeping your claims reasonable, you need to avoid faulty arguments.

Hasty Generalization.   When writers make hasty generalizations, they make claims based on too few examples. For instance, if you know two people who told you a particular teacher is very good, you would have to get the opinions of other students before taking a class from that teacher. Or if a friend of yours was mugged on campus, you could not conclude from that one incident that your school has a crime problem. People commonly make hasty generalizations; they should be avoided in writing.

Personal Attack.   If you have ever followed a political campaign, you have probably heard candidates complain that their opponents are attacking them personally, rather than sticking to the issues. If you were writing an essay arguing for strict gun control laws, you would not be very convincing if you said people against gun control are violent people who get an ego boost from carrying a gun. Here you would be attacking your opponents, instead of arguing the issue.

Either-Or Arguments.   In almost every argument, there are many possibilities. An either-or argument fails to see more than two. For instance, on the issue of financial aid, you should not write:

If financial aid cuts continue, no one will be able to attend college.

Such an argument is simply not true because some students would borrow the money, others would work for it, and some have families who can afford college expenses without financial aid. You can avoid either-or arguments by toning down your claims. In this case, you could argue that *some* students will not be able to attend college. Also, you could show other possibilities: students having to work longer hours while in school or taking a semester off to work to save money.

After this = because of this.   This type of argument assumes that because something happened after something else, the first event caused the second. For example,

Because Helga started dating Darren, she had no time for her friends.

Unless there is evidence that Darren is forbidding Helga to see her friends or taking so much of her time that she can't see them, this claim is faulty. There could be many other reasons Helga stopped seeing her friends. She may have studying to do, be working a job, and so on. This does not mean that you cannot claim that one thing caused another, but when you do so, be sure to have evidence to back up your claim.

Non Sequitur.   This term is Latin for *does not follow.* In such statements, one part of an argument has nothing to do with another:

There cannot be a drug problem in the United States. The government is spending billions of dollars to fight drugs.

Though the amount the government spends fighting drugs may influence the amount of drugs entering the country and people's attitudes about them, there could still be a drug problem.

Organizing an Argument

An argumentative essay can use any of the strategies previously discussed. You saw how the problem-solution essay on campus crime is an argument and how a comparison-contrast of two automobiles can be an argument. A narrative could also be an argument. If you told the story of people starving in a Third World country, that narration could be used to argue that more effort needs to be directed toward alleviating world hunger. A classification essay, too, could argue if you were identifying the classes to make a claim about them.

You use invention for an argumentative essay the same way you do for any essay. Once you have your invention notes, you arrange your arguments in an order that takes the reader from the least important to the most important. For instance, in the paper on campus crime, you would want to talk about burglary first because it is a nonviolent crime; muggings would come next because they are a violent crime; and rape would come last because it includes psychological as well as physical violence and can destroy lives.

Exercise 5.8

Choose one of the topics below, make a set of invention notes, and organize the notes in the best order for an essay arguing your opinion on the topic. State your overall opinion as your thesis.

1. Welfare
2. The draft
3. Car insurance rates for young people
4. Abortion
5. Funding for AIDS research
6. Students' role in university government

Mixing Strategies

If you read an essay, you can often identify the organizing strategy that the writer has used during the process. But at times you can see more than one strategy. For instance, in analyzing causes, a writer might compare and contrast one cause with another. Or, as previously mentioned, an essay might stop to define something for the reader. Likewise, while the problem-solution paper on campus crime would also be an argument, it could compare the campus to others, classify types of crimes, or narrate the stories of crime victims.

Usually one strategy will clearly dominate the essay, and you will be able to identify the essay by the strategy it reflects. However, when an essay uses more than one strategy, it does not mean that the essay lacks organization but that the writer's purpose and thesis require that the topic be thought about and presented in many ways. For example, examine these paragraphs on computer diskettes:

The two most popular types of personal computers are those using 5.25″ floppy diskettes and those with 3.5 hard diskettes. The floppy diskettes, as the name implies, are flat, flexible 5.25 squares with a hole in the center. They look something like a 45-rpm record in its jacket, though the jacket of the floppy diskette is soft plastic that cannot be removed. The smaller, hard diskettes are 3.5″ squares, feel like hard plastic, and sometimes are partly covered with a smooth metallic substance that looks like stretched tinfoil.

Computers using floppy diskettes have become very popular, but the computer industry is promoting the smaller, hard diskettes. When Apple introduced the revolutionary Macintosh computer, it used the hard diskettes. Following the Macintosh, IBM introduced hard-diskette systems, and industry analysts predicted that the floppy diskette would soon be obsolete. These predictions seemed true when nearly all the new laptop computers came out with the hard diskettes. However, since so many people already own machines that require floppy diskettes, they remain widely used today.

Though floppy diskettes are still used, hard diskettes offer more advantages. They hold more data, they are much more durable, and because most new systems use them, they will not soon become obsolete.

In the first of these paragraphs, we can easily see the writer comparing and contrasting the two types of diskettes by how they look and feel. In the second paragraph, however, the writer shifts to narration to show us how the hard diskette was introduced to replace the floppy. In the third paragraph, the writer begins to argue the advantages of the hard diskettes. The purpose of the whole essay might be to compare and contrast the two diskettes to argue that one is better than the other. The point is that the writer's purpose may require many strategies to complete the overall strategy of comparing and contrasting.

Once again, it is important to remember that strategies are ways of thinking. During invention, this writer probably thought about what each diskette looked like, how each was introduced, the advantages and disadvantages of each, and so on, and this range of thinking led to the mixed organization.

Although we can identify strategies as organizational patterns in writing, if you think of the strategies only in this way, they become products. To use the strategies as you write, you must focus on them as thinking processes and remember that the topic and your purpose determine what strategy you use. Sometimes you need not even be aware that you are using a strategy. If, in your hometown, you direct a stranger how to get somewhere, you do not stop and say to yourself, "My topic is getting to point B, so I will analyze the process of travelling from point A to point B." Rather, your mind automatically thinks in terms of process because of your purpose and your audience's need.

Exercise 5.9

In the last exercise, you made and organized some invention notes for an argumentative essay. Looking over those notes, devise a thesis and purpose. Then ask yourself what strategy these suggest and what other strategies you could use to develop particular points.

Writing Assignment

Throughout this chapter, you have worked on exercises that required you to make notes and write a thesis sentence for an essay using one of the strategies of organization. Use the invention notes that you made for *one* exercise to write a rough draft using a particular strategy. Plan on a final paper of about 500 words. Assume an audience of fellow students.

Key Terms

Essay Strategies: Ways of thinking about and organizing the information in an essay.

Narrating: An essay strategy in which the writer presents information in chronological order to tell a story.

Chronological: According to the order of time.

Analyzing Processes: An essay strategy in which the writer shows how to do something or how something works.

Analyzing Causes: An essay strategy in which the writer traces the causes that lead to an effect.

Comparing and Contrasting: An essay strategy in which the writer shows the similarities and differences between two things.

Classifying: An essay strategy in which the writer divides the information into classes.

Defining: An essay strategy in which the writer shows the audience what something is by placing the thing in a class and then showing how it differs from other members of that class.

Arguing: More of a purpose than a strategy, arguing involves writing an essay that presents an opinion on a topic.

Ethical appeal: A strategy for arguing in which the writer uses facts to appeal to the reader's sense of fair play.

Logical appeal: A strategy for arguing in which the writer uses facts to appeal to the reader's sense of logic.

Emotional appeal: A strategy for arguing in which the writer appeals to the reader's feelings.

Conceding and rebutting: A strategy for arguing in which the writer admits the truth of one of the opposition's points but then counterattacks with a related point.

Hasty generalization: A faulty claim in which the writer makes a claim based on too few examples.

Either-or argument: A faulty claim in which the writer fails to recognize more than two possibilities.

Personal attack: A faulty strategy in which the writer attacks his opponent personally rather than discussing the issue.

After this = because of this: A faulty claim in which the writer assumes that an event happening after a previous event was caused by the first event.

Non sequitur: A claim that is unrelated to the statement before it.

chapter six
Writing Timed Essays

We have been discussing writing that affords us a tremendous luxury—time. For example, if an executive has to write a report each month, there are thirty days between reports. Novelists sometimes take years to write a novel. When teachers assign term papers, they usually announce the assignment weeks or months before it is due. Even a short essay written overnight allows you a few hours to invent, draft, revise, and edit. But there are writing situations when writers must write against the clock: a reporter meeting a deadline, a policeman filing a report on an automobile accident, a business person writing a memo to address an immediate problem, a student writing an answer to an essay exam.

When people face a particular writing situation often, the process they use becomes second nature. The police officer writing an accident report, for example, does not need to brainstorm to list the vehicles involved. Nor does the officer have to worry about strategies for organization because he or she probably has discovered through experience one strategy that works well for nearly all accident reports. People who can produce a particular kind of writing quickly have internalized the writing process for that situation. By *internalize*, I mean they have had so much practice that they go through the process almost unconsciously.

In college, there are basically two situations where you have to write against the clock: in-class essays and examination questions. As you gain experience, you will become more skilled in both these situations, perhaps even internalizing the processes they call for. At first, however, they can be very intimidating because you fear you will run out of time or will not produce your best writing. It is true that you probably will not write your best under the pressure of time, but you can learn some strategies that will enable you to use what you know about the writing process to write quickly, clearly, and coherently.

In-Class Essays

In many writing classes, teachers assign essays to be written in class so that students will gain the experience they need to do well on essay examinations in other classes and to write quickly on the job. There are generally two kinds of in-class essay assignments: preassigned essays and impromptu essays. Each has different demands, so we will examine them separately.

Preassigned Essays

When you write a pre-assigned essay in class, you are given the topic one or more days before you have to write the essay. In some cases, you may be allowed to bring in a page or two of notes, though not a draft; other times, you are asked to rely on memory.

When a topic is preassigned, invention becomes the most important part of the process. You can take the topic home, work through your invention strategies, write a thesis, and plan a pattern of organization. In fact, during invention, you should treat the essay just as you would an essay to be written out of class. Then condense your invention notes so that you can commit them to memory or so that they fit on the page, or pages, that you are allowed to bring to class.

Though you may use any of the invention strategies to arrive at a thesis, you should probably end with an ordered brainstorming list. For example, suppose you were given this topic:

Although the cost of attending college is high, students are still getting their money's worth. Argue for or against this claim.

You could explore this topic with any of the invention strategies, perhaps producing several pages of notes. However, if you are allowed only a few or no notes, you need to boil the topic down to a few basic points that can jog your memory. Suppose that after thinking about the topic you decided to agree. A final brainstorming list that you can memorize or bring to class might look like this:

Thesis (agree): College is expensive, but the benefits outweigh the costs.

Becoming educated

Economic opportunity
Social life
Extracurricular offerings

This list is short enough to memorize if you had to. Of course, in writing the paper you would flesh out these sections with details that you thought about during invention. For example, you might have put under extracurricular activities a long list of cultural events, clubs, dances, sporting events, and the like. But were you to try memorize all of the examples for each category, you could lose sight of your main points. In other words, the items on the list should serve as triggers to the material you prepared during invention.

The topic on the cost and benefits of college contained a built-in thesis defined by your agreement or disagreement with the statement. However, sometimes you may be assigned a broader topic that you have to narrow down. Suppose your teacher gave you the subject of campus security and said that you would have to write an essay on some aspect of it in class. Although this topic might not seem broad, it can include many things, depending on the size and location of the campus: problems of security, such as violence, rape, burglary; parking regulations and the patrolling of parking lots; relations between students and security officers; and security in particular areas, such as the library or dormitories. The point is that when you have only fifty to ninety minutes to write, you need to narrow your topic as much as you can.

Although you may prepare well for an in-class essay assigned beforehand, you have to draft the essay in fifty minutes or an hour, and more than likely, the draft will have to stand as the final copy (even though you may be given the opportunity to revise it some other time). As you draft, you should use the points on your brainstorming list, whether in notes or memory, to trigger the content of your paragraphs.

Because you will not have time to organize each paragraph as you would at home, begin writing and let one example generate another. Given time, you might organize your examples differently; writing against the clock, your primary goal is to generate sufficient content. This does not mean you should not pause occasionally to look over what you have written, but you should not allow yourself to get stuck trying to think of a better example when you have one at hand. Writing what you do know may jog your memory and lead to the point you are trying to think of. In short, keep moving.

Though you can't do much, if any, revision in such a short time, try to plan the essay so that you have five or ten minutes to read and edit your paper before turning it in. You probably won't catch all your errors, but you may fix a couple that could distract a reader.

Impromptu Essays

The "impromptu" is a more difficult type of in-class essay. The word *impromptu* comes from French, meaning *in ready*. In English, it means *not rehearsed, spontaneous*. In a writing class, it means the instructor gives you a topic, or a choice of topics, and asks you to write an essay. Impromptu essays are difficult because they do not allow much time for the writing process, but you can use parts of the process to guide you.

Invention and Impromptus.　In an impromptu situation, the writing topic itself can sometimes suggest a thesis and a strategy for organization. For example, here are two impromptu topics assigned by a colleague of mine near the end of a first-semester writing course:

> **1.** Define a problem you anticipate having in the future and explain how you will solve it.
> **2.** What has been your most difficult class this semester and why?

If you look carefully at these topics, you will notice that the second one is a question, but the first one tells you to do something. This difference is important. If you read the first carefully, you will notice that it just leads you to a thesis and provides a strategy for organizing the paper. You are to start by defining and end by explaining how to solve the problem. Your thesis should then reflect this pattern. For example:

> I expect that in the next year my commitment to religion will be tested as I enjoy all of the social life college has to offer; thus, I must learn to balance the two by using restraint.

With this thesis, the student could quickly make a short brainstorming list for each part of the paper:

> Problem
> 　raised religious
> 　like spiritual benefits of religion
> 　want to maintain my commitment to religion
> 　some aspects of college social life may lead me astray
> Solution
> 　pick the right friends

pick the right social functions to attend

show restraint partying

continue to attend church

It should take no more than five minutes to make such a list if you have chosen a topic that you know about. The student could then begin writing, using each item to generate examples to develop the essay.

The second topic above is posed as a question. It could lead you immediately to a thesis if you answered both parts of the question. For instance, here are two possible thesis sentences. Notice how the first part of each answers the "what" of the question while the second part answers the "why" :

1. Life Science 101 was my toughest course this semester because of my lack of background in the subject and the volume of material covered.
2. My most difficult course last year was physical geography because I did not get along with the instructor.

With a thesis sentence, each of these students could then come up with a brainstorming list. The thesis can also control the way you think about the topic and, in turn, generate the organization of the paper. Note the word *because* in each thesis. It suggests a paper that will analyze causes.

How long should you spend on invention for an impromptu? For an hour class, no more than ten minutes. Because you have so little time, it is probably best to use brainstorming lists because they are faster than other invention strategies. Of course, you won't have time to make multiple lists. Make just one list and, if need be, number the points in the order you will present them. Impromptu essays do not allow you much time for invention, but the few minutes you spend on it are worthwhile. If you just start writing as soon as you have read the topic, there is no telling where you might end up. Remember, most readers would rather read something short but organized than something long and rambling.

Exercise 6.1

Choose one of the following topics, and write a thesis and brainstorming list in less than ten minutes. Then write down what strategy for organization the topic suggests.

1. It is sometimes said that during the first semester of college, a student matures more than he or she has through four years of high school. Do you agree or disagree with this statement?
2. Older students who return to college often work harder and earn better grades than traditional freshmen even though they often have responsibilities, such as jobs and families. Why, do you think, is this statement generally true?
3. Compare and contrast two cars, students, politicians, breakfast cereals, game shows, or styles of dress.
4. It is sometimes said that there is a thin line between love and hate. Relate a situation in which you experienced your reaction to crossing that line.
5. Students learn about many processes in their classes: for example, how a certain war started, how a company becomes a corporation, how a certain muscle functions, how a product is marketed. Pick a process you learned about in another class and analyze it.
6. Classify your instructors in terms of *one* of the following features: teaching ability, clothing, body type, attitude toward students.
7. What is the most important problem facing the United States today and why?
8. Who is the most overrated professional athlete and why?
9. Who is the most underrated professional athlete and why?
10. Narrate an incident in which you learned that life is more complex than you thought it was.

Drafting an Impromptu.   An impromptu, of course, requires you to write quickly, but you can't rush through it as if you were freewriting. Keep checking your invention list, and try to stick to it unless you come up with strong additional points as you are writing. Try not to stray too far from the list because, unlike a draft written out of class, an impromptu does not allow time for switching paragraphs around or reshaping your organizational strategy. Again, that's why invention is so important in an impromptu. As you draft, you should probably stop after each paragraph and reread it quickly. Doing so can help you remember where the next paragraph is going. However, do not stop and read individual sentences unless you are really stuck. If you catch an obvious error, correct it; otherwise save editing for last.

Revising an Impromptu.   As mentioned, impromptus do not allow time for revision, unless perhaps you have a couple of hours to write. In most cases, the first draft is the only draft. However, as you write, you can do some revising of the brainstorming list, perhaps changing the order of a paragraph or two. Or when rereading a paragraph, you might quickly combine a couple of sentences if needed. Otherwise, impromptus do not leave you time for major revision.

Exercise 6.2

In no more than thirty-five minutes, write a brief essay from the thesis and brainstorming list you formulated in exercise 6.1.

Editing an Impromptu. You cannot thoroughly edit an impromptu, but if you save yourself about five minutes, you can probably catch and correct some errors in a short essay. Try to focus on particular errors that you know occur in your writing. For example, if you know you have trouble with pronoun usage, concentrate on finding such errors (see Chapter 16). Also, look for major sentence errors, such as fragments, comma splices, and run-on sentences (see Chapters 13 and 14), because they distract most readers (and lower your grade with most teachers) more than any other errors. If you concentrate on errors that usually give you trouble and on major sentence errors, you can clean up your essay quite a bit in five or ten minutes. But don't expect to catch every comma error or misspelling.

Exercise 6.3

In five minutes, edit the essay you wrote in the previous exercise. Then count the number of errors you caught, and examine what kind of errors they were.

Essay Examinations

College examinations use all kinds of questions-true-false, multiple choice, one-word answer, matching. These require short, objective answers. Many instructors, however, want to know if students can discuss the material as well as remember facts about it. These instructors use essay questions. Essay questions may require from a short paragraph of six lines to a three-page essay, depending on how much time is allotted for the exam. In a one-hour class, you might expect to write one or two essays along with some short answers. A final exam, which can run two hours, could require you to write two or three longer essays. Writing essay examinations scares many students, but actually essay questions are easier to write than impromptu essays.

Writing an impromptu essay requires that you come up with ideas about the topic quickly. When you respond to an essay question—if you have kept up with the course and have studied sufficiently—you already have much information at hand when you begin the exam. You won't know the questions beforehand, but there is much you can do to answer them clearly and specifically.

Preparing for Essay Questions.   First, use the invention strategies to cover the material when you study. As you review class notes and textbooks, pick out the points you believe are important. Try to focus on the points the professor has spent the most time on in class. Then, using pen and paper, try out some invention strategies to explore these points.

Compare these two essays from a history text asking students to discuss the Stamp Act as a cause of the American Revolution:

Answer one

The Stamp Act was another tax that the colonists thought was unfair. A lot of important people from all over the colonies got together to protest it, and there were speeches made to stir everyone against it. The colonists saw this law as a violation of their rights that was illegal according to the British constitution. Then they boycotted British products until Parliament repealed the Stamp Act, and they all celebrated together.

Answer two

The Stamp Act was passed by the British Parliament in 1765. It required that the American colonists pay a tax ranging from a half-penny to one pound on all public papers, including legal documents, advertisements, pamphlets, business papers, and so on. This law caused more trouble than earlier taxes because it taxed the businesses inside of the colonies, while earlier taxes had only added to the cost of goods imported from Britain. Since this tax affected powerful people such as businessmen, bankers, lawyers, and journalists, the protest against it was forceful. These men organized into "Sons of Liberty" organizations that tried to stop the British Admiralty Court from enforcing the act. Merchants organized boycotts against British products, colonial legislatures drew up resolutions against the tax, and great speakers such as Patrick Henry and Samuel Adams made public speeches to stir the public against it.

Representatives of nine colonies met in Massachusetts and sent a protest to Parliament, claiming that the law was illegal. Because they were not represented in Parliament, they demanded that taxes inside the colonies should only be passed by colonial legislatures. These protests, the boycott, and Benjamin Franklin's speech before Parliament convinced the British that the Stamp Act was doing more harm than good.

When the Stamp Act was then repealed, there were celebrations all over colonies. The reaction to the Stamp Act is important because it showed the Americans, for the first time, that they could stand up to the British if they united together.

After reading these two answers, you will have little doubt which one earned the better grade. Although the information in the first answer is correct, because it is not developed with specific examples, the history teacher has no way of knowing if the student knows any more than he or she has written. In contrast, the second answer gives the date of the Stamp Act, tells exactly what it taxed, tells whom it affected most, names important people involved in the protest, shows why the colonists thought is was illegal, and then states why it was important in uniting the colonies against Britain.

Obviously the writer of answer two knows the subject, but the invention strategies can help bring that knowledge forth. As you know, invention strategies can help you examine a subject systematically. For example, the journalist's questions force you to ask "Who? What? When? Where? Why? How?" Assume that the history teacher had spent much time on the causes of the American Revolution. The journalist's questions could produce much of the information in answer one if applied to the Stamp Act:

What happened? Stamp Act taxed public documents such as wills and business papers. Ranged from a halfpenny to one pound. First tax on something other than British imports. Colonies banded together in protest. Boycotted British goods and made speeches against it. Sons of Liberty groups formed to prevent the tax from being enforced. When tax was repealed, people celebrated all over the colonies.

When did it happen? 1765

Who did it? British Parliament. Who had to pay it? Businessmen, lawyers, merchants, anyone who wrote public papers. Rich and powerful people. Patrick Henry, Samuel Adams, and Benjamin Franklin all made protest speeches against the tax.

Why? Parliament passed the tax to make money from the colonies. Colonists protested, felt tax was illegal because they had no representation in

Parliament. Thought taxes on things inside the colonies should only be passed by colonial governments.

Where? Protests against the law happened all over the colonies. Nine colonies met in Massachusetts to send a protest to Parliament. Franklin spoke before Parliament in England.

How? How did the tax and the repeal affect the colonies? Made them even more angry at England, brought them closer together, and let them know that united they could stand up to England.

The writer of essay two may have had such a knowledge of the Stamp Act that using the *"five Ws + H"* method would not have been necessary. But even if she did know the material that well, going through the journalist's questions would help her remember the specific details that make her answer so good. In contrast, the student who wrote the weak answer probably could have improved it a great deal if he had used the questions when studying.

If you use invention strategies to study, you will examine the material very thoroughly and will enter the examination prepared. But be sure to write things down so that you can review them more carefully and remember them more easily when the exam comes. Just rereading your text and notes and thinking about them won't help nearly as much as using pen and paper.

Exercise 6.4

Most writing courses do not give essay exams on the textbook and class discussions; instead, you are graded on the essays you write. But for practice, we will use the following questions for some of the subsequent exercises. For this exercise, use an invention strategy to explore one of the questions thoroughly. In parentheses, you will find the time limit and the chapter where the material appears.

1. Analyze the writing process (30 minutes; Unit I, Introduction)
2. Compare and contrast brainstorming and freewriting as invention strategies (15 minutes; Chapter 1)
3. Explain the difference between general and specific writing, providing examples of how each works in an essay (25 minutes; Chapter 3)
4. What is clustering, and what are the advantages and disadvantages of it as an invention strategy? (20 minutes; Chapter 1)
5. What is the writing situation, and how does it affect the way you write? (20 minutes; Chapter 2)

6. What effect does the audience have on the way the writer writes? (20 minutes; Chapter 2)

A second method of preparation is to list significant points and begin to think about them using the strategies for organization. This will help you see relationships between points and enable you to anticipate questions. For instance, are there issues or people the instructor might ask you to compare and contrast? Are there points that can be classified? What items might the instructor ask you to define? Have you covered anything that could be analyzed as a process? This type of thinking and listing is extremely important because the strategies reflect the way people think, the professor as well as you. Thus, the strategies for organization can reflect the kinds of questions you will be asked.

Finally, try to write sample questions. For example, in an introductory psychology course, you would have studied many different theories of psychology. Write a question asking that you classify them. Write another question asking that you compare and contrast two major ones. Write another question asking you to define a theory. Write one asking you to analyze the process of one of the famous experiments you studied. In writing these questions, you may get lucky and write a question that will show up on the test, but that's not the point. Rather, by writing questions, you think about the important relationships in a given field, whether it is psychology or physics. Finally, you can practice writing sample answers to the questions if time allows.

Exercise 6.5

Read a chapter from one of your textbooks and write three essay questions that you think you would be asked if you were being tested on the chapter.

Writing the Essay Exam. Before you begin writing, read all the questions first, noting how many points each is worth (that's often listed) and which questions you know the most about. Figure out roughly how much time you can spend on each question. This is important. Some students will foolishly spend time to write two or three pages on a short essay question worth only ten points and then have time to write only a page on a question worth thirty points. Finally, begin answering the question you know most about, numbering it so that the professor knows which question you have started with (rarely do professors care about the order in which you answer the questions). Writing on the question you know most about has two purposes: it will give you confidence, and it may jog your memory on points that apply to questions you do not know as much about.

Before you answer the question, remember to examine it to see if it suggests a thesis or an organizational strategy, just as you do with an impromptu topic. If you have used the organizational strategies to study before the test, finding them in the questions should not be too difficult. For example, the following questions come from various courses, but the way each is worded suggests the organization of its answer:

> Explain how read-only memory (ROM) works. (computer science)
>
> Compare and contrast the design of 1940s men's double-breasted suits with the double-breasted suits of the 1960s. (fashion design)
>
> What is insider trading, and how does it work? (economics)
>
> What was the Back to Basics movement of the 1970s and how is it similar to and different from the Cultural Literacy movement of the late 1980s? (education)
>
> Why did President Truman relieve General MacArthur of his command during the Korean War? (history)

If you examine these questions carefully, they tell you how to organize your answers. The first obviously wants you to analyze a process: how something works. The second straightforwardly asks for a comparison-contrast. The third and fourth, however, are more difficult because each has two parts. You can assume, however, that in each you will begin with a definition before writing the process analysis on insider trading or the comparison-contrast of the Back to Basics and Cultural Literacy movements. The fifth question would allow you to start immediately with a thesis, which you could then develop with specific causes.

Unfortunately, not all essay questions will immediately suggest a pattern of organization. Compare these questions with the previous ones on the same subject:

> Discuss the design of the 1940s men's double-breasted suit and the design of the 1960s double-breasted suit.
>
> Explain insider trading.

Examine the Cultural Literacy movement of the 1980s in light of the Back to Basics movement of the 1970s.

In these questions, the words in the directions are less specific. Does *discuss* mean you are to compare and contrast the suit designs? Does it mean you are to define and analyze how arbitrage houses work? Does *examine* mean you are to compare and contrast the two educational movements or show how one caused the other? When you get a question worded as generally as these, don't just begin writing all you know on the subject. Take a minute to think about how you could organize what you have to say. Though general questions do not clearly say so, they are probably looking for specific, well-organized answers.

Exercise 6.6

Write down the strategy or strategies for organization suggested in each question in exercise 6.4.

Some Additional Tips.   Sometimes problems will arise when you are taking an essay exam. Even when you have tried to plan your time, you can run short. If you run out of time and still have more to say, add a sentence telling what additional points you would have covered given the time. For instance, suppose that in comparing the men's double-breasted suits, you had covered the width of the lapels, the cut of the shoulders, the patterns and colors, the fit of each, and so on, but you still had much to say about the kinds of fabrics each was made of. Instead of not mentioning fabric at all, you should add a sentence saying something like this: "I was getting ready to compare the fabric types when time ran out." Such a sentence will not get you full credit, but it shows you knew more about the question than you were able to get down. Who knows? You may earn an extra point or two.

Another common problem can occur when you have finished an answer and realize you have left out something in the middle of the essay. If you have time, you can write the paragraph at the end of the essay and then draw an arrow and write a note showing where it goes. While this is not great form, it allows you to show what you could have done given more time.

Finally, the worst problem of all can arise: You read a question and feel you can't answer it at all. Rather than skip it, you should start writing something about any part of the question you know anything about. For instance, the last question in the examples asks why Truman fired MacArthur as American commander in Korea. If you could not remember any of the reasons for his firing but could remember MacArthur's success as commander earlier in the war, you could start writing about that. While you would not be answering the question, the act of writing about MacArthur might enable you to remember more about him to the point that you remember the events that led to him being fired. In this sense, you would be "writing your way into the question," for when writing we often jog our memories, recall information, and come up with ideas. Even if you do not end up answering the question, you would at least show that you know something about MacArthur. Of course, such questions should be answered last so that you do not waste time writing an answer that is off the topic when you might be using your time to work on questions you know.

Exercise 6.7

Pick the question in exercise 6.4 that you know the *least* about and try to "write your way into it."

Anxiety and Timed Writing

Any writing can cause anxiety. When you are asked to write in a specific amount of time, you may feel even more anxious, especially when you know an essay question will affect your grade or that an impromptu will be graded by your writing teacher. But there are some consolations. Most writing teachers do not expect your best work on impromptu essays, and as experienced writers themselves, they will read (and grade) your paper knowing the difficulties you face. As for essay exams, the better an answer is written, the higher grade it will usually receive. At the same time, most graders of essay exams do not expect an essay written in thirty minutes to be a highly polished writing. If your essay answers the question clearly, is fairly well organized, and includes specific details, you will probably do well. Though timed essays do not allow you the luxury of using all you know about the writing process, what you do know about it can help.

Writing Assignments

1. Write an essay answering one of the questions in exercise 6.4. Follow the time specified next to the question.
2. In no more than thirty minutes, write an answer to the question you wrote in 6.5.

Key Terms

Preassigned Essay: An essay for which you are given the topic in advance but that you will have to write in class.

Impromptu Essay: An essay written in class on a topic assigned that day.

unit two

Essays for Reading

The following four essays can enable you to see how strategies for organization are reflected in final essays. Cheva Schroyer Dunkin uses comparison and contrast to explore her reactions to her daughter and memories of herself. Bernadette Pankey analyzes a process to show us how a professional news reporter goes about an important task. Kim Robertson argues her opinions of advertisements, while Khim Hiam Lim uses narration to tell a story that taught him about his relationships with his father and mother. As you read the essays, consider how the students' thoughts on the topics produced the strategies for organization evident in their final products.

Momma Did It, Too
Cheva Schroyer Dunkin (freshman)

Sipping my coffee, I watched my teenaged daughter rock back and forth to the beat of something wild and strange. She seemed so far away, so distant, so different from me, but was she? Each generation, through fads and fashions, asserts an identity that fades with maturity.

Her hair was teased until it stood out and around her face like a porcupine's quills. "Ron" in bold red letters ran down her right shirt sleeve. A huge red heart monopolized the front of her shirt between "I" and "Ron," proclaiming her love for him. Pleated Lee jeans snugly fit her trim frame. White Reebok tennis shoes and red socks completed her outfit—almost. Rips stretched across her jeans exposing both knees, making a U-turn up toward her thigh. Strings and fringed edges implied unbridled recklessness begun by her hair.

After she left, I sat wondering what had happened to the teenagers of today. "In my day," I whispered to myself, then stopped, for I began to remember my teenage years.

I wore my hair in a high, fluffy ponytail that swayed back and forth like a horse tail swatting flies. My nylon cardigan was worn backward, with the pearl buttons outlining my spine. The manufacture's tag showed at my neck like a "white badge of fashion." Can-can petticoats, faithfully dipped in sugar water, made my six-yard circular skirt stand out around me. I looked like an umbrella. Around my ankle I wore a dog collar—a symbol of importance to the world of my unavailability. I wore mine through both loops, meaning I was going steady. Black-and-white saddle oxfords and white bobby sox completed my attire. I danced to the rock-and-roll beat of Bill Haley's "Rock Around the Clock" and Fats Domino's "I Found My Thrill on Blueberry Hill."

I remember my parents starting a sentence with "In my day" and finishing with a lecture about my generation. But it wasn't long before they found out they had nothing to worry about; I was just going through adolescence. Fads and fashion mark the teenagers' time in the sunshine of youth. Jobs, homes, bills, and three-piece suits will have to wait till sundown.

Questions for Study and Discussion

1. What might be on a brainstorming list or cluster diagram for this paper?
2. What is the thesis of Dunkin's essay? At what point does it appear in the paper? Is it repeated elsewhere?
3. How do Dunkin's examples support her thesis?
4. Cite at least three examples of effective use of specific details.
5. What strategy for organization does Dunkin use?
6. Is this essay an example of successive or alternate coverage?
7. Would successive or alternate coverage be more effective for this essay?
8. Dunkin wrote this essay for an audience of classmates; many were traditional college students not much older than her daughter, while others were closer to her age. How does her use of details meet the needs of both groups?
9. Do you agree or disagree with what Dunkin says about fads and fashion in the last paragraph? Why?
10. Why does Dunkin also refer to her own parents?
11. Freewrite for five minutes about your relationship to someone older or younger than you are.
12. Using your freewriting as a basis, make a list of similarities and differences you share with this person.

Following in the Footsteps of a Radio News Reporter
Bernadette Pankey (sophomore)

As people listen to the news on the radio, they often take for granted the five to ten interviews which are heard throughout the newscast. Listeners may hear the police chief describing an escape attempt or a young woman explaining how she won the title of queen at the local fair. These short pieces of tape add interest to the overall news broadcast. The radio news reporter responsible for conducting the actual interviews must put a lot of time and effort into them, even though listeners will hear only five seconds of tape.

Most stations receive press releases announcing events or meetings. These press releases often serve as a basis for a story. The reporter must read the copy thoroughly, writing down any questions. The press release will contain a number to call for more information, but the reporter should call the person or company discussed in the copy directly because the person at the press release number usually knows little more than what appears in the copy.

Before calling, the reporter must make sure the "phoner," or tape machine, is turned on. The machine uses reel-to-reel tape, but it functions like a cassette tape recorder. The reporter must then turn the counter, the narrow black box containing numbers, to zero. The counter allows the reporter to know where the interview is located on the tape, making it easier to find after the interview.

The speaker monitor, a knob usually located nearest to the small, round speaker, should be turned down. If the reporter leaves the knob turned up, an irritating squeal will be heard. The round knob next to the main control panel is called the select switch. This knob must be turned to the position reading "source." The VU meter, the black needle within the small glass case, will then monitor the voices coming through the telephone. The VU meter allows the reporter to know if the voices are too high or too low. If the needle goes all the way to the right side of the red section, the levels are much too high. With the needle in this position, the voices will be distorted. If the needle goes all the way to the left side in the white section, the levels will be too low, and the recording will not be able to be heard. It is best to have the VU needle in the middle, allowing it to move into the red section occasionally. The reporter must then push the record, play, and pause buttons of the main control panel. The reporter is then just a phone call away from the interview.

After contacting the desired person, the reporter must notify him or her that the interview will be taped for on-air use. Some people may hesitate to answer any questions knowing that their voice will be heard over the radio. The reporter must assure the person that he or she will sound just fine and that the information will be used fairly.

Once the person consents to a taped interview, the reporter releases the pause button. The reporter should listen to the source's answer to prepared questions and also ask whatever questions come to mind during the interview. The reporter must also try to get the person to elaborate on answers instead of merely answering with a "yes" or "no" or brief statement. At the conclusion of the conversation, the reporter should verify the person's title and the correct pronunciation of his or her name. The reporter should then thank the person for taking the time to answer the questions.

After the reporter hangs up the telephone, he or she must then check that the conversation was indeed taped. To find out, the reporter must simply rewind the tape to zero on the counter, turn the select switch to "tape," turn up the monitor knob, and push "play" on the control panel. The reporter should then hear his or her voice, as well as the person interviewed.

The reporter reenacts this same interviewing procedure at least once a day, usually more often, just to hear five seconds of the interview played over the air. Of course, the credit goes to the news broadcasters, leaving all of the reporter's hard work unnoticed. But hearing the tape, the reporter gains satisfaction from a job well done.

Questions for Study and Discussion

1. What is Pankey's strategy for organization?
2. Does Pankey assume the reader will be conducting interviews, or is she describing just what the reporter does? How can you tell?
3. What equipment is needed to conduct the interview? What details does Pankey use to describe how the equipment is used?
4. What are the other important details for each step?
5. What details tell us that Pankey assumes her audience knows little or nothing about the topic?
5. What is Pankey's thesis and when does she first state it?
6. The first and last paragraphs do not cover steps in the process. What is their purpose?
7. What is the logic of Pankey's paragraph divisions? What do her paragraphs have in common?
8. Pick out some words that tell you Pankey is organizing the paper in chronological order.
9. Who is Pankey's audience, and what is her purpose?
10. Do you think you could perform this process having read Pankey's essay? Why or why not?
11. Interview a classmate on some process he or she knows how to perform. List the steps and write a brief paragraph explaining the process.
12. Have a third classmate read your paragraph and comment on whether he or she feels your paragraph explains the process clearly.

Misled
Kim Robertson (freshman)

"Lose 20 pounds in one week!" "Softer skin in seven days or your money back!" These are just two examples of slogans used by companies to advertise today. Thumbing through the current issue of *Glamour* magazine, I was shocked to see that over three-fourths of the contents were advertisements. After noticing this, I started paying more attention to advertisements elsewhere. Once while watching a one-half hour television show, I counted seven commercials. I believe that many of the commercials and advertisements are misleading and sometimes simply untrue. Although there may be some truth to advertising, I feel that most advertisements today are so far from reality as to be misleading.

For instance, for amusement, I occasionally glance through a tabloid such as the *National Enquirer* or *Star*. The most recent ad I saw claimed that with the aid of a particular product, a person could lose 20 pounds in one week. All the person needed to do was send a check or money order for $32 to the company and receive a bottle of pills that he or she was to take two of before each meal. The ad was surrounded by "before" and "after" pictures of men and women in oversized pants, smiling proudly at their massive weight loss.

In another magazine, *Redbook,* I spotted an ad that could make my skin flawless and smooth without clogging my pores. Maybelline suggests that using Ultra Performance make-up will result in "perfect" skin. In the corner of the page, there is a model with beautiful skin smiling seductively into the camera.

Television commercials are even worse than print ads. One that did not only turn me away from the product but also insulted me was for Vanish toilet bowl cleaner. The commercial began with a mean-looking toilet bowl growling at a woman with a cleaning brush. The woman then said, "You won't defeat me this time" and with one magic squirt and swoosh of the Vanish cleaner, the bowl was suddenly smiling and sparkling as the woman flexed her arms in glory.

These ads show that advertising today seems to be nothing more than page after page of convincing actors or camera trickery.

As for the weight loss ad in the *Enquirer,* unfortunately, many desperate, overweight people probably sent in their $32 and received (4 to 6 weeks later) a bottle of miracle pills to make them thin. Not only is it probably impossible to lose 20 pounds in one week, but trying may be very dangerous. The advertisement probably did not let consumers know that they had to follow a strict liquid diet and do massive amounts of exercise as part of this program. The people used as examples in the picture were probably either actors or people who had lost a large amount of weight over an extended period of time.

The advertisement concerning Maybelline make-up was not quite as bad but still was misleading. The company wants women to believe that after using the make-up their skin will look like the picture of the model. Realistically, there may be some improvement, but most women will not necessarily have "perfect" and flawless skin after sampling their product.

In comparison to reality, the Vanish commercial is plainly ridiculous. First, as far as I know, toilet bowls do not talk, nor do they growl when you try to clean them. Second, the commercial gives the impression that after one quick spray of Vanish the toilet bowl will be immaculate. Anyone who has scrubbed a bowl knows differently.

Most Americans may not be fooled by advertisements that are too stupid to be real. But a large group of people do not catch the "fine print" that the advertisers keep from them. Advertising sets trends and establishes norms for our society. People are unconsciously convinced that they are supposed to look or dress a certain way, and the advertising industry takes advantage of these notions. I realize that ads need to catch the consumer's eye, and to do that they must be interesting enough to remember, but most advertisements could get the point across without being misleading. I think that with more honest ads, Americans would take advertising more seriously.

Questions for Study and Discussion

1. List at least six items that would be on a brainstorming list or cluster diagram for this essay.

2. What is the thesis of this essay, and how would the items on the brainstorming list or cluster diagram lead to it?

3. Why does Robertson begin her paper with claims from ads? Why does she then tell us how she counted ads in magazines and on television?

4. Evaluate the effectiveness of Robertson's choice of examples. Do they seem typical? What choice of details helps support Robertson's claim?

5. What is the dominant strategy of organization used?

6. Although Robertson is primarily arguing, what other strategy or organization is evident?

7. Cite examples when Robertson uses effective strategies for arguing; for a logical, ethical, or emotional appeal; for conceding and rebutting.

8. Do you find any examples of faulty strategies for arguing—hasty generalization, personal attack, and so on?

9. Cite some ads that you would point out to help prove Robertson's claim.

10. Cite some ads that you would point out to disprove her claim.

11. Choose one ad that you find misleading, and make a brainstorming list that could support your argument.

12. Choose one ad that you find fair and accurate, and make a brainstorming list that could support your argument.

Care
Khim Hian Lim (freshman)

When I was ten years old, my father was teaching in high school. Every afternoon after he had conducted a test, he would stay in his room for a couple of hours until he had finished marking all the papers or at least most of them. Sometimes, instead of taking a break, he fell asleep until we woke him up for dinner. I could feel the pressure and hard time my father had when he needed to mark the test papers for almost two hundred students. The time I tried to "help" him I learned more about my relationship with my parents than I learned about grading tests.

One day, after school, I went into my father's room. I saw him leaning against the back of the couch taking a nap. I approached the table beside him and saw stacks of test papers on the desk. I realized that he was having a hard time again. It was nearly time to eat, so I gradually woke him up, and we went into the dining room together.

On the table were my favorite dishes; however, my mind could not stop thinking over and over of what my father had been doing for the past couple of hours. After dinner, my parents went out to buy some groceries. I walked into my father's room and began to work.

I took out the answer sheet and noticed that there were two sections on the test; section one had essay questions and section two had multiple-choice questions. My father had explained to me before that from a number of choices the student has to pick the correct one. I decided that I could grade the multiple-choice test. "It's so simple. It's nothing," I told myself. All I needed to do was just match the letters on the answer sheet with the letters on the test papers. Therefore, I began to be a temporary teaching assistant.

Suddenly, I saw another answer sheet under a pile of papers. It had different letters than the sheet I was using. "Oh, no!" I shouted. There were two versions of the test, Test A and Test B, but I had marked all the papers according to Test A answers only. I was entirely awake at this time. I knew I had made a tremendous error. I was nervous and started to pray.

Just when I wanted to think of a solution, my parents came back. "It's the end of the world!" I screamed. When my father discovered the incident, his face turned red and he slammed the papers on the floor. My mother glanced at me once, smiled, and told my father that all I had done was try to help. "Yes! Yes! Mum, you are the most understanding woman in the world!" I thought. My father frowned and walked from the room. Eventually, he accepted my apologies and I went to bed immediately.

Questions for Study and Discussion

1. Lim's thesis says he learned about his relationship with his parents. What exactly do you think he learned?

2 Compare and contrast the reactions of Lim's mother and father.

3. Lim's essay does not have a lot of specific details, but those he uses are effective. Cite some examples. Can you think of any additional details that might make the essay more effective?

4. What is Lim's primary strategy for organizing this essay?

5. Give examples of words that signal chronological order.

6. Though the essay is primarily narration, are any other strategies present?

7. Lim was a college student when he wrote this essay, but what uses of language and illustrations of behavior indicate his age at the time the incident happened?

8. Explain the title of the essay. To whom does the title apply?

9. Choose an incident that taught you about your relationship with an elder and make a brainstorming list leading to some thesis about the relationship.

unit three:
Writing Paragraphs and Sentences

Earlier chapters have provided you with some experience in writing essays. Your focus in the previous assignments was on the whole essay, on developing a thesis in an extended piece of writing. In this unit, however, we will focus on the parts that come together to make up an essay: paragraphs and sentences. Learning about these parts will help you improve the whole.

Just as you probably had some idea of what an essay is before you read about essays in the last chapter, you probably have some idea of what paragraphs and sentences are, but the discussions in this unit will expand and clarify your definitions, show you how paragraphs and sentences work in an essay, and provide strategies for writing them.

What Is a Paragraph?

We will start with a short definition to focus the discussion in the chapters that follow: A paragraph is a short piece of writing on a very limited topic, and although some paragraphs can stand alone, most are parts of a larger piece of writing, such as an essay.

Paragraphs vs. Essays

Sometimes a college writing assignment may ask you to write only one paragraph, such as a short answer to a question on a test or regarding a reading assignment. Most writing assignments in college require essays. You already have some idea of the differences between the two, and perhaps you have recognized some similarities as well. Knowing the differences and similarities can help you to write both paragraphs and essays.

The first thing to remember is that a paragraph is usually part of an essay. For instance, in Chapter 4, one of the essays we planned was to argue that tabloids provide harmless entertainment. In fulfilling this purpose, the essay would have to cover various items in the tabloids. Some items, if limited enough, could be covered in one paragraph—the advertisements, for example. Larger items, such as the articles, would require, say, one paragraph for each type. Together, all the paragraphs would add up to support the thesis about tabloids.

Naturally, a paragraph is shorter than an essay. A paragraph will have a topic of its own, but the topic will be more limited than the topic of the whole essay. For example, one paragraph in the tabloid essay might show how articles on the supernatural, though unbelievable, are entertaining, while the essay would be showing how the tabloids as a whole are entertaining.

Though paragraphs and essays differ, they share several similarities. First, a paragraph, like an essay, covers one topic, even though that topic will be more limited than an essay topic. Just as an essay must develop its topic according to the writer's purpose and the reader's needs, each paragraph in the essay must also work to fulfill the writer's purpose and the reader's needs. Second, just as an essay has a main idea, so does a paragraph, and the main idea of a paragraph will serve to develop the main idea of the whole essay, as you will see in the next chapter.

Paragraphs have different functions in essays. Some work as introductions, making the reader familiar with your topic and leading into the thesis of the essay; others develop the body of the essay; and others function as conclusions—but all contribute to the total content and form of the essay.

What Is a Sentence?

You may remember the grade school definition of a sentence as "a group of words expressing a complete thought." Most sentences do express complete thoughts, and keeping that definition in mind can be helpful. But in this unit, you will also learn how to define a sentence in terms of grammar. You will also learn about sentence structure—how sentences are put together in paragraphs. Finally, you will receive many tips on how to write and revise sentences so that they flow and are clear, concise, and direct.

chapter seven
Writing Body Paragraphs

When we examine essays, we can generally classify paragraphs according to their function: They either introduce the topic, develop and support the thesis, or conclude the essay. The number of paragraphs in an essay depends on the writer's topic, thesis, and purpose. As a writer develops a thesis, the paragraphs emerge accordingly. In this chapter, we will discuss body paragraphs and give you some practice writing them.

The Length of Body Paragraphs

If you read a newspaper, you will notice that writers often use one- or two-sentence paragraphs. These short paragraphs are used in order not to strain the eyes of readers. Because newspapers have long, narrow columns of small print, writers have to indent for new paragraphs often. Otherwise, the reader would have difficulty separating the lines.

In college essays, however, the length of a paragraph depends on its purpose as part of the essay. Writers usually use a paragraph to develop a point in an argument, to signal a shift in time in a narrative, to cover a step in a process, and so on. For example, if you were writing an essay on how aerobic exercise develops the heart, lungs, and skeletal muscles, you might have a section on each of these. And for each, you would probably have at least one paragraph. Thus, the indentations for paragraphs in your essay would not be governed by the reader's eyes but by your purpose. Also, in reading an essay, your audience would expect a shift in the topic when a new paragraph begins.

Once in a while, an essay writer will use one- or two-sentence paragraphs to emphasize an idea or to make a transition from one section of an essay to the next, but most often paragraphs in essays continue until the point is fully developed.

Because the writer's purpose governs the length of paragraphs in essays, a paragraph will usually contain from fifty to 200 words. These numbers are rough estimates, and it would be foolish to count words in a paragraph to see if it fits this rule. To develop a point in detail, however, a writer usually needs at least fifty words. And unless a paragraph is very well written, many readers will have difficulty following a paragraph beyond 200 words. Just remember that a paragraph probably should not run longer than three-quarters of a typed page or one full, handwritten page.

If you are covering a point in your essay and you find that the paragraph is getting rather long, see if you can divide it in two at some logical place. For example, let's return to the essay on the effect of aerobics. If you were writing the section on skeletal muscles, you might find that you used about 200 words just explaining how certain exercises develop flexibility before you even got to a discussion of how they strengthen muscles. In this case, it would be wise to start a new paragraph for your discussion of strength. Even with this break, each paragraph would still have a single topic—one on how aerobics develop flexible muscles, another on how they strengthen them.

Exercise 7.1

The paragraph below is about airline hubs. It runs a bit long. Read it carefully, and then mark the spot where you think it could logically be divided into two paragraphs.

> Today large airlines use a hub system. Hubs are airports where an airline will house most of its planes, provide most of its maintenance, and originate most of its flights. From its hub, the airline schedules several flights that reach out like spokes to other airports that are not its hub. For example, St. Louis is a Delta hub. Delta flights from St. Louis extend in all directions to other airports. An airline will also fly from one of its hubs to another on longer flights. A Delta plane traveling from Atlanta, Delta's major hub, to Los Angeles will likely stop in St. Louis to take on more passengers, receive maintenance, and perhaps refuel. Travelers have mixed feelings about the hub system. Some complain that it creates congestion that leads to delays in taking off and landing and contributes to the danger of midair collisions. Hubs also result in fewer direct flights for travelers. On some nondirect flights, travelers even have to change planes. Other travelers like hubs because they allow airlines to expand service and to keep fares as low as possible.

Just as paragraphs can be too long, they can be too short. For instance, examine the following paragraphs:

People tend to have strong feelings about air travel. Some people hate to fly. They fear air travel and spend the flight listening for any little noise that may seem odd, reciting prayers in their minds, and gripping the arms of their seat for dear life on takeoff and landing.

Other people love to fly. They find takeoff and landing exhilarating. They relax and enjoy the scenery from a window seat, thinking of air travel as a pleasant experience and marvelously efficient means of transportation.

In reading these two paragraphs, we can identify their topic in the first sentence: people's feelings about air travel. If we look at the second paragraph, we can see the same topic still being developed. Even though the second paragraph focuses on people who enjoy flying, the topic is still feelings about flight. If these paragraphs were much longer, we might consider breaking the topic into two: fear of flying and love of flying. But because they are short, we can combine them under the larger topic and do not have to worry about creating a paragraph too long for our readers to follow. If we left these paragraphs separated, we would end up with a choppy effect. Worse yet, we would confuse readers, because when they see a new paragraph, they expect some significant change in the topic.

As you draft and revise your essays, consider the length of your paragraphs. If you have spent a lot of time on invention, you probably won't have any trouble. But sometimes you will need to consider whether paragraphs need to be separated or put together as you revise your completed draft.

Topic Sentences

As you know, an essay has a thesis sentence stating its main idea. Often each paragraph in an essay will have a *topic sentence,* which states the main idea of a paragraph within an essay. Be careful not to confuse topic sentences with the general topic of a whole essay or with its thesis, which says something about the essay topic.

Each paragraph also has a topic that is part of the larger topic of the whole essay. Each topic sentence is a subpoint of the point made in the thesis. For instance, if you started with the thesis that living in a campus apartment is preferable to living in a college dorm, one of your paragraphs might have a topic sentence saying that apartment living provides more flexibility and variety when it comes to meals. Another paragraph might have a topic sentence arguing that apartments allow for more privacy. Each topic sentence would be one specific point used to develop the thesis. So remember: A topic sentence is more specific than a thesis sentence. If you remember Hayakawa's ladder diagram on general and specific language, think of the topic sentence as a rung or two below the more general thesis sentence.

Although a topic sentence is more specific than a thesis sentence, it is more general (less specific) than the rest of the information in the paragraph. For example, after stating the topic sentence that apartments allow for more flexibility and a greater variety of meals, you would then need specific details and examples to support this topic sentence, which in turn supports the larger thesis that apartment living is preferable to dorm living.

Exercise 7.2

The following groups of sentences could form paragraphs if the sentences were arranged in the right order. Read each group and underline the sentence that would be the topic sentence if you arranged the sentences in order to form a paragraph. Remember that the topic sentence will be the most general sentence in the paragraph.

1. The lenses must be inserted and removed carefully.
   Soft contact lenses require proper care.
   Nonpermanent lenses should be removed and cleaned every evening.
   Soft-lens wearers must make sure their hands are clean whenever they handle their lenses.
2. With a computer, a writer does not have to worry as much about making mistakes because it is easy to correct them.
   Writers can revise as they go along and then check a printed draft before making more revisions.
   Computers also allow writers to move sentences and paragraphs to parts of the essay where they would fit more effectively.
   Computers can help people improve their writing.
   Unlike staring at a blank page, working on a computer can be fun, and when people like to write, they will improve.
3. Because the sun is so hot, people have to take precautions when going out, and air conditioning is a must indoors.
   The climate of Florida is not as pleasant as most people think.
   As a peninsula, Florida enjoys ocean breezes, but the moisture also contributes to high humidity.
   Floridians must be concerned about hurricanes, which can cause

massive property damage, personal injury, and even death. Though warm weather may be nice in the winter, the summers get unbearably hot.

Exercise 7.3

In the previous exercise, you chose the most general sentence as the topic sentence of a paragraph. Following are paragraphs in which the italicized topic sentence is so general that it is vague or inaccurate. Rewrite the topic sentence to make it more specific and thus more closely related to the information in the paragraph.

Women have made great advances. Colleges and universities around the country admit more women into professional schools each year. Women today are increasingly entering such fields as medicine, business, finance, and law. Though women are still striving to be paid salaries equal to those paid to men, their presence, influence, and future in professional fields are rapidly expanding.

The Pontiac GTO was a neat car in the 1960s. It had a 389-cubic-inch engine and could be ordered with either a large four-barrel carburetor or three two-barrels. With either setup, the engine rumbled at even cruising speeds. Most GTOs also had four-on-the-floor with Hurst powershift linkage, enabling a hot driver to burn rubber in every gear. The styling was as impressive as the car's power, with sleek lines, a low-slung chassis, and an air scoop in the middle of the hood.

It is easy to get around in large cities. Subway systems usually enable passengers to travel to almost any point in the city in a short time. In addition, subway fares are inexpensive, often no more than a dollar. For that dollar, the rider usually can transfer from one line to the next without paying an additional fare. Transfers thus make it possible to travel great distances cheaply. Most subway systems provide maps free or for an inexpensive fee. These maps enable even a tourist unfamiliar with the city to figure out which lines go where, and, of course, subway personnel will always provide directions.

Placement of Topic Sentences

Topic sentences can be placed almost anywhere in a paragraph: first, second, third, or even last. Sometimes writers even split them, revealing part of the main idea in the first sentence before completing the idea in the last sentence of the paragraph. Some paragraphs do not even state the topic in a single sentence but imply a main idea through the combination of all the sentences.

Topic Sentence First.   Beginning writers often like to place the topic sentence first in a paragraph. Experienced writers use this method, too. One advantage of placing the topic sentence first is that the reader will know what is coming. Look over these two paragraphs, one by a beginner, one by a professional:

Though yo-yos are no longer popular, they were once a terrific form of childhood amusement. Today's kids would rather sit indoors playing video games, but in my neighborhood, summer meant that most kids would be out in the street competing with one another to amaze with yo-yo tricks such as "walk the dog," "rock the cradle," and "around the world." A true yo-yo master could put on shows that would draw crowds on a street corner and make him the envy of every kid in the neighborhood.

Nothing posed a more serious threat to the bald eagle's survival than a modern chemical called DDT. Around 1940, a retired Canadian banker named Charles L. Broley began keeping track of eagles nesting in Florida. Each breeding season, he climbed into more than 50 nests, counted the eaglets, and put metal bands on their legs. In the late 1940s, a sudden drop-off in the number of young produced led him to conclude that 80 percent of his birds were sterile. Broley blamed DDT. Later, scientists discovered that DDE, a breakdown product of DDT, causes not sterility but a fatal thinning of eggshells among birds of prey. Applied on cropland all over the United States, the pesticide was running off into waterways where it concentrated in fish. The bald eagles ate the fish, and the DDT impaired their ability to reproduce.

Jim Doherty, "The Bird That Became Our National Symbol"

In each paragraph, the writer begins with a general point in the topic sentence and then follows with specific examples for support. Such paragraphs are fairly easy to write and read. Thus, you can't go wrong when you place the topic sentence first.

Topic Sentence Second or Third.   Sometimes a writer will use a sentence or two to lead up to the topic sentence. Usually these lead-in sentences refer to the discussion in the essay's previous paragraphs. In other words, these sentences provide a sort of bridge. Examine this example:

How can you be less food-centered? For one thing, you can find alternatives to eating. Draw up a list of at least five, and preferably a dozen or more, activities that please you—going for a walk in the country, sailing, talking to your best friend, reading the latest mystery novel, whatever. Make sure that the list contains several things that are as easy to do as eating. Now every time you have a desire to eat, do something from your list first.

Junius Adams, "Think Thin and Get Thin"

This paragraph, from a how-to essay on losing weight, followed a paragraph in which the author discussed how people, from infancy, are taught to be "food-centered." The question looks back to the topic of that paragraph before Adams moves forward to the topic sentence of finding activities to substitute for eating. You can see that the first sentence cannot be the topic sentence because it does not mention substitute activities. The first sentence, however, leads up to the topic sentence, placed second, telling us to find alternatives.

Topic Sentence Last.   Sometimes a writer can use arguments, examples, or specific details to lead up to the topic sentence. This method can be effective because the topic sentence works as a "clincher" to emphasize the point of the paragraph. Read this beginner's paragraph, and the professional example that follows:

My psych teacher assigned three chapters this week and promised a test on Friday. My English teacher hit us with another essay assignment. My golf teacher told us we have to play one round this week and have our scorecard signed by the clubhouse attendant. I have to interview people in three different professions this week for my career counseling class. It seems most college professors think their class is the center of a student's life.

The anthropologist Ray Birdwhistell has undertaken a study which he calls "kinesics," which is the systematic examination of gesture and body motion in communication; this is a rich area about which many students of human behavior have been much excited. But there is a danger in going too far in this direction—in going overboard to the extent of saying that words are of no importance. There are thousands of things children must know and enjoy that it is not possible for them to get without words.

S. I. Hayakawa, Through the Communication Barrier

In the first paragraph, there would be nothing wrong with putting the topic sentence first, but it is probably more effective coming last because after the series of examples, the sentence on professors packs more punch than it would if it came first. In Hayakawa's paragraph, he uses examples of something he does not fully endorse—studying kinesics—to set up his belief that words are essential for children.

Exercise 7.4

Underline the topic sentence in each paragraph.

1. Most new cars have electronic ignition systems that require special instruments to test. Many have fuel injection systems that must be precisely timed by professionals. With the increased popularity of front-wheel drive and air conditioning, engines are mounted sideways with the air unit in front of them, making it difficult to reach even simple parts in need of general maintenance. With these new developments in automobiles, it is becoming more and more difficult for people to work on their own cars.

2. People feel safer behind some kind of physical barrier. If a social situation is in any way threatening, then there is an immediate urge to set up such a barricade. For a tiny child faced with a stranger, the problem is usually solved by hiding behind its mother's body and peeping out at the intruder to see what he or she will do next. If the mother's body is not available, then a chair or some other piece of solid furniture will do.

   Desmond Morris, Manwatching

3. Ever since Harry S. Truman was the first President to use television, network television has been the key conduit for political messages. In recent years, however, local and independent cable operations have become more important. In 1984, for example, local television burst out of its role as a bit player in the presidential election drama. This was first seen in the Democratic primaries, as candidates flew around the country, timing their arrival to coincide with the local evening news, going to live local voters in upcoming primaries, often keeping waiting the television news teams of the more prestigious networks.

   Paul A. Dawson, American Government

4. Cats are loose in their morals, but not consciously so. Man, in his descent from the cat, has brought the cat's looseness with him but has left the unconsciousness behind—the saving grace which excuses the cat. The cat is innocent, man is not.

   Mark Twain, "The Lowest Animal"

Implied Topic Sentences. Sometimes a paragraph will not state the topic sentence. This does not mean the paragraph does not have a topic but that for some reason the writer has not felt the need to include it in the paragraph. When this is the case, we say the topic sentence is *implied*. Take, for example, the following paragraph:

Vic's Lunch Room was more of a long hall than a room. Seats lined the counter, with a row of cramped booths on the opposite wall with about a two-foot corridor in between, where slovenly waitresses in dowdy uniforms and hairnets carried trays of greasy meatloaf or watery soup. Behind the counter in front of a blackened stove, Vic stood sweating and unshaven in an apron stained with the week's specials, growling at the customers, factory workers and any of the street people who could scrape up enough money for the slop that passed as a hot meal.

In reading this paragraph, you probably noticed that each sentence contains specific details: the size of the place, the food, and the appearances of the waitresses, Vic, and the customers. But there is no one sentence that tells us the point of the paragraph. Nevertheless, we can see the point: Vic's is not a place where most people would want to eat.

Implied topic sentences can save the writer from stating an obvious point. But if you choose to leave your topic sentence implied, make sure that the information in the paragraph clearly implies one point that the reader can see without confusion.

Exercise 7.5

In each of the following paragraphs, the topic sentence is implied. Write a sentence for each that expresses the implied topic sentence.

1. The hot cheese bubbles as it mixes with the bright red sauce and clumps of tomato, all surrounded by a rising rim of golden crust. Sausage and pepperoni dot the surface glistening with a hint of oil, while slices of peppers and onions crisscross through the cheese. All the ingredients contribute to the unmistakable aroma that tickles the nostrils and tantalizes the tastebuds.

2. There was, for example, the turn-of-the-century trainman who replaced a faulty coupling with a pair of jeans; the Wyoming man who used his jeans as a towrope to haul his car out of a ditch, the Californian who found several pairs in an abandoned mine, wore

them, and discovered they were sixty-three years old and still as good as new. . . . And then there is the particularly terrifying story of the careless construction worker who dangled fifty-two stories above the street until rescued, his sole support the Levis' belt loop through which his rope was hooked.

Carin Quinn, "The Jeaning of America—And the World"

3. To bunt a baseball, you must first "square-up" to the pitcher. This means that as the pitcher goes into his windup, you move your back leg forward and your front leg back so that you are facing the pitcher, who should be able to read the letters on your uniform. While moving into this stance, slide your top hand up the bat to a position about three to four inches below the label. Hold the bat waist high in front of you in a position parallel to the ground. Just as you should wait for a strike when hitting, a strike is the best pitch to bunt. If the pitch is too high, you are likely to pop it up. If it is too low, you will have trouble making contact with the ball. So look for a good pitch. As you bunt the ball, angle the bat toward the first or third base line depending on where you want the ball to go. Try to bunt the ball with a slight downward motion to ensure against the pop up. When the bat touches the ball, draw the bat back. This will deaden the ball, making it roll slowly to allow you more time to reach first base before a fielder picks up the ball.

Topic Sentences and the Writing Process

As you plan, draft, and revise the paragraphs in your essays, pay close attention to your topic sentences at each point in the writing process. Some writers, for instance, plan possible topic sentences once they have a thesis and a set of invention notes. Other writers begin with the notes and do not worry about topic sentences until they are drafting. Whatever you do, always reconsider your topic sentences during revision. This set of questions can help:

1. Does the topic sentence express the main idea of the paragraph clearly?
2. Is there anything in the paragraph that does not fit the point of the topic sentence?
3. Is the topic sentence more specific (as it should be) than the thesis sentence of the essay?
4. Is the topic sentence more general than the other sentences in the paragraph?

During revision, you should also check the placement of your topic sentences. For example, adding a lead-in sentence before the topic sentence can create a needed connection between the paragraph and the one before it. Maybe the topic sentence can be moved to the end of the paragraph to emphasize your point, or placed first to make sure the reader knows where the paragraph is going. You may find you can cut the topic sentence and leave the point implied, or you might want to add a topic sentence when an implied point is not quite clear.

Three Qualities of a Good Paragraph

As you draft and revise paragraphs in your essays, you will need to consider three qualities that make a paragraph effective: development, unity, and coherence.

Development

You already have some sense of paragraph development: knowing that you should include specific details and all the information the reader needs. A paragraph shows adequate development when it fully covers a limited topic to achieve the writer's purpose, support the thesis, and meet the reader's needs. In this sense, development has to do with specific details and examples, which we discussed fully in Chapter 3. You may also remember the two paragraphs answering the essay question on the Stamp Act in Chapter 6. The weaker one was not developed fully enough to show the instructor all the student knew about the Stamp Act. The stronger one used enough detail to serve the writer's purpose—defining the Stamp Act—and to meet the reader's needs.

Let's look at another example. In Exercise 7.5, you read a paragraph instructing readers on how to bunt a baseball. Suppose the paragraph had been written like this:

Turn toward the pitcher, and hold the bat in front of you. Wait for a good pitch, and tap the ball softly.

Only a person who knew a lot about bunting could follow these directions because the paragraph lacks development—and such a person would not need directions to begin with. In contrast, the directions in Exercise 7.5, because they are fully developed, could instruct someone—a Little Leaguer, for instance—who knew very little about bunting.

Exercise 7.6

The following paragraphs lack development. Choose one and revise it for an audience that knows very little about the topic. You will need to add specific language and examples of your own.

1. Video games have become very popular. Unlike the early games, they now work like arcade games. Nintendo and Atari are two kinds, and each has all kinds of games.
2. To do laundry, sort out your clothes and put them in the washer. Then add soap and turn the washer on. When they are done, put them in the dryer.
3. Discipline in some high schools is a problem. Corporal punishment has been proven ineffective, and some consider it inhumane. Some students act very wild and keep others from learning. They are not afraid of the punishments schools use.

Unity

When a paragraph has unity, it has one topic and does not shift from that topic, even though the examples may differ. For instance, the following paragraph talks of three different players, yet the topic focuses on one main idea that applies to all three players:

> The greatest NBA players are not only great shooters but also great passers. Earvin "Magic" Johnson of the Los Angeles Lakers earned his nickname for his passing more than his shooting. Larry Bird of the Celtics, though one of the greatest shooters in NBA history, could take the crowd's breath away with "no-look" passes that made him seem to have eyes in the back of his head. Detroit Pistons' guard Isiah Thomas often dazzles his opponents with passes behind his back or even through the opponent's legs. While many NBA stars have been fine shooters, only the greatest are blessed equally with the ability to pass.

This paragraph discusses three different players, but it is unified by the focus on passing. All three examples work together to support the topic sentence that the best NBA players are great passers.

When you are drafting an essay, keeping a paragraph unified can be difficult because one example or idea can lead to another that does not fit the topic of the paragraph. For instance, in discussing the example of Magic Johnson, the writer might have been tempted to add that in addition to being a great passer, Johnson is an excellent rebounder. That's true, but because the topic of the paragraph focuses on passing, the point about rebounding does not belong.

As you revise your draft, consider the unity of each paragraph. If you have development that does not fit your topic, remove those examples to unify the paragraph. Also, consider the possibility of using the examples elsewhere in the essay. For instance, if you were writing an essay whose purpose was to define what makes a truly great NBA player, the point on Johnson's rebounding ability could be used in another paragraph on rebounding as part of greatness.

Exercise 7.7

In each of the following paragraphs, cross out any sentences that break up the unity of the paragraph.

1. Ceiling fans have become very popular since the first energy crisis of the early Seventies. More and more homes and businesses use ceiling fans to save energy and reduce heating and air-conditioning bills. In the famous Bogart movie *Casablanca*, ceiling fans were in all the buildings to fight the African heat. In summer, ceiling fans can be set to pull cold air upward—it normally drops—and keep it circulating; thus, rooms stay cooler and the air conditioner does not run as often. In winter, the fans can be reversed to drive warm air downward—it normally rises—to warm a room more effectively. Some people also consider a ceiling fan an attractive addition to the decor of a room.

2. It is very likely that in the first half of the next century the United States will elect a woman president. Women were granted the right to vote only seventy years ago. Since then, there have been many representatives, senators, and mayors of large cities who are women. In the 1970s, Ella Grasso was elected governor of Connecticut, becoming the first woman in that state to hold that office. Margaret Chase Smith may have been the greatest female senator. In the 1984 presidential election, Geraldine Ferraro was the first woman nominated by a major party to run for vice-president. With such progress since 1920, it is inevitable that a woman will achieve the presidency in the U.S. sometime in the next fifty years. The highest office has often been

held by women in other countries—for example, Margaret Thatcher in England, Golda Meir in Israel, Indira Ghandi in India, and the many queens throughout history.

3. Legalized gambling has spread in the United States in the past twenty years. At one time, Nevada was the only state where gambling was legal, other than at racetracks. About twenty years ago, New York started a state lottery, and many other states followed, establishing lotteries of their own. Some people are against legalized gambling on religious grounds; others think it contributes to crime. Today many states run lotteries, with varieties of games, including the popular Lotto, in which winners can collect millions of dollars. Legalized gambling prevents organized crime from profiting from illegal gambling.

Coherence

You probably have heard the word *cohesion* before. It refers to the way parts work together to form a whole. Often the word is used in its adjective form, *cohesive*. If we hear of a cohesive family unit, we know that family members work together to keep the family whole. If a sportscaster speaks of a cohesive team, he or she means the players work well together as a team. The word *coherence* is similar, but it usually refers to logic and ideas.

Paragraphs need coherence, which occurs in a paragraph when each sentence follows logically and clearly from the one before it and leads likewise to the sentence following it. For a paragraph to be coherent, first it must have unity. Remember the sentences you crossed out in the previous exercise. None of them followed from the sentence before or led to the sentence after.

In addition, paragraphs achieve coherence through transitions. Simply defined, *transitions* are words that signal the connections between paragraphs in an essay and among sentences in a paragraph. There are two types of transitions that you should be aware of: (1) the repetition and variation of key words, and (2) transitional words and phrases.

Repetition and Variation of Key Words. If you stick to the topic of your paragraph, you will often repeat the key words in your idea without thinking about them. Sometimes, you will vary the key words, though. For example, you might substitute *riding a bike* for *bicycling*. Let's have a look at a paragraph on bicycling. The topic sentence focuses on bicycling as exercise, so *bicycling* and *exercise* are the key words. As you reread the paragraph, note the connections between key words, which are in bold type or italics.

Bicycling is terrific *exercise*. When you **ride a bike,** you *exercise* all of the leg muscles and most of the muscles of the upper body. In addition, **bicycling** *exercises* the lungs and the heart. Thus, **bicycling** is both a muscular and aerobic *exercise*.

From these connections, you can see how throughout the paragraph the repetition holds together the two parts of the idea in the topic sentence— bicycling and exercise. You also have an example of variation in the second sentence when *bicycling* is changed to *ride a bike*.

Seeing the connections in this paragraph should have been easy, because the idea was fairly simple. Let's try a more difficult paragraph. Read the topic sentence first, and note the key words: references to home run hitters are in bold type; references to the big swing are in italics; and references to strikeouts are circled. Examine the way these words are repeated and varied:

Home run hitters need a <u>big, powerful swing</u>, but such a <u>swing</u> reduces the chances of making contact with the ball and thus leads to more strike-outs. **Babe Ruth** had a compact <u>swing</u>, but **he** <u>swung</u> very hard with a quick, <u>snappy stroke</u> of the bat that either knocked the ball into the stands or missed it completely. Like **Ruth, Mickey Mantle** took a powerful cut at the ball, but **he** also <u>swung</u> with a much longer arc, bringing the bat back farther, stretching his arms farther from his body, and ending with a long follow through. Any one who ever saw **Reggie Jackson** bat knows how hard **he** <u>swung</u>. **He** seemingly began his <u>swing</u> form somewhere back behind the catcher and often ended it with <u>a wild sweep</u>. This <u>swing</u> either launched the ball into the upper deck or left **Jackson** on one knee as the umpire called strike three.

This paragraph is fairly long, yet because of the repetition and variation of the key words, we are able to follow it. Here you will also note more variation: for instance, *big, powerful swing* is varied a number of times, but the variations still convey that part of the idea. Likewise, *strikeout* appears (circled) as *missing it completely* and *strike three.*

Exercise 7.8

Read the following paragraphs carefully. Then circle the key words in the topic sentence. Finally, connect them to the repetitions and variations in the rest of the paragraph.

1. Catalog showrooms are discount retail stores that sell general merchandise, using as their main promotional pieces large catalogs mailed to prospective customers. The customer identifies the items he or she wishes to purchase, either from the catalog or an in-store display, and the order is filled from a warehouse attached to the showroom. Although they carry general merchandise lines, catalog showrooms tend to feature items on which they can offer large discounts—jewelry, luggage, small appliances, toys, and sporting goods.
   Thomas C. Kinnear and Kenneth L. Bernhardt, Principles of Marketing

2. Our world is becoming more and more complex, and communication contributes to that complexity. Electronic communication continues to become more sophisticated, efficient, and rapid. Not only are people talking to machines, but machines are talking to machines. Messages bounce off satellites and flash around the world in fractions of seconds. Communications can now be carried on a thin sheath of optical fibers one-tenth the diameter of the copper cable that was formerly required. Tiny microcomputer chips hold more data than whole library buildings. The advances in the various fields of electronic communication are fantastic.
   Norman B. Sigband and David N. Bateman, Communicating in Business

3. How does one determine whether a law is just or unjust? A just law is a man-made code that squares with the moral law or the law of God. An unjust law is a code that is out of harmony with the moral law. To put it in terms of St. Thomas Aquinas: An unjust law is a human law that is not rooted in eternal law. Any law that uplifts human

personality is just. Any law that degrades human personality is unjust. All segregation statutes are unjust because segregation distorts the soul and damages the personality.

Martin Luther King, "Letter from Birmingham Jail"

Transitional Words and Phrases

Transitional words and phrases are any words that purposely show connections between sentences. They work like highway signs, signalling to the reader that here is a place to turn or that the discussion will continue this way. You have probably used these words often in conversation and writing, but you probably have not thought about them. Sometimes they emerge naturally as you think and write. Other times you might have to add them while revising to tighten the connection between one sentence and another. Study the list and examples that follow:

1. *In addition, also, moreover, furthermore, and* (yes, you can start a sentence with *and*), *indeed, in fact:* This group signals that you are adding another point or example.

Spike Lee is a controversial filmmaker. *In fact,* his movie *School Daze,* about blacks in college, received criticism from some black leaders and educators because they believed black students were portrayed as wanting to be white. *Furthermore,* in 1989, the movie *Do the Right Thing* depicted a race riot in Brooklyn's Bedford-Stuyvesant area.

2. *Thus, therefore, consequently, as a result:* These words signal an effect that comes from a cause in the previous sentence(s).

As a result, Lee was often questioned about the title of the movie.

3. *Of course, no doubt, certainly, doubtless, granted:* These words give in on a point or recognize a point just off your main point.

Of course, the title was only one controversial element in the movie. The title, *no doubt,* was only one controversial element in the movie.

4. *Still, nevertheless, notwithstanding:* These return the discussion to your point after you have left it (see the sentences above and below).

Still, it provoked some people to think that Lee was advocating racial violence.

5. *Yet, however, but, on the other hand, on the contrary, in contrast:* These words signal a difference or contrast.

However, many elements in Spike Lee's movies advocate the need for better understanding and sensitivity among people of all races.

Now let's put some of these sentences together to form a paragraph:

Spike Lee is a controversial filmmaker. *In fact,* his movie *School Daze,* about blacks in college, received much criticism from black leaders and educators *because* they believed black students were portrayed as wanting to be white. *Furthermore,* in 1989, the movie *Do the Right Thing* depicted a race riot in Brooklyn's Bedford-Stuyvesant area. *As a result,* Lee was often questioned about the film's title. *Of course,* the title was only one controversial element in the movie. *Still,* the title provoked some people to think that Lee was advocating racial violence. *However,* many elements in Spike Lee's movies advocate the need for better understanding and sensitivity among people of all races. Whatever Lee's message, he produces films that cause people to think.

In reading this paragraph, we can see the writer's conflicting feelings about Spike Lee. On the one hand, the paragraph respects Lee's ability to make films that cause people to think. On the other hand, there is a concern about the messages of Lee's movies. Because of this conflict, the writer's ideas shift back and forth between respect and concern. Here the transitions help. Read the paragraph without the transitions and notice how choppy and unconnected many of the ideas seem:

Spike Lee is a controversial filmmaker. His movie *School Daze,* about blacks in college, received much criticism from black leaders and educators because they believed black students were portrayed as wanting to be white. In 1989, the movie *Do the Right Thing* depicted a race riot in Brooklyn's Bedford-Stuyvesant area. Lee was often questioned about the film's title. The title was only one controversial element in the movie. The title provoked some people to think that Lee was advocating racial violence. Many elements in Spike Lee's movies advocate the need for better understanding and sensitivity among people of all races. Whatever Lee's message, he produces films that cause people to think.

Although the first couple of sentences in the paragraph make sense, as the discussion of *Do the Right Thing* begins, the conflict between respect and concern is more difficult to follow without the transitional words. The ideas are still in the paragraph, but we, as readers, have to sort them out and piece together the conflict. In short, there are no signposts to tell us which way the writer's thoughts are going.

Although transitions are important, every sentence you write need not contain transitional words and phrases. In fact, too many of them can sometimes confuse the reader, just as too many roadsigns in one place can confuse a driver. Often the repetitions and variations of key words will make your paragraph cohesive. Still, it is helpful to become aware of transitional words and phrases and the ways they add cohesion.

When you are drafting a paper, some transitional words and phrases will appear naturally because your thought patterns often add and shift information. When you are revising a paper, you might find that adding a transitional word or phrase can tighten the relationship between sentences and make your point clear.

Exercise 7.9

Here are some pairs of sentences. Add a transitional word or phrase to the second sentence in order to tighten its connection to the first sentence.

1. Writing can be difficult. It can cause anxiety.
2. Students know the writing will be graded. They fear their reader as a judge. They should imagine their reader as a person who wants to be informed and entertained.
3. The teacher has to evaluate the paper. If students forget about evaluation and concentrate on writing, good grades will follow.

Exercise 7.10

Write a short paragraph using the sentences from Exercise 7.9.

Paragraph Checklist

We have said quite a bit about paragraphs—so much, in fact, that as you revise your paragraphs you could not possibly remember it all. The list of questions below can help you to recall the general considerations that you need to be aware of as you revise.

1. What is the paragraph's purpose? That is, what is the one point it is trying to make? How is that point connected to the thesis of the whole essay?
2. Does the paragraph have a single identifiable topic? In other words, is there one main idea that it is trying to get across?
3. Is the main idea expressed clearly in a topic sentence? Or if the main idea is implied, will it be evident to the reader?
4. Is the topic of the paragraph limited enough to be covered specifically?
5. Is the topic fully developed, given your purpose and the reader's needs?
6. Does the paragraph have unity? Is there any information that could confuse the reader because it does not belong in the paragraph?
7. Is the paragraph coherent, with key words repeated and varied and transitional words and phrases used when needed?
8. Should the paragraph be divided into two or more paragraphs?
9. Should the paragraph be combined with another paragraph?

Writing Assignments

1. Choose a paragraph from a paper you have previously written, and revise it to improve development, unity, and coherence.
2. Below are three pairs of sentences. The first of each pair could be a thesis sentence for an essay. The second could be a topic sentence for one body paragraph in the essay. Choose one of the topic sentences and write a paragraph of at least 100 words.

a. Thesis: The cleanliness of a city depends on government and citizens.
Topic Sentence: Litter is a problem that can easily be solved when government and citizens work together.
b. Thesis: Parents contribute greatly to the success or failure of their children in school.
Topic Sentence: There are several ways parents can teach children to value reading.
c. Thesis: Music videos range from the cheerful and harmless to the offensive and repulsive.
Topic Sentence: Some of the better videos rely on humor for their effects.

Key Terms

Paragraph: A relatively short piece of writing that can stand alone but usually is part of an essay.

Body paragraph: Any paragraph that follows the introduction and leads to the conclusion. Each body paragraph helps to develop and support the thesis of the whole essay.

Topic sentence: A sentence that states the main idea of the paragraph.

Implied topic sentence: A topic sentence that is not stated in the paragraph, but all the information in the paragraph points to one idea that could be stated.

Development: A paragraph has adequate development when it contains enough information—examples and details—to achieve the writer's purpose and enable the reader to see the main idea.

Unity: A paragraph achieves unity when it sticks to its main idea.

Coherence: A paragraph achieves coherence when each sentence follows clearly from the sentence before it and leads clearly to the sentence following. Coherence refers to the way sentences work together to form the whole paragraph.

Repetitions and variations: Key words in a paragraph that are repeated exactly or in varied forms to keep the paragraph on topic and to add coherence.

Transitional words and phrases: These show connections between sentences as the reader moves from one sentence to the next. A few examples are *however, consequently, indeed, in fact, as a result,* and *in addition.*

chapter eight
Writing Introductions and Conclusions

The body paragraphs discussed in Chapter 7 support and develop the thesis of an essay once the topic has been introduced and the thesis has been stated. They also lead up to a final paragraph or two that conclude the essay. In a relatively short essay, an introductory paragraph—or simply an *introduction*—comes before the body paragraphs. Another paragraph, called the *conclusion*, follows the body paragraphs and closes the essay. In longer essays, introductions and conclusions may run to three or more paragraphs. But for our purposes, think of an introduction and a conclusion as one paragraph each. Introductions and conclusions have different purposes than body paragraphs, but they work with them to create the overall structure of the essay.

Introductions

How do I begin? Many writers have asked themselves this question. And many beginning writers are often so stumped by it that we should start by discussing how *not* to begin. The weakest introductions discuss the writer's difficulty with the topic and/or talk directly to the teacher. For example:

> I am having trouble with this topic because I really do not care much about drug problems. I read in the papers about drugs, but they don't affect me much, so I do not think about them. But since I have to write something, I guess I will argue that no matter what the government does, some people will always take drugs.

The problem with this introduction is that it disregards the audience and the fact that writing is a kind of social interaction. For this writer, the teacher is the only audience, and the paragraph fails to address what the audience wants to know about: the topic. Although the teacher may be your reader, you should write as if you were writing to the whole class or to anyone interested in your topic. Also, the audience does not really care to know that the writer had trouble with the topic—it wants to know about the drug problem.

Another problem occurs when writers start introductions too far from the topic:

> Since the beginning of time, there were people taking drugs. Cavemen probably ate leaves and roots that got them high. In ancient times, the Roman orgies included drugs as well as alcohol. Once Europeans had contact with the Orient, opium was imported to Europe. Since America began, people always had drugs, and it was only in the twentieth century that they became illegal. Some people today think legalizing drugs would solve the drug problem, but this supposed solution would do more harm than good.

This introduction is on the right track in that it defines the topic in the introduction, but it needs to begin closer to the issue of the thesis: the question of legalizing drugs today. Going back to the beginning of time does not move the introduction, nor the readers, to the thesis very quickly, and by covering so many years—actually centuries—the essay ends up with a vague and general opening that does not relate closely enough to the thesis.

Introductions are not easy, but because they provide the reader with a first impression of your essay, they are certainly important, and you should take much care in writing them. Sometimes it is best to start writing the body of the paper once you have a thesis and add your introduction last. That way, you know what the body of your paper says, and you can then write a good introduction to lead into it. If you do write the introduction first, revise it carefully after you have written the body. Either way, your readers will expect an introduction.

You do not just plunge into a hot bath; you get in gradually. Readers like to get into an essay the same way. That's why a paragraph to introduce your topic and "set up" your thesis will add to the effectiveness of your essay.

Introductions serve four purposes:

1. To get the reader's attention.
2. To move the reader into your paper by defining the topic before you state the thesis.
3. To limit your essay by moving from a general discussion of the topic to the specific thesis that your paper wants to illustrate.
4. To state your thesis before moving to the body paragraphs that illustrate it.

The following paragraph is a possible introduction for an essay on student work-study programs. To show you how one type of introduction works, each sentence is numbered and an explanation of its purpose follows.

1. Millions of college students each year work part-time to contribute to the payment of their tuition. 2. From jobs behind fast-food counters to establishing small businesses of their own, students constitute an important part of the nation's work force. 3. Many students participate in college work-study programs, which allow them to earn money working for their school without the inconvenience of leaving campus. 4. Funding for work-study jobs should be increased because they are necessary for the success of many college students.

1. The first sentence raises the subject area of students working to pay tuition.
2. This sentence limits the subject to the kinds of jobs students hold.
3. The third sentence introduces the topic of work-study jobs.
4. This sentence says something about the topic and thus is the thesis.

This type of introduction is sometimes called the *funnel* because it begins with a wide subject area and gradually narrows it down to a limited topic. In other words, it starts general and becomes more specific with each sentence until the reader finally reaches the specific thesis.

The funnel is a common and effective way to begin an essay, but there are many strategies for writing an introduction. In fact, the number of strategies is limited only by the writer's imagination. Clever writers are always coming up with new ways to begin. Here are a few strategies that writers have used effectively. The thesis in each is italicized to show you how the introduction leads to it. In your own essays, there is no need to underline the thesis unless your teacher asks you to.

Selecting

When you write an introduction using selection, you begin with a straight forward statement about the subject area. You then give brief, specific examples within that subject area. The final example becomes the thesis of the paper. Study the following introduction:

Each generation of rock 'n' roll fans has its favorite groups and performers. People who grew up in the Fifties usually believe that Elvis truly was "The King." Fans of Sixties rock point to the unparalleled musical versatility and political consciousness of The Beatles. In the Seventies, Bruce Springsteen became "The Boss," a title many of his fans feel he still holds. Michael Jackson, though a pop star since childhood, achieved legendary status in the Eighties, and Prince emerged as another rock giant. Rock music certainly has produced some talented groups and performers, *but of all of these, The Rolling Stones truly deserve their self-proclaimed title—"World's Greatest Rock 'n' Roll Band."*

As you can see, the opening sentence introduces the subject of the essay as rock performers and limits the subject to a topic on people's attitudes toward them. The writer then gives brief examples of great rock performers from each decade before introducing his thesis on The Stones. Note the transitional word *but*. It is used to contrast the thesis to the introductory examples; that is, it *selects* The Stones from a group of performers and limits the paper to them.

Exercise 8.1

Using the selection method, write an introduction for an essay on one of these thesis sentences.

1. Pollution is the major problem in _____ .
2. _____ was the best team in football in the 1980s.
3. Proper study habits are the key to academic success.
4. _____ is the most difficult course for entering freshman at _____ .
5. Dogs make the best pets.

Narrating

Another way to introduce your thesis is to tell a brief story—to narrate—about yourself or someone you know. In the introduction below, the writer uses the tragic story of a friend to set up a thesis on drunk driving:

As a twenty-seven-year-old attorney working in the prosecutor's office, Andrea LeBeau was an intelligent woman with a successful future ahead of her. One night last December, Andrea tried to beat a red light in the new 280Z she had purchased after a year on the job. Unfortunately, Andrea's daring was the result of "a few drinks" at a friend's Christmas party. She broadsided another car, suffering fatal injuries and leaving the other driver laid up in the hospital for months with a broken leg and pelvis. One would think an intelligent young attorney would know better. *Drunk driving affects people of all ages and classes.*

This introduction leads to the thesis by using the story of someone most people would not expect to drink and drive. Narrating can be an effective way to begin because it personalizes an impersonal topic by providing the story of an individual rather than a faceless group.

Exercise 8.2

Choose one of the thesis sentences in the previous exercise, or a thesis of your own, and use narration to introduce it.

Describing

Like narrating, describing a person, place, or thing can effectively make a topic more personal and thus get the reader's interest before introducing your thesis.

Person

Andrea LeBeau was a young woman who, as the television commercial cliché goes, "had it all." She was tall, with lush brown hair, beautiful dark eyes, and a figure that evidenced her daily workouts and prowess on the tennis courts. As intelligent as she was beautiful, Andrea had graduated in the top ten percent of her law school class and was rising rapidly in the prosecutor's office. For all her attributes, Andrea treated everyone with respect and good cheer. At twenty-seven, Andrea is dead, the victim of her own drunk driving. *Drunk driving is a problem that includes all ages and classes of people.*

A place

From the parking lot, I could see the towers of the castle of the Magic Kingdom standing stately against the blue sky. To the right, the tall peak of The Matterhorn rose even higher. From the left, I could hear the jungle sounds of Adventureland. As I entered the gate, Main Street stretched before me with its quaint shops evoking an old-fashioned small town so charming it could never have existed. I was entranced. Disneyland may have been built for children, but *it brings out the child in adults*.

A thing

Loops of steel hurtle fifteen stories in the air like the tentacles of some technological monster. Long spines of track zig-zag from one loop to the next. It's the Vortex, King's Island's largest roller coaster, and *riding it is one of life's most exciting two minutes*.

In each introduction, the specific details bring the topic to life and set up the thesis. Note that the first example, on the young attorney, sets up the same thesis as was used with narration. In other words, different kinds of strategies can be used no matter what your thesis.

A descriptive introduction can work with a serious topic, such as the one in the first example, or with an informal topic, such as a narrative on visiting Disneyland or riding a roller coaster. But whatever the topic, you need vivid details to get the reader's attention.

Exercise 8.3

Choose one of the thesis sentences from Exercise 8.1, or a thesis of your own, and write an introduction using description.

Asking Questions

Raising a question or a series of questions is often a good way to begin an essay. Because a question appeals to the natural curiosity of people, it can be a handy way of getting your reader's attention and introducing the topic.

Single question

How would you like to earn millions of dollars a year and pay no taxes? Each year, we read stories in the press of millionaires who have so many tax deductions that they end up with an income tax of zero—a great deal, if you can get it. But most likely you cannot. John Q. Worker, if he is lucky enough to be making $500 a week, will be even luckier to see $400 of that in his paycheck. *Designed for the wealthy few, the tax laws in America are badly in need of reform.*

Series of questions

Do you want to live in the country? Do you want to wake up in the morning to the fresh air and sound of birds? Sound great? Do you want to drink well water that tastes like the pipes that carry it into your home? Do you want to drive ten miles to the nearest store for a bag of potato chips? Do you want to haul your weekly garbage another ten miles to the nearest dump? If you still want to live in the country, then you will have to find out for yourself that *country living is not as pleasant as most people think.*

Beginning with questions is fairly easy, so don't overuse the strategy. There's nothing wrong with it, but some students fall back on it too often and do not get practice in the other strategies. As you develop as a writer, you should learn to use all the strategies—and even come up with some new ones of your own. Nevertheless, questions are an old standby for beginning an essay.

Exercise 8.4

Use a question or series of questions to introduce one of the thesis sentences you have worked with in previous exercises.

Surprising or Shocking the Reader

This strategy attempts to get the reader's attention quickly with the opening statement. The statement can range from something mildly surprising to something downright shocking. As you know, when most people hear something surprising or shocking, they immediately want to hear more. Thus, this strategy can gain your reader's attention quickly and effectively.

Surprising statement

A computer is a dumb machine! Although we may marvel at the speed and efficiency with which computers process information and perform calculations, the computer is a slave, capable of doing only what its human operator tells it to. Computers may run amazing programs, but without the human programmer the computer can do nothing. They may process beautiful words, but the beauty comes from the writer's talent. These are just a couple of examples of how *the computer has been overestimated in recent years.*

Shocking statement

Hitler was a hero. Maybe not to people today, but in the 1930s, for many unwitting Germans, he was the man who was leading Germany back to prosperity and greatness. Of course, these Germans later found out their leader was a monster. We always hear how societies need heroes, but *when taken too far, hero worship destroys both hero and followers.*

In both examples, the first sentence opens the reader's eyes (and ears). In the first, most readers will want to read on to find out why the writer believes computers to be dumb. The second introduction comes from a term paper written for a psychology professor. The rest of the paper analyzed how the dynamics of hero worship can be destructive. There was nothing startling about the analysis itself, but you can be sure that after reading the first sentence, the professor read on with interest.

Exercise 8.5

Use a shocking or surprising statement to introduce one of the thesis sentences you have been working with.

Quoting

If you are familiar with a quotation from a famous person of history or a present-day celebrity, quoting this person can help move the reader into your essay. Readers will quickly identify with widely known quotes, such as John F. Kennedy's "Ask not what your country can do for you, ask what you can do for your country," or Martin Luther King's "I have a dream." Even if the quote is not widely known, it can still add authority to your introduction.

> "God is dead," wrote philosopher Frederick Nietzsche in the late nineteenth century. Nietzsche, now himself dead, was responding to the many scientific discoveries that had begun to challenge the teachings of the Bible and other holy books. While science has often challenged religion, *unless it can explain the secrets of humanity's relation to the universe, people will always have a need for religion.*

When you use a quotation, be sure that it fits your thesis. In the introduction above, the quotation is used as a contrast. That's fine. Other times, your thesis might agree with the quotation. For example, if you were arguing that people should contribute more time to volunteer service, you could set up this thesis using the Kennedy quotation mentioned above.

Exercise 8.6

Use a quotation to write an introduction to one of the thesis sentences you have been working with. Do not overlook quotations from popular-culture figures, such as entertainers and sports stars. If you have trouble coming up with a quotation, use *Bartlett's Familiar Quotations* or a similar reference book.

Referring to Something You've Read

As a college student, you have been doing a lot of reading. Often your reading can help you to begin an essay of your own. For example, in the following paragraph, the writer refers to a book by Truman Capote to set up a thesis on capital punishment:

> In his book *In Cold Blood*, Truman Capote tells the story of the brutal murder of a Kansas family in their own home by two exconvict drifters. Although this book enables us to reach some understanding of the killers and to see them as humans, the description of the murders prevents us from

wanting anything less than the death penalty for them. Though even mur-derers are human, *the loss of life suffered by the victims makes capital punishment just punishment.*

Referring to something you've read can be an effective introductory strategy. By considering your thesis in terms of something you have read, you can see your own ideas more clearly. Also, your readers will begin with the impression that you have some authority on the topic because you have read about it. In other words, your reading will support your personal opinions.

Exercise 8.7

Refer to something you have read to introduce one of the thesis sentences you have been working with. You can refer to a book or to a newspaper or magazine article.

Exercise 8.8

Following are some possible thesis sentences. If the thesis sentences have blanks, fill them in with whatever you want. Choose one thesis and then write two different introductions for it. For example, you could write one with a famous quotation and another with the funnel method. This is just an example; choose any two types of introductions you want, but make sure you choose only one thesis.

1. It is necessary that every educated person have experience and skill in writing.
2. _____ is the best athlete in _____.
3. Some television preachers pervert Christian principles.
4. Many young people today have more concern for others than most people think.
5. Too many young people today seem to care only about themselves.

Exercise 8.9

Write a new introduction for one of the essays you have previously written for this class.

Conclusions

Just as an essay should begin with an introductory paragraph, it should end with a concluding paragraph, a conclusion. And just as introductions can be weak, so can conclusions. Again, problems will arise if you talk about your troubles in the conclusion. For example:

> I have said all I know about why people should buy American instead of foreign cars. This is a difficult topic to prove, but I have tried to give good reasons, and I can't think of anything else.

Like the introduction we looked at earlier, this conclusion shares your problems with the reader when you should stay focused on the topic and thesis at one of the most important points in the paper—the end.

You should also avoid making claims for the success of your paper. For example:

> My paper proves that people should buy American cars instead of foreign cars. My examples have shown that American cars are better.

If the examples did prove your point, they should stand on their own. You should not have to tell the readers.

A third type of weak conclusion lacks development and states the obvious: Drug use should be stopped or reduced in America. It hurts people, so something should be done about it.

This writer has the right idea in restating her thesis, but the sentences lack punch. They are obviously true, but without development, the conclusion is flat and could not leave much of an impression on an audience. Remember that a conclusion is the last thing the audience reads; thus, it should leave a lasting impression.

Purposes

1. Concluding paragraphs enable you to stress the importance of the thesis of your essay. Often they repeat your thesis but in different words to emphasize it once more.
2. Conclusions also give your essay a sense of completeness so that the reader does not feel that you have dropped the topic abruptly before developing it fully.
3. Conclusions give you one last chance to leave a lasting impression on the reader.

Qualities

1. Often conclusions restate the thesis in different words or imply the thesis.
2. In most cases, conclusions are more general than the body paragraphs.
3. Like introductions, conclusions for short essays (500–700 words) should be no more than 100–150 words.

Like the strategies for beginning an essay, the strategies for ending one are limited only by the writer's imagination. Writers are always coming up with new and clever ways to write conclusions. The following strategies are a few that writers have used effectively.

Echoing Your Introduction

Sometimes you can conclude a paper by having the reader recall your introduction. Your conclusion, then, works as a kind of echo. This strategy works because it reminds readers of your thesis and gives the essay a kind of "wholeness." Think back to the narrative introduction with the thesis on adults enjoying Disneyland as much as children. Assuming the writer spent most of the essay discussing what he did there that day, here is a possible conclusion for that essay:

> I had thought I would spend a few hours at Disneyland, but here I was at 1:00 A.M., closing time, leaving the front gates with the now dark towers of the Magic Kingdom behind me. I could see tired children, toddling along and struggling to keep their eyes open as best they could. Others slept in their parents' arms as we waited for the parking lot tram that would take us to our cars. My forty-year-old feet ached, and I felt a bit sad to think that in a couple of days I would be leaving California, my vacation over, to go back to my desk. But then I smiled to think that for at least a day I felt ten years old again.

As you can see, the writer recalls a couple of things from the introduction: the parking lot and the towers of the Magic Kingdom. But note that he also implies the thesis—that adults enjoy Disneyland—by claiming to have felt like a boy of ten.

Exercise 8.10

Choose an essay you have written for class, and rewrite its conclusion by echoing its introduction.

Challenging the Reader

Another effective way to conclude is with a challenge to your readers to take action or to change the way they think. In the following conclusion of an essay on jury duty, the writer challenged readers to meet their obligations when called upon to be jurors:

> Though serving on a jury is not only a civic responsibility but also an interesting experience, many people still view jury duty as a chore that interrupts their jobs and the routine of their daily lives. However, juries are part of America's attempt to be a free and just society. Thus, jury duty challenges us to be interested and responsible citizens.

The closing sentence puts the reader on the spot. To reject the writer's conclusion is to shirk one's civic duties; to accept the challenge is to accept the writer's thesis. Note also that the writer's thesis is evident in the beginning of the paragraph before the challenge is issued.

Exercise 8.11

Rewrite the conclusion you wrote in exercise 8.10, this time making a challenge to the reader.

Looking to the Future

Most of the time your essay will cover a topic from the past or in the present. To conclude an essay, however, you can look ahead and predict possible future outcomes from your topic. The following conclusion would work well for an essay arguing that more and better students should enter the teaching profession.

> Without well-qualified teachers, schools are little more than buildings and equipment. If higher-paying careers continue to attract the best and brightest students, there will not only be a shortage of teachers, but the teachers available may not have the best qualifications. Our youth will suffer. And when youth suffers, the future suffers.

This conclusion would work well because it emphasizes the problem discussed in the essay. The essay, of course, would have to provide support that would make such predictions believable. That is crucial. If you use this strategy, make sure that your predictions are within reason. Don't exaggerate, but at the same time don't be afraid to predict possible outcomes of your topic.

Exercise 8.12

Pick a conclusion from an essay you have written and rewrite it to predict the future, or rewrite one of your conclusions from the previous exercises.

Posing Questions

We have discussed earlier how to start an essay with a question or series of questions. You can also conclude an essay this way. (However, if you use questions in your introduction, it is not wise to use the same strategy in your conclusion.) Let's examine two examples, one on the topic of campus drinking and another on political advertising.

Questions first

Why do so many college students drink? Why do they drink so much? Psychologists might say that drinking enables them to overcome their social problems, providing a false sense of confidence. Sociologists might say that students are like the rest of American society, where per capita alcohol consumption is among the highest in the world. The students themselves might say that they are just trying to find a release from academic pressures. Whatever the reasons, drinking on college campuses has reached epidemic proportions.

Questions last

Campaign advertisements should help us understand the qualifications of the candidates and their positions on the issues. Instead, most tell us what a boob or knave the opposing candidate is, or they present general images of the candidate as a family person or God-fearing American. Do such advertisements contribute to creating an informed electorate or a people who choose political leaders the same way they choose soft drinks and soap?

Both of these conclusions use the questions effectively. The first starts with the questions and then gives possible answers, while the second ends with a question for the reader to consider. In both conclusions, the questions force the reader to ponder the thesis of the essay.

Exercise 8.13

Write two different conclusions for a paper that you have already written for this class.

Writing Assignment

Think about the place where you grew up. How is it typical? Different? What thesis does it illustrate? Write a short essay (500 words) showing how your neighborhood or area illustrates, or does not illustrate, something about the way Americans live. Be specific in developing your paragraphs so that your neighborhood does not sound like any similar place. Give as much attention to the introduction and conclusion as to the body paragraphs. Assume that you are writing this essay to be included in a book about American life. Your purpose is to show an educated audience how your town or neighborhood does or does not fit stereotypes of American living, e.g., the happy suburban family, the good country folk, the ethnic neighborhood, the tough urban slum, and so on.

Key Terms

Introduction: A paragraph (or paragraphs in a longer essay) that gets the reader's attention, limits the topic of the essay, and states the essay's thesis.
Conclusion: A paragraph (or paragraphs in a longer essay) that stresses the importance of the thesis, gives the essay a sense of completeness, and leaves a final impression on the reader.

chapter nine
Sentence Structure

Thus far, you have been concentrating on writing whole essays and the paragraphs and sentences that make up those essays. You have also spoken tens of thousands of sentences throughout your life. Sentences are a key element in writing: Good sentence structure can make an adequate essay good and a good essay excellent.

Some beginning writers may be good at writing individual sentences but have trouble putting them together into effective paragraphs and essays. Other beginning writers may learn to organize and develop essays and paragraphs, but they may not be as effective as the writer wants because the individual sentences in them do not express the ideas as smoothly, clearly, and grammatically as they should. This chapter will focus on sentence structure, how parts of sentences fit together to form the whole.

As you know, each word has a function in a sentence, a purpose for being there. There are many grammatical terms that describe these functions. You probably have studied these terms in elementary and high school, but if you have forgotten some of them, don't worry. Writing good sentences does not require you to know every single term to describe the functions of words in sentences. There are some terms, however, that are helpful because they describe the most important parts of sentences: subject, verb, clause, phrase, and modifier. As you progress through this chapter, you will learn these terms, and we will introduce a few others to help these make sense. Knowing the terms themselves will not necessarily make you a better writer, but the concepts the terms represent will help you as you write and revise your sentences.

Kernel Sentences

Consisting of one subject and one verb, kernel sentences are the shortest and simplest of all English sentences. Kernel sentences consist of two or three words, with a subject first and a verb second:

Subject	+	verb
Julian		works.
The baby		cried.
Dogs		bark.
The sun		rose.
Archie		screamed.

Because they are so short, these kernel sentences may seem a bit odd to you. After all, only small children speak consistently in kernel sentences, and rarely are kernel sentences used in writing. But these kernels are complete sentences— each has a subject and a verb. The subject is the doer, and the verb shows what the subject did. We will discuss subjects and verbs more completely later; for now, examine how the kernels function as parts of larger sentences:

Julian, who studied forestry at Oregon State University, now *works* managing timber forests for Weyerhauser, a large paper manufacturer.

Suffering severely from colic, *the baby cried* throughout the night, keeping its worried parents awake.

Dogs, no matter what their breed, usually *bark* if a stranger enters the home.

The desert *sun rose,* a burning orange disk flat against the clear summer sky.

Alone at night in the dark woods, *Archie,* a city boy, *screamed* wildly upon hearing something coming through the brush.

Though these sentences are now longer, the kernel is still the most important part because it expresses the main point of the sentence. For this reason, identifying kernels can help you revise your sentences.

Exercise 9.1

Underline the kernels in each of the following sentences.

1. During the first three months of pregnancy, the embryo, at first tiny and misshapen, begins the changes leading to its final form.
2. After a strenuous game of tennis, Alison drank a tall glass of lemonade.
3. Eldon Stewart, a heart surgeon from Texas, recently joined the staff at Central General Hospital.

4. Rhode Island, though the smallest state in the U.S., has several excellent colleges and universities.
5. Bread baked at home tastes better than bread from the store.

Subjects

As you saw in the kernel sentences, every sentence has a subject—the first word you underlined in each sentence in the last exercise. Let's define subject:

> The subject of a sentence is the word or words which do something or which something is said about. A subject can be a person, a group of people, a place, an idea, an activity:

Person:
Carl Lewis starred in the 1984 and 1988 Olympics.

People:
Some politicians do not tell the truth.

Place:
Russia has more land than the United States.

Thing:
Lead weighs more than other metals.

Idea:
Einstein's theory of relativity changed the way science perceives the universe.

Activity:
Chopping wood is strenuous exercise.

Simple vs. Complete Subjects

When we looked at kernel sentences, each one had a *simple subject* —one word that does something or about which something is said. Compare these pairs of sentences:

The students formed a study group.

simple subject

The students from Reeve Hall formed a study group.

simple subject

complete subject

Students were elected to lead the group.

simple subject

Students earning the best grades in each subject were

simple subject

complete subject

elected to lead the group.

All were satisfied with the group's leaders.

simple subject

All of the members were satisfied with the group's leaders.

simple subject

complete subject

Studying prepared the group members for exams.

simple subject

Studying different subjects prepared the group.

simple subject

complete subject

Comparing these sentences, you probably have figured out that while the simple subject is the one word that the sentence is about, the *complete subject* includes the simple subject and all the words that go with it before the verb. Knowing how to tell the simple subject from the complete subject can help you to choose the right verb form (see Chapter 14), but more importantly it can help you when you revise sentences. When a sentence is unclear or awkward to read, you can sometimes isolate the simple subject and cut words from the complete subject to make a clearer sentence. You can then use the words you cut as the basis for another sentence. For example:

The book I needed for psychology class and which was very thick and contained several color pictures cost more than I had left.

This sentence is difficult to read because there are too many words between the simple subject *the book* and the verb *cost*. The cost of the psychology book is one main point, so it should be limited to one sentence. But there is also another point: the features that made the book expensive. This information needs to be sorted out and placed in another sentence:

The book I needed for psychology was very thick and contained several color pictures. It cost more money than I had left, so I could not buy it until I received my financial-aid check.

Exercise 9.2

Circle each simple subject and underline the complete subject.

1. Many of the countries of Eastern Europe have communist governments.
2. European countries aligned with the Soviet Union form an alliance called the Warsaw Pact.
3. Before 1989, each of these countries had a communist government.
4. Since 1989, these countries have undergone great changes.
5. Glasnost, a policy of openness, was promoted in the Soviet Union by Premier Gorbachev.
6. Nations such as Poland and Yugoslavia abandoned communism for new forms of government.
7. Romania, another Warsaw Pact nation, had a repressive form of communism before a revolt in 1990.

8. The communism practiced in China differs from that of European countries.
9. The large population of China makes the country difficult to govern.
10. Protests against the repressive Chinese government in 1989 led to even more repression.

Exercise 9.3

Circle the simple subjects and underline the complete subjects in a paragraph of your own writing.

Compound Subjects

In the following sentence, who is performing the action? *Althea and Tony washed the car.* Here you can see that more than one person is doing something. *Washed* is the only verb, but the sentence has two subjects because two people performed the action together. Thus, a compound subject is any subject in which more than one person, place, thing, idea, or activity performs the same action or has the same thing said about them. Study these examples:

> *Jennifer, Magda, and Lisa* decided to take chemistry together.
> *Oranges and grapefruits* are natural sources of Vitamin C.
> *Prime Minister Margaret Thatcher of England and President Ronald Reagan* were great friends and allies.
> *Willie Mays of the Giants, Mickey Mantle of the Yankees, and Duke Snider of the Dodgers* played centerfield for their respective teams during the 1950s.
> *Fans and sportswriters* alike argued over who was the best centerfielder of the three.

Exercise 9.4

Underline the compound subjects in these sentences.

1. New York, Los Angeles, and Chicago are the three largest cities in America.

2. In the summer, joggers picnickers, and sightseers flock to McCormick Park.
3. Of all the forms of government, monarchy and dictatorship have been most prevalent throughout history.
4. Democracy and communism have spread only in the twentieth century.
5. Spain and Russia were monarchies prior to the twentieth century.
6. A tall woman in a black leather coat and a stocky man with short hair were seen driving off from the scene of the robbery.
7. In the last two years, Mothers Against Drunk Driving (MADD) and Students Against Drunk Driving (SADD) have done much to change people's perceptions of driving under the influence of alcohol.
8. New York, New Jersey, California, Illinois, and Ohio are just a few of the states with severe penalties for drunk driving.
9. Pyramid, Magnum, Malibu, and Cambridge are low-cost brands of cigarettes introduced in the late 1980s.
10. The weasel and beaver are both rodents.

Exercise 9.5

Write five sentences of your own using compound subjects.

Verbs

Along with a subject, every sentence must have a verb. Without a verb, nothing can be said about a subject. There are two kinds of verbs in English sentences: *action verbs* and *linking verbs*. In a sentence in which the subject does something, there will be an action verb. In a sentence in which something is said about the subject, there will be a linking verb. Compare these two sentences:

> Action verb: Alicea Ramirez *teaches* mathematics at the local university.
> Linking verb: Alicea Ramirez *is* a mathematics teacher at the local university.

These sentences seem almost identical, but in the first, *teaches* is an action verb because the woman is doing something—teaching. In the second, something is said about her—that she is something. Often the difference between sentences with action verbs and ones with linking verbs is much clearer. Compare:

> Mike Tyson is a great boxer.
> Mike Tyson knocked out most of his opponents.

English contains far more action verbs than linking verbs. The most common linking verbs are forms of the verb *to be:* am, is, are, was, were, will be, has been, have been, had been. Other common linking verbs are forms of *feel, appear, look,* and *seem.* Knowing the difference between action and linking verbs can help you write and revise sentences. As we will see in the next chapter, action verbs usually work more effectively than linking verbs because they are more specific.

Exercise 9.6

Circle the verb in each sentence, and above the circle put an A if the verb is an action verb or an L if it's a linking verb.

1. The American Indians were a proud and noble people.
2. The Indians lived life much differently than Europeans.
3. First of all, they were closer to nature.
4. They hunted for most of their food.
5. Though primarily hunters, they also grew some crops.
6. The coming of Europeans to America corrupted Indian culture.
7. Europeans introduced the Indians to such vices as alcohol.
8. To the Europeans, the Indians seemed uncivilized.
9. The expansion of the United States drove Indians from their lands.
10. The treatment of the Indians is one of the great injustices in American history.

Exercise 9.7

Write two sentences with action verbs and two with linking verbs.

Compound Verbs

Just as a sentence can have more than one subject, it can have more than one verb. When a subject or a compound subject has more than one verb, the sentence has a compound verb. Study these sentences:

> We *ate* and *drank* all evening.
> The police *questioned* the suspect and *charged* him with the robbery.
> Howard *cleaned* the gutters, *mowed* the lawn, *weeded* the garden, and *swept* the sidewalks.
> Danielle and Christopher *met* in September and *married* the following June.
> Ernesto *entered* community college but after one year *transferred* to the state university.

As you can see, sometimes the verbs forming a compound verb can be close together, as in the first sentence, or far apart, as in the last sentence. No matter how far apart the verbs are, if the subject is performing both actions, the verbs are compound. For example, in the last sentence, Ernesto is the person who both entered and transferred. The words in between just tell what he entered and where he transferred.

Exercise 9.8

Underline the parts of the compound verbs in these sentences.

1. Computers store and retrieve information.
2. Anita wanted to become a ballet dancer but injured her leg.
3. The team traded two young players for a veteran pitcher and then went on to win the pennant.
4. The AIDS virus enters the blood and attacks the cells.
5. A grandfather clock enhances the decor of any room and usually keeps accurate time.
6. The angry child cried, screamed, and stamped his feet.
7. Nylon carpet is inexpensive and wears well.
8. The car bucked and sputtered and finally stalled.
9. Inexpensive disposable pens and cigarette lighters were introduced in the 1960s and soon became popular.
10. After a hard day of working construction, Hank drove straight home, ate a big meal, and went to bed.

Exercise 9.9

Write five sentences using compound verbs.

Predicates

You probably remember the word *predicate* from your previous studies of English. Most elementary school children know that sentences contain subjects and predicates, though they may not be sure what that means. Simply defined, a predicate is the verb plus any phrases that follow it. Like subjects, predicates can be described as either a *simple predicate* or a *complete predicate*. The simple predicate is the verb itself; the complete predicate includes the verb and any words or phrases that follow it. The words following the verb in the predicate are called the *complement*. Study these examples:

Knowing how to identify simple predicates will help you isolate the verb in a sentence—an important skill as you begin to develop smooth and grammatically correct sentences.

Exercise 9.10

In these sentences, circle the simple predicate (the verb) and underline the complement.

1. Pine forests spread throughout northern Maine.
2. Many people in northern Maine work in the logging industry.
3. Pine is a staple of the logging industry in Maine.
4. Wisconsin produces many dairy products.
5. In fact, Wisconsin calls itself the "Dairy State."
6. Cheese, however, is Wisconsin's most famous dairy product.
7. Colorado boasts a large mining industry.
8. The state is also a haven for tourists.
9. Its many beautiful mountains attract hikers, campers, and sightseers.
10. In the winter, thousands of people visit Colorado to ski.

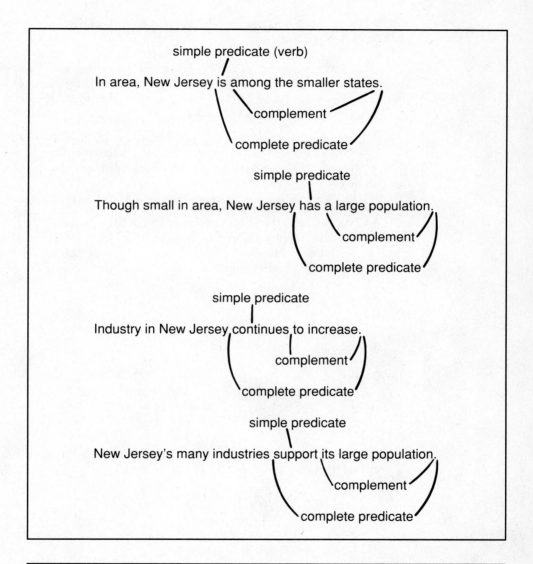

Exercise 9.11

Circle the simple predicate and underline the complete predicate in a paragraph of your own.

Direct Objects

The words in complements can be described in various ways, depending on the verb in the sentence. Often action verbs are followed by direct objects. A direct object receives the action of the verb. You can tell a direct object by asking what or whom the verb affects. For example:

> The knight killed the *dragon*. (What was killed? The dragon.)
> Sandra bought a new *car* last week. (What was bought? A car.)
> The people elected *George Bush* President. (Who was elected? George Bush.)
> Evelyn knew a *secret* about Eric. (What did Evelyn know? A secret.)

As you can see, the direct object receives the action. Notice, however, that the action can be physical or mental. In the first sentence, the object—the dragon—is killed while in the last, it is merely something known.

Though action verbs often have direct objects, sometimes they do not. Compare these pairs of sentences:

Object:

> Jose Feliciano sang the national anthem at the 1968 World Series. (What did he sing? The national anthem.)

No Object:

> Jose Feliciano sang at the 1968 World Series. (What did he sing? The sentence does not say; it tells us only where he sang.)

Object:

> Janet swam the breaststroke competitively throughout her high school years. (What did she swim? The breaststroke.)

No Object:

> Janet swam competitively throughout her high school years. (What did she swim? We are told only when she swam.)

Object:

> Paul cooks very spicy meatballs. (What does Paul cook? Meatballs.)

No Object:

> Paul cooks with a lot of spices. (We are not told what Paul cooks, only how he cooks.)

Object:

> Anthony Trollope wrote many novels. (What did he write? Many novels.)

No Object:

> Anthony Trollope wrote very quickly. (We are told only how Trollope wrote.)

When a predicate contains a direct object, you can always tell who or what the verb affects. When there is no direct object, the complement will tell you only when, where, or how the action took place.

Exercise 9.12

Underline the direct object in each sentence.

1. Plaque causes tooth decay.
2. During regular cleanings, dentists remove plaque, using small picks.
3. Feeling the pick against the teeth, the patient experiences discomfort.
4. A small buffing tool polishes the teeth after cleaning.
5. Regular cleanings ensure healthy teeth.
6. In recent years, dentistry has overcome people's fear of dentists.
7. High-speed drills make visits to the dentist less painful.
8. Preventative measures, such as fluoride treatments, have reduced the number of cavities in children.
9. Despite advances in dentistry, many people still fear dental work.

Exercise 9.13

Circle the direct objects in sentences in a paragraph of your own. Remember that not all sentences have direct objects.

Exercise 9.14

Some of the following sentences contain direct objects; some do not. Underline the direct objects when they occur; write NO next to sentences without direct objects.

1. Autumn brings cooler temperatures.
2. In autumn, leaves fall from the trees.
3. People rake leaves into piles before bagging them for disposal.
4. Years ago, people would burn leaves.
5. Some people enjoy the aroma of burning leaves.
6. However, the smoke from burning leaves pollutes the air.
7. Most cities and towns have laws against leaf burning.
8. Some towns set aside one day a week for leaf burning.
9. Dry leaves burn rapidly.
10. Leaves blow all over the streets on windy days.

Predicate Nouns and Adjectives

Linking verbs are often followed by either predicate nouns or predicate adjectives. As you know, a noun is a word that functions as the name of a person, place, thing, idea, emotion, etc. (Abe Lincoln, Germany, book, democracy, love). An adjective is a word that functions to describe something (a *tired* boy, *pink* house, a *short* rest). Study these examples:

> Dr. Donald DeBakey is a *surgeon*. (noun)
> Dr. DeBakey is *famous* for heart surgery. (adjective)
> Medicine is a *science*. (noun)
> Science is *valuable* to society. (adjective)
> The price seems a *rip-off*. (noun)
> The price seems *unfair*. (adjective)

Exercise 9.15

In the following sentences, circle the direct object and write DO next to the sentence, or circle the predicate nouns and adjectives and write PN or PA next to the sentence. If a sentence does not have a direct object, predicate noun, or predicate adjective, write NO next to it.

1. In ancient Rome, around 78 B.C., two generals, Pompey and Crassus, struggled against each other.

2. Each wanted control of the military.
3. Pompey won the struggle.
4. Crassus, however, became rich in politics.
5. A few years later, Crassus, Pompey, and Julius Caesar banded together in the First Triumvirate.
6. The Triumvirate was an alliance that enabled the three men to rule Rome.
7. Crassus died in battle in 53 B.C.
8. Pompey was now afraid of the growing popularity of Caesar.
9. The army was loyal to Caesar in the struggle between the two men.
10. Thus, Caesar seized control of the government for himself.

Exercise 9.16

Return to the paragraph of your own in which you circled direct objects. Underline any predicate nouns or adjectives, and identify them with PN and PA.

Phrases

Simply defined, a phrase is any two or more words that *does not contain a subject and a verb*. A kernel sentence contains only a subject and a verb, but as you know, most sentences contain more than two or three words. Phrases fill out sentences, modifying the subjects and verbs. To modify means to change. When we say a phrase is a modifier, we mean it changes the way we think of the subject and verb by adding information to it. For example, compare these sentences; in the second sentence, the modifying phrases are italicized and numbered:

Kernel: Ellen went.
  [1]*Having recovered from a long illness,* Ellen went [2]*to Florida* [3]*for a restful vacation.*

The second sentence has three phrases. The first phrase modifies Ellen, telling us more about her. The next two phrases tell about the verb and where Ellen went and why. When you write your own sentences, you will use phrases as well as subjects and verbs. Knowing the difference between a phrase and a subject or verb will enable you to revise your sentences to make them smoother and clearer.

Exercise 9.17

Underline the phrases in these sentences.

1. Confused by the many road signs, Daryl pulled over to the side of the road, feeling lost.
2. He reached in the glove compartment to find a map.
3. He drove down the road after finding his location.
4. Seeing the sign for Carterville, he eased across two lanes toward the exit.
5. Despite the delay, he arrived on time for the wedding.
6. After parking the car, he walked up the steps of the church and entered.
7. Wanting to remain unseen, he sat in the back on the left side.
8. At the sound of the organ, Michelle came through the doors on her father's arm and walked slowly up the aisle to the strains of "Here Comes the Bride."
9. Remembering their three years together, Daryl thought of his mistakes with her and wanted to cry.
10. Before the end of the ceremony, he left, feeling a sharp pain cutting through his stomach.

Exercise 9.18

Underline the phrases in a paragraph of your own writing.

Types of Phrases

As the previous exercise showed you, phrases add much information to sentences. There are many different kinds of phrases, and you do not need to memorize them. But we will discuss some of them and their functions in sentences.

Participle Phrases: Participle phrases contain a verb form that usually ends in *-ed* or *-ing*. (For more on participles, see Chapter 15.) Though containing a verb form, participle phrases are not the verb of the sentence. Rather, they work as modifiers, are the subject or object of a sentence, or act as a predicate adjective or noun.

Participles as modifiers:

Convinced of the man's guilt, the judge sent him to prison. (Here the phrase modifies the subject, judge, adding the reason why the judge sent the man to prison.)

The police were following a woman *wearing a red hat.* (Here the phrase modifies the object *woman,* telling us what she was wearing.)

The newly married couple went *shopping for furniture.* (This phrase modifies the verb, telling us where they went.)

As subjects (note that only participles ending in *-ing* can be subjects):

Taking out an auto loan is nearly a necessity with today's car prices. (Because the phrase is what the sentence is about, it is the subject.)

Mastering the violin requires years of practice. (What requires years of practice? Mastering the violin, expressed in a phrase.)

As objects (again, note that only participles ending in *-ing* can function as objects):

Tabitha enjoys *running in marathons.* (The phrase expresses what Tabitha enjoys.)

Getting a driver's license requires *taking a test.* (The phrase is the object of *requires.*)

As predicate nouns and adjectives (participles ending in *-ing* function as predicate nouns, while participles ending in *-ed* function as predicate adjectives):

Bobby's favorite hobby is *building model airplanes.* (The participle phrase works like a noun because it tells us the activity that is the boy's favorite hobby.)

Georgia seems *tired of her job.* (The phrase here works as an adjective because it tells us how the subject seems.)

Exercise 9.19

Underline each participle phrase. Then identify its function by writing above it M for modifier, S for subject, DO for direct object, PN for predicate noun, or PA for predicate adjective. Sentences can have more than one participle phrase. (Note: Be sure not to confuse the verb form of a participle phrase with the main verb of the kernel sentence.)

1. Ruling France for 49 years, King Louis XV knew little about the common people.

2. The French middle class was disgusted with Louis's corrupt government and decadent lifestyle.
3. Following Louis XV, Louis XVI continued ignoring the needs of the middle class.
4. Embittered enough to revolt, the middle class began recruiting the necessary support of the peasants.
5. After trying to persuade Louis XVI to enact reforms, the people formed a National Assembly.
6. Declaring this assembly illegal, Louis XVI called his troops to Paris.
7. The people of Paris, fearing the troops, began arming themselves.
8. A mob of people stormed the Bastille, a fortress-prison, looking to secure weapons.
9. Storming the Bastille, many people were killed.
10. The storming of the Bastille, on July 14, 1789, is viewed as Independence Day in France.

Exercise 9.20

Underline and identify any verb phrases in a paragraph of your own.

Prepositional Phrases.   Prepositional phrases consist of a preposition and a noun, pronoun, or a word functioning like a noun. The word or words following the preposition are called the *object of the preposition*, not to be confused with the direct object of a verb. For example,

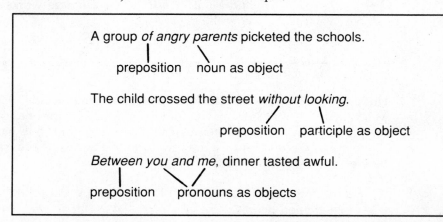

A group *of angry parents* picketed the schools.

  preposition   noun as object

The child crossed the street *without looking*.

  preposition   participle as object

Between you and me, dinner tasted awful.

  preposition   pronouns as objects

Prepositional phrases work as modifiers. In the first sentence above, the phrase *of angry parents* modifies the subject *group*. The phrase *without looking* modifies the verb *crossed*, telling how the child crossed the street. In the third, *between you and me* modifies the whole sentence.

Prepositional phrases also commonly follow forms of linking verbs:

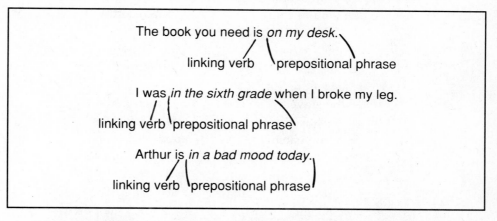

Of course, several prepositional phrases can appear in one sentence. Sometimes they follow one right after the other, but in every case they serve as modifiers. They are never subjects, verbs, or objects. Examine this sentence. The prepositional phrases are marked off and arrows point to the words they modify:

The variety | of cultural activities | in ancient Greece | reflect a high degree |

of civilization | although technology was | in its infancy |.

There are many words that function as prepositions. Most are single words, but sometimes two words together function as a preposition:

aboard the train	*against* him
about the boy	*ahead of* me
according to experts	*among* the workers
across the sea	*around* the block
after her	*as well as* you

at the movies	*instead of* a party
because of the rain	*into* the woods
before our dinner	*like* diamonds and pearls
behind the car	*near* the tree
below the shelf	*of* a good family
beneath the counter	*off* the record
beside his chair	*on* the chair
besides Victor	*onto* the porch
between the women	*out* the door
beyond all doubt	*outside* his expertise
by the stove	*past* their bedtime
despite our efforts	*rather than* a car
down the hatch	*through* the window
during the winter	*throughout* your life
except the bears	*to* the store
for a fee	*under* the bed
from a big city	*underneath* the porch
in a cup	*until* next time
in addition to money	*up* the creek
in case of fire	*upon* her principles
in front of the television	*with* a smile
in place of the original	*within* a month
inside the house	*without* care
inside of a week	

You need not worry about memorizing all of these prepositions because you already know them—you have used them all your life. You also know that they are followed by objects (you would never say, "I am college in"). Sometimes, when many prepositional phrases appear in a sentence, you might have trouble picking out the subject and verb to find the kernel sentence. In writing your own sentences, you always need to be sure you have a kernel sentence, so you need to be able to identify the prepositional phrases that are not part of the kernel.

Exercise 9.21

Underline all the prepositional phrases in each sentence. Then circle the words that remain. These words will be your kernel sentence and, in some sentences, a direct object.

1. After four years of college, Marty worked for an accounting firm on the West Coast.
2. Marty had decided on a career in accounting before his junior year.
3. As a freshman, he had been enrolled in the prelaw program.
4. In 1776, the American colonies declared their independence from Great Britain.
5. Fenway Park in Boston is one of Baseball's oldest stadiums.
6. A group of noisy students was in the dorm halls last night at 1:00 A.M.
7. Before the arrival of the dorm director, they woke many of the students on the floor.
8. A few of the students on the floor slept through the disturbance.
9. On Wednesday at 2:40, the police found a car in a ditch on the south road to Marlinton.
10. Snow fell for ten hours straight during last week's blizzard.

Noun Phrases. As you know, a phrase is any group of two or more words that does not have a subject and verb, but these phrases can include nouns. The simplest form of noun phrase is a noun and the word *a, an, or the.* Other noun phrases include adjectives (descriptive words) as well:

> a tall man
> a fat white cat
> the old stuffed chair

A noun phrase thus can be defined as a noun and the words that modify it. Noun phrases appear in a sentence anywhere that single nouns do. They can serve as:

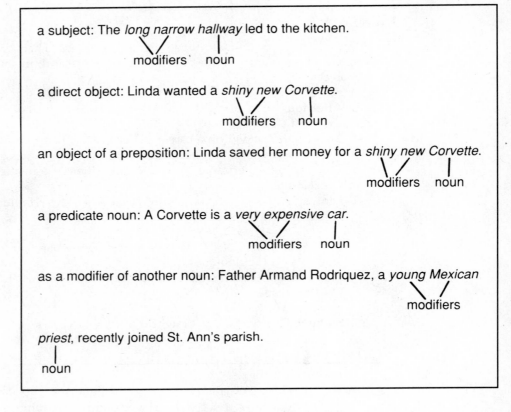

a subject: The *long narrow hallway* led to the kitchen.
modifiers   noun

a direct object: Linda wanted a *shiny new Corvette*.
modifiers   noun

an object of a preposition: Linda saved her money for a *shiny new Corvette*.
modifiers   noun

a predicate noun: A Corvette is a *very expensive car*.
modifiers   noun

as a modifier of another noun: Father Armand Rodriquez, a *young Mexican*
modifiers

priest, recently joined St. Ann's parish.
noun

In each sentence, the modifiers add to our knowledge of the noun, thus changing our view of it. In the last sentence, the whole noun phrase modifies the noun before it: Father Armand Rodriguez. Without the noun phrase, we would not know the priest's name or age group.

Exercise 9.22

Underline any noun phrases in the following sentences.

1. In medieval times, feudal governments were widespread.
2. Powerful feudal warlords would rule a large or small area, protecting the local people.

3. In return, the local people, peasant farmers, would pay heavy taxes to the warlord.
4. At times, feudalism was a highly uncivilized form of government.
5. Sometimes, greedy, evil warlords would levy taxes of outrageous amounts.
6. The poor, unarmed peasants had no choice but to pay.
7. Though medieval times were often brutal, people made important advances.
8. Poor and hungry peasants numbered in the millions, but slavery was almost nonexistent.
9. Central governments took a long time to develop because of feudalism, a system of warring lords.
10. The church, the major power in medieval times, had as much influence as the feudal lords.

All of the phrases we have discussed fit together with kernels—subjects and verbs—to form sentences. Remember that a phrase, no matter what kind, cannot form a complete sentence by itself. Phrases must be attached to a subject and verb to form a sentence.

Clauses

A clause is any group of words that contains at least one subject and one verb. Thus, all kernel sentences are considered clauses. Clauses may also contain several phrases along with the subject and verb. Thus, some clauses are sentences. However, there are different kinds of clauses, and it is important to know them because some can stand alone as sentences and some cannot.

Independent Clauses

Independent clauses contain at least one subject and one verb, and they can stand alone as complete sentences. That is why they are called *independent*. They can be as short as a two-word kernel or very long, containing a kernel and many modifiers. Examine these sentences. In each, the subject and verb are in italics:

> *War kills.*
>
> Because of nuclear weapons, a *war* between superpowers probably would *kill* millions of people quickly.

Both of these sentences are independent clauses because of the subject *war* and the verb *kills* or *kill.* The second, however, is much longer because it includes a direct object and many modifiers, particularly prepositional phrases. But the first sentence, though just two words, is an independent clause and complete sentence because it has at least one subject and one verb that state a fact and thus make sense.

Like any other clauses, independent clauses can have compound subjects and/or compound verbs:

> Compound subject: *Hitler and Mussolini* formed an alliance during World War II.
>
> Compound verb: The enemy *bombed* the cities and *mined* the harbors.
>
> Compound subject and compound verb: *Runaway inflation* and the *hostage crisis* in Iran *tarnished* Carter's presidential image and *led* to his defeat in the 1980 election.

Independent Clauses and Coordinating Conjunctions.

Independent clauses can stand alone as sentences. They can also be joined by coordinating conjunctions to form compound sentences. A *compound sentence* is any two or more independent clauses joined by coordinating conjunctions. Coordinating conjunctions are the words *but, and, for, nor, or, so,* and *yet.* Examine these compound sentences:

> You may never be another Hemingway, *but* you can learn to write well.
>
> New Yorkers sometimes look down on other Americans as bumpkins, *and* other Americans sometimes view New Yorkers as pretentious snobs.
>
> The child went to bed early, *for* his parents had company.
>
> She does not like drinking, *nor* does she like going into bars. (Note that when *nor* joins the clauses, the verb comes first and the subject second in the second clause.)
>
> The key players must recover from their injuries quickly, *or* the team will have little chance to win the conference title.
>
> It was raining heavily in the morning, *so* they decided to cancel the afternoon picnic.
>
> Ramona grew up fifteen minutes from New York, *yet* she never visited the Statue of Liberty.

A compound sentence can add variety to your writing and draw together related points. Remembering coordinating conjunctions is not difficult, and beginning writers have invented nonsense words from the first letter of each to help remember them:

But	**F**or	**B**ut
And	**A**nd	**O**r
For	**N**or	**Y**et
Nor	**B**ut	**F**or
Or	**O**r	**A**nd
So	**Y**et	**N**or
Yet	**S**o	**S**o

Bafnosy, fanboys, and *boyfans* are not words, of course, but any one of them will work as a device for remembering the coordinating conjunctions. Also remember that when you join two independent clauses with a coordinating conjunction to form a compound sentence, you must put a comma before the conjunction: independent clause + comma + coordinating conjunction + independent clause = compound sentence.

Exercise 9.23

Join each pair of independent clauses to form a compound sentence. Try to use each conjunction at least once.

1. The wind howled. The snow fell.
2. The temperature dropped to below zero. The sun was shining brightly against a blue sky.
3. The biblical teachings of Christianity advocate poverty and humility. Some televangelists have luxurious and flamboyant lifestyles.
4. We might go to Aruba on vacation. Maybe we will go to the Bahamas.
5. "M*A*S*H" was an extremely popular television show in the 1970s. It gained an even larger audience from syndicated reruns.
6. Lori is a premed major. She plans to become a surgeon.
7. Nadia wants to graduate in three years. She must take courses every summer.
8. The ancient Greeks did not shoe horses. They did not use them to pull wagons.
9. Burt decided to go to college. He wanted a good job.
10. The paint was peeling off the house. Most of the gutters were rusted through.

Exercise 9.24

Write seven compound sentences, using a different coordinating conjunction in each.

Independent Clauses and Conjunctive Adverbs.   Another group of words—conjunctive adverbs—can join independent clauses to form compound sentences. You have seen these words in the last chapter when they were discussed as transitions between sentences. Conjunctive adverbs can also be used to join sentences with a semicolon. Here are several sentences using some of the most common conjunctive adverbs:

The car had rust around all the wheel wells; *also,* the right front fender was dented.

Lenny flunked three courses; *consequently,* he was placed on academic probation.

General Douglas MacArthur was a daring military leader; *furthermore,* his charisma won the confidence of the public.

The girl sassed the teacher all day; *finally,* she was sent to the principal's office.

Aluminum wiring was found to cause fires; *hence,* its use was discontinued in new construction.

In retrospect, President Lyndon Johnson did much for the country; *however,* while in office he was plagued by the Vietnam War.

President Johnson should be remembered for promoting civil rights legislation and integration; *instead,* he is most often remembered for escalating the war.

Los Angeles, like many large cities, suffers a high rate of crime; *nevertheless,* the city attracts millions of tourists each year.

First, the furnace broke down; *next,* the pipes froze.

Home prices must drop in large metropolitan areas; *otherwise,* few people will be able to buy homes.

College tuition rises annually; *still,* the cost is worth it in the long run.

The demonstrators marched around the building; *then* they stormed it.

Keith lost his job; *therefore,* he will have to postpone buying a new car.

Lynette earned straight *A*'s this semester; *thus,* she was named to the dean's list.

Conjunctive adverbs, like coordinating conjunctions, help you to combine independent clauses to draw relationships between them. Beginning writers often worry about trying to remember all the conjunctive adverbs so that they do not forget to use semicolons with them. Remembering them all is not necessary. Just remember the seven coordinating conjunctions, and if you are not using one of them, you need a semicolon rather than a comma. Another useful trick is to remember that coordinating conjunctions have two or three letters while conjunctive adverbs have at least four letters.

Whether you choose a coordinating conjunction or a conjunctive adverb as a connector is up to you. Using the conjunctive adverb makes the sentence a bit more formal because the semicolon is a less common form of punctuation than the comma. Generally, it is wise to vary your use of connectors to achieve variety in your sentences.

Exercise 9.25

Using conjunctive adverbs and semicolons, combine the following pairs of independent clauses into sentences.

1. The weatherperson forecasted a warm, sunny day. It has been cool and cloudy.
2. Marcia was a very good writer and had a strong grasp of grammar. She was hired to tutor other students in English.
3. Folklore is fun to study. We can learn a great deal about cultures and ethnic groups through their folktales and folkways.
4. Maria wanted to attend an Ivy League university. She enrolled in a state college.
5. Teachers earn less than most other professionals. Fewer students are planning to become teachers.
6. The Indian scout heard horses in the distance. He saw the cavalry troops advancing across the plain.
7. Montana is a very large state. Its population is very small compared to that of most states.
8. The team played poorly all year. The coaching staff made some foolish decisions.
9. The patient fought the cancer for months. He died.
10. You must dress and speak well for an interview. You won't have a chance to get the job.

Exercise 9.26

Using conjunctive adverbs and semicolons, write five compound sentences of your own.

Dependent Clauses

Like independent clauses, dependent clauses contain at least one subject and one verb. Unlike independent clauses, however, dependent clauses cannot stand alone as sentences—they need another clause to lean on to complete their meaning. Compare:

Independent Clause:
　　Fewer people purchased homes.

Dependent Clause:
　　when mortgage rates went up

Dependent + Independent Clause:
　　When mortgage rates went up, fewer people purchased homes.

The first sentence is an independent clause: It has a subject *people* and a verb *purchased,* and it makes sense by simply stating a fact. The next clause is really not a sentence because as soon as the word *when* is added, the reader expects more information if the sentence is to make sense. What happened when mortgage rates went up? Despite having a subject and a verb, this group of words cannot make sense by itself. In the last sentence, it *depends* on the independent clause to complete the meaning and make sense.

Dependent clauses are also called *subordinate clauses. Subordinate* means to be below something. For example, workers are subordinate to their boss. In the case of clauses, a dependent clause is subordinate to an independent clause because it, unlike an independent clause, cannot stand alone as a sentence. Dependent clauses are formed when we add a *subordinating conjunction* to a subject and verb. Thus, a dependent clause can be defined as a subordinating conjunction plus at least one subject and one verb. The following list shows you most of the subordinating conjunctions functioning as part of a dependent clause:

Subordinating conjunctions:

After	*After Coach Matt resigned*, the school never had another winning wrestling team.
Although	*Although Congress will pass the bill*, the President will veto it.
As	*As the committee allocates funds*, it records expenditures.
As if	He criticized the government *as if it were responsible for all of his problems.*
As soon as	*As soon as the public tires of one sex symbol*, a new one emerges.
As though	The teacher hands out assignments *as though they took five minutes to complete.*
Because	*Because she planned the party well*, everyone had a good time.
Before	You should have your car checked *before you leave on vacation.*
How	*How Charles Manson controlled his followers*, few people can understand.
If	*If you follow every new leader who comes along*, you will soon lose your identity.
Since	*Since the paint factories closed*, Paintville has become a ghost town.
So that	I bought a new battery *so that my car would start on cold days.*
Though	She appears very sophisticated, *though she is actually quite naive.*
Unless	*Unless you are ill*, you should attend all classes.
Until	No grades will be assigned *until all work is completed.*
When	*When the going gets tough*, the tough get going.
Whenever	Fan support increases *whenever the team starts winning.*
Wherever	The police followed him *wherever he went.*
While	She was writing her report *while her children were sleeping.*

When a dependent and an independent clause form a sentence like these, the sentence is called a *complex sentence.* You need not remember that, but you should remember that EVERY SENTENCE NEEDS AT LEAST ONE INDEPENDENT CLAUSE. Even if you have two or three or more dependent clauses together, they cannot make a sentence unless they are connected to an independent clause.

This does not mean dependent clauses are weak. Actually, they are quite strong because they allow you to show clear relationships between themselves and the information in the independent clause. Compare these sentences:

The police arrived, and the mob began to get ugly.
When the police arrived, the mob began to get ugly.
The mob began to get ugly when the police arrived.

The first sentence is compound, with two independent clauses joined by *and*. The second and third sentences are complex, with one clause subordinated—made dependent by the addition of *when*. The complex sentences here would be more effective than the compound because they express an exact time relationship that is missing in the compound sentence. In this case, *when* is a more exact word than *and*.

Whether you start a complex sentence with the dependent or independent clause is your choice. It depends on what you want to stress most. Usually the last part of a sentence carries the most force. Also, in deciding which clause to put first, you should consider sentence variety. Four sentences in a row beginning with the dependent clause could get monotonous. Note also that when you begin with the dependent clause, you place a comma between it and the independent clause. In contrast, no comma is used when you begin with the independent clause.

Exercise 9.27

Choose five pairs of sentences from exercise 9.25 and use a subordinating conjunction to join each pair into a complex sentence.

Exercise 9.28

Write five complex sentences of your own.

Relative Clauses

Relative clauses are another type of dependent clause. Relative clauses contain either a relative pronoun and at least one verb or a relative pronoun and a subject and verb. Thus the patterns for relative clauses are:

Relative pronoun + verb = relative clause
Relative pronoun + subject + verb = relative clause

You may not know what relative pronouns are, but actually you use them all the time in speaking and writing. Here is a list:

who	whoever	which	what
whom	whomever	that	whose

Because they are dependent clauses, relative clauses can never stand alone as complete sentences. However, they can function as subjects, objects, or modifiers in other clauses. Also, with a linking verb, they can function like a predicate noun. As relative clauses function in the larger sentence, they also have sentence parts within them.

Beginning writers sometimes find relative clauses confusing because they function as part of a larger sentence but have sentence parts within them. That *can* be confusing, but you need not worry about it. You are actually quite experienced using relative clauses. You do not have to know all the parts; you just need to know that relative clauses are dependent and thus cannot stand alone as complete sentences.

In using relative clauses, you should note that they work best as modifiers and direct objects. When used as subjects or like predicate nouns, they can create awkward sentences. For example, the first sentence above would read

---

As subjects:

Whoever wins the race receives the large gold trophy.

relative pronoun   verb   direct object

What you need is a long vacation.

relative pronoun   subject   verb   predicate noun

As objects:

The dog discovered *that the cat had eaten his food.*

relative pronoun   subject   verb   direct object

I wonder *whose car broke down today*.

relative pronoun   subject   verb

Vicki dates *whomever she wants*.

relative pronoun   subject   verb

As modifiers:

I know a man *who worked building the Alaska Pipeline*.

relative pronoun   verb

People *who drink and smoke heavily* suffer heart attacks

relative pronoun   compound verb

more often than people *who do not*.

relative pronoun   verb

Julie Anastas, *whom I met in biology class*, has decided to

relative pronoun   subject   verb

transfer to a school *that offers a zoology major*.

relative pronoun   verb   direct object

As predicate nouns:

The reason for my tardiness is *that my alarm clock failed to go off*.

relative pronoun   subject   verb

The problem with the car has been *that it stalls on hills*.

relative pronoun   subject   verb

more smoothly if it said, *The winner of the race receives the large gold trophy.* Also, the last sentence would be more direct if it simply said, *The car had been stalling on hills.* These are matters of style that will be discussed further in the next chapter. For now, remember that relative clauses are common in English sentences and that they function effectively as modifiers and objects.

Exercise 9.29

Underline the relative clauses in these sentences.

1. Epicurus, a Greek philosopher, believed that people should accept the world as it is.
2. People should be judged on their own merits rather than on whom they associate with.
3. Religious groups who emphasize the humanist concept of individualism have always been at odds with mainstream religion, which usually preaches submission to God.
4. Louis XIV, who was known as the Sun King, ruled France for seventy-two years.
5. It was not just that Roberto Clemente was a great player but that he played with a spirit that inspired his teammates and delighted the fans.
6. The court concluded that companies who polluted the river would be liable for damages to wildlife.
7. Despite the North's victory at the Battle of Gettysburg, Lincoln was disappointed that the Union forces missed an opportunity to capture the South's army.
8. The Watergate hearings in 1973 showed that even Presidents are not above the law.
9. The prosperity that Americans enjoyed in the 1950s was much like the prosperity of the 1920s; both were the result of a postwar economy that was fueled by confidence in the nation's power and stability.
10. The Federalist party, which is now forgotten by most Americans, was a major force in early American politics.

Exercise 9.30

Combine each pair of the following sentences by making the second sentence a relative clause. After each pair of sentences, you are told whether the relative clause will function as an object or modifier. Study the examples first:

Example:
We knew about Mark. Mark was leaving town. (object)
Combined with second sentence as relative clause: We knew that Mark was leaving town.

Example:
The troops fought fiercely to win the battle. The troops were prepared. (modify troops)
The troops who were prepared fought fiercely to win the battle.

1. Craig bought a 1957 Chevrolet for just $800. The car was in mint condition. (modify Chevrolet)
2. The police found out. Oscar DeLeon, a Colombian drug dealer, was in town. (object)
3. The sofa costs over a thousand dollars. Jill and Peter want to buy it. (modify sofa)
4. *Star Wars, ET,* and *Batman* were all popular films. They were released in the summer and directed at a young audience. (modify films)
5. Most people believed the rumor. The Hamiltons were getting divorced. (modify rumor)
6. Most people believed. The Hamiltons were getting divorced. (direct object)
7. The Mazda Miata captures the spirit of earlier sports cars, such as the Triumph TR4 and the MGB. It was introduced in 1989. (modify Miata)
8. *Miata* means *reward.* It is a Japanese word. (modify Miata)
9. The school purchased computers with a government grant. The school was in an impoverished area. (modify school)
10. The church asked something. All parishioners contribute to a fund for a new playground. (object)

Exercise 9.31

Write five sentences containing relative clauses.

Writing Assignment

Write an essay of 500–600 words that argues why the profession your major will prepare you for is important to society. If you have not yet chosen a major, choose a profession that you think you would be suited for and would enjoy. Assume an audience of other students who might be considering this profession.

Key Terms

Kernel sentence: A two- or three-word sentence containing a subject and a verb.
Subject: The word in a sentence or clause that performs an action or about which something is said.
Simple subject: The subject without the words modifying it.
Complete subject: The subject and all the words modifying it.
Compound subject: Two or more words that perform an action or about which something is said.
Verb: The word that signifies the action performed by the subject or that links the subject to what is said about it.
Action verb: A verb showing a physical or mental action.
Linking verb: A verb linking the subject to what is said about it.
Compound verb: Two or more verbs showing the action performed by the subject or linking the subject to what is said about it.
Predicate: The verb and all the words following it in a clause or sentence.
Simple predicate: The verb by itself.
Complement: The words that modify a verb in a predicate.
Direct object: The word or words that receive the action of a verb.
Predicate noun: A noun, or word functioning like a noun, following a linking verb and telling what the subject is.
Predicate adjective: An adjective, or word functioning like an adjective, following a linking verb and describing the subject.
Phrase: Any group of words that does not contain at least one subject and one verb.
Participle phrase: A phrase that begins with a verb form ending in -ed or -ing and that can serve as a subject, direct object, or modifier.
Prepositional phrase: A phrase that begins with a preposition followed by a noun or noun phrase.
Object of a preposition: The noun or nouns following the preposition in a prepositional phrase.
Noun phrase: A phrase including a noun and its modifiers that can function as a subject, direct object, or modifier.
Clause: Any group of words with at least one subject and one verb.
Independent clause: A clause that can stand alone as a sentence.
Coordinating conjunction: One of seven connecting words—*but, and, for, nor, or, so, yet* —that can join independent clauses with a comma to form a compound sentence.

Conjunctive adverb: A connecting word—such as *consequently, however, then, thus,* etc.—that can join independent clauses with a semicolon to form a compound sentence.

Compound sentence: Two or more independent clauses joined by coordinating conjunctions or conjunctive adverbs.

Dependent clause: A group of words with at least one subject and one verb that cannot stand alone as a sentence because a subordinating conjunction has been added to the beginning of it.

Subordinating conjunction: A word—such as *after, because, since, when,* etc.—that functions to make a clause dependent on another clause to complete the meaning of the sentence.

Complex sentence: A sentence that contains at least one dependent and one independent clause.

Relative clause: A type of dependent clause that contains either a relative pronoun plus a verb or a relative pronoun plus a subject and a verb and that functions as a subject, direct object, predicate noun, or modifier.

Relative pronoun: One of eight words—*who, whom, whoever, whomever, whose, what, which,* and *that*—that form a relative clause when linked to a verb or to a subject and a verb.

chapter ten
Writing Good Sentences

In the previous chapter, you learned about sentence structure—how words, phrases, and clauses fit together to form sentences. That information can help you write good sentences, but sometimes a sentence may have all its parts in order and still be ineffective if it is indirect, wordy, choppy, or awkward. There are several strategies that you can learn for writing good sentences; this chapter will provide you with many of them.

Writing Direct Sentences

The basic kernel of every English sentence is the subject and verb. You learned in the last chapter that without the kernel, there is no sentence. When you write sentences, first make sure that the person or thing you want to write about is the subject. Second, that the action performed by the subject is the verb. Keeping these guidelines in mind will enable you to write clear and direct sentences.

Choosing the Subject

The subject is one of the two most important parts of a sentence. Because a sentence is primarily about the subject, you should make sure that whatever you want to emphasize occupies the subject position in the sentence. When writers fail to choose the proper subject, they end up with indirect sentences:

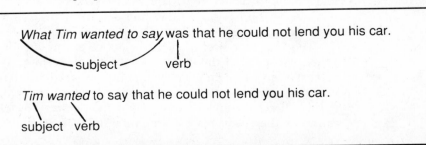

In the first of these sentences, the italicized words from *what* to *say* make up the complete subject; the verb is *was*. The second sentence makes *Tim* the subject, as it should, because he is the person the sentence is about. The verb is now *wanted,* directly stating what Tim felt. Compare two more:

A clarinet is the instrument Jill learned how to play.
     /   \
subject   verb

Jill learned to play the clarinet.
    \   \
subject   verb

Again the first sentence does not use the best subject. The sentence is about Jill, but she is stuck in the middle of the predicate. In the second sentence, Jill is now the subject, followed immediately by the verb expressing what she did. Examine one more pair:

From religion, *some people get* a sense of their place in the universe.
               / |
          subject   verb

Religion provides some people with a sense of their place in the universe.
    | |
subject   verb

Here the proper subject of the sentence—*religion*—is stuck in a prepositional phrase at the beginning of the sentence. The writer uses *people* as the subject, placing the focus on them. The second sentence clears up the problem by making *religion* the subject and adding a verb—*provides*—to express what religion does for some people.

The first sentence in each pair above exemplifies how people often speak. When we speak at the spur of the moment, we are not always sure what our subject is, so we begin with the first thing that comes to mind and then think our way through the sentence. In an everyday conversation, most listeners will not mind indirect sentences as long as they understand us. However, you should try to choose the best subject when you write. When you have a sentence that does not sound quite right, identify the person or thing you are talking about and make that the subject.

Exercise 10.1

Rewrite each of these sentences so that the subject refers to what the sentence is about.

1. Holy communion is the sacrament Catholics consider most important.
2. Being born again is the thing fundamentalist Christians believe necessary for salvation.
3. Many beliefs are different among different forms of Christianity.
4. One thing that is sacred to one group may not be sacred to another.
5. Freedom of religion is a right that all Americans have.
6. The separation of church and state is one thing that the Constitution provides for.
7. Freedom of religion is not something that every country enjoys.
8. In some countries, the law is that people must practice only the state religion.
9. Religious freedom is the reason that the Puritan settlers came to America.
10. But what happened was the Puritans soon became intolerant of other religions.

Avoiding Illogical Subjects

Subjects and predicates must fit together logically in sentences—that is, together they must make sense in terms of both meaning and grammar. Sometimes writers will mistakenly couple a subject and a verb that cannot fit together. One type of illogical construction occurs when the writer mistakenly adds a preposition to a participle phrase (a phrase ending in *-ing*) and uses them as the subject:

Illogical:
   By practicing will make you a good musician.

Logical:
Practicing will make you a good musician.

Logical:
By practicing, you will become a good musician.

The first sentence is illogical because if you break it down to a kernel it would read: By practicing will make. We do not have to know that prepositional phrases cannot be subjects to know that this sentence does not sound right. In contrast, *practicing* is the subject in sentence two. In sentence three, the prepositional phrase is still there, but now the subject *you* has been added.

Illogical: The rookie's first game was only six points.
                          subject   verb

Logical: The rookie's total in his first game was only six points.
                 subject   verb

Logical: The rookie scored only six points in his first game.
             subject   verb

Illogical constructions also commonly occur when a linking verb joins a subject to a predicate that does not make sense. For example:
The first sentence is illogical because the subject *game* cannot *be* six points. To avoid this error, remember that a linking verb works like an equal sign between the subject and the word following the verb. In the second sentence, the subject *total* is equal to *points*. In the third sentence, the rookie is now the subject who does something: scores six points. Now the sentence makes sense because a person can score points while a game cannot.

Exercise 10.2

Rewrite the following sentences so that they are logical. If a sentence is logical, put an L next to it.

1. In rescuing the child from the fire was brave.
2. Through a flaming hoop was the dog's first trick.
3. Before leaving on vacation, Alice cleaned house.
4. After lifting weights will make you feel strong.
5. The doctor's opinion was indigestion.
6. The price of the car was too high was my opinion.
7. The Beatles first number-one record was "I Want to Hold Your Hand."
8. The band's performance was rock music.
9. A nurse is a difficult job.

Choosing the Verb

Because the verb expresses what the subject is or does, it is extremely important. The verb should tell, as vividly and directly as possible, about the subject. Often a verb can be grammatically correct but still not be the best choice. Choosing the best verbs adds muscle to your sentences, making them more clear and direct.

Using Strong Verbs. Some verbs do not express any action at all; other verbs express very little action. Thus, they tend to add little to your writing. Some of these verbs are forms of *to be, to have,* and *to make.* Sometimes an action verb can replace one of these verbs, making the sentence more vivid and direct, though the forms of *to be, to have,* or *to make* would not be incorrect. You can not eliminate all forms of *to be, to have,* and *to make.* They are integral to the language, and without them we could not communicate many ideas. However, when you use these verbs too often, your writing begins to lack punch. Substitute an action verb whenever you can. Compare these pairs of sentences:

The second sentence of each pair uses an action verb that was a noun in the first sentence. Often when you have a weak verb, a *potential action verb* will be hiding somewhere in the sentence in the form of a noun. Nouns can sometimes be changed to action verbs by eliminating a suffix from the word. *Suffixes* are letters added to the end of a word to change its function as a part of speech. Eliminating suffixes also changes the word's function. Cutting the following suffixes from nouns enables you to form verbs (though sometimes you may have to change a letter or two to complete the change):

Suffix: -tion

noun	*verb*
aggravation	aggravate

Roller coasters were always a fascination for my brother.

subject   verb (past form of to be)

Roller coasters always fascinated my brother.

subject   verb (action)

Kevin has a collection of stamps.

subject   verb (form of to have)

Kevin collects stamps.

subject   verb

Heavy snow and subzero temperatures are regular occurrences in

compound subject   verb (form of to be)

northern Minnesota.

Heavy snow and subzero temperatures occur regularly in

compound subject   verb (action)

northern Minnesota.

The President made an announcement that he would veto any bill

subject   verb

raising taxes.

The President announced that he would veto any bill raising taxes.

subject   verb

creation	create
graduation	graduate
illustration	illustrate
registration	register
satisfaction	satisfy

Suffixes: -ance or -ence

noun	*verb*
attendance	attend
allowance	allow
defiance	defy
disappearance	disappear
performance	perform
reliance	rely

Suffix: -ment

noun	*verb*
argument	argue
arrangement	arrange
disarmament	disarm
placement	place
statement	state

Suffix: -er or -or

noun	*verb*
actor	act
director	direct
driver	drive
listener	listen
painter	paint
singer	sing

Exercise 10.3

Rewrite each sentence so that the italicized word becomes the verb. In some cases, you will have to change other words or add or subtract words to the sentence.

1. Your essay was a *demonstration* of competence.
2. Eric's grades are an *indication* of his effort and intelligence.
3. Cutting class is an *avoidance* of responsibility.
4. The mayor made a *suggestion* that the city hire more fire fighters.
5. The design of the building was a *combination* of modern and traditional architecture.
6. This week's assignment was just a *continuance* of last week's work.
7. Eisenhower was the *leader* of the Allied Forces in World War II.
8. Rick's choice of career was a *disappointment* to his parents.
9. The workers had *resentment* about Stanfield's promotion.
10. Farley and Stoner were the big *losers* in last night's poker game.

Exercise 10.4

Replace weak verbs with stronger verbs in at least three sentences of an essay you have written for this class.

Active-Voice vs. Passive-Voice Verbs.   A verb is in the active voice when the subject performs the action of the verb. A verb is in the passive voice when the subject receives the action of the verb. These sentences illustrate a verb in the active and passive voices:

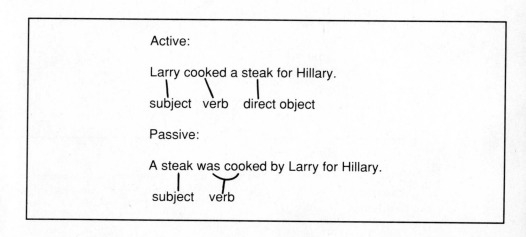

In the first sentence, Larry, as the subject, performs the action, and the verb is in the active voice. In the second sentence, the steak dinner is the subject, but it is not doing anything. Rather, something is being done to it—it is being cooked. Thus, it receives rather than performs the action. You can remember the distinction if you apply it to people rather than verbs. Someone who lives an active life is someone who is always doing something. A passive person, in contrast, sits back and lets things be done to him or her. In most cases, choose active-voice verbs. They express action and emphasize the subject in fewer words, making your sentences more direct.

Exercise 10.5

Rewrite these sentences with passive-voice verbs to make them active. If a verb is in the active voice, place an A next to the sentence. A sentence may have more than one verb that needs to be changed.

1. The bank was robbed yesterday by three men wearing ski masks.
2. Cancer is feared by most people.
3. The paper was typed by Mona in less than an hour.
4. The game was won with a last-second touchdown pass.
5. Happy about his test grades, Leon celebrated with his friends.
6. The early settlers were often attacked by Indians, and the Indians were often attacked by the early settlers.
7. Because his car was parked in a driveway, Jim was given a ticket by the police.
8. The Louisiana Territory was purchased for the United States by the Jefferson administration.
9. The son of a poor coal miner, D. H. Lawrence became a famous writer in the first decades of the twentieth century.
10. *Madame Bovary*, a controversial novel in its time, was written by Gustave Flaubert, one of France's greatest writers.

Exercise 10.6

Find three sentences with passive-voice verbs in an essay you have written, and rewrite them so that the verbs are in the active voice.

Eliminating Wordiness

In substituting strong action verbs for weaker verbs and in changing verbs from active to passive voice, you usually eliminate some words from the sentence. Whenever you can write a sentence in fewer words, do so. Wordiness occurs in sentences when the writer includes words unnecessary to the meaning. Of course, all sentences need not be short. A long sentence will not be wordy if every word is pulling its weight. As you draft an essay, you may have trouble avoiding wordiness. When you revise, you should try to eliminate as many wordy constructions as you can. Eliminating wordiness takes practice, but a few strategies can help you get started.

Cut Redundancy

Redundancy occurs when a phrase contains words that needlessly repeat the meaning of other words. Redundancy clutters sentences and wastes the reader's time. The italicized words illustrate redundancy:

> Her blouse was blue *in color.*
> The room was large *in size.*
> Steve was *physically* sick with the flu.
> Many students majored in *the field of* business in the 1980s.
> Louie was wearing the same *identical* jacket as Joe.
> Paulette's grandparents moved to *the state of* Florida.
> Tim put his hat on *his head* and left the room.
> Juan enjoys working *his job* as a mail carrier.
> Workers *who are employed* at Starlight Electric earn high wages.

As you can see, without the italicized words, the sentences would say the same thing in fewer words.

Exercise 10.7

Cross out any redundant words or phrases.

1. Jeanette painted her room a pale shade of blue.
2. The problems of the homeless who live on the streets drew public attention in the 1980s.

3. The field of psychology offers many interesting subjects of study.
4. In today's modern world that we live in, a college education has nearly become a necessity in any profession or professional endeavor.
5. The army destroyed and defeated its enemy quickly and efficiently.
6. The sport of gymnastics requires tremendous agility.
7. At the young age of seven, I was afraid to be alone by myself in the dark.
8. The mother was tired of the child's silly and foolish tricks.
9. Felipe moved to the city of Los Angeles in the month of September to go to school at UCLA.
10. The ship left the port of San Francisco at 5 A.M. in the morning.

Cut Flabby Phrases

Flabby phrases contain more words than needed to express the meaning; they usually can be replaced by a much shorter phrase or a single word. Unlike redundancies, they do not repeat meaning, but they still clutter up sentences and require more of the reader.

Flabby Phrase	*Substitute*
at this point in time	now
at that point in time	then
by means of	by
due to the fact that	because
for the reason that	because
for the purpose of	to
in the final analysis	finally
in the event that	if
in order to	to
am of the opinion	believe
until such time as	until

In examining this list, you might think that the phrases are obviously wordy and that you would not write them, but in the heat of drafting a paper, writers can easily lapse into using such phrases. If you are careful, you can usually catch them as you draft and revise.

Exercise 10.8

Change any flabby phrases to single words.

1. At this point in time, President Bush is of the opinion that taxes need not be raised.
2. Until such time as you pay your bill, your credit privileges are suspended.
3. In the event that it rains, the party will move indoors.
4. The guests moved indoors in order to avoid the rain.
5. In the final analysis, we decided against buying a Yugo due to the fact that it was too small for our family.
6. You can reach Chicago from New York by means of Interstate 80.
7. You need only a pair of pliers in order to change your car's air filter.
8. Harry went to a tailor for the purpose of buying a custom-fitted suit.
9. The trooper pulled the car over for the reason that its tail lights were not working.
10. Vince was of the opinion that he would not declare a major until such time as he was sure what he wanted to study.

Eliminating Expletive Constructions

Expletive constructions are *there are, there is, here is, here are, it is,* or any past or future forms of these: *there were, here was, it will be,* and so on. Expletive constructions commonly begin sentences, and you can not eliminate all of them in your writing—nor should you try. However, sometimes expletives add needless words to sentences. Usually wordiness occurs when an expletive is used with a noun followed by a relative clause:

> *There was* only one student *who* could not attend class yesterday.
> *There are* some politicians *who* think more of their own interests than of those of their constituents.
> *It is* a fool *who* believes in luck.

In these sentences, the expletives add nothing and should be cut. When you cut the expletives, you must also cut the relative pronouns (*who, which, that,* etc.):

> Only one student could not attend class yesterday.

Some politicians think more of their own interests than of those their constituents.

Only a fool believes in luck.

Expletives also can occur without a relative clause. Compare these sentences:

Wordy: It is fun to water-ski.
Direct: Waterskiing is fun.
Wordy: It was early in the morning when the fire started.
Direct: The fire started early in the morning.

You may think that eliminating expletives does not change a sentence much. After all, only three words are usually cut from each sentence. In a nine-word sentence, however, those three words amount to one-third of the length of the sentence. Even with longer sentences, any time you can cut three words, you are reducing wordiness significantly. Consider that a 500-word essay probably contains about thirty sentences. Three words from each would add up quickly. Of course, beginning writers often hate to cut anything because they have worked so hard to get the words on paper. However, you are always better off writing a shorter essay than a long one with a lot of needless words.

Exercise 10.9

Eliminate any expletive constructions. You may have to rearrange words or add a word to make a new sentence.

1. It was nearly midnight when we arrived home.
2. There are many days when Roy wants to sleep in.
3. There is a student in our class who is a former Marine.
4. There are a lot of times when words can be cut from sentences without losing any meaning.
5. It is thrilling to ride a motorcycle at high speeds, but it is also very dangerous.
6. There are some people who love opera; there are others who hate it.
7. It was Elliot who left the meeting early.
8. It wasn't I who ate the whole pie.
9. There is nothing that can prevent you from improving your writing if you work hard.
10. It was last Saturday when we went to the play.

Exercise 10.10

Examine a piece of your own writing. If you find any expletive constructions, rewrite the sentences to eliminate them.

Reducing Clauses to Phrases

As you may remember, clauses are any group of words that contains at least one subject and one verb. Dependent clauses contain at least one subject and one verb preceded by a subordinating conjunction: *although, because, until, when,* etc. (see Chapter 9 for a complete list). Relative clauses, another form of dependent clause, contain either a relative pronoun and a verb or a relative pronoun and a subject and verb. Dependent and relative clauses are important components of sentence structure, and you should not try to cut them all. But at times, you can reduce a clause to a phrase to eliminate words from your sentences. Compare these sentences:

Because Dick was feeling sleepy, he went to bed early.

        dependent clause

Feeling sleepy, Dick went to bed early.

participle phrase

After Lance lost his dog, he vowed never to own another one.

        dependent clause

After losing his dog, Lance vowed never to own another one.

participle phrase

Westerhaus ✓

Finchams ✓

Dietz

Loomis

Johnson
Hanssen

Grams ✓

Del

— When _____ person,
it's also (who), not
that

NO slang

— Keep the tense in every sentence
the same (past/past, present/present

pronouns

- When talking about a person, it's who/whom, not that

- no slang
- keep the tense in every sentence the same (past/past, present/presen

- pronouns
- editing symbols: A, $\underline{a}$, ^, ~~apple~~ e,
  fragment. ¶,
- plagiarism
- keep true to assignment.

- you/you, we/we,
- subject-verb agreement
     is/are

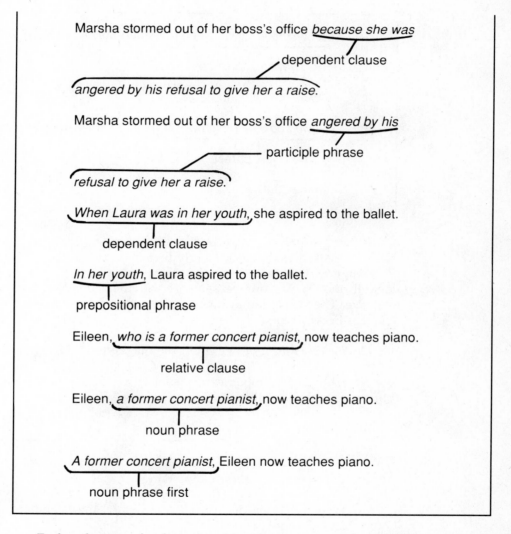

Marsha stormed out of her boss's office *because she was*

dependent clause

angered by his refusal to give her a raise.

Marsha stormed out of her boss's office *angered by his*

participle phrase

refusal to give her a raise.

When Laura was in her youth, she aspired to the ballet.

dependent clause

In her youth, Laura aspired to the ballet.

prepositional phrase

Eileen, *who is a former concert pianist,* now teaches piano.

relative clause

Eileen, *a former concert pianist,* now teaches piano.

noun phrase

A former concert pianist, Eileen now teaches piano.

noun phrase first

Each reduction of a clause to a phrase cuts two words: the subject and verb of the clause. The phrase then modifies the subject of another clause. For example, the phrase *angered by his refusal to give her a raise* tells us how Marsha felt as she stormed out of the office. When you reduce a clause to a phrase, you need to be sure that the phrase can modify the subject that is left in the next clause. Compare these sentences, for example:

As we drove down the highway, the Statue of Liberty was

dependent clause

visible on the right.

Driving down the highway, the Statue of Liberty was visible

participle phrase

on the right.

Although shorter, the second sentence now causes a problem. The phrase cannot modify the Statue of Liberty because it cannot be driving (unless it's a very large car). Phrases must have something in the sentence that they can logically modify. The original sentence with the dependent clause, then, is more effective. The clause could, however, be reduced to a phrase if we made some changes in the second clause:.

Driving down the road, we could see the Statue of Liberty on our right.

Now the phrase modifies the subject *we*. Because people can drive, the phrase now has something it can modify logically.

Exercise 10.11

Reduce the clauses in italics to modifying phrases.

1. *When the Bartons travelled through Europe,* they photographed many famous sights.
2. Ingrid Grueter, *who was formerly a cook in Germany,* opened a restaurant in Ft. Worth, Texas.
3. *Because she is a skilled writer,* Selina decided she would major in journalism.
4. *Though the boys were too young to attend an R-rated movie,* they tried to get in to see one.
5. Bill Reade, *who was my best friend in college,* now manages a large supermarket.

6. *After Richard won $10,000 in the lottery,* he heard from friends he had not seen in years.
7. Nolan Ryan reached a milestone in 1989, *when he struck out his 5,000th batter.*
8. Anthony, *who is the best writer in our class,* entered an essay contest sponsored by the Optimists Club.
9. Lucy called the restaurant for reservations *before she went to dinner.*
10. Making lasagna, *which is my favorite dish,* is not very difficult, but it takes time.

Combining Sentences

When you write sentences, you should strive to achieve a mature style. This does not mean you should write long sentences with a lot of big words, but it *does* mean that you should avoid writing a lot of short sentences, which creates choppiness. For beginners, sentence combining often can improve style and clarify your point.

Combining Short Sentences for a More Mature Style

If you remember the first books you read as a child, you know that they contained very short sentences:

See Dick run. See Jane run. See Spot run. Dick and Jane run with Spot.

Written for first-graders, these sentences fit the audience, but to an adult they seem ridiculous. As a beginning writer in college, you would never write such sentences. Because you are older, you naturally have developed a more sophisticated control of sentences. In fact, in speaking, you probably use much more complex sentence structure than you realize. For instance, if you had to express the action of the short sentences above, you would probably say something like, "Dick and Jane are running with their dog, Spot." In writing, however, beginners sometimes need to combine sentences so that their written style is as mature as the way they speak. Consider the following examples:

Our plumber did a good job of fixing our sink. His name was Mr. Sawicki. He charged us only twenty dollars.
Melissa is a good friend of mine. She is majoring in agriculture. She wants to prepare for veterinary school after she graduates.

In each set, the sentences are too short, creating a choppy effect that would distract most adult readers. The sentences could easily be combined:

Our plumber, Mr. Sawicki, did a good job of fixing our sink and charged us only twenty dollars.

Melissa, a good friend of mine, is majoring in agriculture to prepare for veterinary school after she graduates.

In each of these examples, three sentences were combined to make one. Learning how to combine sentences can improve your style, making your writing more mature.

Exercise 10.12

Combine each group of sentences into one sentence. Do not be afraid to change the order of the information. Just concentrate on writing the best sentence you can from the short sentences.

Example:
Benjamin Franklin was a teenager.
He worked in a printing office.
The printing office belonged to his brother.
The printing office was in Boston.

Combined:
As a teenager, Benjamin Franklin worked in his brother's printing office in Boston.

1. Benjamin Franklin read.
   He read a great deal.
   He worked in a printing office.
2. It was in August.
   It was in 1721.
   Franklin was fifteen years old.
   Franklin founded a newspaper.
   He founded it with his brother.
3. The newspaper was called the *New Courant*.
   The newspaper came out weekly.
   It satirized political leaders.
   It satirized religious leaders.

4. Franklin wrote for the newspaper.
   He wrote satires.
   The satires angered leaders.
   These leaders were religious.
5. It was 1723.
   Franklin was seventeen.
   He moved to Philadelphia.
   He started his own business.
   It was a printing business.
6. Franklin was curious.
   He was curious about everything.
   He encountered everything in his daily life.
7. He investigated electricity.
   His investigation brought him fame.
   He was famous around the world.
   He was not satisfied with fame.
   He wanted to apply knowledge of electricity.
   He wanted to apply it to everyday life.
8. Franklin was also an inventor.
   He invented the lightning rod.
   He did this in 1756.
   He later invented a stove.
   It was called the Franklin stove.
   Franklin stoves are still used today.
9. Franklin attended the first Continental Congress.
   The Congress wrote the Declaration of Independence.
   Franklin helped.
10. It was late in Franklin's life.
    He was known around the world.
    He was known as a thinker.
    He was known as a patriot.
    He was known as an inventor.

In working on this exercise, you may have thought that you do not write such short sentences. And you are right. As an adult, your sentences are rarely so short. But combining such sentences can help you realize how longer sentences are made from a lot of short ones. Also, you may have realized that each group of short sentences could be combined in more than one way, which is a valuable lesson. Compare the different ways the sentences in the exercise can be combined:

Benjamin Franklin was a teenager.
He worked in a printing office.

The printing office belonged to his brother.

The printing office was in Boston.

When he was a teenager, Benjamin Franklin worked in his brother's printing office in Boston.

Benjamin Franklin, when he was a teenager, worked in Boston in his brother's printing office.

As a Boston teenager, Benjamin Franklin worked in his brother's printing office.

Benjamin Franklin, as a teenager, worked in his brother's Boston printing office.

Benjamin Franklin worked in his brother's printing office when he was a teenager in Boston.

As you can see, there are many ways to write this sentence, and you can probably think of others. The more versions of a sentence you can see, the easier it is to shape a sentence as smoothly and clearly as possible. Notice here that some parts of the sentence can be moved around. When you write and revise sentences, try to be aware of the parts you can move and the parts you cannot.

Exercise 10.13

Rewrite three sentences from the previous exercise as many ways as you can. Some sentences will allow for more versions than others.

Combining Longer Sentences to Show Meaning Relationships

Combining shorter sentences, as you did in the exercise, can help you to see how sentences work and to avoid a childish style. While the sentences in your draft are usually longer than those in the exercises, often they can be combined to make your meaning clearer. Examine the following pairs of sentences:

Sports cars can make driving more fun than just getting from one place to another.

Insurance for sports cars costs much more than for conventional cars.

The railroad gates were not working. Leigh drove through the crossing and was nearly hit by a train.

In each set of sentences, the pairs are related. In the first set, the second sentence contrasts with the first, providing an advantage and then a disadvantage of owning a sports car. But because the sentences are separate, the reader must draw the contrast. In the second set, there is a causal relationship, but again the reader must figure out the connection between the sentences. Compare the combined versions to the original pairs:

Sports cars can make driving more fun than just getting from one place to another, but insurance for sports cars costs much more than for conventional cars.

Because the railroad gates were not working, Leigh drove through the crossing and was nearly hit by a train.

The combined versions do not add new information, but when combined, the sentences show the connections between the first piece of information and the second. In the first set, the word *but* lets the reader know that the second part of the sentence will contrast with the first part. In the second set, adding *because* to the first sentence makes it depend on the second to complete the meaning. What happened *because* the railroad gate was not working? Leigh drove through the crossing and was nearly hit by a train. Combining sentences makes connections for the reader. In addition, the combined versions eliminate the choppy and immature style of the first sets.

In Chapter 9, you learned about coordinating conjunctions and conjunctive adverbs, which can connect sentences. We will review these connectors:

Coordinating Conjunctions (used after a comma)	Conjunctive Adverbs (used after a semicolon)
but	accordingly
and	also
for	consequently
nor	furthermore
or	moreover
so	nevertheless
yet	then
	therefore
	thus
	still

Whether you choose a connector that takes a comma or one that takes a semicolon depends on the writing situation. The connectors used with semicolons tend to be more formal, so if the writing situation is formal, use one of them. In less formal situations, prefer connectors that can be used with the comma. Or if you have already written a lot of one type of sentence, use the other type of connector to create variety.

Combining to Show Contrast. The following connectors contrast—show a difference between—information in one sentence and in another that follows. For example:

Ulysses S. Grant distinguished himself as a great leader in the Civil War, *but* he was not a very good President.

As you can see in this example, the first part of the sentence shows us something Grant did well, while the second part shows something he did poorly. Thus, there is a contrast between Grant's military career and his political career. Any of the connectors above could show this contrast:

Ulysses S. Grant distinguished himself as a great leader in the Civil War, *yet* he was not a very good President.
Ulysses S. Grant distinguished himself as a great leader in the Civil War; *however*, he was not a very good President.
Ulysses S. Grant distinguished himself as a great leader in the Civil War; *nevertheless*, he was not a very good President.
Ulysses S. Grant distinguished himself as a great leader in the Civil War; *still*, he was not a very good President.
(Remember that sentences combined with *however*, *nevertheless*, and *still* are punctuated with a semicolon.)

Sometimes one connector may work better than another. You could write, for example:

The children wanted to go on a picnic, but it was raining.

The same sentences connected with *nevertheless* would not sound quite right:

The children wanted to go on a picnic; nevertheless, it was raining.

When you use connectors to show contrast, make sure the contrast is clear.

Exercise 10.14

The following pairs of contradictory sentences were taken from students' writing. Combine each pair of sentences twice to show contrast, using a different connector in each. Compare the sentences you make in the combinations. Are some connectors better than others in certain sentences?

Example:

Pasta is a very nutritious food. The oils used in pasta salads often contain harmful fats and cholesterol.

Pasta is a very nutritious food, but the oils used in pasta salads often contain harmful fats and cholesterol.

Pasta is a very nutritious food; however, the oils used in pasta salads often contain harmful fats and cholesterol.

1. As a child, I wanted to become an astronaut. When I was in high school, I learned that most astronauts have backgrounds in math and science, my worst subjects.
2. Listening to opera, I thought it was boring. I attended an opera and found it quite entertaining.
3. "The Cosby Show" has been popular for years. It is not an accurate picture of most blacks because few are as well off as the Huxtable family.
4. I don't think I'll ever like writing. I like writing in this journal because I can say what's on my mind.
5. Mr. Edwards taught social studies. In college, he had majored in English literature.
6. My parents were not rich. They always bought me nice clothes if the other kids had them.
7. I never could afford to travel. I toured Italy when I won a trip in a raffle.
8. I think the essay explained a thesis sentence. I had trouble reading it, so I don't understand.

Exercise 10.15

Combine the sentences in the previous exercise by placing one of the following subordinating conjunctions at the beginning of the first sentence: *although, even though, granted that*. Then join the next sentence to the first with a comma.

Example:
> Pasta is a very healthy food. The oils used in pasta salads often contain unhealthful fats and cholesterol.
>
> Although pasta is a very healthful food, the oils used in pasta salads often contain unhealthful fats and cholesterol.

Exercise 10.16

Revise the following paragraph by combining sentences to show contrast where needed. Try to use both methods previously discussed.

> Most of the American colonists supported the revolution. Some remained loyal to England. The loyalists, as they were called, helped the British troops by spying on the revolutionaries. They had to be very careful because most of their neighbors were supporters of the revolution. When the war ended, the loyalists fled the United States and settled in England. They were not enthusiastically accepted by the English people.

Exercise 10.17

Revise a paragraph or section of a paper you have written for this or any other course by combining sentences to show contrast where needed.

Combining to Show Causes and Effects. Just as combining can show contrast between sentences, it can help you show a cause-effect relationship. In the following sentences, what happens in the first *causes* the effect expressed in the second:

> The neighborhood had shabby housing, no recreational facilities for children, and a high crime rate. We hoped to move as soon as we could afford to.

Most readers can guess that the conditions described in the first sentence cause the desire to move expressed in the second sentence. But the reader has to do the work that the writer should be doing. Thus, the sentences should be combined to show the cause-effect relationship that they imply. One way to combine them is by using the following punctuation and connecting words

, so
; consequently
; therefore
; thus

The neighborhood had shabby housing, no recreational facilities for children, and a high crime rate, *so* we hoped to move as soon as we could afford to.

The neighborhood had shabby housing, no recreational facilities for children, and a high crime rate; *consequently*, we hoped to move as soon as we could afford to.

The neighborhood had shabby housing, no recreational facilities for children, and a high crime rate; *therefore*, we hoped to move as soon as we could afford to.

No matter which connector you choose to combine these sentences, the combination draws a cause-effect relationship, saving the reader the trouble of making the connection.

Exercise 10.18

In each pair of sentences, the first sentence states a cause and the second states an effect. Combine each pair to show a cause-effect relationship.

1. My financial-aid check arrived late. I couldn't buy my books immediately and fell behind in my classes.
2. I worked part-time at McDonald's. I did not earn much money.
3. The recruiters said that my education, not basketball, was most important. My mother thought they cared about me.
4. A lot of people think teenagers from the ghetto just want to fight and steal. These people won't give ghetto kids a job.
5. Toxic-waste dumps are not welcome in many communities. They are often located in areas where the population is sparse.
6. My sister dropped out of high school and had a child. She has had trouble finding a good job and bettering herself.
7. The Vietnam War was fought in a dense jungle. Many of the U.S. Army's major weapons, such as tanks and field artillery, were nearly useless.

8. In the late nineteenth century, workers earned low wages and had no rights or benefits. Labor unions were formed to combat injustices in the workplace.

You can also show cause-effect relationships by adding *because* or *since* to the beginning of the first sentence and then replacing the period between the sentences with a comma. For instance:

Because the neighborhood had shabby housing, no recreational facilities for children, and a high crime rate, we hoped to move as soon as we could afford to.

In this revision, the first clause now becomes dependent on the second; that is, the second clause describes the effect of the cause expressed in the first clause. You also could reverse the order of the clauses and still maintain the causal relationship:

We hoped to move as soon as we could afford to *because* the neighborhood had shabby housing, no recreational facilities for children, and a high crime rate.

Which clause you put first is up to you. Either way, both parts of the sentence are tightly linked, enabling the reader to see the cause-effect relationship.

Exercise 10.19

Rewrite the first five sentences in exercise 10.18, this time adding *because* to the first clause and changing the period between the sentences to a comma. Rewrite the last five, placing the dependent clause (the one with *because*) second.

Combining to Coordinate Information. When we combine sentences to join similar information, we are coordinating—putting together similar pieces of information. For example, each of the sentences states an advantage of owning a Honda Civic:

The Honda Civic costs little to operate.
It maintains its value upon resale.

These are not bad sentences by themselves, but they are closely related and could be joined to stress the relationship between them. There are two ways to link them:

1. Join them with a comma and *and*.
2. Join them with a semicolon and either *furthermore, moreover,* or *in addition*.

Coordinating related sentences can help you to connect ideas so that your reader can see the relationship between them. Also, coordination helps avoid a choppy style and adds sentence variety to your writing.

Exercise 10.20

Combine these sentences to coordinate related information.

1. Washington's troops were short of food and supplies. They soon would face a winter of hardship.
2. I have been writing a great deal in my journal. I feel it improves my writing of essays.
3. In a pure capitalist system, the citizens control the wealth. The government collects taxes only to finance basic programs.
4. Trying to domesticate a wild animal can be dangerous. It is not fair to the animal.
5. Banks earn money investing depositors' money. Depositors earn interest in return.
6. You have to get up early on a farm. You have to be willing to work hard for long hours.
7. Learning a trade such as plumbing does not take as long as earning a four-year degree. Plumbers make as much money as, or more than, many college graduates.
8. Wrigley Field is one of the oldest stadiums in baseball. Like most stadiums of the past, it is located in a residential neighborhood.

Rewriting Awkward Sentences

Sometimes sentences just do not sound right, though you cannot tell exactly what's wrong with them. Sentences that don't need to be combined may still need to be rewritten because they do not make your point clearly or they sound awkward. Let's examine some sentences from a paper that a student wrote for a class in educational counseling. The student was assigned to discuss some aspect of peer pressure that high school counselors needed to know about. The thesis argued that peer pressure can cause teenagers to have sex before they want to or are ready for it. The three sentences below are different versions of the beginning of a paragraph on how peer pressure among males occurs in the locker room:

> There are many specific areas where peer pressure to have sex are noticed, the locker room being one of these.
> In the locker room, guys always pressure each other to have sex.
> In the locker room, young men always pressure each other to talk about their sexual experiences with their girlfriends.

Looking over the first sentence, the student decided that it had many problems. In the thesis and at other points in the essay, he had said that peer pressure occurs in many areas, so he did not need to say so again. He also discovered that he had used a passive-voice verb and that there were no people in the sentence. Also, the place being discussed, the locker room, was tacked on at the end of the sentence. His second sentence makes some improvements: He now identifies the locker room in the opening phrase and makes the guys in it the subject. But the student sees that this sentence also needs revision—first, because it sounds as if he is saying the guys are trying to have sex with each other, and second, because he finds the word *guys* rather casual in view of his audience. The third sentence, as you can see, solves both problems. It is clear and appropriate to his purpose and audience.

As you draft an essay, sometimes you can spot a problem sentence and revise it before you go on, but after writing the draft, you should read your essay aloud. Are there any sentences that could be smoother? Clearer? Can you change the order of any parts of the sentences? Cut words? You need to ask these questions whenever you find a sentence that does not sound quite right. Trust your ear.

Exercise 10.21

Read over the papers you have written for this class. Find five sentences that sound unclear or awkward and revise them.

Writing Assignments

1. Write an essay of approximately 500 words in which you analyze the behavior and values of a particular social or ethnic group. Be sure to limit your topic sufficiently. "Americans," for example, would be too broad a topic. "Older students returning to college," in contrast, would work. Assume that a sociology class is your audience.

2. Some social critics argue that men, as well as women, have benefited from the women's rights movement of the last twenty years. Write an essay in which you argue that this claim is true or not true. Assume an audience of males.

Key Terms

Active voice: A sentence is in active voice when the subject performs the action expressed in the verb.

Passive voice: A sentence is in passive voice when the subject receives the action expressed in the verb.

Illogical constructions: A combination of subject and verb in which the subject is incapable of doing what the verb expresses.

Suffix: Letters added to the end of a word to change its function in a sentence.

Wordiness: The inclusion of unnecessary words in a sentence.

Redundancy: The use of words or phrases that unnecessarily repeat the meaning of a previous word or phrase.

Flabby phrases: Phrases that contain unnecessary words and that can be replaced by a shorter phrase or a single word.

Expletive constructions: Constructions such as *it is* and *there are*, used to begin sentences.

Sentence combining: A technique combining short sentences into longer ones or combining longer sentences to show contrasting, cause-effect, or coordinate relationships.

Choppiness: The use of too many short sentences in a row.

unit three

Essays for Reading

As in the previous units, the following four essays were written by students. Camille Costa argues the positive and negative effects of television on young viewers. David Vaughn uses humor to discuss a serious point in a narrative about a teacher's behavior. Carol Somerville also uses narrative to recount an experience while growing up. In an argument mixing humor and seriousness, Michael S. Godwin warns against the dangers of relying on interpretations of nonverbal cues in courtship. As you read each essay, note how each writer chooses examples and details to fit his or her purpose. Also, note the variety of sentence structures and their appropriateness in these essays.

Television: A Product of Its People
Camille Costa (freshman)

As a group, Americans do not like to be told what to do or what to think. Individually an American has the freedom to become a millionaire or one of the homeless. American television is a product of American people, and, like those people, television has both positive and negative aspects. I agree with Neil Postman when he says that the media, particularly television, is "pervasive and powerful" and yet the enemy of foundations and traditions. But though Postman's claim is generally true, much of the effect of television depends on how much people watch it and how they react to it.

True, much television undermines traditional values. Marital affairs, deceit, dishonesty, violence, and sexual promiscuity are the norms in a lot of programs. Soap operas, for example, could easily distort a child's viewpoint. Children are impressionable and easily persuaded. Most parents spend many years instilling morals in their children, teaching them not to lie, cheat, steal, or be violent. Soap opera characters lie, cheat, steal, murder, and then get by with no punishment, leading the child-viewer to believe that one can benefit from these negative actions. Seeing evil prevail over good could quickly distort a child's value system.

Last summer, I babysat for a seven-year-old boy named Doug. He was addicted to daytime television, and I think television may have affected his view of the world. His parents, both middle-class American teachers, adhered to traditional values. Doug did not. He frequently lied, cheated at games, and often would take things that did not belong to him. Unlike other children his age, Doug seldom went outdoors but instead preferred to stay inside and watch soap operas. In my opinion, Doug's personality and perception of the world were altered by the conniving people he saw on television. Doug's parents tried to combat this problem, but with little effort or success. He may have been a healthier, happier, more sociable child had he been required to read books once in a while instead of being allowed to watch so much television.

American television does not affect just viewers in the United States but has an international impact. Last year, my high school foreign-language teacher, Mrs. Witmer, told my class of the problems with taking tour groups of students through Spain. Young Spanish males who had been influenced by American television attempted to be inappropriately intimate with the girls on the tour. These young men assumed the female students to be as promiscuous as the women on television. The young males would not only make sexually suggestive remarks but would actually follow and touch the unsuspecting girls. The tour guide apologized to my teacher and then explained that these men see American women on television as typical of all American women and girls.

Another example of how the American medium undermines traditions even in foreign countries came from my friend Anya, an exchange student from Sweden who attended my high school last year. She told me that her mother, like many people in her country, was an avid fan of the soap opera "Dallas." Anya's mother, who previously dressed in traditional Swedish attire of layers of clothing, decided to have some dresses made that looked like the ones worn by Miss Ellie. Also, according to Anya, her mother was worried about her being a foreign exchange student because she thought that most Americans were like the ones on "Dallas." Each time Anya called home, her mother would repeatedly quiz her about the boys at our high school. The mother expected to hear how Americans were deceiving and manipulating her daughter. It came as a great surprise when Anya informed her mother that everyone in my hometown had been compassionate and generous.

Of course, nothing is all bad, and television has its good points. Along with the violence, sex, drugs, and lies, television programs often communicate a positive message. "Sesame Street," for instance, can benefit young children. It teaches good morals and shows people being rewarded for doing good deeds. Seeing this, children learn that good behavior is rewarded. Television also helps with the airing of antidrug and anticrime commercials. The advertisements do not promote drug abuse and crime but instead make them look harmful and unappealing. This message should reach people in all age groups, and what better way to convey it than through television, the medium that seems to reach everyone.

Television also provides some educational programs, such as "Wild Kingdom," "Nova," and "National Geographic Specials." These programs allow the viewers to see new lands, explore faraway countries, learn about other cultures, and discover interesting animals that they never knew existed. Most Americans never get the chance to travel to New Guinea or Antarctica. Through these programs, people can learn new things about foreign places that they might otherwise never see. One could argue that the viewer could learn about these places by reading a book or looking at a photograph, but reading can not always compare to the splendor of a moving image on a TV screen. Of course, the question is, how many children and adults watch the beneficial programs rather than the junk?

In many ways, I agree with Neil Postman. Yes, television often undermines families' efforts to instill traditional American values of honesty, fidelity, and loyalty. Many programs depict criminals and unethical businessmen as glamorous heroes. The long-term effect of such negative role modeling may be extremely harmful on children. Yet television also has another side that Postman fails to consider. The educational bonus offered to many has no parallel in modern history. The capacity of television to educate the masses is amazing. Television, like so many man-made devices, is neither good nor evil: The question remains as to how humankind uses this ''pervasive and powerful'' medium.

Questions for Study and Discussion

1. What is Costa's thesis? To what extent do you agree or disagree with her?

2. Does your experience of viewing television coincide with Costa's claims?

3. Do you think Costa portrays television fairly?

4. Cite examples that you find convincing in Costa's paper. Which examples do you find most convincing? Least convincing?

5. How does Costa's introduction lead to her thesis? Have you seen this strategy, or a similar strategy, in Chapter 8?

6. Point out the topic sentences in Costa's body paragraphs. Where does she usually place them? Are they effective?

7. How is the topic sentence in the third paragraph placed differently than the others? Why?

8. How does Costa's conclusion echo her introduction? Do you find this strategy effective for this paper?

9. Costa's essay is an argument, but what other strategy for organization is evident? How does her feeling about the topic determine the organization?

10. Is Costa finally pro- or antitelevision, or does her argument rest on another issue besides television itself?

11. In a brief freewriting, describe a television show that you believe undermines traditional values.

12. In a brief freewriting, describe a television show that you believe has a positive effect on viewers.

Gulag Fourteen
David Vaughn (freshman)

One of the most interesting events of my life was my escape from Gulag Fourteen. Last semester, I had the unusual privilege of studying the Russian language under a professor I'll refer to as Doctor Demento, or Dr. D, as she was affectionately known to her students. At the beginning of the semester, I assumed Dr. D. was trying to be informal so that she could establish a good relationship with the class, but that idea quickly faded. I gradually went from thinking she wasn't playing with a full deck to realizing that the only card she had left was a joker.

One of my earliest clues that something was wrong came the first day of class. Dr. D. was calling roll when halfway down the list she stopped and said to one student, "Your first name is just like the song." She then proceeded to sing, in its entirety, a song no one else in the class had ever heard.

As the semester progressed, her eccentricity became more apparent. For example, she explained to the class that the Swiss syndicate had attempted to assassinate her three times. The explanation took a little over half of a class period when we were scheduled to review Russian verbs. Daily she would choose some irrelevant topic to expound on. If we were lucky, we would get ten minutes of class time a day. Once she spent twenty-five minutes telling the class that the Swiss Army's uniform has the color red on it.

In no time, a class that had started at more than thirty students had been reduced to a dozen. The classroom, room fourteen, was quickly nicknamed Gulag Fourteen. Soon the students started complaining to Dr. D about her teaching methods. For almost a week after a mass complaint, our Russian class ran almost like a normal class. Unfortunately the normality soon ended, and we received a half-hour lecture on how she didn't see her first husband's face until after they were married. She explained that she was too shy to look him in the face before they were married. Shortly thereafter, she started giving lectures on the German notes that had been left on the board from the previous class. This was easy to overcome. Every day we would go in and erase the board; if we forgot, we could count on a German lecture.

As the semester progressed, Dr. D. would continue to go off on tangents, and the class would march to the department head with red faces and clenched fists. If the semester had been any longer, the university would have witnessed the first lynching of one of its professors. Fortunately, for Dr. D., the semester ended.

Our final examination shocked us all. Not only did she add vocabulary we had never studied, but she also asked questions about Russian history, culture, and politics. She had never taught these or even indicated they would be on the final. When asked about the test, she told us to figure out the vocabulary, and because we were students of the Russian language, we should have studied history, culture, and politics outside the class, even though she hadn't told us to.

When we got to the end of the exam, we felt better. The last line asked us to list on the back of the exam what we had learned from the class. Halfway through our test, Dr. D. left the room. Since we were more concerned with revenge than cheating, we jointly decided upon what should be put on the backs of our exams. We listed everything we had learned, from the ice storms of Geneva to the decadence of socialist Europe.

After the final exam, the number of students planning to take a second semester of Russian dropped from four to zero. So ends the tale of Gulag Fourteen. Based on my grade, a C, I suppose you could say I escaped exceptionally well. Still Gulag Fourteen will best be remembered for the person who ran it, affectionately known as БОЛШОЯ СУКА , which is better left untranslated.

Questions for Study and Discussion

1. Part of Vaughn's purpose is obviously to entertain an audience of fellow students with humor. But is there also a serious part of this purpose?

2. What is Vaughn's thesis? Why is it worth writing about?

3. Cite examples that work to convey the humor of the situation?

4. How do these examples also imply serious problems, regarding both the class and the instructor?

5. How does Vaughn organize the paper? How does the situation itself determine the organization?

6. Which of Vaughn's paragraphs state topic sentences directly?

7. Which paragraphs imply a topic sentence without stating one?

8. Why, or why not, is Vaughn's conclusion effective?

9. Do you think the students in this class could have taken other measures to try to improve Dr. D's teaching?

10. Have you ever been in a similar situation? What did you do? Write a short paragraph explaining your experience with an eccentric teacher or boss.

Dragons and Dustballs
Carol Somerville (sophomore)

Whush, whirl, whirr, whirr! These were the intriguing sounds that called me to my brother's bedroom, commonly called the dormer room. These joyful noises signified that Greg was playing with his Erector Set. Ah, the Erector Set, the magical toy that transformed metal, wire, gears, and lots of other good stuff into

Ferris wheels, merry-go-rounds, and other mechanical items that I did not recognize. That magical kit was indeed a sacred toy to be treasured.

Greg had a tendency to be possessive of all his gadgetry; in fact, he was downright miserly. We had vicious battles over whether or not I, a mere five-year-old girl, could enter the dormer room while the merry-go-round was in motion. One day I got up my courage and asked Greg if I could help him build something. Actually, my suggestion was more dumb than brave. Greg was furious with such a stupid idea. I was hurt and angry that he would not let me help. We created such a ruckus that my mother came to referee. She ruled for Greg. I was not to play with the Erector Set because my mother said that I was too young to know how to use it correctly. It was a sad day.

Surprisingly, the sun did rise the next day, and I had partly recovered from the prior day's disappointment. The direct approach had not worked, so I decided I would have to be sneaky. I would commit the unthinkable act; I would play with the Erector Set when Greg was not home. I would create a mechanical wonder that would disgrace his double Ferris wheel.

As with any great plan, this one had obstacles. Greg knew how much I wanted to play with the Erector Set, so to keep it safe while he was gone he hid it in his vault, alias the crawlway. The crawlway, which led to a door to the roof, was accessible only through Greg's bedroom, so it was a part of his personal domain. It was the only place in the house that I had not explored because I was terrified of it. It was a dark, low, cavelike place that only rats, bats, snakes, bears, monsters, dragons, and Greg dare enter. Was playing with the Erector Set worth the risk of going into the crawlway? It was a tough choice, but I decided that the reward was worth the risk.

I found a flashlight to guide me on my dreaded journey. I went into the dormer room and opened the little door to the crawlway. It was dark and scary, but I entered the little space. I finally understood why it was called a crawlway; I could not stand up. For a few minutes, I sat very quiet, waiting for some unknown creature to attack. I waited and waited, and nothing happened. Eventually, I turned on my flashlight, and much to my surprise there was nothing in the crawlway but me, dustballs, and the Erector Set. I was having such a good time not being eaten by dragons that I had nearly forgotten my mission, to get the Erector Set. I moved to the end of the crawlway, grabbed my reward, and scurried out to play.

I was quite excited when I opened the box and took out all the pieces. It was not too long before I realized that I had a problem. I did not have any idea how to build a Ferris wheel, or anything else for that matter. The directions were not a lot of help since I had not yet learned to read. I played with various parts until I got bored. Soon deciding that the Erector Set was not as much fun as I thought it would be, I put all the pieces back in the box and put it back in the crawlway.

When Greg got home from school that afternoon, he was quite surprised to find that I had set up housekeeping in the crawlway with my dolls. "What are you doing in there?" he asked. "I'm playing. What's it look like I'm doing?" I replied. "I can see that, but the monsters will eat you if they catch you in there," he said. "They will not! There's no such thing as monsters anyway," I retorted. He was so surprised at my reply that he never even asked if I had played with his cherished Erector Set.

Questions for Study and Discussion

1. Explain Somerville's title. How well does it fit the essay?

2. Somerville never states her thesis directly, but a thesis is implied. How would you express it?

3. What is Somerville's purpose in this essay? Who is her audience?

4. What do you think of Somerville's introduction? How does it fit in with the rest of the paper?

5. How does Somerville organize this essay? How does the experience determine the organization?

6. Explain why Somerville starts new paragraphs when she does.

7. Cite examples of effective use of specific detail.

8. Somerville effectively varies her sentence structure and length. Cite examples of her effective use of short sentences.

9. Why do you think Somerville plays in the crawlway after discovering that it is harmless?

10. In a brief freewriting, describe a similar childhood experience of your own. Try to think of a time when you discovered something about how the world really is, as opposed to how you had perceived it.

Head Games

Michael S. Godwin (freshman)

Proverbs warns us to be wary of seductive glances that will lead us to ruination. Apparently there is a lot of seductive glancing still going on because preachers are still shouting the same warning from the pulpits today. Leftover attitudes from the Victorian age necessitate the use of veiled language with the opposite sex, causing us to send and receive mixed messages that foul the process of establishing the ground rules for courtship. We have become so afraid of injuring one another's egos that we have become unwilling to use precise terminology to communicate with members of the opposite sex.

Do-it-yourself psychology books spend many pages to convince us to "read" the language of the body. They exhort us to pay attention to posture, dress, eye contact, and hand gestures. My personal experience with this advice is unsatisfactory. When I concentrate on nonverbal communication, I invariably miss the real message. I have analyzed myself out of more potential relationships than I care to remember! I still have trouble differentiating between a longing glance and the vacuous stare of the severely nearsighted.

School dances were terrifying experiences for me. I was painfully shy and usually went to the dances alone. I had perfected the slouch and the shuffle that told everyone that I was uninterested in their adolescent mating rituals. But my posture was far from the truth. I noticed everything, and I was plotting my moves in accordance with the latest self-help manual. At a spring oldies dance, I met my dream girl! Carol was a beauty, and she was talking to me! She frequently held my hand as we moved around the gym. She leaned toward me when we spoke. Her eye contact was intense and smoldering. We danced, and my libido raced. At the end of the night, I asked her out, but she turned me down! It seems that this teenage queen had lost her contact lenses. She was nearly blind without them. The handholding she explained as a safety device. She couldn't see where she was going. I had been a sort of leader-dog.

Another way to send a mating call, without actually voicing one, is with the use of colognes and after-shave lotions. I was convinced that because Russian Leather contained something called musk it had to work. It did two things. First, I got a rash after repeated use. Second, when my date was forced to inhale my heady bouquet in the confines of a closed car, she regurgitated her dinner.

With our ridiculous mating rituals, we have nearly eliminated the beauty, candor, and simplicity of straightforward English in expressing our emotions with a member of the opposite sex. As overly intellectual animals, we have filtered, strained, and complicated the exchange of signals between the sexes in a quest for convention and social "cool." Gone is the directness of Mae West's invitation to, "Come up and see me some time" and her ribald question, "Is that a pistol you're packin' or are you just very glad to see me?" Admittedly, Mae West was a parody, a put-on, and an unconventional role model—but she was undeniably exciting, and her famous one-liners effectively removed any confusion over the lady's intent.

We can continue to play the head games of courtship, but they are hazardous to our mental health. Our divorce rate is soaring. Psychiatrists are overloaded, and psychologists are treating more clients every year. I believe that the key to survival for both sexes is a return to a more direct and simple form of communication than the coy games we now suffer.

Questions for Study and Discussion
1. Identify Godwin's purpose and audience.
2. What is Godwin's thesis?

3. How does Godwin introduce his thesis? How effective is the introduction?

4. How effective are Godwin's examples in supporting his thesis?

5. What, according to Godwin, is the problem with communicating through body language? Are there times when body language is effective?

6. Discuss Godwin's organization of the essay.

7. Does Godwin suggest a solution to the problem he claims exists?

8. Godwin's essay is at once humorous and serious. How effectively does he mix the two attitudes?

9. In a brief freewriting, recount an experience you have had that supports Godwin's thesis.

unit four
Revision

By now you have a general idea of what revision is about. In Chapter 1, you learned that revision is part of the writing process—the part when you "re-see" your writing and make changes according to your purpose and your audience's needs. And in other chapters, you saw how revision can make writing more specific or be used to improve an essay, paragraph, or sentence. Before proceeding into our detailed discussion of revision, let's review what you know already. First, revision is not the same as editing. When you edit, you check your writing for misspelled words, grammar and punctuation errors, and so on. When you revise, you change larger matters having to do with the content, organization, and style of your essay. Second, you know that revision is the part of the writing process that usually comes after drafting. But you also know that because the parts of the process sometimes overlap, some revision can take place as you are writing your draft. Third, you know that to revise a draft, you need to wait awhile before doing so—at least some hours, if not overnight. This period of waiting will enable you to re-see the draft so that you can make any necessary changes. Finally, you know that during revision it is important to receive feedback from others—friends, relatives, classmates, your teacher—by having them read and respond to your essay.

Along with knowing something about revision, you have seen examples of revised writing. Remember in Chapter 3 how the writer of the paragraph on Chicago museums revised to focus the topic on one museum, the Museum of Science and Industry? If you recall, the writer's first draft tried to cover all of the city's major museums. Though it made a general statement about each, it had very little focus and few specific details. In revising—re-seeing—the first paragraph, the writer realized that for the audience to understand the attractions of each museum, each general idea from the first paragraph would have to be developed with specific details. Thus, the revisions consisted of separating the general ideas and developing each one with additional details in a paragraph of its own. In short, the writer separated ideas and added details to fulfill the purpose of the writing and to meet the audience's needs.

With the writing you have done in this course, in other courses, or on your own, you have probably gained some experience in revising. If you think about that experience, you know that when revising you consider many different aspects of your writing—from as large a matter as reorganizing the paper to as small a matter as rewriting part of a sentence. Good revision, in other words, requires many different considerations. And though part of the larger writing process, revision is a process itself—a process within a process, so to speak. In this unit, we will discuss revision as a process and see how student writers engage in it.

chapter eleven
Revision as Process

Revision leads to changes, and change implies a process. You have probably heard the expression "in the process of change," this or that happened, or you may have heard someone say something "changed in the process." These expressions can apply to almost anything—the changes in someone's outlook during the education process or the changes in the design of a house during the building process, for example. These changes are the result of re-seeing—the student seeing his or her ideas about democracy differently as the result of a political science course, or the architect seeing his or her ideas about a house differently once the house has begun to take shape.

Now add writers to our examples. A former writing teacher of mine once told me that "for a good writer, a piece of writing is never finished; it's just abandoned." He meant that good writers are always re-seeing what they have written and looking for ways to say it better. But finally, because of a deadline, the writer must "abandon" the writing and let it stand as it is. Of course, if the writer has allowed time to make any necessary revisions, the writing will probably be a successful product. The point is, experienced writers are always looking for ways to make their writing even better. They see their writing as always in the process of change until a deadline prevents them from changing it anymore.

While most experienced writers revise a great deal, beginning writers usually do not revise very much. As we saw in Chapter 1, beginners tend to think that experienced writers just sit down, write something, and are finished. The beginners then try to write this way themselves because they do not know how much experienced writers revise—either while drafting or after a draft is completed. I sometimes kid beginning writers by telling them that their final paper is just their rough draft copied over neatly. Usually this joke makes them realize that changes need to be made—revision needs to be done—in the rough draft before the writer can begin thinking about a final copy.

Revision, as experienced writers know, is hard work. Most beginning writers do not avoid revision because they are lazy but because they do not know *how* to revise or *what* to revise. When you revise a first, second, or even third draft, you need to reconsider—and make necessary changes in—the content, organization, and sentence structure of your essay. And all of these changes must be done according to the requirements of the writing situation: your purpose, role, and audience. This seems like a lot to consider in the revision process, and it is, but if we examine them one at a time, you will gain a better understanding of how and why you revise.

Revision and the Writing Situation

Any change you make on an essay relates directly to one or more of the elements of the writing situation: purpose, role, and audience. If you add more details to strengthen a point, you are assuming your audience needs these details and will not get the point without them. If you cut a sentence, you are assuming the audience does not need the sentence to make sense of what you are saying. Suppose you start with a thesis that points out a problem, but then in revising you change the thesis to one that calls for a solution to a problem. As a result, your purpose in writing changes. If in revising a term paper, you substitute a neutral or formal word for a slang word, you are making the substitution to conform to your role as college student because you know students do not use slang in term papers. Nor does your audience, the professor, expect slang. Thus the substitution is the result of both your role and the needs of your audience.

Revising for Your Audience

It is difficult to separate your purpose and role from your concerns about audience. But when you revise, it is wise to reconsider your initial thoughts about your audience. Let's review the audience analysis questions from Chapter 1 to see how they can help during revision:

1. Who is my audience?
   a. What do they know about the topic?
   b. What references can I assume they will know?
   c. What references must be explained?
2. What is my audience's attitude toward what I am writing?
   a. Are they most likely to agree?

> **b.** Are they most likely to disagree?
> **c.** Are they neutral?
> **3.** How do I want my audience to use my writing?
>   **a.** To inform themselves?
>   **b.** To entertain themselves?
>   **c.** To make a decision?
>   **d.** To solve a problem?
>   **e.** To change their views or behavior?

If you review these questions *after* you complete your draft, you can often see the places in your writing that need revision. For instance, I once wrote a letter to a company from which I purchased a stereo. My letter described the problem with the stereo in reasonably complete detail. However, I then closed the first draft of the letter telling the reader I hoped he or she would help me. But how? I never said. Did I want a new stereo? Did I want my money refunded? Did I want the name of a local service center that could fix the stereo? As it turned out, I had taken the stereo to the local service center twice, and neither time was it repaired properly, so I wanted the reader to authorize either a replacement of the stereo or a refund. When I revised the letter I made this clear. If I had not, the company probably would have told me to go to the same service center I had gone to in the first place.

In effect, in my first draft, I was not aware of what I wanted the reader to do. If the reader had seen the first draft, he or she would have assumed the stereo needed to be fixed and would have "solved the problem" by sending me to the service center. However, I not only wanted the reader to solve the problem but to do so by making a decision on whether to authorize a refund or a replacement. In this case, keeping in mind *how the reader was to use the writing* (question 3 on audience analysis) was extremely important.

Exercise 11.1

Assume you are writing the letter asking the company to replace the faulty stereo. Your audience is a consumer affairs representative for a national chain of electronics stores. The stores sell various brands and products ranging from telephone answering machines to widescreen televisions, and your audience must deal with complaints about all of them. Examine the items below. If you think an item should be included in the letter, write *yes* next to it and explain why. If an item should not be included, write *no* and explain your answer.

1. The exact date of purchase:_____
2. The brand and model number:_____
3. The color of the stereo:_____
4. The name and address of the store where the stereo was purchased:
   _____
5. Reference to other items that you have purchased at that store:_____
   _____
6. The specific problem with the store:_____
   _____
7. The number of times and dates repairs were made:_____
   _____
8. What songs were playing when the stereo malfunctioned:_____
   _____
9. The name and address of the service center:_____
   _____
10. Your taste in music:_____

Exercise 11.2

Following is a draft of a letter written in response to exercise 11.1. It is badly in need of revision. Revise the letter using what you have learned from the previous discussion and exercise.

August 17, 1989

Ms. Mary Tune
Consumer Affairs
Electroland Stores
Oxnard, California 93030

Dear Ms. Tune:

Last month, I bought a stereo at my local Electroland store. I was really happy to buy it because I am into rhythm-and-blues music, and I knew to get the best sounds from my large collection of R & B albums, I needed a good stereo.

At first, the stereo played real well, and I particularly enjoyed the bass sounds, but then the turntable started slowing down, distorting the music. Of course, I was bummed out, so I took the stereo back to Electroland. They sent me to another place to get it fixed. I was told the problem was just a loose belt and that it would be fixed in a couple of days. It was fixed, and the stereo worked well for a week or two, but then the turntable started slowing down again. I then had the turntable fixed again, but in a few days it was slowing down again. So I went back to the Electroland store where I bought the stereo, but they told me they couldn't do anything and that I had to write to you. That's how I got your address.

I hope you will help me out. I'm tired of all this hassle and I just want to be able to listen to my favorite records.

Exercise 11.3

Examine a paper written for this or any other class. See if you can find parts of the paper that need to be revised to meet the needs of your audience more effectively. Using the audience analysis questions, jot down a list of revisions you could make to accommodate your audience more effectively.

Revising to Clarify Your Role and Purpose

As you revise a paper to meet the needs of your audience, you will also be reconsidering your role and purpose. If you think about the writing situation of the letter in exercise 11.2, you know some information the reader needed was left out while other information that the reader did not need was included. You should be able to identify the writer's role as dissatisfied consumer, but in the unneeded information, you can also see that the writer has mixed in another role: rhythm and blues fan. Though the writer may love this type of music, the reader, who probably reads dozens of letters a day, probably does not care what kind of music the writer likes. The reader, as a consumer affairs representative, is concerned with the writer as consumer and should not be asked to spend time seeing the writer in another role. Also, since the writer's purpose is to have the stereo replaced, the love of rhythm and blues is not part of the purpose of the letter.

As you read through the following paragraph, see if you can identify the writer's role and purpose. Then look for information that does not fit either one:

Driving a tractor-trailer is not an easy job. First of all, the driver must be able to shift a transmission which can have anywhere from ten to twenty-four different gears. Each shift must be double-clutched, meaning the driver must push down the clutch, move the gearshift to neutral before releasing the clutch, and then push down the clutch again before shifting to the next gear. All this must be done in a split second so that the truck does not stall. *Peterbuilt,* the best brand of truck, also has the easiest transmission to shift because the gears are very smooth and the clutch has a hydraulic release. Also, truck drivers must be skillful at using their brakes. Unlike a car's brakes, truck brakes are controlled by air, and thus they are very powerful and can throw the truck into a skid if a driver applies them too quickly. Yet a truck without air brakes would be a menace to highway safety. Along with knowing how to apply the brakes, a truck driver must learn how to steer properly, using a very large steering wheel to keep the semi in its lane and to guide it safely around corners.

You probably did not have much trouble seeing that the writer's role is that of someone knowledgeable about truck driving and that the purpose of the paragraph is to inform a less knowledgeable audience about the difficulties of driving a tractor-trailer. Perhaps the writer wants us to respect truck drivers more. But what is the writer's role and purpose in the sentence stating that *Peterbuilt* trucks are the best? Is the writer now persuading or informing? Does the sentence stick to the paragraph's purpose? Also, how does the statement about trucks without air brakes fit the writer's role and purpose? As this paragraph shows, when you revise your writing, just as in the invention stage, you must keep your role and purpose clearly in mind.

Exercise 11.4

The paragraph below was written to explain why insurance companies set particular rates for automobile insurance for different groups of drivers. The writer's role is that of student. His purpose is to show the professor he knows why rates are highest for single males from age eighteen to twenty-five. Revise the paragraph to fit this role and purpose. What information does not belong? What wording needs to be changed?

Insurance rates for single males from eighteen to twenty-five are the highest of any group of drivers, and there are many reasons. These dudes have the most accidents, and they are most often arrested for driving and drinking. No one should drive drunk, and anyone who does should be put in jail. Drivers at this age also rank among the highest in number of speeding tickets, and a large proportion of these males are gear heads who like to drag race with high performance cars. Single males between eighteen and twenty five buy the largest percentage of high performance cars. A lot of them should not even be allowed on the road.

Exercise 11.5

Choose any topic you like and write a paragraph of about a hundred words. Make sure your role and purpose are clear, but then add a sentence or two that does not fit either the role or purpose. Have a classmate do the same, and when you are finished, trade paragraphs and identify the information that does not fit the writer's role and purpose. Be prepared to explain why.

Exercise 11.6

Examine a paper written for this or any class that you feel would be improved with more revision. See if you can find information that does not fit your role and purpose in writing the paper. Revise any parts of the paper where this problem occurs.

Revising for Better Content

When you revise your writing to meet the needs of your audience more effectively or to clarify your role and purpose, you are often tinkering with the content of the paper so that it meets the needs of the writing situation. However, sometimes you may have your role, purpose, and audience clearly in mind, but still the content of your paper does not do the job of communicating what you want to say. When we talk about the content of the paper, we are talking more about *what* the writer has to say and less about *how* he or she says it.

Adding and Expanding Information and Ideas

Sometimes the problem with a piece of writing is that it does not say enough to meet the audience's needs. Information must be added, or information already in the paper must be expanded. Below is a paragraph from the first draft of an essay on popular music in the sixties:

> A lot of Sixties music had a protest message. Bob Dylan's songs dealt with racism and war, such as "The Ballad of Emmett Till" and "Masters of War."

Richie Havens was another protest singer. The Beatles had some protest songs too, such as "Bungalow Bill."

This paragraph was written by a student in his early thirties and directed to an audience of classmates in their late teens and early twenties who knew little about sixties music. The writer's purpose was to educate the audience to see the value of the music, so his role was that of an authority on the subject. The role, purpose, and audience seem clear, and the paragraph has a clear topic sentence backed by some examples. But most of the students in the audience had questions. Why and how were the Dylan songs about war and racism? Who was Richie Havens? Were there other protest singers? And even though the student's audience was familiar with the Beatles, most of them had never heard "Bungalow Bill." In short, if the writer was to fulfill his purpose in educating the audience (and his role as authority), he would have to consider what additional information his audience would need. His revised paragraph looked like this:

A lot of Sixties music had a protest message. Bob Dylan wrote songs against racism and war. For instance, "The Ballad of Emmett Till" told the story of the awful lynching of a young black man in Mississippi. Also, "Masters of War" condemned people who made money from wars. Richie Havens was another protest singer. He was black, and his most famous protest song, "Freedom," was often sung at civil rights demonstrations. Joan Baez had a hit with "I Shall Be Released," a song written by Dylan about the unjust imprisonment of protesters. Even the Beatles wrote and sang protest songs. "Bungalow Bill" made fun of General William Westmoreland, who was the commander of American troops in Vietnam.

In this revised version of the paragraph, the writer has added another example, on Joan Baez, and has expanded and explained the previous examples. His audience now knows what the Dylan songs were about, who Richie Havens was and why he was important at the time, and what "Bungalow Bill" was about. Although the writer still gives only a sample of protest songs in the sixties, this sample provides enough information to enable his audience to see his point.

Using Invention Strategies to Add and Expand

When we broke the writing process into steps in Chapter 1, we placed the invention strategies first because first you have to come up with—invent—ideas and information about your topic. However, you also know that the parts of the process can also overlap. This overlapping occurs when you revise because you use the invention strategies--the first step in the process--to help you add and explain information during revision.

In revising the paragraph on protest in sixties music, the student could have used brainstorming, clustering, or even the journalist's questions to come up with the information added to the paragraph. For example, in the draft, he mentioned that Richie Havens was another protest singer, a statement which did not tell us much. By brainstorming or clustering about Havens, he might have come up with the following list or cluster diagram:

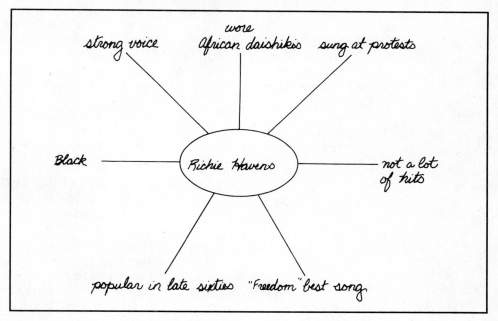

Brainstorming List
Strong voice
Not a lot of hit songs
Well known mostly in the late Sixties
Black man
Often wore African dashikis
Best song: ''Freedom''
Often sang ''Freedom'' at civil rights protests

Journalist's questions

Who:	Richie Havens
What:	sang protest songs, particularly the song "Freedom"
When:	late Sixties
Why:	as a black, to protest problems of civil rights
Where:	in concerts and at civil rights demonstrations
How:	with a strong voice, wearing African dashiki

As you can see, the invention strategies give the writer the needed details. From these, the writer can pick the details that best support the topic sentence stating that much of the music of the Sixties carried a protest message. These can then be added in the appropriate places in the draft and included in the revised version of the paragraph. Of course, revision does not always require you to go back to the invention strategies, but when you see a need for—or readers ask for—more information, the strategies can help you come up with it.

Exercise 11.7

The following three paragraphs need information added or expanded. For each paragraph, raise questions that could help the writer revise. Do this exercise either on your own or with two or three other students.

1. Trains are not a very good way to travel long distances. They take too long to get from one place to another. If you have to ride overnight on the train, you probably won't be very comfortable. You see nice scenery, but after a while even the scenery gets boring.

2. My son's paper route helped him make money, but it was an inconvenience for me. I always had to make sure he was up on time to deliver the papers before he went to school. People would call our home bothering me when he forgot to leave their paper. Sometimes when he could not deliver the papers, I delivered them for him, and he had a big route with many customers. It wasn't worth the money he made.

3. Steroid use among athletes is foolish. Athletes see steroids as a way to build up their bodies and improve their performance. They do not consider the side effects, such as heart problems. Using steroids can also cause death.

Exercise 11.8

Now that you have raised questions about these paragraphs, choose one and revise it by adding information that would make it more informative. Use the invention strategies if you have trouble coming up with information. Once you have rewritten the paragraph, have a classmate point out how the information you have added improves the paragraph and what information is needed to improve it even more.

Exercise 11.19

Revise a paragraph from an essay you have written for this or another class, adding and expanding information where needed.

Cutting Unnecessary Information

When we discussed revision as part of the writing situation, some of the revisions you made in the exercises required you to cut material. Remember the letter writer's references to rhythm and blues. Beginning writers—and many experienced writers, too—often find that cutting is the most painful part of revision. After all, writers (whether beginners or experts) put a lot of work into writing, so cutting out something they have labored to write can be painful. But many times cutting information can improve a piece of writing significantly. There are many reasons to cut information, but two stand out:

1. when you have more details or examples than the reader needs to get the point, and
2. when you have unnecessarily repeated an idea.

Cutting Unnecessary Details. In Chapter 3, you learned about the need to be specific in your writing. Specific writing requires you to use enough examples to enable the reader to see your point. When your readers disagree with you, you probably need more examples to convince them to accept, or at least seriously consider, your point. When readers agree or are neutral, you can probably get away with fewer. But when do you have enough examples and details? When do you have too many? This is a tough call. It takes practice and experience to know exactly. A good rule of thumb is that it is better to have too much information than too little, but if you consider the needs of your audience carefully, you will usually know when you have too much.

Sometimes too many details can distract the reader from your main point. Consider the following paragraph:

> In the past few years, McDonald's has tried to improve the decor of their restaurants to make them seem like fancy restaurants. Recently I was in a McDonald's in northern Indiana that was decorated to look like the dining room of an old riverboat. It had many mirrors edged in an imitation gold leaf, brass bells and replicas of gas lanterns on the walls, and scalloped moldings and railings. There were about a dozen of the mirrors and about two dozen each of the bells and lanterns, one over each booth. Another McDonald's I visited, this one in Ohio, had a modern decor. The walls were done in pink and mauve, there were numerous plants, and modern paintings hung above each booth. These paintings were not Picasso copies or anything that radical. Instead, they abstractly portrayed mountains or beaches, done suggestively in bold lines and broad patches of color rather than in the realistic detail of landscapes. Another McDonald's was decorated to suggest an old railroad station with . . .

This writer obviously has an eye for detail, but as you read through this paragraph, you may have begun to forget the writer's main point: that McDonald's is upgrading the decor of its restaurants. Even if you didn't lose sight of this point, do you really need the estimate of how many mirrors, lanterns, and bells there were in the restaurant decorated like a riverboat? Doesn't just knowing they were there enable you to get the point? Similarly, do you need a detailed description of the paintings to see that the second restaurant had a modern decor? Don't forget what we said in Chapter 2: Show rather than tell, but also remember that showing doesn't mean losing your point, and the reader, in a forest of details.

Exercise 11.10

Revise the paragraph below, cutting unnecessary details.

> As kids, we shuddered when we walked past old Mr. Speers's house, for we were sure it was haunted. In front of the house there was a fence with sharp pointed spikes on top of it. It was about five feet high, and the spikes were at least three inches long. A twenty-foot path of broken gray stones crossed

a yard full of dead weeds—including broadleaf, crabgrass, and dandelions—and leafless, thorny bushes spread against the house. The porch sagged across the front of the house, and there were spaces where spindles were missing from the broken railings. The rickety steps led to a carved oak door with a heavy brass knocker. I never looked, but I was sure the carvings on the door were pictures of fiends and devils. The dusky-blue velvet curtains in the windows looked like they belonged in an old funeral parlor. But it was hard to see the curtains because of the thick cobwebs in the windows themselves. The roof of the house was high and peaked with turrets on each side. These turrets were round and pointed at the top. Under the eaves of the roof, blackbirds nested and screamed like tormented souls. These birds would swoop down as if they wanted to attack us. All the gutters around the roof were rusty. The house had once been painted a pale gray, but the paint was faded and chipped. In some spots, the bare, weathered wood showed through the paint.

Cutting Unnecessary Repetition of Ideas.   Sometimes you may repeat yourself to make sure the reader gets the point, but be careful not to repeat yourself too much. Readers lose patience when they are told something more times than they need to know it. Read the following paragraph for examples of unnecessary repetition:

The design of baseball mitts has changed tremendously since the game was first played, making fielding much easier. The first mitts, used in the latter part of the nineteenth century, were little more than a leather glove, like those worn today in cold weather. Without padding or webbing, they offered little protection and thus hindered a player's ability to field sharply hit balls. Because the old mitts were just five-fingered gloves made of leather, they were effective only in catching slow ground balls or pop flies, so players could not field as well. Today's mitts are much larger, sometimes measuring as much as eighteen inches from the heavily padded heel to the top of the wide basketlike webbing that bridges the forefinger and thumb. They still have five fingers, but the fingers are as much as eight inches long, stiffly padded, connected to each other by a rawhide stitch, and hinged at the palm to allow the player to smother the wickedest grounder or the sharpest line drive. The large size and heavy padding of modern gloves enables players to be better fielders. Today's baseball gloves are far superior to the first gloves and make fielding easier.

The purpose and point of this paragraph are clear: The writer is comparing the original baseball mitts to today's to show how the changes in the design make fielding easier. We get this idea in the topic sentence, but then it reappears three times in the last two sentences of the paragraph. Also, in the middle of the paragraph, the writer says the old gloves were like the leather gloves people wear in winter. He then repeats himself, saying they were just five-fingered leather gloves. Part of this writer's problem is that he is afraid to let his specific details show his general ideas; thus, he unnecessarily repeats them.

Exercise 11.11

The following paragraph repeats its general idea more than it should. Revise it to eliminate repetition.

> Nursing is not the glamorous job that the media sometimes show it to be. In movies and television shows, female nurses are usually pretty women with cheery smiles and great dispositions. They flirt with doctors and usually end up marrying or having a romance with one. Sometimes, they are shown making life-and-death decisions about a patient when the doctors are not around. This is a very glamorous picture, but it doesn't happen that way. A nurse's job is not very glamorous. In reality, because the nurse may often work long hours, or even double-shifts, she won't care whether she looks very pretty or not, so she is not very glamorous. These hours, along with the never-ending demands of the patients, can wipe the smile off the face of even the most cheerful nurse. As for romances with doctors, the nurse's life is not this glamorous. The truly professional nurse is not on the job to flirt with doctors. And instead of making life-and-death decisions, the average nurse spends most of her time emptying bedpans, administering medication, filling out charts, and moving heavy patients so the bed linen can be changed, which is not glamorous either. So a nurse's job is tough, not glamorous like on TV or in the movies.

Rearranging Information

Sometimes a paragraph or essay may have all the information it needs, but the information may not be presented in the best possible order and needs rearranging. For instance, you could be narrating and place material out of chronological order, or you could be persuading but not have your points arranged to create the most impact. Compare the first draft and revised versions of the following paragraph:

First draft:

When I returned from Christmas break, a water pipe had burst, and my dorm room was a mess. There was a big puddle of dirty water in the middle, and the tiles were all coming up. The bottom mattress had stains on it, and there was a rusty spring hanging down from the soaked bunk above. Then I looked up and saw all these wet stains on the ceiling. The dresser had mold all over it, and there were some soggy old magazines in front of it. They smelled from all the dampness from the water.

Revised version:

When I returned from Christmas break, a water pipe had burst and my dorm room was a mess. The floor tiles were coming loose in a big puddle of dirty water. This puddle started in the middle of the floor and ran into a pile of soggy magazines in front of the dresser. As for the dresser, there was slimy gray mold all over it. When I turned around, I saw the bunks. The mattress on the top one was soaked, and it had a rusty spring hanging from it. Even the bottom one had water stains. The whole room had a sickening moldy smell. Then I looked up and saw a stain that covered almost the whole ceiling and cracks that the water had dripped through from the pipes.

These paragraphs may not seem very different to you. You probably noticed a few added details, such as the words "slimy gray" describing the mold, or the expansion of the example about the ceiling. But if you looked more closely, the examples have been rearranged quite a bit to improve the organization. Notice that in the second sentence of the revision the writer reverses the order of the loose tiles and the puddle. We now see the tiles *in* the puddle, and mentioning the puddle second allows her to lead into the third sentence, which is also about the puddle. That sentence then gives us an idea of the size of the puddle but also leads us over to the magazines and the dresser, which is described in the fourth sentence. We then get the details on the bed and ceiling. Overall, the revision moves us across the floor to one side of the room where the dresser is, back to the other side where the bed is, and finally up to the ceiling to the cause of the problem, the broken pipe, first mentioned in the topic sentence. In other words, we see the room as the student did. In contrast, because the rough draft presents the details randomly, it is more difficult to follow.

In Chapter 7, you learned that paragraphs read better when they have coherence—when one sentence follows logically from the one before it. The revised paragraph above works better because it has coherence. You also learned in Chapter 4 that transitions—both transitional words and repetition of key words—add to coherence. When you rearrange information in a paragraph or in a whole essay, it is important that you check your transitions because sometimes the rearrangement requires that new transitions be added.

In the above revision, note the transitional phrases added at the beginning of sentences four, five, and seven: *As for the dresser; When I turned around; Even.* The first two help locate the reader as the writer's eyes move about the room, while the last emphasizes the extent of the damage. So while the rearranged examples improve the paragraph, the transitions help the reader to see the rearrangement.

Exercise 11.12

Here are some questions that can help you judge whether sentences in a paragraph need to be rearranged. Apply these questions to each of the sentences in a paragraph you have written. Jot down notes about the purpose and place of each sentence in the paragraph. Then revise the paragraph for the best possible arrangement.

1. Is the sentence the topic sentence? If so, is the topic of the paragraph clear and limited? Is the sentence smoothly written?
2. Is the sentence an example? If so, is the example concrete and specific?
3. Is the sentence one part of a longer example? If so, is it linked clearly to the other parts?
4. Does the sentence follow clearly from the sentence before it? If not, why not? Should a transition be added, or should the sentence be moved?
5. Does the sentence lead to the sentence following it? If not, why not? Should a transition be added, or should the sentence be moved?

All the examples so far have discussed content in paragraphs, assuming that the paragraphs were parts of a larger essay. Whether you are adding, cutting, or rearranging content, the same principles that apply to individual paragraphs apply to the whole essay. For instance, a student of mine came into my office one day with a term paper she had written for an Afro-American studies course. The purpose of her paper was to show how Tuskegee Institute, the first black college in America, started out as a vocational school and gradually developed into a full-fledged university. She had received the paper back with a poor grade, but the professor was allowing her to revise and resubmit it. When we went over it, she was able to see that she had done a good job showing Tuskegee's original vocational curriculum and its broad curriculum during the last few decades.

However, she had skimmed over the 1930s, a decade when the school increasingly added liberal arts courses. In her revised version of the paper, she added more than two pages of discussion on this important period in the school's development.

While this student added content to her essay, some students cut whole paragraphs, even pages, when the information is not relevant to the purpose of the paper and the needs of the audience. As for rearranging information, if it makes a better paper, there is nothing wrong with moving a paragraph or more from the end of the paper to the beginning, from the beginning to the end, or whatever is called for to put the paragraphs in the best possible order.

In the next chapter, you will see two students revising. As you read through parts of their drafts, and their completed essays, note that they apply the same principles of revision to the whole of the essay as they apply to its individual parts.

Writing Assignments

1. Revise the first paper you wrote in this course. Then write a brief paragraph discussing why you made your revisions and how they improved the paper.

2. Write a letter to a friend about something related to college: grades, studying, social life, etc. Then revise the letter so that it would be appropriate to send to your parents.

3. Write an essay advising beginning freshmen on what they need to know about revision. Consider the purpose, need, and strategies for revision.

Key Terms

Adding and expanding: During revision, to put in additional information, examples, and ideas where needed. You can add and expand to clarify your purpose and/or to meet the needs of your audience.

Cutting: Taking out information, examples, or ideas that stray from your purpose and thesis or that are not needed for your audience to understand your point.

Rearranging: Moving sentences from one part of a paragraph to another or moving paragraphs to different places in the essay to achieve the best possible organization.

chapter twelve
Student Writers Revising

Just as writers will vary their writing processes to fit their personalities, they will also have different habits when revising. Some writers make very rough drafts after little invention and then revise large chunks of the essay. Others make lots of invention notes and plan their organizing strategy so thoroughly that revision requires only work on sentences and perhaps the adding and cutting of a few details. By now, you should be familiar with your own habits, both in the whole of the writing process and in revision. In this chapter, you will see how two students revised essays. As you read through their essays and revisions, think about how you revise.

"A Sticky Situation," E. Brian Miller

E. Brian Miller's essay, "A Sticky Situation," responds to a topic asking students to write an essay in which they show how a frightening childhood experience enabled them to learn something. Though Brian was a nineteen-year-old freshman when he wrote this essay, his drafts leading to the completed essay show that he had the maturity, energy, and intelligence to revise his work into a polished student essay. Read the complete essay first, and then examine the comparisons that follow.

A Sticky Situation

On a warm autumn day in October 1972, like any kid my age on such a day, I was outside playing. The sun was shining brightly, and the leaves on the trees were blowing softly in the moderate wind of a very comfortable fall day. Little did I know that I would have a frightening experience that would teach me a lot about the relationship between parents and children.

Shortly after lunch, my mom dressed me up and sent me outside to help my dad, who was fixing the pump on our well. I patiently "helped" him, as only a five-year-old could, for the better part of twenty minutes. But I was totally bored with this activity and was searching anxiously for anything that looked like a possible escape. Finally, my dog, a black-and-brown beagle named King, ran by making it very obvious that he wanted to play, so off I went.

I ran after King, but as soon as I would catch up to him he would take off faster than before. We ran through every inch of the eight acres on which our house was located. King led me through the woods and into the east meadow. We stopped there for a while and rested in a thicket of tall grass, but as soon as we were comfortable, King bolted away with me giving chase. The dog was chasing a rabbit that led us along the creek forming the north boundary of our property. The brush along the water was extremely rough, and it was becoming hard for my young body to keep up with the lively animals.

After our run along the creek, I followed King into the cornfield directly west of our home. We romped through the ten-acre plot and left nothing to chance, exploring everything but not finding the rabbit. Our exploration complete, we headed for home. However, all of a sudden I didn't seem to be moving. I had unknowingly wandered into a quagmire of mud. Then, my little red boots were caught in an inescapable suction. I was trapped.

In the meantime, my dad had asked my mom if I was with her; my mom said that she thought I was with my dad. Panic struck my parents. Hastily, they began to search around the immediate area. Their little boy was nowhere to be found. My dad then jumped into his truck and raced up and down the road fronting our property, while my mom hurried down to the creek, but I was not there either. At this point, they were frantic; bad thoughts entered their heads. "What if he has fallen in the creek and drowned? What if he has wandered out to the road and been hit by a car? Where could he be?" they wondered. They were ready to call the police and fire department. Just then, my dad heard King barking in the cornfield to the west (my loyal dog had stayed at my side), and he glimpsed the tassel of my red stocking hat ever so slightly through the corn stalks. They had found me.

Their search had taken only thirty minutes, but during this seeming eternity I had cried myself dry. The dried tears combined with the mud made my face an awful sight. Having King at my side was the only thing that kept me from being completely petrified. As my dad got to me, I was still crying dry tears, but the only words I could muster were, "I'm stuck in the mud." As I was pulled from the mud, my boots made a sound like a balloon snapping. He then took me home for a big bowl of soup and mug of hot chocolate.

Needless to say, I learned some valuable lessons from this experience. First of all, I learned never to wander away from home without telling my parents, but more importantly I learned how much I meant to them and how frightening it was to be a child alone.

Revising a Section: From Freewriting to Final Copy

Brian's final essay is a polished copy of his second draft. His first draft was very rough, almost freewriting. If we compare the sections of each draft, in which he discusses following his dog, we will see how the details of his experience, the organization of his essay, and the structure of his sentences gradually take shape.

First Draft:

soon after

I ~~began playing with~~ King and followed him all over our eight acres. Then he went into a cornfield. He was chasing a rabbit and who knows what else. Like the naive youngster I

Expand: add details on the chase

was, I followed him everywhere, all over this ten-acre plot of corn. King must have lost the rabbit or got tired because finally he turned around toward home. I eagerly followed. Then it happened as I was following him. I stepped smack in the middle of a quagmire of mud. My little red boots instantly were submerged five inches ~~and~~ I was trapped.

Draft 2:

I ran after King, ~~and~~ *but* as soon as I would catch up to him he

would take off faster than before. We ran through every inch

of the eight acres on which our house was located. King led

me through the woods and into the *east* meadow ~~in the east~~. We

stopped *t* here for a while and rested in ~~the~~ *a* thicket of tall grass,

but as soon as we were comfortable, King bolted away ~~again~~. *with me giving chase.*

We ended up along the creek. *The dog was chasing a rabbit that led* The brush along the water *us along a creek forming the north boundary of our property*

was extremely rough. It was becoming hard for my young

body to keep up with the lively animals.

After our *I ran* ~~stroll~~ along the creek, I followed my dog into the

cornfield directly west of our home. We romped through the

ten-acre plot and left nothing to chance ~~as we~~ explored *ing* every-

but not finding the rabbit.

thing, ~~But with~~ *O* ur exploration complete, we headed for

and I followed.

home, ~~However~~, I didn't seem to be moving. I had *unknowingly* wandered

into a quagmire of mud. *Then* ~~Now~~ my little red boots were caught

better word?

in the (unconquerable) suction. I was trapped.

Draft 3:

I ran after King, but as soon as I would catch up to him he would take off faster than before. We ran through every inch of the eight acres on which our house was located. King led me through the woods and into the east meadow. We stopped there for a while and rested in a thicket of tall grass, but as soon as we were comfortable, King bolted away with me giving chase. The dog was chasing a rabbit that led us along the creek forming the north boundary of our property. The brush along the water was extremely rough, and it was becoming hard for my young body to keep up with the lively animals.

    After our run along the creek, I followed King into the cornfield directly west of our home. We romped through the ten-acre plot and left nothing to chance, exploring everything but not finding the rabbit. Our exploration complete, King turned for home, and I followed. However, all of a sudden, I didn't seem to be moving. I had unknowingly wandered into a quagmire of mud. Then, my little red boots were caught in an inescapable suction. I was trapped.

The most obvious change, of course, is the expansion of draft one from one to two paragraphs. By adding the information about stopping in the meadow and chasing the rabbit along the creek, Brian creates for his audience a stronger sense of his surroundings and his experience. Notice, too, how the references to east, west, and north and the specifics on the size of the property and cornfield create a large place for a little boy to run into trouble. Also, the paragraph adds suspense to the narration as it delays the revelation of the frightening experience.

    As Brian expands the material with each revision, he also improves his sentence structure and word choice. In the second and third drafts, for example, he separates the sentence "I was trapped" from the previous sentence. Standing alone in contrast to the longer sentences of the rest of the paragraph, the short sentence calls attention to itself to emphasize his predicament. Note also how he combines sentences at the end of the first paragraph to avoid choppiness.

    As for word choice, Brian rightly questions his choice of the third word in the second paragraph of draft two. Running after a dog and a rabbit certainly is not a *stroll*, nor is it an *excursion*. In the final draft, the use of *run* is simpler but more accurate. Likewise, in the last sentence of the final draft, the word *inescapable* is more accurate than *unconquerable* used in the second draft.

    Brian's revisions were equally thorough and effective on all sections of the paper, as you will see in completing the following exercises.

Exercise 12.1

Note the revisions in the draft and final versions of the introduction to "A Sticky Situation" and write down possible reasons for them.

Draft version:

It was a warm autumn day in October 1972. The sun was shining brightly, and the leaves on the trees were blowing briskly in the moderate wind, which made the temperature very comfortable for a fall day.

Final version:

On a warm autumn day in October 1972, like any kid my age on such a day, I was outside playing. The sun was shining brightly, and the leaves on the trees were blowing softly in the moderate wind of a very comfortable fall day. Little did I know that I would have a frightening experience that would teach me a lot about the relationship between parents and children.

Exercise 12.2

This section from Brian's first draft discusses how his parents searched for him, how he felt while stuck, and how they found him. Compare it to the same section in the completed essay and write down how his revisions have improved organization, development, and sentence structure.

My parents searched the house and immediately around it. I was nowhere to be found. My mom went all over our property to the creek. My dad drove around in his truck, and they still couldn't find me.

I was all out of tears by now and the dirt and dried tears made my face a sorry sight. I was trying to cry but nothing would come out. All I could say was "I'm stuck in the mud."

Mom and dad were now petrified—what if I had fallen in the creek and drowned? They were just about to call the police and fire department when my dad looked to the corn field and saw me through the stalks of corn. When they finally got there I was still crying dry tears and saying, "I'm stuck in the mud."

"From Full-Time Mom to Reentry Woman," Elaine Pies

Elaine Pies wrote "From Full-Time Mom to Reentry Woman" when she was a thirty-eight-year-old sophomore at Indiana State University. Her purpose was to show other married women returning to school how she and her family adapted to the changes brought about by her going to school. Read her entire essay first, and then examine the sections from the drafts and the explanations that follow.

From Full-Time Mom To Reentry Woman

According to Jeanne Fisher-Thompson and Julie A. Kuhn in an essay on the status of women in higher education, the reentry woman is defined as "any woman who has interrupted her education after high school or during college for at least a few years, and is now reentering or seeking to reenter a college or university for the purpose of completing a degree." After more than twenty years of marriage and seventeen years of child rearing, I am assuming this identity, namely, "reentry woman." As a full-time student at Indiana State University, I find this role to be both challenging and satisfying. In addition, I have discovered that the reentry students are the focus of much research, and researchers have found that campus support groups are needed to meet the financial, emotional, and educational needs of women with families. Without the necessary reassurance that such groups offer, many women drop out of college. But I have found on my own that another support group may be even more important: the family itself. So I feel fortunate to have a very effective support system in my own home. Not only is my husband in favor of my enrollment at ISU, but our four sons share much enthusiasm for my commitment to earning a college degree even though my enrollment makes our home life hectic, to say the least.

My first experience of entering postsecondary education began when I enrolled in the Women's External Degree program at Saint Mary-of-the-Woods College. There was much flexibility in this program due to the off-campus, self-directed study which allowed me to remain in my home. But though I could remain home, taking courses required my family and me to make many adjustments. The time I generally set aside for reading an extra story or watching another television program with the boys was spent in a cloistered area (if such a place can be found in a busy household). My daily chores, which my family had once taken for granted, now seemed important as the heaps of laundry accumulated in the basement while an assignment in "Introduction to Philosophy" couldn't wait. Consequently, the entire family developed a new understanding of domestic chores and also began to realize that Mom was very serious about her new career. They soon learned that study time was sacred and knew I tolerated few interruptions. However, when seven-year-old Zachary brought me a cup of tea while I was muddling my way through my psychology textbook, I couldn't refuse his act of love and took advantage of that intrusion to share a treasured moment with an inquisitive child.

Since I have been reading articles about reentry women, I noticed that child care is cited as a common problem. The year I was taking courses through St. Mary's external degree program, I was also providing day care for three children beside my own. Three of my four were in school most of the day, but with the three I was taking care of, plus my youngest, I still had at least four children around the house all day. But I needed the day care money to pay for my courses, so I had to do the best I could. Each day as I cleared away the remnants of lunch and mopped up rivulets of milk that ran down chair legs, I looked forward to the children's nap time. These peaceful interludes in my hectic days provided times to read assignments or work on papers that always seemed to be due immediately. I was amazed at the amounts of work that I could accomplish before my school-age boys burst through the front door in a flurry of papers and backpacks, signaling the end of naps and study time. What a transition! Within five minutes I went from Cardinal Ratzinger's theological concepts to little boys' hugs and "Cartoon Carnival."

When my youngest son, Daniel, entered grade school, I decided to give up the day care service and enroll at Indiana State University part time, and by the next semester, full-time enrollment seemed appropriate. Again, this change in my status brought many changes for me and my family. Meeting class schedules, preparing assignments daily, and interacting with the younger students were only a few of the adjustments that I had to make. (My family had a different list, of course.)

What a sense of relief I experienced as I learned that most of my professors understood many of the complications that an older student encounters. Just beginning a new semester, a project, or preparing for exams seemed to be enough to stimulate a series of family illnesses or other crises. The possibilities and probabilities of confusion were often overwhelming, but fortunately most of my professors understood when Daniel's virus or Zachary's flu caused me to miss class or to ask for permission to complete an assignment late.

Prior to becoming a student at Indiana State, I had not considered the possibility of individual attention and consideration from the professors. Now, I am experiencing the benefit of instruction and guidance from men and women who will help me to realize my potential. The professors at Indiana State have been, and continue to be, constant sources of motivation and affirmation. Perhaps being a nontraditional student heightens my eagerness to take advantage of the open communications with my professors. How reassuring it is for me to know that I can schedule a conference without difficulty, or that I might drop in during office hours with my questions and problems. Without such contact from the faculty, my education would not be nearly as pleasant.

Now that I have been on campus for three semesters, I also feel accepted by the younger students. Being labeled a "curve buster" and harassed by a few students in a psychology class is the only unpleasant response that I have encountered. This incident occurred on the first day of my first semester on campus. I was the last person to enter the classroom due to a trek across the unfamiliar campus. As I came into the room, one of the young men turned, looked at me, and feigned a headache. "Oh, no, a curve buster. There go our chances of a low curve in here!" he groaned. I didn't understand why he found me threatening. Later, a friend informed me that the younger students know that most older students take their courses very seriously, so this young man assumed I would earn top grades, thus raising the grading scale. As the semester progressed, I began to make friends in this class—even with the young man who didn't want me to be a part of it—and by the end of the term, I was asked to join the study session that was planned before finals.

Although attending college full time can be fulfilling, there are also various discontinuities and role conflicts that reentry women must understand and resolve whenever possible. For example, sometimes I feel guilty and question my ability to fulfill both roles, mother and student. "Am I neglecting my home and family?" Or, "Will I ever be able to prepare for an exam the way that I want to?" Finding time for a seemingly insignificant task, such as pegging Clint's Levis or mending my husband's blue jacket, often seems impossible. However, the little projects seem to be the ones that frequently mean the most to my crew. Obviously, when seventeen-year-old Greg wants a high school term paper typed and needs it the next day, I don't experience guilt for refusing his request. But when he is involved in a school activity, the role of mother dominates the role of student. Besides, the mom in me enjoys seeing the ninth-grade play that Clint directed or discussing Zach's book report more than the student in me enjoys exploring Merton's "modes of adaptation" for Sociology 200. Still, there are times when I'm with the kids that I feel I should be studying and times when I'm studying that I feel guilty for not being with the kids.

Planning and organization are surely important to maintaining a moderate sense of order in the family, and remaining flexible is the only way that I have learned to cope with the stress that is inevitable. Regardless of the course load that I take, Zachary must be taken to the orthodontist or Daniel to his trumpet lessons. Or I have to attend Greg's track meets (I wouldn't miss such an exhilarating experience!) or take the snake (the one Daniel has in a big glass jar) to school for show-and-tell. The list is endless. With so much "running" to be done, contrary to the attitudes of some parents, I am thrilled that my teenage son, Greg, can drive! Now that leaves us to shuffle the family vehicles.

This can present as much stress as Greg's driving alleviates. For example, one day Greg took his father to work and then took the truck to meet his own work schedule, while I drove the car to the college library. So Mark, my husband, was left without a way home from work. Greg and I each thought the other one was to pick Dad up. Consequently, as I drove home the figure that I thought I recognized walking down the road was indeed familiar! Mark had walked most of the four miles home. Why hadn't he "phoned home" and left a message? Between Clint, Zachary, and Daniel talking to their friends, our phone was easily tied up for some time, even with calls supposedly limited to ten minutes each. How fortunate for Mark (and the boys) that the weather was warm and pleasant for his evening stroll.

Such scheduling mishaps seem comical in retrospect, just as unused symphony tickets and declined dinner invitations continue to be a necessity if I am to achieve the quality of education that I desire. Without a doubt, many students in similar situations wonder, "How will we accomplish everything?" When I feel this way, I just think that if parenthood did not help me to learn how to defer gratification, pursuing a college education certainly has.

Despite the upheavals my education sometimes causes, my going to college has also benefitted my sons. As Greg, Clint, Zachary, and Daniel watch my efforts and see my determination to earn a college degree, I believe they will be affected in the best possible ways. Certainly they are responsible for more of the mundane household chores than when I was at home all of the time, and the older boys are becoming very good cooks. All of the boys' work around the house will provide them with practical skills that they will use as adults. Furthermore, they are helping me toward my goal, learning to be responsible for themselves, and continuing to realize the importance of setting goals and getting an education.

For several years before I began my college education in Saint Mary of the Woods College's off-campus program and then at Indiana State University, I wondered if attending college was possible for a full-time mother and a woman in her thirties. Definitely! Even on those days when I don't get all of the assignments handed in, or when spaghetti is on the menu for the third time in one week, my education is worth the effort. The reentry experience provides a sense of accomplishment and creative involvement in my own life that is exceptionally satisfying. Being a college student over thirty is a fantastic part of my life, whether I am referred to as nontraditional student, reentry woman, or my favorite label—Mom.

Revisions of Paragraphs

On the following pages, you can compare Elaine's revisions from one draft to another. Following each are explanations of the changes based on conversations I had with her. As you read and compare the paragraphs, see if you agree with her strategies.

Introduction: Draft 2

According to Jeanne Fisher-Thompson and Julie A. Kuhn in a paper on the status and education of women, the reentry woman is defined as "any woman who has interrupted her education after high school or during college for at least a few years, and is now re-entering or seeking to re-enter a college or university for the purpose of completing a degree." After more than twenty years of marriage and seventeen years of child rearing, I am assuming this identity, namely, "re-entry woman." As a full-time, non-traditional student at Indiana State University, I find this role to be both challenging and satisfying. In addition, I have discovered that the re-entry students are the focus of much research, *and researchers have that* ~~Our various needs—financial,~~ *campus groups that are needed to meet the financial, emotional, and* ~~emotional, and educational— are studied in depth. From this information~~ *educational needs of women with families* ~~one significant fact appears repeatedly.~~ The need for support ~~groups~~

exists, whether advocating revised ~~financial~~ aid or promoting curriculum

~~changes that are~~ more compatible with the routines of women ~~with families~~ *But I have found that another support group may be even more* ~~and jobs. Without the necessary reassurance that such groups offer, many~~ *important - the family itself.* *fortunate that* ~~women drop out of college.~~ So I feel that ~~my good fortune is apparent.~~ I

have very effective support system in my own home. Not only is my

spouse in favor of my enrollment at ISU, but our four sons (10 to 17 years

old) share much enthusiasm for my commitment to earning a college

degree *even though my enrollment makes our homelife hectic, to say the least.*

Draft 3:

According to Jeanne Fisher-Thompson and Julie A. Kuhn in a paper on the status of women in higher education, the reentry woman is defined as "any woman who has interrupted her education after high school or during college for at least a few years, and is now reentering or seeking to reenter a college or university for the purpose of completing a degree." After more than twenty years of marriage and seventeen years of child rearing, I am assuming this identity, namely, "reentry woman". As a full-time student at Indiana State University, I find this role to be both challenging and satisfying. In addition, I have discovered that reentry students are the focus of much research, and researchers have found that campus support groups are needed to meet the financial, emotional, and educational needs of women with families. Without the necessary reassurance that such groups offer, many women drop out of college. But I have found that another support group may be even more important: the family itself. So I feel fortunate that I have a very effective support system in my own home. Not only is my husband in favor of my enrollment at ISU, but our four sons (ten to seventeen years old) share much enthusiasm for my commitment to earning a college degree even though my enrollment makes our home life hectic at times, to say the least.

Elaine does not make major changes from the second to final draft of her introduction, but the changes are important. In the first sentence, she merely changes a couple of words to make the sentence read more smoothly, but in the middle of the paragraph, she combines a lot of information on support groups into one sentence. However, the two most important changes come at the end of the introduction. First, she adds the sentence stating that she has discovered the family may be the most important support group. Second, by adding the point on how hectic school has made her family's life, she expands the thesis to cover much of what the paper is about.

Third Paragraph: Draft 1

As I continued to read articles about the re-entry woman, I noticed that child care was cited as the most common concern among this group. Being enrolled in an external degree program alleviated that worry for me. Moreover, I could

? continue as (care giver) for other children. That service pro-

vided an income which paid much of my tuition. Each day as I

cleared away the remnants of lunch, and mopped up rivulets

of milk that ran down chair legs, I looked forward to the

children's nap time. These peaceful interludes in my hectic

days provided times to read assignments or work on papers

that always seemed to be due immediately. I was amazed at

the amounts of work that I could accomplish before the older

children burst through the front door in a flurry of papers and

backpacks, signaling the end of naps and study time. What a

transition! Within five minutes I went from Cardinal Ratzin-

ger's theological concepts to little boy's hugs and Cartoon

Carnival.

make clear how many kids I took care of and how many were at home at once

Draft 2:

The year I was taking courses through St. Mary's external degree program, I was also providing day care for three children beside my own. Three of my four were in school most of the day, but with the three I was taking care of, plus my youngest, I still had at least four children around the house all day. But I needed the day care money to pay for my courses, so I had to do the best I could. Each day as I cleared away the remnants of lunch and mopped up rivulets of milk that ran down chair legs, I looked forward to the children's nap time. These peaceful interludes in my hectic days provided times to read assignments or work on papers that always seemed to be due immediately. I was amazed at the amounts of work that I could accomplish before my school-age boys burst through the front door in a flurry of papers and backpacks, signaling the end of naps and study time. What a transition! Within five minutes, I went from Cardinal Ratzinger's theological concepts to little boys' hugs and "Cartoon Carnival."

Comparing these two paragraphs, you can see Elaine making notes to herself to revise the paragraph so that it is clear how she was earning money providing day care and how many children she had at home at a time. In the first draft, the term *care giver* is confusing, and readers can't tell how many of her children Elaine is taking care of. She knew how many, but she also knew her audience would need to know.

Also, she cuts her first sentence completely. Why? At the time the paragraph refers to, she had not yet begun to read articles about reentry women. She also felt that at this point her paper was focused primarily on her experience. But if you look back to the final draft, you will see that the sentence is put back in. There, however, she revises it to make clear that she only began reading the articles recently. In addition, though the paragraph still focuses on her experience, the first sentence indicates that other reentry women are concerned about child care, too. Thus, putting the sentence back in enables Elaine to more effectively follow her purpose: to show other reentry women that others share their problems. In short, the first sentence helps to show that Elaine's experience is typical.

Paragraph 4: Draft 1, Cut from following drafts

The new role that I found so stimulating also required me to carefully consider the projects that I volunteered for or the sewing jobs that I accepted. As an "at-home-mom," I was frequently asked to mend costumes, cushions, or curtains for one or another of the teachers at the school that my sons attended. I suppose "yes" had become a conditioned response. Thus, when Mr. Nation (the principal) asked me if I would mend an article for the children, I said, "Certainly." The article was delivered in a bag;

however, it was not the usual brown bag from our neighborhood grocery but an ominously large, black trash bag! The object of my stitchery was a parachute—a massive, survival orange parachute that the children used for playground activities! It took more than an hour to locate all of the tears in the fabric. Just the thought of the precious nap times that the mending would consume impressed the importance of investigating a request more thoroughly before committing myself to volunteer my time now that I was taking courses.

Though this paragraph is very specific and tells an interesting story relating to Elaine's thesis, it was cut because the example was not typical enough, and she had already made the point on balancing home life and off-campus courses. She also needed to get on to the discussion of enrolling in Indiana State because on-campus study would be more typical of the experience of other reentry women. So in cutting the paragraph, Elaine again kept her purpose and audience in mind.

Writing Assignments

1. Compare a draft of your own with a final copy of the same paper. Write a paper describing the changes you made and your reasons for making them.

2. Revise a paper you have previously written that you feel could have been better with revision.

unit four

Essays for Reading

The following essays—one written by student Marcia Lightle, the other by professional writer Donald Murray—both discuss revision. Both writers, student and professional, argue the value of revision while showing how they go about it. As you read through the essays, compare what these writers say to the discussions in Chapter 11 and to your own habits of revision.

If at First You Don't Succeed . . .
Marcia Lightle (sophomore)

You have spent several hours writing a paper, and you think your essay sounds pretty good. Are you finished? If the final copy is going to be more than just "pretty good," then you must be willing to take the next step in the writing process: revision. Revision is not just copying the words from a messy draft onto a fresh page; that is transcription. Revision is the step in which you read what you have written, separate the good from the bad, smooth out the wrinkles, and consider what changes you can make to improve the paper.

Even the best writers understand that their first drafts are not their best drafts. James A. Michener, the famous author of historical novels, says of his craft, "I do not consider myself a good writer. Anyone who wants reassurance of this should read one of my first drafts. But I'm one of the worlds great rewriters." Michener's assessment of himself should tell you that any word you write can be changed.

Sure, it is easy to fall in love with a first draft. Often when I am enthusiastic about a topic, I believe that all of my ideas are worth putting on paper and I end up with a tangle of information. On the other hand, when I struggle for days with a topic, I become frustrated, trying to pull together a lot of loose ends. In either case, in revision I try to make sure that my ideas form a single thread running throughout the paper.

When I get tired of drafting or revising, I set the paper aside. There is nothing wrong with needing to put a paper down for a while to set your ideas in order. Do anything: Go for a walk, talk on the phone, or work on other homework. If you have the time, do not look at the paper until the next day. If you are pressed for time, try to take at least an hour break. Come back to your work when you have a fresh perspective.

Why does a break make so much difference? Have you ever read over one of your graded essay tests and wondered how you could have written it? When

I have, I found that part of the problem was that I couldn't revise because a test is a high-pressure situation with only time to think about the questions. Writing a rough draft is something like taking an essay test, but with writing you have a chance to take your time and let the ideas simmer before you put them down, and then you can revise your draft before anyone reads it. Keep in mind that a rough draft is just that: rough. It will take polishing in order to shine.

When I revise, I read the paper twice. During the first reading, I focus on my thesis, main ideas in paragraphs, and supporting ideas. While taking a break from reading, often I think of new ideas that I can work into an existing paragraph or that could be an idea developed in its own paragraph. I also consider these ideas and other examples in relation to my thesis.

Sometimes you will read a revised draft and notice that your ideas have changed the main idea from the original thesis. There is nothing wrong as long as you change the thesis so that it is consistent with the supporting ideas when you write the final draft. You might not even discover your real thesis until you reach the conclusion and "see the light." If this happens, go back to the first paragraph, insert the new thesis, and then read the paper through, checking to see that all your supporting ideas are focused and "flow" coherently.

Does all this revision sound like a lot of work? Revision is work, but your effort will pay off in a polished final essay and probably in a high grade. I wrote several drafts of this essay before I got to the one you are reading. When you write an essay, think of yourself as a writer. You create the essay; it is your responsibility to see that what you put on the page is what you want the reader to understand. Remember that you can have control over your writing; use revision to your advantage to maintain that control. You have a right to be a perfectionist.

Questions for Study and Discussion

1. Lightle begins with a definition of revision in which she says what revision is not. What is the difference between revision and transcription?

2. How does Lightle define revision? How is her definition similar to or different from the definition in Chapter 11?

3. Why do you think Lightle includes the quotation from James Michener, the historical novelist?

4. What difficulties does Lightle face when she is enthusiastic about a topic? How does she overcome them?

5. Why does Lightle recommend taking breaks when revising?

6. According to Lightle, writing a draft is similar to writing an essay on a test. To what extent do you agree or disagree?

7. How many times does Lightle read her paper during revision? What does she focus on during each reading?

8. What does Lightle say to do when you find that your thesis has changed during the draft?

9. What does Lightle mean when she says "think of yourself as a writer"?

10. Freewrite a paragraph explaining how your revision process is similar to or different from Lightle's? Then revise the paragraph.

The Maker's Eye: Revising Your Own Manuscript
Donald Murray (professional)

When the beginning writer completes his first draft, he usually reads it through to correct typographical errors and considers the job of writing done. When the professional writer completes his first draft, he usually feels he is at the start of the writing process. Now that he has a draft, he can begin writing.

The difference in attitude is the difference between amateur and professional, inexperience and experience, journeyman and craftsman. Peter F. Drucker, the prolific business writer, for example, calls his first draft "the zero draft"—after that he can start counting. Most productive writers share the feeling that the first draft—and most of those that follow—is an opportunity to discover what they have to say and how they can best say it.

To produce a progression of drafts, each of which says more and says it better, the writer has to develop a special reading skill. In school we are taught to read what is on the page. We try to comprehend what the author has said, what he meant, and what are the implications of his words.

The writer of such drafts must be his own best enemy. He must accept the criticism of others and be even more suspicious of it. He cannot depend on others. He must detach himself from his own page so that he can apply both his caring and his craft to his own work.

Detachment is not easy. Science fiction writer Ray Bradbury supposedly puts each manuscript away for a year and then rereads it as a stranger. Not many writers can afford the time to do this. We must read when our judgment may be at its worst, when we are close to the euphoric moment of creation. The writer "should be critical of everything that seems to him most delightful in his style," advises novelist Nancy Hale. "He should excise what he most admires, because he wouldn't thus admire it if he weren't . . . in a sense protecting it from criticism."

The writer must learn to protect himself from his own ego, when it takes the form of uncritical pride or uncritical self-destruction. As poet John Ciardi points out, "the last act of the writing must be to become one's own reader. It is, I suppose, a schizophrenic process, to begin passionately and to end critically, to begin hot and to end cold; and more important, to be passion-hot and critic-cold at the same time."

Just as dangerous as the protective writer is the despairing one, who thinks everything he does is awful, terrible, dreadful. If he is to publish, he must save what is effective on his page while he cuts away what doesn't work. The writer must hear and respect his own voice.

Remember how each craftsman you have seen—the carpenter eyeing the level of a shelf, the mechanic listening to the motor—takes the instinctive step back. This is what the writer has to do when he reads his own work. "The writer must survey his work critically, coolly, as though he were a stranger to it," says children's book writer Eleanor Estes. "He must be willing to prune, expertly and hard-heartedly. At the end of each revision, a manuscript may look like a battered old hive, worked over, torn apart, pinned together, added to, deleted from, words changed and words changed back. Yet the book must maintain its original freshness and spontaneity."

It is far easier for most beginning writers to understand the need for rereading and rewriting than it is to understand how to go about it. The published writer doesn't necessarily break down the various stages of rewriting and editing, he just goes ahead and does it. One of our most prolific fiction writers, Anthony Burgess, says, "I might revise a page twenty times." Short story and children's writer Ronald Dahl states, "By the time I'm nearing the end of a story, the first part will have been reread and altered and corrected at least 150 times. . . . Good writing is essentially rewriting. I am positive of this."

There is nothing virtuous in the rewriting process. It is simply an essential condition of life for most writers. There are writers who do very little rewriting, mostly because they have the capacity and experience to create and review a large number of invisible drafts in their minds before they get to the page. And many writers perform all of the tasks of revision simultaneously, page by page, rather than draft by draft. But it is still possible to break down the process of rereading one's own work into the sequence most published writers follow and which the beginning writer should follow as he studies his own page.

Many writers at first just scan their manuscript, reading as quickly as possible for problems of subject and form. In this way, they stand back from the more technical details of language so they can spot any weaknesses in content or in organization. When the writer reads his manuscript, he is usually looking for seven elements.

The first is *subject*. Do you have anything to say? If you are lucky, you will find that indeed you do have something to say, perhaps a little more than you expected. If the subject is not clear, or if it is not yet limited or defined enough for you to handle, don't go on. What you have to say is always more important than how you say it.

The next point to check is *audience*. It is true that you should write primarily for yourself, in the sense that you should be true to yourself. But the aim of writing is communication, not just self-expression. You should, in reading your piece, ask yourself if there is an audience for what you have written, if anyone will need or enjoy what you have to say.

Form should then be considered after audience. Form, or genre, is the vehicle which will carry what you have to say to your audience, and it should grow out of your subject. If you have a character, your subject may grow into a short story, a magazine profile, a novel, a biography, or a play. It depends on what you have to say and to whom you wish to say it. When you reread your own manuscript, you must ask yourself if the form is suitable, if it works, and if it will carry your meaning to your reader.

Once you have the appropriate form, look at the *structure,* the order of what you have to say. Every good piece of writing is built on a solid framework of logic or argument or narrative or motivation; it is a line which runs through the entire piece of writing and holds it together. If you read your own manuscript and cannot spot this essential thread, stop writing until you have found something to hold your writing together.

The manuscript which has order must also have *development.* Each part of it must be built in a way that will prepare the reader for the next part. Description, documentation, action, dialogue, metaphor—these and many other devices flesh out the skeleton so that the reader will be able to understand what is written. How much development? That's like asking how much lipstick or how much garlic. It depends on the girl or on the casserole. This is the question that the writer will be answering as he reads his piece of writing through from beginning to end, and answering it will lead him to the sixth element.

The writer must be sure of his *dimensions.* This means that there should be something more than structure and development, that there should be a pleasing proportion between all of the parts. You cannot decide on a dimension without seeing all of the parts of writing together. You have to examine each section of the writing in its relationship to all of the other sections.

Finally, the writer has to listen for *tone.* Any piece of writing is held together by that invisible force, the writer's voice. Tone is his style, tone is all that is on the page and off the page, tone is grace, wit, anger—the spirit which drives a piece of writing forward. Look back to those manuscripts you most admire, and you will discover that there is a coherent tone, an authoritative voice holding the whole thing together.

When the writer feels that he has a draft which has subject, audience, form, structure, development, dimension, and tone, then he is ready to begin the careful process of line-by-line editing. Each line, each word has to be right. As Paul Gallico has said, ". . . every successful writer is primarily a good editor."

Now the writer reads his own copy with infinite care. He often reads aloud, calling on his ear's experience with language. Does this sound right—or this? He reads and listens and revises, back and forth from eye to page to ear to page. I find I must do this careful editing at short runs, fifteen or twenty minutes, or I become too kind with myself.

Slowly the writer moves from word to word, looking through the word to see the subject. Good writing is, in a sense, invisible. It should enable the reader to see the subject, not the writer. Every word should be true—true to what the writer has to say. And each word must be precise in its relation to the words which have gone before and the words which will follow.

This sounds tedious, but it isn't. Making something right is immensely satisfying, and the writer who once was lost in a swamp of potentialities now has the chance to work with the most technical skills of language. And even in the process of the most careful editing, there is the joy of language. Words have double meanings, even triple and quadruple meanings. Each word has its own tone, its opportunity for connotation and denotation and nuance. And when you connect words, there is always the chance of the sudden insight, the unexpected clarification.

The maker's eye moves back and forth from word to phrase to sentence to paragraph to sentence to phrase to word. He looks at his sentences for variety and balance in form and structure, and at the interior of the paragraph for coherence, unity, and emphasis. He plays with figurative language, decides to repeat or not, to create a parallelism for emphasis. He works over his copy until he achieves a manuscript which appears effortless to the reader.

I learned something about this process when I first wore bifocals. I thought that when I was editing I was working line by line. But I discovered that I had to buy reading (or, in my case, editing) glasses, even though the bottom sections of my bifocals have a greater expanse of glass than ordinary glasses. While I am editing, my eyes are unconsciously flicking back and forth across the whole page, or back to another page, or forward to another page. The limited bifocal view through the lower half of my glasses is not enough. Each line must be seen in its relationship to every other line.

When does this process end? Most writers agree with the great Russian novelist Tolstoy, who said, "I scarcely ever reread my published writings, but if by chance I come across a page, it always strikes me: all this must be rewritten; this is how I should have written it."

The maker's eye is never satisfied, for he knows that each word in his copy is tentative. Writing, to the writer, is alive, something that is full of potential and alternatives, something which can grow beyond its own dream. The writer reads to discover what he has said—and then to say it better.

A piece of writing is never finished. It is delivered to a deadline, torn out of the typewriter on demand, sent off with a sense of frustration and incompleteness. Just as the writer knows he must stop avoiding writing and write, he also knows he must send his copy off to be published, although it is not quite right yet—if only he had another couple of days, just another run at it, perhaps . . .

Questions for Study and Discussion

1. What, according to Murray, is the difference between beginning writers and professional writers?

2. What is the purpose of the first draft for professionals?

3. How are writers similar to such craftsmen as carpenters and mechanics?

4. Briefly summarize Murray's definitions of *subject, audience, form, structure, development, dimensions,* and *tone.*

5. How do Murray's definitions relate to what you have learned about purpose, role, and audience?

6. How does Murray say writers must read their drafts?

7. What did Murray say he first learned from wearing bifocals?

8. To what extent does Marcia Lightle, the author of the previous essay, subscribe to what Murray says?

9. Compare Murray's ideas on revision to the revisions you saw in the student revisions in Chapter 12. Do the students seem to follow strategies Murray recommends?

10. Write a brief paragraph in which you explain how your writing, as Murray says, "is never finished."

unit five
Editing

In editing your writing, you probably have looked into this unit earlier, either at your teacher's request or on your own. Although you will do some editing as you draft and revise, editing is usually the last step of the writing process. Thus, this is the final unit of the book. When you are editing, your goal is make sure all the language follows standard-English forms. What is standard English? Before we can answer that question, let's look at forms of English that are not standard.

The English language is spoken in many different ways around the world. Even here in the United States, groups of people speak the language somewhat differently. The most obvious differences are in pronunciation. As you probably know, a person from New York does not pronounce words the same way a person from Georgia does. Similarly, some of the forms used by different groups will vary. For example, a person from a rural area of the Midwest might say, "The workers *was* tired at the end of the day." A young urban person might say, "The workers *be* tired at the end of the day." In contrast, other people would say, "The workers *were* tired." Similarly, working-class people might say, "He *don't* seem to be a good candidate for mayor," or "It *don't* look like the sun is going to come out today," while other people would say, "He *doesn't* seem" or "It *doesn't* look."

The way a group of people talks is called a *dialect*, and groups of people who speak the same dialect make up *speech communities* (see Paul Roberts's essay at the end of this unit). Dialects can be determined by various factors: class, geography, race, nationality. Because the United States has many groups of people, there are many American dialects of English. The pronunciations and forms in these dialects are not so different that people from different groups cannot understand each other. For example, you may think people from a certain group sound a bit funny, but if you think you can't understand them, you probably are not trying very hard. It is wrong to think that the dialect of others, or your own, is just a form of bad grammar and that people who speak it are inferior. If you are aware that you speak a dialect, your goal should not be to change the way you speak, for when you are around your family and the people you have grown up with, you will need the dialect to remain part of the group. Rather, you should keep the dialect for situations when you need it, but you should also learn to speak and write the standard English you will need in college and on the job.

Standard English is the language used in government, business, school, and the news media. It is also the language of power. Some linguists argue that standard English allows for better communication and that it is capable of expressing more-complex ideas. Other linguists say that all dialects communicate equally, that all are just as capable of expressing complex ideas, and that standard English became the standard form of the language because it is the version of English used by the upper-middle and upper classes. Whatever the case, the rules of standard English are not written in stone by some supreme being running the universe, and some people have succeeded quite well without mastering standard English. Standard English, however, is very powerful because generally it is used by the people with the best jobs and the most influence in the country. It would be nice if we could all use our own dialects. Unfortunately, if we want successful careers, we have to use standard English.

As we discuss editing in this chapter, we won't be looking so much at errors as we will be looking at nonstandard forms. Errors are errors only when you are trying to use one dialect and you mistakenly use a form of another. For example, in the working-class neighborhood in New Jersey where I grew up, it is common to address a group of people with the pronoun *youse*. In standard English, the pronoun form for addressing a group is *you*, without the *s*. If I were writing a report to other professors at my university, I would be in error if I addressed them as *youse* because I would be using a nonstandard form in a piece of writing that should be written in standard English, the language of colleges and universities.

As a beginning writer, particularly if you have grown up with a nonstandard dialect, you may find editing one of the most bothersome parts of writing. You finish an essay, you believe it develops a thesis, you feel it is thoughtful and interesting, but you worry that you have used nonstandard forms that could distract the reader from getting your point. While organizing and presenting interesting ideas are the most important elements of writing, a piece of writing that is full of nonstandard forms will not be very effective.

One simple way to edit is by sound. Read your paper aloud, listening for words or sentences that do not sound right. For instance, suppose you wrote, "The U.S. Constitution give us the right to vote." Reading this sentence aloud, you would probably catch the error because in speech you probably say, or hear others say, "Constitution gives." Read your paper aloud at least once during editing, but be sure to read exactly what is on the page because sometimes we read sentences as they should sound rather than as they actually appear.

Though editing by sound is helpful, some errors cannot be heard. Read this sentence aloud: The schools curriculum attracted me. If you realized that there should be an apostrophe before the final *s* in *schools*, you caught that error by sight because there is no difference in the way you hear the plural form *schools* and the possessive form *school's*. Another common error you cannot hear is the confusion of words that sound the same but have a different spelling and meaning: *do/due, for/fore/four, its/it's, know/no, to/too/two,* and *their/there/they're,* to name a few. When you edit, read the paper two or three times *looking* for errors that need to be seen.

You need not be a grammar whiz to edit nonstandard forms. First of all, you probably do not make as many errors as you think you do. Most beginners tend to have trouble with only two or three forms, but because they use each one over and over, they feel as if they have made many errors. This unit covers common lapses from standard English and gives you enough background in grammar so that you can learn to reduce, if not eliminate, nonstandard forms. Remember, however, that while learning to write standard English takes time, if you keep an error log (as was suggested in Chapter 1) and if you review the appropriate sections of this unit each time you identify nonstandard forms in your writing, you will gradually eliminate them.

chapter thirteen
Editing Fragments

If you have read Chapters 9 and 10, you already know quite a bit about sentences. The goals of those chapters were to show you how sentences work and how to write clear, well-constructed sentences—something all writers, from beginners to experts, want to do. Unfortunately, though, sentences sometimes are written in nonstandard English without your realizing it. These sentences may even be clear and smoothly written but may not follow standard English rules. The goal of this chapter is to show you how to identify one type of nonstandard sentence—the fragment—and how to edit fragments to follow the forms of standard English.

A *fragment* is any group of words that cannot stand alone as a sentence but that is punctuated as a sentence. Fragments can distract readers to the point where they cannot make sense of what you are trying to say. In Chapter 9, you learned many ways to describe sentences. Before we discuss how to edit fragments, we will review the basic sentence parts.

Subjects and Verbs

As you will remember, standard English sentences must have at least one subject and one verb, though many have more than one of each. Knowing how to identify subjects and verbs is valuable because it helps you to make nonstandard sentences standard. The exercises and discussion that follow will help you become skillful at identifying subjects and verbs.

Subjects

Exercise 13.1

Fill in the blank spaces with any words that fit. Don't worry about having the "correct" answer; just add something that fits.

1. _____ earn very high salaries.
2. _____ is the President of the United States.
3. In the 1960s, _____ helped lead the civil rights movement for black people in America.
4. During World War II, _____ was the evil leader of Germany.
5. _____ is one of the best singers I ever heard.
6. _____ goes swimming as much as she can as soon as_____ gets hot.
7. _____ does not like winter in Minnesota because _____ falls almost every week and _____ often drops to below zero.
8. _____ won the TV ratings poll last week, but _____ think that _____ is a better show.
9. _____ celebrate the Fourth of July each year, and in many towns across the country _____ fill the sky with bright colors and loud noise.
10. _____ and _____ were the two best Presidents this country ever had.
11. _____ and _____ like to dance, but _____ , _____ and _____ would rather just listen to the music.
12. _____ should be aware of the dangers of drugs because _____ can kill.
13. _____ , _____ , and _____ are my favorite foods.
14. _____ loves listening to the Rolling Stones, but _____ and _____ prefer younger groups.

In filling in the blanks, you added the subjects of the sentences. Let's review the definition of subject presented in Chapter 9:

The subject of a sentence is the person, place, thing, idea, or action that does something, that performs an action. For example: The *Los Angeles Lakers* won two straight NBA championships in 1987 and 1988. (The *Lakers* did something.) The subject can also be the person, place, thing, or idea that something is said about. For example, *Jogging* is good for the lungs. (Something is said about the action of jogging.)

Every word that you put in the blanks was a subject. Thus, either it was doing something or something was being said about it. For example, if you filled in a woman's name in the first blank of example #6, the woman does something: goes swimming. If you wrote *the weather* or *the temperature* in the second blank, you filled in a thing that does something: gets hot. Compare these subjects to the one in number 2. When you filled in the name of the President, you were filling in a person that something was being said about. Although he is not doing anything in the sentence, something is being said about him. Identifying subjects may seem fairly easy, but because it is so important in editing sentences, you should practice it a little more.

Exercise 13.2

Underline each subject in the following sentences. If a subject is performing an action, put an A above it. If something is being said about a subject, put an S above it. Remember that a sentence can have more than one subject.

1. Lance chose to go to the local community college even though he knew he could get into the state university.
2. He figured he could get a good job with an Associate's degree, and the community college was less expensive.
3. Computer games can be challenging and fun.
4. But young people should not neglect their schoolwork to play them.
5. Mary and Elliot purchased an older home, which they restored to its original condition.
6. The home was a bargain, but it needed a lot of work.
7. After a year of renovation, the home looked beautiful.
8. Some people believe that old homes are built better than new ones.
9. Homemade ice cream is very easy to make if you use an electric ice cream maker, but few people make it anymore.
10. Honduras, El Salvador, and Nicaragua are countries few Americans ever thought about before the late 1980s.

Exercise 13.3

The following sentences are longer and more difficult than those in the previous exercises. Next to each is a number telling you how many subjects it contains. Underline all the subjects in each.

1. (1) With a wingspread of up to six inches, the Polyphemus is one of the few huge American silk moths, much larger than, say, a giant or tiger swallowtail butterfly.

    Annie Dillard

2. (4) My remarks about society may have seemed too pessimistic, but I believe that society can only represent a fragment of the human spirit, and that another fragment can only get expressed through art.

    E. M. Forster

3. (3) I told her that, in his autobiography, Mahatma Gandhi stated that eating meat made people lustful.

    Paul Theroux

4. (4) Coffee, tea, cocoa, and cola drinks are all drugs.

    Adam Smith

Exercise 13.4

The following paragraph, by Theodore H. White, describes John F. Kennedy's arrival at the television studio for his 1960 presidential debate with Richard Nixon. Underline all the subjects you can find.

Senator Kennedy arrived about fifteen minutes after the Vice-President; sat for the camera; and his advisors inspected him, then declared they were satisfied. The producer made a remark about the glare of the senator's white shirt, and Kennedy sent an aide back to his hotel to bring back a blue one, into which he just changed before air time. The men took their seats; the tally lights on the cameras blinked red to show they were live now.

Verbs

Now that you have reviewed subjects, we will work on verbs, an equally important part of the sentence to know as you edit fragments.

Exercise 13.5

Fill in the blanks in the sentences below.

1. Jesus Christ _____ in Bethlehem.
2. Roger Maris _____ 61 home runs in 1961 to set a major league record, surpassing Babe Ruth, who _____ 60 in 1927.
3. A new house today _____ much more than it _____ five years ago.
4. Antonio _____ an essay for his history class, and his teacher _____ it.
5. Mike Tyson _____ the youngest man to win the heavyweight boxing championship.
6. Amelia Earhart _____ planes great distances at a time when few women _____ the opportunity to become pilots.
7. Jessica _____ to school in the morning, _____ a part-time job all afternoon, and _____ each night.
8. To make money, some kids _____ lawns in the summer, _____leaves in the fall, and _____ snow in the winter.
9. I _____ that students must _____ to earn good grades in college.
10. Our psychology class _____ Sigmund Freud, who_____ that sexual urges control much of human development and behavior.

You probably realized that you have filled in the verbs in these sentences. As you remember, verbs are the words in a sentence that show either action—what the subject is doing—or a state of being—what the subject is or was. Compare the following sentences to grasp this difference. The verb is italicized in each:

Action: Alice Walker *writes* novels. Being: Alice Walker *is* a talented and respected novelist.

In the first sentence, Walker writes, and writing is an action. The second sentence tells what she is, rather than showing an action she does. Like subjects, verbs are a necessary part of each sentence: Each sentence must have at least one subject and at least one verb, even though many sentences have more. Knowing how to identify subjects and verbs, as mentioned before, will help you to write standard English sentences and to edit fragments. For now, get some more practice in identifying verbs. Go back to the exercises in which you underlined subjects and put two lines under each verb.

Editing Fragments

When you can identify subjects and verbs, you should not have much difficulty editing sentence fragments. A sentence fragment is a group of words that is punctuated with a period as if it were a complete sentence. Actually, it is only part of a sentence—thus the name fragment. We often speak in fragments, even when using standard English. For example, if a friend asks where you had lunch and you answer, "At the cafeteria," you are answering in a sentence fragment. However, in the context of your conversation, the fragment makes sense. If you were writing a letter and wanted to tell a friend where you had lunch, to make sense you would have to write, "I ate at the cafeteria." Now, with the subject *I* and the verb *ate,* you would have a complete sentence. Sometimes fragments are used in advertisements, but in most kinds of writing, fragments prevent the reader from understanding your meaning.

Exercise 13.6

The following groups of words are punctuated as sentences. Some of the groups have subjects and verbs and could therefore be sentences; others are either missing a subject or verb, so they are fragments. In the space next to each, write S if the group of words is a sentence, and write F if the group of words is a fragment. Remember, a sentence will have both a subject and a verb.

1. After playing cards until late in the evening._____
2. George McGovern, a former presidential candidate._____
3. Computer word processing is becoming the most common way to write in the business world._____
4. An earthquake registering 5.6 on the Richter scale._____

5. Sandra Day O'Connor, the first female Supreme Court justice. _____
6. Sunday Silence won the Kentucky Derby in 1989._____
7. Using the writing process makes writing less difficult._____
8. To edit sentence fragments._____
9. To shop in Greeley's Corner Market is to take a step back in time. _____
10. Buying a new car with no money down._____

If you identified the fragments correctly, you identified groups of words that do not have both a subject and a verb; therefore, they do not make a complete statement that makes sense. They might have a potential subject or a potential verb, but without both, they are fragments. Thus, they need to have words added to become sentences.

Take number 10, for example. When we read it, we want to ask, "Who is buying a new car with no money down" or "What about buying a new car with no money down?" If we add a few words, we can answer these questions and make complete sentences:

Annette is buying a new car with no money down.

Now the sentence shows action with *Annette* as the subject and *is buying* as the verb. Or we could answer our second question by making *buying* the subject:

Buying a new car with no money down is difficult to do.

Now we have added the verb *is,* saying something about the subject and making a complete sentence. In correcting the fragment, we changed a phrase to a sentence. As you learned in Chapter 9, any group of words that lacks both a subject and verb is called a *phrase.* There are several kinds of phrases. When punctuated as sentences, phrases are fragments.

Participle Phrases as Fragments

The fragment that we edited above resulted from the writer punctuating an *-ing* phrase (technically called a participle phrase) as a sentence. Similarly, beginning writers sometimes punctuate an *-ed* phrase (a past-participle phrase) as a sentence. Compare these fragments:

Earning a degree in business.
Confused by the many road signs.

As you saw in the example on buying a car, editing an *-ing* fragment was fairly easy. In the first example, we just added a subject and the helping verb *is* to the beginning of the fragment. In the second, *Buying* became the subject and we added the verb *can be*. We can also edit an *-ing* fragment a third way: by adding it to another sentence before or after it in the paper. Suppose the student had written:

Annette got herself deeply in debt. *Buying a new car with no money down.* She must pay nearly $300 a month.

In the context of the other two sentences, the fragment makes sense, so it is more difficult to detect. You must be very careful when looking for fragments. Once you identified this one, it would be very easy to fix. Compare these edited versions:

Annette got herself deeply in debt, *buying a new car with no money down.* She must pay nearly $300 a month.
Annette got herself deeply in debt. *Buying a new car with no money down,* she must pay nearly $300 a month.
Annette got herself deeply in debt. *Because she bought a new car with no money down,* she must pay nearly $300 a month.

When you look for *-ing* fragments, remember three points:

1. Words ending in *-ing* can be the subject if there is another verb form following:

   Exercising regularly *requires* discipline.

2. Words ending in *-ing* can be the verb only if a helping verb comes before it (see Chapter 15 for more on helping verbs):

   Jimmy Connors already *was playing* tennis when he was four years old.

3. Phrases with *-ing* words can modify part or all of the sentence:

   Rebelling against England, *the American colonies declared* their independence in 1776.

Exercise 13.7

Some of the following items are fragments with *-ing* words. On a separate sheet of paper, correct each one using all three ways discussed. For the third way, you will have to write your own sentences. If an item is correct, write down just its subject and verb.

1. Going to a carnival.
2. Living only in Australia, koalas resemble teddy bears.
3. Casey Stengel was one of major league baseball's most successful managers, guiding the New York Yankees to ten pennants in sixteen years.
4. Earning a salary that will enable you to support a family.
5. Drinking milk.
6. Sleeping through his alarm, Greg missed his morning class.

Editing fragments with words ending in *-ed* is similar to editing fragments with *-ing* words, but there are only two ways to do so. Examine the fragment and the two corrected versions that follow:

Anthony had never driven in a large city before. *Confused by the many road signs.* He became hopelessly lost.

Anthony had never driven in a large city before. *He was confused by the many road signs.* He became hopelessly lost.

Anthony had never driven in a large city before. *Confused by the many road signs, he became hopelessly lost.*

In the first correction, we added the subject *he* and the helping verb *was* to the fragment. In the second, we connected the fragment to another sentence. We could not, however, make the fragment a subject, as we did with *-ing* phrases, and then add a verb because the sentence thus made would not be standard English:

Confused by the many road signs made him hopelessly lost.

We may be able to figure out what this attempted sentence means, but we know that it does not sound right.

Exercise 13.8

On a separate sheet of paper, correct each *-ed* fragment using both ways you have learned. For the second way, you will have to write your own sentence and connect the fragment to it. If a sentence is correct, write down its subject and verb.

1. Tired from a long day at work.
2. The small child, frightened by a large dog, ran home crying.
3. Covered with snow, the woods looked quiet and peaceful.
4. Filled with money.
5. The old house was painted a crazy shade of blue.
6. Cleaned thoroughly with hot, soapy water.
7. Converted into apartments that were rented to college students wanting to live near campus.
8. Divorced for the second time in five years, Michael was disillusioned with marriage.
9. Joshua lay down, tired from a long day of work.
10. Discovered in 1492 by Christopher Columbus, an Italian explorer sailing under the flag of Spain.

Exercise 13.9

In this paragraph, correct any *-ing* or *-ed* fragments you find by attaching them to the sentence before or after or by adding a subject and helping verb.

At one time, the sea was as challenging and mysterious as outer space is today. People feared that ships that ventured too far would fall off the end of the earth. Disappearing forever. Not convinced that the earth was flat. Columbus decided to sail west. Looking for a route from Europe to India. Scoffed at by the Italian government, Columbus appealed to Queen Isabella of Spain. She supplied him with three small ships and crews. Believing in his courage, if not in his wisdom. Having faced many hardships along the way but assuring himself a place in history. Columbus, as we know, reached America, not India.

Noun Phrases as Fragments

Sometimes a fragment occurs when the proposed sentence has a noun and a few other words that modify it. Together these words make up a *noun phrase*. For example:

> The new girl from Texas
> The tall man in the fur hat
> A large red barn
> Lonny Duchamp, the best athlete on campus
> A car that breaks down often

In the context of a paragraph, such phrases can mistakenly be punctuated as sentences, but they are not sentences because they do not have both a subject and a verb. There are three ways to correct this type of fragment:

> 1. Add a verb after the noun: The new girl *is* from Texas. (*girl* is the subject, and *is* is the verb)
> 2. Add a subject and verb before the noun: *Andrea dislikes* the new girl from Texas. (*Andrea* is the subject, *dislikes* is the verb, and *the girl* becomes the object of Andrea's dislike)
> 3. Connect the noun to the previous sentence, using a comma: *Yesterday, the class met Felicia Alvarez,* the new girl from Texas.

Exercise 13.10

Correct the fragments that are noun phrases. Be sure to use each of the three ways discussed. If a sentence is not a fragment, put an S next to it and underline the subject and verb.

1. A large snake lying in the grass.
2. The cups filled to the brim with steaming coffee.
3. A roaring thunderstorm late in the evening.
4. Edna Ferber, an American novelist.
5. The greatest hockey player of all time.
6. The roaring waters of Niagara Falls indicate nature's power.
7. A loaf of stale bread and three slices of ham.
8. The jockey guiding his mount into the starting gate.

9. A burnt piece of steak.
10. A holiday celebrated by most Christian people.

Dependent Clauses as Fragments

The fragments you have just worked on were all phrases. Punctuated with a period, a phrase is a fragment because, as you know, a sentence must have at least one subject and one verb. Also, a sentence will usually be a statement that makes sense, in context, by itself. In grade school, you may have learned that a sentence must express a complete thought. That idea can be helpful when you are editing for fragments; keep it in mind as you work on the next exercise.

Exercise 13.11

The following groups of words all have at least one subject and one verb, but some of them are not sentences because they do not make sense by themselves. Mark S (for sentence) next to each group that makes sense and F (for fragment) next to each group that causes you to want more information.

1. Although computer programmers earn good salaries._____
2. Participating in aerobic exercise regularly can strengthen the lungs and heart._____
3. When the party was over._____
4. When the party was over, the house was a mess._____
4. Woodworking can be fun._____
5. Because the band was too loud._____
6. Even though the students had read the assignment._____
7. If space travel becomes a reality for the average person._____
8. Everyone ran from the building when the fire alarm sounded. _____
9. After the firefighters arrived._____
10. Since the dog ran away._____

If you were able to separate the sentences from the fragments, you also were able to tell the difference between sentences and dependent clauses. A *clause*, as we said in Chapter 9, is any group of words that contains at least one subject and one verb. You also may remember that there are basically two types of clauses: independent and dependent.

An *independent clause* has at least one subject and one verb and makes sense by itself as a complete thought or states a sensible fact in context. For instance, "I rode my bicycle this morning" has the subject *I* and the verb *rode*, and it tells us a complete piece of information. An independent clause will always be a complete sentence. Understand this rule and you will avoid fragments: *To be a sentence, a group of words must have at least one independent clause.*

The fragments you marked in exercise 13.11 all have subjects and verbs, but they do not make sense by themselves because they leave us asking for more information. A dependent clause also has at least one subject and one verb, but it does not make sense by itself because it starts with a subordinating conjunction that leaves us asking for more information. For instance, in number 10, we have the subject *dog* and the verb *ran away*, but the word *since* makes us wonder what happened *since* the dog ran away. The word *since* is a subordinating conjunction, as defined in Chapter 9. Added to a subject and verb, such words create dependent clauses, and a dependent clause cannot form a complete sentence by itself. It *depends* on an independent clause to complete its meaning. For example:

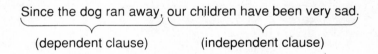

Since the dog ran away, our children have been very sad.

(dependent clause)   (independent clause)

Now we have joined the dependent clause to an independent clause—*our children were very sad*—to form a standard English sentence.

There are two ways to correct fragments that are dependent clauses:

1. Add an independent clause to complete the thought.
2. Cut the conjunction to create a statement of fact:

~~Since~~ The dog ran away.

Exercise 13.12

Edit each fragment using both techniques suggested above.

1. Whenever I go to bed very late.
2. Because the weather has been warm.
3. As soon as I had finished studying.
4. After Victoria's mother died.
5. When Bruce was seven years old.
6. Since my typewriter has been broken.
7. Before I spend my money on clothing.
8. Although I enjoy attending college.
9. If Todd learns to mind his manners.
10. Now that I am getting older.

In editing each fragment in the previous exercise, you first added an independent clause. In editing your own writing, the independent clauses are usually there before and after the fragments, so a third way to correct a fragment is simply to connect it to the sentence before or after it, just as you did in correcting fragments with -*ing* and -*ed* phrases.

Exercise 13.13

Correct the fragments in this paragraph by connecting them to complete sentences.

Executive privilege is the President's right not to appear before congressional committees. Some political experts have criticized this privilege. Because they think the President should not be able to withhold information from Congress or the public. The Iran-Contra hearings brought the question of executive privilege into the news. When it was proposed that President Reagan supply Congress with information about what he knew about the activities of Oliver North. Earlier in the Reagan administration, Congress had cited Anne M. Burford (Reagan's head of the Environmental Protection Agency) for contempt. After she refused to provide information about the EPA's role in enforcing the laws requiring corporations to clean up toxic waste.

Relative Clauses as Fragments

As you may remember, a relative clause is a type of dependent clause used most often to describe a noun or to serve as the direct object of a verb. For example:

> John Akers, *who made the honor roll each year,* was accepted to the college of his first choice. (Here the relative clause describes John Akers.)
> Mary's guidance counselor recommended *that she take advanced math courses.* (Here the relative clause is the object of the counselor's recommendation.)

Relative clauses are easy to identify because they always begin with *who, whom, whoever, whomever, what, which, that.* Most commonly, fragments occur in relative clauses beginning with *who* or *which.* The easiest and best way to edit a relative clause punctuated as a fragment is to add it to the sentence *before* it.

Nonstandard

The Chamber of Commerce held a dinner to honor Tamita Sims. Who started the first all-black business in the city.

Standard

The Chamber of Commerce held a dinner to honor Tamita Sims, who started the first all-black business in the city.

Exercise 13.14

Edit the relative-clause fragments in this paragraph by connecting them to the sentences before them.

One shrewd investment available to anyone is baseball cards. Which years ago were just bought and traded by young boys for the fun of it. Today, the value of some cards is quite high. Rookie cards are particularly valuable if the player goes on to have a great career. Which is predictable in many cases. One such player is New York Yankee Don Mattingly. Who began playing in 1982 and quickly became a star. By 1989, a Mattingly rookie card was worth over $50 on the collectors' market. Baseball cards no longer are just for kids but are collected by investors. Who buy and sell them each year at card shows around the nation and through advertisements in collectors' magazines.

We have seen two basic types of fragments: phrases, which are groups of words without a subject and verb, and dependent clauses, which do have a subject and verb but do not make sense by themselves. You probably did pretty well in telling the difference between the sentences and fragments in the exercises, but to make your knowledge pay off, you need to be able to identify fragments when they appear in your own writing. This can be more difficult because sometimes the fragments make sense in the context of the sentences before and after them. Still, they will distract a reader and hinder you from getting your meaning across. To practice editing fragments in your writing, complete the following exercises.

Exercise 13.15

Examine a piece of writing you have done for another class. See if you can find any fragments, whether your teacher has marked them or not. Edit the fragments to form standard English sentences.

Writing Assignments

1. As fast as you can, freewrite a paragraph of fifty to seventy-five words on anything you like. When you are finished, see if you find any fragments. If you do, edit them to form standard English sentences.
2. Write a paragraph of about 100–150 words, purposely including sentence fragments. Then edit the fragments so that all sentences are in standard English.

Key Terms

Subject: The person, place, thing, action, or idea that the sentence shows performing an action or that the sentence says something about.
Verb: The word in a sentence that shows the action the subject performs or that expresses a state of being about the subject.
Phrase: Any group of words that does not have both a subject and a verb.
Clause: Any group of words that contains both a subject and verb.
Independent clause: A group of words that has a subject and verb and that can stand alone as a sentence.

Dependent clause: A group of words that has a subject and verb but that does not make sense by itself. Dependent clauses begin with subordinating conjunctions, such as *although, because, while,* etc.

Relative clause: A type of dependent clause beginning with *that, which, who, whom, whoever, whomever,* or *whose.* Relative clauses cannot stand alone as sentences.

Fragment: A phrase, a dependent clause, or a relative clause punctuated with a period as if it were a complete sentence.

chapter fourteen

Editing Comma Splices and Run-on Sentences

Like fragments, comma splices and run-on sentences are nonstandard forms of English sentences. Comma splices and run-ons are distracting and can turn your reader's attention away from your true meaning. Editing comma splices and run-ons is not difficult, as you will see in this chapter.

Editing Comma Splices

A **comma splice** occurs when a writer uses only a comma to join two or more independent clauses. Commas are not powerful enough by themselves to join two independent clauses. Here are some examples:

1. Eldon loves pizza, his brother loves burgers. (Two short independent clauses connected with only a comma.)
2. Sharon brought potato chips to the party, they were gone in ten minutes. (The subject of the second clause—*they*—is a pronoun. See Chapter 16 for more on pronouns.)
3. Although the car started, it ran poorly and later stalled out, a tune-up might solve the problem. (The sentence starts with a dependent clause [Although . . . started] followed by an independent clause to form a good sentence, but then another independent clause [a tune up . . . problem] is tacked on with only a comma.)

Editing Comma Splices with Coordinating Conjunctions

In Chapter 9, you learned about the seven coordinating conjunctions: *but, and, for, nor, or, so, yet.* We called these BAFNOSY words—a nonsense word formed by the first letter of each of the conjunctions to help us remember them. Placed after a comma, any of the BAFNOSY words can turn a comma splice into a standard-English sentence. Note the corrections of the previous examples:

1. Eldon loves pizza, *but* his brother loves burgers.
2. Sharon bought potato chips to the party, *and* they were gone in ten minutes.
3. Although the car started, it ran poorly and later stalled out, *yet* a tune-up might solve the problem.

Coordinating conjunctions are very helpful when you edit comma splices, but be sure you pick the one that best illustrates your meaning. Here are the meaning relationships that the conjunctions create:

but contrasts different things or actions: The television had a clear picture, *but* the sound was full of static.

and connects similar things or actions: The wind was blowing fiercely, *and* snow was coming down heavily.

for shows a cause: I was tired, *for* I had worked hard.

nor connects negative elements: American blacks have not always had civil rights, *nor* have American Indians.

or shows alternatives: The insurance company must pay for fire damage, *or* Peter will sue.

so shows an effect of a cause: Not many tickets were sold, *so* the concert was cancelled.

yet shows contrast and is used like *but:* Arnold was on a diet, *yet* he kept eating chocolate.

Exercise 14.1

Using coordinating conjunctions, edit the following comma splices. Be sure that you use a conjunction that results in a sentence that makes sense. If a sentence is correct, put a C next to it.

1. All of the Indiana Jones movies were released in the summer, teenagers go to the movies a lot in the summer.
2. *Star Wars* sold millions of tickets as a summer movie, it set a box office record.

3. If you understand a few basic rules, correcting comma splices is not difficult, it does not take much time either.
4. Comma splices can hurt grades as well as the clarity of your writing, it is wise to edit for them carefully.
5. Phillip was dating a woman much older than he, she did not look or act her age.
6. His parents did not approve of the relationship, he continued to date her anyway.
7. Because of the snowstorm, classes were cancelled in all the local schools, most children were very happy.
8. Karate and aikido are both martial arts, aikido concentrates on defense.
9. Although you are feeling ill, you should go to work, you will be fired if you miss again.
10. Toxic waste is dangerous, it must be disposed of carefully.

Editing Comma Splices with Conjunctive Adverbs

Conjunctive adverbs are another group of transitional words that allow writers to join two independent clauses (see Chapter 7). However, to use a conjunctive adverb to join two sentences, you must insert a semicolon before it (a comma after it is optional). Many comma splices occur when beginning writers use a conjunctive adverb with only a comma before it:

> The tuxedo David had picked out for the prom cost more than he could afford, therefore, he had to borrow money from his parents.

The independent clause is tacked on with *therefore* and a comma. Since *therefore* is not a coordinating conjunction, it, and words like it, requires a semicolon to join sentences. Only a coordinating conjunction (BAFNOSY) can join independent clauses with a comma.

> The students wrote first drafts of their essays, then they began the revision process.

As in the previous example, we have two sentences joined with a comma and a word that is not a coordinating conjunction (BAFNOSY). Such comma splices occur often with *then* because the word is used so much. *Then* is a conjunctive adverb; so you must put a semicolon before it. (Remember that there is no *T* in BAFNOSY.)

Therefore and *then* are just two of many conjunctive adverbs. Here are some of the many more: *accordingly, also, besides, consequently, finally, furthermore, hence, however, indeed, likewise, nevertheless, next, now, similarly, thus.* Don't worry if you cannot remember all of these words. You don't have to. Just remember the seven coordinating conjunctions—the BAFNOSY words—and if you do not have one of them connecting two independent clauses, you will know that you need a semicolon rather than a comma.

Exercise 14.2

Using conjunctive adverbs, correct these comma splices. As you did in the previous exercise, make sure your sentences make sense. If you have trouble thinking of the right conjunctive adverb, look back over the list. If a sentence is correct, place a C next to it.

1. The tent leaked severely, we got soaked from the thunderstorm.
2. Some people love to go camping, they romanticize it, thinking they are getting close to nature.
3. Camping can be enjoyable, I prefer a vacation at a resort with hotels, swimming pools, and nightlife.
4. When you pitch a tent, you stand it up on poles, you pull the tenting material tightly outward and down to the ground.
5. You make sure the tent is tight, then you hammer pegs through the tent loops into the ground.
6. Camping is better if the weather is warm, you have to be prepared for dropping temperatures during the night.
7. When camping, you must have the necessary supplies and equipment; however, you cannot have more than you can carry.
8. Some people see vacations as a way to escape civilization, they go camping.
9. On a camping trip you can go hiking, you can go fishing if you have tackle, a license, and access to a lake or pond.
10. Millions of Americans camp every year, national parks and campgrounds are becoming overcrowded.

Editing Comma Splices with Semicolons

Whenever you find a comma splice, you also can edit it simply by replacing the comma with a semicolon and no conjunctive adverb. For example:

Comma Splice
Alice drove a Cadillac, her brother Bill preferred a Lincoln.

Edited with a Semicolon
Alice drove a Cadillac; her brother Bill preferred a Lincoln.

Whether you use the semicolon by itself or with a conjunctive adverb is your choice, but the semicolon works best when the sentences are not too long and the meaning relationship between them is clear. In any case, when you use this method of editing, do not add a coordinating conjunction.

Exercise 14.3

Using the semicolon, correct the comma splices below.

1. Mr. Putnam enjoys cigars, he sends to South America for them.
2. These cigars are hand-rolled, most cigars are machine-rolled.
3. Some people love the smell of a cigar, others hate it.
4. The Lone Ranger wore a mask, Tonto did not.
5. The mother applied iodine to her son's skinned knee, he screamed.
6. Cherry bombs are dangerous, they have cost more than one child a finger.
7. Angela took up the guitar, she learned fast.
8. In a month, she could play ten songs, in a year, she performed on stage.
9. Stocks can be a risky investment, government bonds are safer.
10. Few people drink lemonade in the summer anymore, soft drinks are in.

Editing Comma Splices with Dependent Clauses

Although you cannot join two independent clauses with just a comma, you can write a standard-English sentence with one dependent and one independent clause. Examine the following sentences:

Comma Splice
The party was exciting, most guests stayed late.

Standard-English Sentence with First Clause Dependent
Because the party was exciting, most guests stayed late.

Comma Splice
The police arrived, the burglar ran off.

Standard-English Sentence with Second Clause Dependent
The burglar ran off *when* the police arrived.

In each of the standard-English sentences, one clause has been made dependent. In the first sentence, adding *because* to the first clause makes it depend on the second clause to complete the meaning. The opposite is true in the second sentence. In both sentences, the dependent clause corrects the comma splice. Note that when the dependent clause comes first, a comma follows, but when the dependent clause is second, no comma is necessary.

Exercise 14.4

Edit these comma splices by making one of the clauses dependent. Be sure that the sentences you create make sense. If you have trouble, review the list of subordinating or "dependent" conjunctions in Chapter 9.

1. Berry Gordy founded the first black record company in the United States, he wanted black artists to enjoy the profits from their talents.
2. Blacks were recording numerous hit records, their white managers were making most of the money.
3. Gordy called his record company Motown, it was located in Detroit, the Motor City.
4. All record companies were owned by whites, Gordy established Motown Records in the early 1960s.
5. More black artists began signing contracts with Motown Records, the company grew quickly.
6. Gordy became one of the most prosperous men in the music business, he remained true to his commitment to black recording artists.
7. Black recording artists had a difficult time, Motown Records did not exist.

8. Motown was established, black soloists and groups had trouble getting a fair contract.
9. Gordy was a smart businessman, he knew a white audience would buy records by black stars.
10. Gordy was a pioneer in the music business, he will probably be elected to the Rock 'n' Roll Hall of Fame someday.

Editing Comma Splices with Periods

One sure way to edit a comma splice is to replace the comma with a period, making two sentences. This method works best when the sentences incorrectly joined by the comma are fairly long. If the comma is joining two short sentences, you would be better off using one of the other methods.

Comma Splice
Feminism has benefited many woman, it has helped men too.

Edited with a Period
Feminism has benefited many woman. It has helped men too.

The edited sentences now comply with the rules of standard English, but because they are short, they create a choppy effect. In this case, it would be better to combine the sentences with a comma and a coordinating conjunction or with a semicolon and a conjunctive adverb. If the sentences are longer, however, using the period can work well:

Comma Splice
During the Vietnam War, young people were more politically active than they are today. Some people say that today's youth are apathetic, but others argue that there is no urgent political cause to arouse young people.

Edited with a Period
During the Vietnam War, young people were more politically active than they are today. Some people say that today's youth are apathetic, but others argue that there is no urgent political cause to arouse young people.

Exercise 14.5

Edit these comma splices by replacing the comma with a period. Be careful to replace the comma that causes the splice.

1. Vermont is a beautiful place to live if you enjoy winter sports, it gets a lot of snow in the winter, so the skiing is excellent, and its many frozen lakes are a skater's dream.
2. On our way to Philadelphia, it was raining so hard that we could barely see the road, the windshield wipers were nearly useless as huge trucks sprayed torrents of water across our windshield.
3. In May, thousands of students around the nation will be graduating from state colleges and universities, many, however, will leave their states to seek employment in other parts of the country because of the demand for mobility in today's job market.
4. During the energy crisis of the 1970s, U.S. auto manufacturers began to market small cars to compete with Japanese and European imports, in the 1980s, they returned to making large cars when gasoline became cheaper and more plentiful.
5. The university lecture series often presents interesting and prestigious speakers, ranging from world leaders to great writers, for example, former British Prime Minister Harold Wilson spoke last month, and next month Maya Angelou will talk about her life and writing.

Exercise 14.6

Using any of the methods you have learned, correct any comma splices that you find in these paragraphs:

The individual inventor was a hero of the nineteenth century, however, we rarely hear about individual inventors anymore. We use computers all the time, who invented them? Though we may associate television with Dumont, there is no single person credited with its invention. Similarly, we associate names such as Goddard and Von Braun with rocketry, still, we don't think of someone inventing the first rocket the way we think of Edison inventing the lightbulb or Bell inventing the telephone.

Younger students often mature more in their first semester of college than they have in all their years of high school. They have so many additional responsibilities to take on, college requires that they have to discipline themselves. If they don't, no one else will help them. Many students enjoy taking on new responsibilities, it makes them feel good about themselves. They gain new self-respect, they realize they can face the difficult tasks of life on their own.

Exercise 14.7

Freewrite for about ten minutes on any topic you want. Edit your freewriting to eliminate comma splices.

Editing Run-on Sentences

Many beginning writers think that a run-on sentence is a sentence that is too long. Actually length really has nothing to do with whether or not a sentence is a run-on. Certainly a run-on can be long, but it also can be short:

Class ended the students left.

Here we have only five words, but the sentence is a run-on. No matter what the length, a run-on sentence occurs when two independent clauses are joined together with *no* punctuation at all.

Some instructors refer to run-on sentences as fused sentences or run-together sentences, but whatever they are called, the error results when two strings of words capable of standing alone as sentences are joined together without punctuation. In the example above, *class ended* is an independent clause because it has the subject *class* and the verb *ended*. Likewise, *the students* is a subject and *left* is a verb. Thus, we have two independent clauses run together with no conjunction or punctuation. Here are a few more examples of run-ons:

1. The boy kicked the dog it bit him. (The second sentence has the pronoun *it* as the subject. Remember that pronouns can be subjects.)
2. Japan would not surrender therefore President Truman gave orders to drop the first atomic bomb. (Here two independent

clauses are tacked together with *therefore* without the necessary semicolon, a common error.)

3. The bomb was dropped on Hiroshima and Nagasaki then the world was shocked by the devastation it caused. (Two sentences are joined with *then* without the needed semicolon.)

When you edit run-on sentences, the first thing to remember is that you will need more than a comma. Beginners often think that if they separate the clauses in a run-on with a comma, they have fixed the sentence. Actually, they have created a comma splice, a form just as nonstandard as a run-on. Run-ons are similar to comma splices in that both join independent clauses in nonstandard ways. In fact, a run-on is a comma splice without the comma. Given the similarities between the two, nearly the same methods can be used to edit run-ons as are used to edit comma splices.

Editing Run-on Sentences with Coordinating Conjunctions

Coordinating conjunctions (*but, and, for, nor, or, so, yet*) are powerful little words because they are the only words in the English language that allow you to join two sentences with a comma. Thus, you can use them to edit run-on sentences:

Run-on
Phil and Alicia decided they wanted to go to Europe they began saving money a year before the trip.

Edited with a Conjunction and a Comma
Phil and Alicia decided they wanted to go to Europe, *so* they began saving money a year before the trip.

Using a coordinating conjunction with a comma is probably the most common method of correcting run-on sentences, and it often leads to nicely balanced sentences that show a relationship between one independent clause and another.

Exercise 14.8

Using commas and coordinating conjunctions, correct these run-on sentences. If a sentence is correct, put a C next to it and underline the comma and conjunction.

1. Ice milk has fewer calories than ice cream it does not taste as good.
2. Shirley is on a diet she eats ice milk when she wants ice cream.
3. She has to eat low-calorie foods she also has to eat small portions.
4. Keith has high cholesterol he eats ice milk, too, because it is low in fat.
5. A high cholesterol level is dangerous it can cause a heart attack.
6. Cholesterol blocks the arteries alcohol raises the blood pressure.
7. Cholesterol and alcohol contribute to heart attacks people should reduce both the amount of fatty foods they eat and the amount of alcohol they drink.
8. Some doctors claim one or two glasses of wine a day is good for a person more than that can raise blood pressure levels.
9. Smoking also is a major contributor to heart attacks if you smoke and drink, you greatly increase your chances of having one.
10. Nutrition is very important as the saying goes, "we are what we eat."

Editing Run-on Sentences with Conjunctive Adverbs and Semicolons

As you know from editing comma splices, a semicolon and a conjunctive adverb (*consequently*, *however*, *nevertheless*, *then*, *thus*, *therefore*, etc.) can join two sentences together. The same is true with run-ons:

Run-on Sentence
When the house caught fire, the firefighters responded quickly there was only minor smoke damage.

Edited with a Conjunctive Adverb and a Semicolon
When the house caught fire, the firefighters responded quickly; *therefore,* there was only minor smoke damage.

Edited with a Semicolon
When the house caught fire, the fire fighters responded quickly; there was only minor smoke damage.

Whether you choose the conjunctive adverb and the semicolon or just the semicolon is up to you. In this case, just the semicolon might be better because the sentences are fairly short and informal. However, with other sentences, you might want to include the conjunctive adverb to draw a tighter meaning relationship.

Exercise 14.9

Correct the following run-on sentences, using semicolons and conjunctive adverbs or just semicolons. Try to use both methods.

1. Synthetic fabrics were developed and became popular in the last half of this century before that people wore clothes made primarily of natural fibers.
2. Synthetic fabrics wrinkle less when washed they require little or no ironing.
3. Many of the things we take for granted were developed in the 1940s and 1950s we assume they have been around forever.
4. World War II spawned much research many new products appeared after the war.
5. Aluminum siding for homes came out in the 1950s vinyl siding was developed about fifteen years later.
6. During the war there was very little development in the automobile industry because auto plants were used to manufacture military vehicles after the war automobile development advanced rapidly.
7. The postwar economy was booming most people had money to buy the latest products.
8. Television and television commercials became common many products enjoyed widespread recognition.
9. People were spending money the economy was growing rapidly.
10. The boom economy of the 1950s carried over into the 1960s and was sustained by the Vietnam War economy the 1970s suffered recession and inflation.

Editing Run-On Sentences with Dependent Clauses

When you find a run-on sentence, another way to edit it is to make one of the clauses dependent.

Run-on
The restaurant served Italian food the owners were Chinese.

Edited with a Dependent Clause
Although the restaurant served Italian food, the owners were Chinese.

Making one clause dependent is a good way to correct a run-on. In these sentences, the relationship between the dependent and independent clauses tends to produce mature style by drawing tighter relationships—(of time, cause, contrast, or condition)—between clauses.

Exercise 14.10

Edit the following run-ons by making one clause dependent. If you have trouble, review the list of subordinating conjunctions in Chapter 9.

1. Before the late 1960s, few people attended college there was very little financial aid.
2. Scholarships were offered to very promising students the government did not offer grants and loans to average students as it does today.
3. National Defense Student Loans have helped many students some students have defaulted.
4. All students should repay their loans if they don't, other students have a harder time securing loans for themselves.
5. Universities began to set open-admissions policies in the late 1960s many more people were able to seek higher education.
6. Increased financial aid was necessary many students entering through open admissions were from poor families.
7. Much financial aid is available today students have to maintain a satisfactory grade point average to remain eligible.
8. Students are denied financial aid their grade point averages fall below the minimum standard.
9. Financial aid is an incentive for students to work hard they are in college.
10. Increases in financial aid will have to continue the cost of a college education rises.

Editing Run-on Sentences with Periods

Just as you can edit a comma splice by replacing the comma with a period, you can edit a run-on by placing a period between the two independent clauses to make two sentences. This type of correction solves the grammatical problem, but, as with comma splices, it can lead to choppy styles unless the sentences being separated are long. The following is a long run-on followed by a correction:

Run-on
Prohibition-era gangster Jack "Legs" Diamond got his start running speakeasies around Albany, New York, eventually building a criminal empire he got the nickname "Legs" because he danced well.

Edited with a Period
Prohibition-era gangster Jack "Legs" Diamond got his start running speakeasies around Albany, New York, eventually building a criminal empire. He got the nickname "Legs" because he danced well.

Here the use of the period works well because combining the sentences would create a rather long sentence. Also, the second sentence brings up a new point on Diamond.

Exercise 14.11

Using a period to make two sentences, edit these run-on sentences.

1. Wyatt Earp, one of the most famous marshals of the Old West was known for bringing law and order to Dodge City, Kansas, a wild town on the route of the cattle drives Earp carried a custom-made pistol, called the "Buntline Special," with a long barrel.
2. Refinishing old furniture is time consuming and difficult because the old finish must be removed with a stripping chemical before the piece can be sanded and refinished working with stripping chemicals requires adequate ventilation because they emit toxic fumes.
3. Slow-pitch softball is a popular game throughout the United States because it is not difficult to play, and the game emphasizes offense there are many different levels ranging from highly skilled semiprofessional leagues to tavern leagues that allow nearly anyone to play.

4. A major controversy in motorcycle safety regards helmet laws, which vary from state to state some states have strict helmet laws, but other states do not require riders to wear a helmet at all.

5. The Nintendo Company made a fortune in the late 1980s by reviving home video games, which had lost popularity after consumers got bored with the first home video games Nintendo's popularity is the result of superior graphics and speed that match those of arcade games.

Practice Editing

In this chapter, you have learned methods for editing comma splices and run-on sentences. The exercises provided you with practice editing each type of non-standard form. If you keep an error log, you will become aware of the particular type of sentence problem that occurs most often in your writing. You can then concentrate on that particular problem. However, when you edit a paper, you should be watching for all types of major sentence errors. Although you may make one or two more regularly than others, any one of them can pop up at any time. To practice editing for both comma splices and run-ons, do the following exercises.

Exercise 14.12

Correct all comma splices and run-on sentences in the brief essay that follows.

Some people drive long distances on vacation, chances are that at some point they will have to go through a major city. The interstate highway system is designed to connect large population areas travelling through most cities, drivers can choose to follow the interstate through the city or drive around it on a road called a beltway or loop, which is a circular highway intersected by the interstate.

Taking the beltway allows drivers to avoid the inner-city traffic they leave the interstate, make a half circle around the city, and then return to the interstate to continue. There is usually less traffic on the beltway. The beltway can save drivers the aggravation of fighting traffic on unfamiliar roads, however, the beltway usually is a few miles longer. Other drivers prefer going through the city because they believe it saves time, also, it affords a view of the downtown.

As drivers approach a large city, they should look for construction signs before they decide to take the beltway or to remain on the interstate. If signs signal beltway construction, the route through the city will be faster and less stressful no one likes to crawl bumper to bumper through miles of construction. Construction on the route through the city could be even worse, costing as much as two hours of driving time.

Whatever route drivers choose, they should drive carefully, making a safe trip is always more important than making good time.

Exercise 14.13

Write a paragraph on a topic of your choice in which you purposely write comma splices and run-on sentences. Then edit the paragraph, changing these to standard English sentences.

Key Terms

Comma splice: Two independent clauses connected with a comma but no connecting word.

Run-on sentence: Two or more independent clauses joined without punctuation or a connecting word.

Coordinating conjunction: The words *but, and, for, nor, or, so,* and *yet,* used with a comma to join two independent clauses. The first letter of each spells the nonsense word *BAFNOSY.*

Conjunctive adverb: Words such as *also, however, nevertheless, thus,* and others that connect independent clauses with semicolons.

Semicolon: A mark of punctuation that looks like a period placed above a comma. It is used to join independent clauses either by itself or with a conjunctive adverb.

chapter fifteen
Editing Verb Forms

As a speaker of English, you use verbs hundreds, even thousands, of times each day. Most of the time you probably use the standard-English forms. In fact, most speakers often use standard-English verbs without really knowing how the verb system works. Yet from reading and hearing others speak, they know which verb forms to use. At times, however, some people use verb forms that are part of a dialect and not standard English.

English has a very complex system of verbs, but you can use standard-English verb forms without knowing all there is to know about this system. To edit problems with verbs, however, you should know the differences among infinitives, main verbs, and helping verbs, along with the difference between regular and irregular verbs. Also, it helps to be familiar with verb tenses and to be able to make verbs agree with their subjects.

Verb Forms

Like all parts of speech, verb forms can be classified and identified by their function in a sentence. You constantly use verbs in all the ways they function, but you may not be aware of the function of verbs as you use them. Knowing the four basic functions of verbs can help you edit nonstandard verb forms.

Infinitives

Infinitives are the basic form of every verb before it is used to show action, show relationships, or mark the time when something happened. Infinitives are easy to identify because they are usually preceded by the word *to: to be, to cry, to eat, to fall, to have, to love, to make,* and so on. (Note, however, that not every word preceded by *to* is an infinitive form of a verb. When *to* is used as a preposition, a noun will follow it in phrases such as *to church, to town, to California,* and so on.)

Although the infinitive is the basic form of a verb, it can never serve as the main verb in a sentence. There is only one good reason to know what an infinitive is: so you won't mistake it for the main verb when you are trying to tell if a group of words is a complete sentence. For example, examine the following group of words:

To discover a cure for cancer someday.

A beginning writer might mistake this group of words for a sentence, thinking that the verb is *To discover*. Although the word *discover* indicates some action, with *to* before it, it can't take a subject. Thus, it can't be a part of the subject-verb construction needed to make a complete sentence. In editing this sentence, you could write:

Doctors hope to discover a cure for cancer someday.

This sentence still has the infinitive *to discover*, but the main verb is *hope*, the subject is *doctors*, and the infinitive *to discover* is now the direct object. Thus, we have a complete sentence. If you know what infinitives are, you won't mistake them for the main verb in a sentence, and you will reduce the possibility of writing unwanted fragments.

Exercise 15.1

Underline the infinitives in the following sentences.

1. Raymond asked his advisor to review his schedule.
2. To try for success is to succeed.
3. Maria wanted to return to college when her son started school.
4. Do you like to go to the movies?
5. The army retreated to higher ground when the enemy started to attack.
6. Everyone wants to have coffee after dinner.
7. In Beverly Hills, people are not allowed to smoke in restaurants.
8. The President planned to veto the bill from Congress.
9. Bullfighters face great danger to entertain the crowd.
10. Anthony began to cut school when his parents were divorced.

Now underline the infinitives in this paragraph:

A 1975 psychological study by Latham and Yuki reported that an intention to reach a specific organizational goal motivates people's behavior at work. Goals help workers to focus attention on a task and to work out strategies for completing the task. To succeed, however, organizational goals must be challenging to the worker, the worker must have the ability to achieve the goal, and the worker must see the goal as attached to a tangible reward.

Main Verbs

In a sentence or independent clause, the word that shows the action or links the subject to the rest of the sentence is the main verb. Main verbs also show *tense*—the time something takes place. Together with a subject, a main verb forms a complete sentence, so every sentence must have at least one main verb. Examine the main verbs in these sentences:

> The United States *produces* more food than any other country.
> The Emancipation Proclamation *abolished* slavery in the United States.
> Art *dropped* twenty pounds in two months.
> Warren will *graduate* next June.
> That movie *had* a weak plot.
> After living in Phoenix for ten years, Wilma will *move* to Tucson next fall.
> Tyrone is *studying* to be an attorney.
> Tyrone *is* in his third year of law school.
> Mr. and Mrs. Colletti are *moving* to Florida next month.
> Andrew Johnson *was* the only President to be impeached.
> Johnson had *been* Lincoln's Vice President before Lincoln was *assassinated*.

Each of the marked verbs in these sentences serves as a main verb. As you can see, main verbs can take many forms. Some show action—and some of them have *-ed* or *-ing* on the end. Others are verbs of being, such as *is* and *was*. But in each case, the main verb either shows action or links the subject to the part of the sentence that says something about it.

Exercise 15.2

Return to exercise 15.1 and place two lines under each main verb.

Helping Verbs and Participles

Sometimes a main verb has one or more verb forms before it, such as *am, are, is, was, were, has, have, had, will,* and so on. These verbs are called helping verbs because they help us understand sentences by marking their tense—the time the action took place (or will take place) or the time something is said about the subject. As a speaker of English, you know how most tenses work from hearing them. Knowing how to identify helping verbs will help you separate them from the main verb. As you remember, when you are editing to find fragments, comma splices, and run-on sentences, it is very important to be able to locate main verbs. Compare the following pairs of sentences. In each pair, the main verb is marked in the first sentence and the helping verbs are marked in the second.

Main verb:	Irene has *decided* to change jobs.
Helping verb:	Irene *has* decided to change jobs.
Main verb:	The bank was *robbed* yesterday.
Helping verb:	The bank *was* robbed yesterday.
Main verb:	Andrew should have *been* in class today.
Helping verb:	Andrew *should have* been in class today.
Main verb:	If you had *wanted* good Chinese food, you should have *gone* to Loo's.
Helping verb:	If you *had* wanted good Chinese food, you *should have* gone to Loo's.
Main verb:	Hurricane Hugo will *go* down in meteorological history as one of the most devastating storms on record.
Helping verb:	Hurricane Hugo *will* go down in meteorological history as one of the most devastating storms on record.
Main verb:	Lionel Johnson is *running* for mayor.
Helping verb:	Lionel Johnson *is* running for mayor.
Main verb:	With some effort, Tracy can *earn* an A in English.
Helping verb:	With some effort, Tracy *can* earn an A in English.

With a little study and practice, you can tell the difference between main verbs and helping verbs. Some verbs, however, are tricky because sometimes they can be used as main verbs or as helping verbs. Examine the following list and examples:

am	Main verb:	I *am* from New Jersey.
	Helping verb:	I *am* writing an essay. (main verb: *writing*)
are	Main verb:	Many of the freshmen *are* business majors.
	Helping verb:	Many of the freshmen *are* majoring in business. (main verb: *majoring*)
do	Main verb:	You *do* well on exams.
	Helping verb:	But you *do* need to study. (main verb: *need*)
had	Main verb:	Lucinda *had* her paycheck in her purse.
	Helping verb:	Lucinda *had* returned from work. (main verb: *returned*)
has	Main verb:	Jeff *has* five hundred dollars in the bank.
	Helping verb:	Since last summer, Jeff *has* saved five hundred dollars. (main verb: *saved*)
have	Main verb:	Most beginning writers *have* a strong desire to learn standard English.
	Helping verb:	Many beginning writers *have* learned to use standard English. (main verb: *learned*)
is	Main verb:	Mrs. Lynch *is* a police officer.
	Helping verb:	She *is* trying to become a detective. (main verb: *trying*)
was	Main verb:	The winning dog *was* a greyhound.
	Helping verb:	The greyhound *was* running fast. (main verb: *running*)
were	Main verb:	The DiMaggio brothers *were* all professional baseball players.
	Helping verb:	We *were* sleeping during the storm. (main verb: *sleeping*)

As you can see from the examples, these verbs can be either main or helping verbs. As you look for verbs when you are editing your paper for sentence errors, make sure each sentence has at least one main verb to go with the subject.

When a main verb is used with a helping verb, the main verb is said to be in the *participle* form. In Chapter 9, participles were discussed as parts of verb phrases used as subjects and modifiers. Verbs in participle form can also be the main verb if they have a helping verb. There are present participles and past participles. You can tell them apart because present participles always end in *-ing* and past participles end in *-ed*. Compare these sentences:

Present Participle as Main Verb
Quentin Dias is *running* for city council.

Past Participle as Main Verb
Dias was *defeated* in his bid for city council.

Exercise 15.3

Underline all helping verbs and circle all main verbs in these sentences. Not every sentence will have both.

Remember: When used with a helping verb, main verbs will be in participle form.

1. The war with the Sioux was one of the last Indian wars.
2. Although the Sioux were granted hunting rights on northern plains, white prospectors tramped through the hunting grounds during the Black Hills Gold Rush of 1875.
3. Because the prospectors were disturbing the hunting grounds, the Sioux tribes banded together to stop them.
4. They were led by the great chiefs Crazy Horse, Rain-in-the-Face, and Sitting Bull.
5. By the spring of 1876, the U.S. Army had sent many cavalry troops to fight the Sioux.
6. George Armstrong Custer led his troops deep into Sioux territory in search of victory and glory.
7. At the Little Big Horn River, Custer thought he had surrounded a small war party of Sioux.
8. But he was wrong; his 265 men had entered the primary Sioux camp.
9. Custer's troops were faced with 2,500 Sioux warriors and were massacred in only a couple of hours.

10. The Battle of Little Big Horn has gone down in history as the worst military blunder of the Indian wars; however, the Sioux viewed it as revenge for the brutal treatment of the Indians by whites.

Examine a paragraph or two of some writing you have done. Underline all helping verbs and circle all main verbs.

Regular vs. Irregular Verbs

Regular verbs are the group of English verbs that take the same endings when used a certain way. For example, when preceded by the subjects *he, she,* or *it,* a regular verb in the present tense has an *s* added to the end, as in the following forms:

He walks. She walks. It walks.

Also, regular verbs have *-ed* added to show that something happened in the past. This is true whether the verb is in the simple past tense or in a past-participle form that takes one or more helping verbs. Compare these forms of regular verbs:

Present	Simple Past	Past Participle with Helping Verbs
I talk	I talked	I have talked
You laugh	You laughed	You had laughed
He jumps	He jumped	He would have jumped
She calls	She called	She had called
It cooks	It cooked	It has cooked
We walk	We walked	We could have walked
You smile	You smiled	You have smiled
They travel	They traveled	They will have traveled

Although each verb is different, notice that in the simple past each has *-ed* at the end. Also, in the participle forms using helping verbs, the *-ed* again appears at the end of the verb. In other words, there is a *regular* way—adding *-ed*—to show the past and other forms of these verbs. That's why they are called *regular* verbs.

Nonstandard forms of these verbs usually occur either from leaving the *-s* off the present form that follows *he, she,* or *it;* adding an *-s* to the present form that follows *we* or *they;* or leaving the *-ed* off the past or past-participle forms. Compare the following sentences:

Present Tense

Nonstandard:	Tony cook dinner when his wife work late.
Standard:	Tony cooks when his wife works late.
Nonstandard:	Professional athletes earns excellent salaries.
Standard:	Professional athletes earn excellent salaries.

Simple Past Tense

Nonstandard:	He talk to the professor about the assignment.
Standard:	He talked to the professor about the assignment.
Nonstandard:	She ask her parents if she could borrow the family car.
Standard:	She asked her parents if she could borrow the family car.

Past-Participle Forms with Helping Verbs

Nonstandard:	They have change their ideas.
Standard:	They have changed their ideas.
Nonstandard:	He would have play in the outfield if his team need him.
Standard:	He would have played in the outfield if his team needed him.
Nonstandard:	The play had end by ten o'clock.
Standard:	The play had ended by ten o'clock.

If you have a problem using *-s* and *-ed* endings in your writing, you need to edit very carefully. Look at the regular verbs in your sentences, and make sure that you add the *-s* if you are using *he, she,* or *it* in the present tense, or the *-ed* if the verb is in the simple past tense or in a past form that uses helping verbs.

Exercise 15.4

Before each sentence, there is an infinitive form of the verb in parentheses. Put the correct main verb in the blank.

1. (to walk) Despite a sprained ankle, Althea _____ all the way home.
2. (to use) Every year, the university _____ tons of paper.
3. (to use) Every year, universities across the nation _____ tons of paper.
4. (to start; to fire) The Civil War _____ when the Confederate forces _____ on Fort Sumter.
5. (to answer) You always _____ the questions correctly.
6. (to play) We _____ basketball on Saturday mornings.
7. (to call) Anthony _____ me last night from Oregon.
8. (to describe; to listen) The victim _____ the mugger to the police officer, who _____ carefully.
9. (to type; to edit; to use) Lester _____ the second draft of his essay; later he _____ it to make sure he had _____ standard verb forms.
10. (to swerve; to crash) A large truck _____ off the road and _____ into a telephone pole.

Exercise 15.5

Change nonstandard verbs to standard forms in the following paragraph.

The U.S. Constitution work as a set of laws that sets guidelines for making other laws. In other words, it provide the "rules of the game" for government, and lawmakers must consider it when they passes new laws. New social problems sometimes causes the Constitution to be challenge. Thus, occasionally Congress amend the Constitution to enable it to allow for problems that the Founding Fathers did not anticipate. Prohibition and its repeal provides two examples. Though problems requiring amendments arises from time to time, the Constitution remains an effective document for government.

Unfortunately for people trying to use standard English, not all verbs are regular. While we add *-ed* to regular verbs to form the past and past-participle forms, *irregular verbs* do not follow a particular pattern. Some irregular verbs have similar patterns, but overall there are no hard-and-fast rules for these verbs. Compare these pairs of regular and irregular verbs:

Infinitive	Present	Simple Past	Past Participle with Helping Verbs
to live	live/lives	lived	has lived
to be	am/is/are	was/were	have been
to rest	rest/rests	rested	have rested
to lie (recline)	lie/lies	lay	has lain
to type	type/types	typed	were typed
to write	write/writes	wrote	had written
to ruin	ruin/ruins	ruined	was ruined
to break	break/breaks	broke	is broken
to own	own/owns	owned	has been owned
to have	have/has	had	has had
to jog	jog/jogs	jogged	had jogged
to run	run/runs	ran	has run

As these comparisons show, irregular verbs are tricky. For the present forms, sometimes you can add an *s* to make the form used with *he*, *she*, and *it*; other times, even the present tense takes different forms, as with the verb *to be*. Also, to form the simple past or past forms used with helping verbs, you can't just add *-ed*. The following list contains many of the irregular verbs.

Infinitive	Present	Simple Past	Past Participle with Helping Verbs
to be	am/is/are	was/were	have been
to beat	beat/beats	beat	has beaten
to begin	begin/begins	began	have begun
to bite	bite/bites	bit	was bitten
to blow	blow/blows	blew	has blown
to break	break/breaks	broke	is broken

Infinitive	Present	Simple Past	Past Participle with Helping Verbs
to bring	bring/brings	brought	were brought
to build	build/builds	built	will be built
to catch	catch/catches	caught	is caught
to choose	choose/chooses	chose	are chosen
to come	come/comes	came	had come
to cost	cost/costs	cost	have cost
to deal	deal/deals	dealt	has dealt
to dig	dig/digs	dug	will be dug
to do	do/does	did	has done
to draw	draw/draws	drew	were drawn
to drink	drink/drinks	drank	has drunk
to drive	drive/drives	drove	had driven
to eat	eat/eats	ate	have eaten
to fall	fall/falls	fell	have fallen
to fight	fight/fights	fought	has fought
to find	find/finds	found	was found
to fly	fly/flies	flew	has flown
to forget	forget/forgets	forgot	was forgotten
to freeze	freeze/freezes	froze	have frozen
to get	get/gets	got	has got/gotten
to give	give/gives	gave	have given
to go	go/goes	went	has gone
to have	have/has	had	has had
to know	know/knows	knew	had known
to lead	lead/leads	led	have led
to lend	lend/lends	lent	will be lent
to lie (recline)	lie/lies	lay	has lain
to make	make/makes	made	has made
to ride	ride/rides	rode	was ridden
to ring	ring/rings	rang	has rung
to run	run/runs	ran	had run
to say	say/says	said	were said
to see	see/sees	saw	have seen
to set (put)	set/sets	set	had set
to shake	shake/shakes	shook	has shaken

Infinitive	Present	Simple Past	Past Participle with Helping Verbs
to sing	sing/sings	sang	was sung
to sink	sink/sinks	sank	has sunk
to sit (chair)	sit/sits	sat	have sat
to speak	speak/speaks	spoke	has spoken
to spring	spring/springs	sprang	has sprung
to steal	steal/steals	stole	has stolen
to swim	swim/swims	swam	have swum
to swing	swing/swings	swung	has swung
to take	take/takes	took	was taken
to tear	tear/tears	tore	is torn
to throw	throw/throws	threw	had thrown
to wear	wear/wears	wore	had worn
to write	write/writes	wrote	have written

This list is certainly long, but there are still more irregular verbs in English! Fortunately, you probably know most of them already because you use them every day. For example, I doubt that you would ever write or say, "I *worn* my new coat yesterday," although you might say "I *seen* it" or "I *done* it" if you hear these nonstandard forms often. You need to find out which irregular verbs give you trouble. The following are some common problems that beginning writers have with irregular verbs.

Confused Forms of *to Be*

There are so many different forms of the verb *to be* that it is very easy to confuse them. Read the following common errors, and note which forms give you trouble:

Present Tense

Nonstandard	Standard
I is, I be	I am
You is, You be	You are
He/She/It be	He/She/It is
We is, We be	We are
They is, They be	They are

Simple Past Tense

Nonstandard	Standard
I were, I be	I was
You was, You be	You were
He/She/It be/were	He/She/It was
We was, We be	We were
They is, They be	They were

Past Participles with Helping Verbs

Nonstandard	Standard
I been	I have/had been
You been	You have/had been
He/She/It been	He/She/It has/had been
We been	We have/had been
They been	They have/had been

Confused Forms of *to Do*

The verb *to do* is used in many different nonstandard forms by speakers from different parts of the country. One particularly troublesome form is the difference between the use of the simple past form, *did,* and the past-participle form used with a helping verb, *done.* Be very careful not to confuse these. As the examples show, *did* should always be used alone, but *done* should always be used with a helping verb.

Present Tense

Nonstandard	Standard
I does	I do
You does	You do
He/She/It do	He/She/It does
We does	We do
They does	They do

Simple Past Tense

Nonstandard	Standard
I done	I did
You done	You did
He/She/It done	He/She/It did
We done	We did
They done	They did

Past Participles with Helping Verbs

Nonstandard	Standard
I have/had did	I have/had done
You have/had did	You have/had done
He/She/It has/had did	He/She/It has/had done
We have/had did	We have/had done
They have/had did	They have/had done

Confused Forms of *to Go*

Very few people confuse present forms of this verb, but the simple past form, *went*, and the past participle used with helping verbs, *gone*, often cause problems. In particular, many people use *went* with a helping verb. *Went*, as the simple-past form, should not be used with a helping verb, while *gone* must always have a helping verb. Compare the uses of these forms:

Nonstandard: Many students *have went* to Florida for spring break.
Some *had went* before the break began.

Standard: Many students *have gone* to Florida for spring break.
Some *had gone* before the break began.

Confused Forms of *to See*

The most common nonstandard use of *to see* occurs when people confuse the participle used with a helping verb, *seen*, for the simple-past form, *saw*. Compare the differences in these sentences:

Nonstandard: I *seen* Phil on his way to work.

Standard: I *saw* Phil on his way to work.
I *have seen* Phil on his way to work.
I *had seen* Phil on his way to work.

Confused Forms Ending in *-n*

For many irregular verbs, the past-participle form used with a helping verb ends in *-n: broken, chosen, driven, frozen, spoken, stolen, taken,* and so on. But often the *-n* is left off and the simple past is used with the helping verb, thus creating a nonstandard form. Compare to the standard forms, and use the standard forms in your writing:

Nonstandard:	The drug ring *was broke* by the FBI.
Standard:	The drug ring *was broken* by the FBI.
Nonstandard:	We *had drove* four hundred miles in one day.
Standard:	We *had driven* four hundred miles in one day.
Nonstandard:	The lake *will have froze* by next week.
Standard:	The lake *will have frozen* by next week.
Nonstandard:	Jim's book *has been stole.*
Standard:	Jim's book *has been stolen.*
Nonstandard:	Mr. Ortiz *had took* his daughter to the doctor last Tuesday.
Standard:	Mr. Ortiz *had taken* his daughter to the doctor last Tuesday.

Exercise 15.6

Cross out the nonstandard forms of irregular verbs, and replace them with standard forms.

1. The boy thought he seen a UFO last night.
2. The car was stole sometime last night after we had went out to the movies.
3. We had knew car thefts was on the rise in our city.
4. The workers who have did their jobs efficiently will earn a bonus.
5. Anton brang a guest home for dinner.
6. After we have ate our dinner, we will meet you at the theater.
7. Beverly Sills had sang at the Metropolitan Opera House many times before she sung in Europe.
8. The plane had flew into a severe thunderstorm.
9. I wish I had not took chemistry and math in the same semester.
10. Protesting the referee's decision, the fans had threw debris all over the court.

Exercise 15.7

Edit the following paragraph so that all irregular verbs are in the standard forms.

I never gone to a water park until last summer when I was visiting California. It were a very large place with ten different-sized water slides and three different swimming pools. One even have waves. One of the water slides were over five stories high, and it was very steep. I wanted to go down it, but I was afraid at first. After I seen little kids going down this slide, I feel foolish, so I done it myself. Well, when I hit the pool at the bottom, I thought my back was broke. After that, I decided to stick to the smaller slides and the pool.

Exercise 15.8

Review papers you have written. Pick a page or two and circle irregular verbs you have used in the standard forms. This will show you how much you know about them. Then look for any nonstandard forms and change them to standard forms.

Verb Tenses

In addition to showing action or linking the subject and predicate, verbs have different forms to show the time a sentence refers to. These forms are called the *tenses* of the verb. The basic verb tenses are the present, past, and future, but there are other tenses to mark more complex relationships of action and time, among them the perfect tenses. You use all of these tenses when you speak, though you may not know the names of each or exactly why you use them.

Present Tense

You have seen many present-tense verbs in the previous discussion of verbs. The present tense has four uses: to refer to something happening at the same time of the writing or speaking, to refer to action that happens regularly or continuously, or to express a general truth:

At the time of writing: As I *work* on this book, the furnace *hums* in the background.
Regular: Kay *eats* a large breakfast every morning.
Continuous: The dogs in our neighborhood *bark* all night.
General truth: The sun *provides* the earth with light.

In most cases, the present tense is formed by using the basic form of the verb from the infinitive. However, an *-s* is added when the verb is used with a singular noun or the pronouns *he, she, it:*

Present tense of *to eat*
Singular: I eat, you eat, he eats, she eats, it eats, the dog eats, acid eats
Plural: we eat, you eat, they eat, hungry people eat

Exercise 15.9

Write one sentence for each of the four uses of present tense.

Past Tense

As you know, regular verbs form the past tense when *-ed* is added. Irregular verbs have other forms (see above). The past tense is used to describe actions completed in the past or ongoing conditions that existed in the past but no longer exist:

Completed action: The people *elected* Lincoln President in 1860.
                      Eric *finished* his paper last night.
Past condition: Prior to Columbus's voyage, Europeans *believed* the earth was flat.

The forms of verbs in the past tense are the same no matter what the subject:

Regular verb: *to cook*
Singular: I cooked, you cooked, he/she cooked, Felix cooked
Plural: we cooked, you cooked, they cooked, the children cooked

Irregular verb: *to run*
Singular: I ran, you ran, he/she/it ran, the horse ran
Plural: we ran, you ran, they ran, the girls ran

Exercise 15.10

Write two sentences for each use of the past tense.

Future Tense

The future tense expresses actions that will happen or actions that are intended but have not yet happened:

Action that will happen: The sun *will rise* again tomorrow.
Action that is intended: Rita *will go* to Mexico next summer.

Whether the verb is regular or irregular and whether the subject is singular or plural, the future tense is always formed by adding *will* to the base form of the infinitive:

to sleep: I will sleep, you will sleep, he/she/it will sleep, the baby will sleep, we will sleep, you will sleep, they will sleep, the cats will sleep

---

Exercise 15.11

Write two sentences for each use of the future tense.

Present-Perfect Tense

Verbs in the present-perfect tense refer to conditions that started in the past and still exist or to an action recently completed at an unspecified time:

Action continued to present: I *have dieted* for three weeks now.
    Action completed recently but at an unspecified time: Anita *has left* for Hawaii.

You form the present-perfect tense by adding the helping verb *has* or *have* to the past-participle form of the verb:

Regular verb: *to laugh*
    Singular: I have laughed, you have laughed, he has laughed, the hyena has laughed
    Plural: we have laughed, you have laughed, they have laughed, the teachers have laughed

Exercise 15.12

Write two sentences for each use of the present-perfect tense.

Past-Perfect Tense

Verbs in the past-perfect tense refer to actions that occurred or conditions that existed in the past but that were completed before some other action or occurrence in the past:

Action: By the time he left Las Vegas, Calvin *had lost* all his money.
Condition: The 1930s brought the Great Depression to America, whereas the 1920s *had been* prosperous years.

No matter what the subject is, the past-perfect tense of the verb is formed by adding *had* to the past participle.

Irregular verb *to leave:* I had left, you had left, she/he had left, the boat had left, we had left, you had left, they had left, the trucks had left

Future-Perfect Tense

Verbs in the future-perfect tense refer to actions or conditions in the future that will have ended before or at the same time as another future event or condition.

> Action: Drew *will have studied* for fifty to sixty hours by the time she completes her exams.
> Condition: When Sam graduates, he *will have been* a college student for almost seven years.

To form the future-perfect tense, you add *will have* to the past participle whether the subject is singular or plural.

> Irregular verb: *to be:*
> I will have been, you will have been, she/he will have been, the house will have been, we will have been, you will have been, they will have been, the Chinese will have been.

Exercise 15.13

Write two sentences for each use of the future-perfect tense.

Exercise 15.14

Identify the tenses of the verbs in a page of your writing, marking them P for present, PA for past, F for future, PP for present perfect, PAP for past perfect, and FP for future perfect. Consider why you used the tenses you did.

Modals

As you saw in studying tenses, the helping verbs help mark the time of sentences. Modals are another type of helping verb, but they indicate *capability, obligation,* or *possibility,* rather than time. Here are some common modals and their uses:

> Capability: can
> Henry *can* fix your car.

Obligation: must, should
Arlene *must* take her children to the day care center before going to work.
Young people *should* respect senior citizens.

Possibility: may, might, could, would
Bonita *may* choose to major in communications.
Austin *would* have helped chop wood.
The old wiring *could* start a fire.

Modals can be added to some tenses but not others. As a native English speaker, you know when a modal sounds right. You would not, for example, write: *"Felicia could is a nice girl,* but she has a bad attitude." You would write: *"Felicia could be a nice girl,* but she has a bad attitude." And while modals work with most past tenses, you would not add one to a verb in the future tense: *"We might will go to the concert."*

Exercise 15.15

Write a sentence for each of the following modal constructions.

1. might have visited
2. can sleep
3. should go
4. would have left
5. must want
6. could have spent
7. may try
8. must have meant
9. should see
10. would argue

Subject and Verb Agreement

One way to describe subjects is to say that they have person and number. **Number** refers to the condition of a noun (or word functioning as a noun) as singular or plural. **Person** refers to whoever or whatever is being talked or written about. **First person** is the writer or speaker expressed as *I*. **Second person** is someone being spoken to, the audience addressed as *you*. **Third person** is just that, a third person or thing being discussed by the writer (the first person) with the audience (the second person). Certain verb forms always follow certain person subjects. When they do, the verb and subject are said to agree. If they do not, there is disagreement between subject and verb. When we discussed regular and irregular verbs, you saw examples of subject-verb agreement and disagreement. We will examine further how disagreement occurs with both types of verbs.

Making Regular Verbs Agree with Subjects

One of the most common errors of subject-verb disagreement occurs with regular verbs in the present tense. Compare these sentences:

Robin **talk** too much about herself. (disagreement)
Robin **talks** too much about herself. (agreement)

Her friends **likes** her anyway. (disagreement)
Her friends **like** her anyway. (agreement)

In each pair, the first sentence contains a nonstandard use of the verb resulting in disagreement of subject and verb. Study the following conjugation to see which verb forms agree with which subjects:

to walk	Singular Subject	Verb	Plural Subject	Verb
First person:	I	walk	We	walk
Second person:	You	walk	You	walk
Third person:	He	walks	They	walk
	She	walks	Phil and Carol	walk
	It	walks	Senior citizens	walk
	Joe	walks		
	The bear	walks		

Finding the right form for a regular verb in the present tense is not difficult because all of the forms are the same except the form used with a singular subject in the third person—it ends in *-s*. However, dialect speakers and beginning writers often confuse this form with others, ending up with sentences that say *he walk, Sid walk, I walks, they walks,* and so on. According to standard English, such sentences have errors in the agreement of subject and verb.

Exercise 15.16

Correct any errors in subject-verb agreement that you find in these sentences. If a sentence contains no error, place a C next to it.

1. Veterinarians uses PCP as an animal tranquilizer, but drug abusers take it to get high.
2. After taking PCP, a person feel relaxed, almost euphoric.
3. But the side effects of PCP includes confusion, violence, and even coma.
4. Americans abuse cocaine more than any other drug.
5. Both rich and poor people finds cocaine a fashionable drug.
6. Cocaine produce mood elevation and feelings of well-being, but prolonged use of cocaine leads to addiction.
7. PCP, cocaine, and other drugs eventually causes physical and psychological problems that leads to insanity in severe cases.
8. Drug dealers earns large profits by taking advantage of the weakness of others.
9. Taking drugs makes some people feel important, but these people do not realize the damage drugs causes to the body.
10. Smart people stay away from all illegal drugs.

Making Irregular Verbs Agree with Subjects

Most irregular verbs in the present tense work like regular verbs with subjects. However, forms of *to be* and *to have* have many different forms and thus lead to many agreement errors, both when they are used as main verbs and as helping verbs. Study these examples:

> Forms of *to be* as main verb
>> You *is* very clever. (disagreement)
>> You *are* very clever. (agreement)

Tommy *are* a fine sculptor. (disagreement)
Tommy *is* a fine sculptor. (agreement)

They *be* early for class yesterday. (disagreement)
They *was* early for class yesterday. (disagreement)
They *were* early for class. (agreement)

Forms of *to be* as helping verbs:
I *is* going fishing this afternoon. (disagreement)
I *am* going fishing this afternoon. (agreement)

Emmett *be* laughing at us. (disagreement)
Emmett *were* laughing at us. (disagreement)
Emmett *was* laughing at us. (agreement)

Forms of *to have* as main verbs
I *has* new golf clubs. (disagreement)
I *have* new golf clubs. (agreement)

Lester *have* a red Firebird. (disagreement)
Lester *has* a red Firebird. (agreement)

Bennie and Tonya *has* a baby daughter. (disagreement)
Bennie and Tonya *have* a baby daughter. (agreement)

Forms of *to have* as a helping verb
You *has* won my loyalty. (disagreement)
You *have* won my loyalty. (agreement)

We *has* bought a new house. (disagreement)
We *have* bought a new house. (agreement)

In each case of disagreement, the form of *to be* or *to have* is coupled with a subject that it does not fit according to standard English. Some of the sentences are acceptable in some dialects; however, they are not standard English. Study the following conjugations to become familiar with the standard-English forms:

to be (present tense)	*Singular Subject*	*Verb*	*Plural Subject*	*Verb*
First person:	I	am	We	are
Second person:	You	are	You	are
Third person:	He	is	They	are
	She	is	The girls	are
	Angela	is	Danielle and Lee	are
	It	is	The cars	are
	The car	is		

to be (past tense)	*Singular Subject*	*Verb*	*Plural Subject*	*Verb*
First person:	I	was	We	were
Second person:	You	were	You	were
Third person:	He	was	They	were
	She	was	The girls	were
	Angela	was	Danielle and Lee	were
	It	was	The cars	were
	The car	was		

to have (present tense)	*Singular Subject*	*Verb*	*Plural Subject*	*Verb*
First person:	I	have	We	have
Second person:	You	have	You	have
Third person:	He	has	They	have
	She	has	The men	have
	David	has	Lou and Denise	have
	It	has	The houses	have
	The house	has		

to have (past tense)
All forms take *had*.

The variety of forms for these verbs makes them more difficult to grasp than the forms of regular verbs. However, it is very important to know them because they are very commonly used in English and, when misused, can cause many errors in subject-verb agreement.

Exercise 15.17

Correct all errors in subject-verb agreement in the following sentences. Circle correct forms of *to be* and *to have*.

1. Alexis de Tocqueville were a Frenchman who visited the United States in 1831.
2. After studying Americans, Tocqueville concluded that they were a people who was dedicated to liberty.
3. Tocqueville wrote a book, *Democracy in America*, that were acclaimed here and abroad.

4. This book have been read by many people who were interested in American culture.
5. Injustices in the United States is still with us, but American citizens has the freedom to express their opinions.
6. Liberals and conservatives has argued for decades about national policies.
7. In recent years, public opinion in the United States have been diverse on such controversial issues as abortion.
8. This difference of opinion has led to many struggles, but it also have illustrated the workings of democracy.
9. Young and old alike is lucky to be able to speak out on abortion or any other issue.
10. If we is angry about something, we has the freedom to express ourselves.

Exercise 15.18

The following paragraph contains a wide variety of errors in subject-verb agreement. Correct them all and circle any verbs that do agree with their subjects.

Both scientific experts and average citizens disagrees about the benefits of nuclear power as a source of energy. For years, we has relied on fossil fuels, such as gas and oil, to produce heat and electricity, but as these have diminished, scientists and engineers has sought to develop other forms of energy. People in coal-mining states argue that we should use more coal, but because coal does not burn clean, it cause air pollution. Others believes that nuclear power is the answer if the government enforce strict standards of safety at nuclear plants. Safety standards has always been in effect, but standards alone cannot prevent accidents. The failure of safety measures were evident in the accident at the Three Mile Island reactor a little over ten years ago. Until then, nuclear reactors was considered safe by most scientists and many citizens. Since the Three Mile Island accident and the 1986 disaster at the Chernobyl reactor in the Soviet Union, many scientists and citizens believes nuclear power is not worth the risk.

Exercise 15.19

Examine a page of something you have written, checking for errors in subject-verb agreement.

Key Terms

Infinitive verb: The basic form of a verb before it is used to show action or time relationships. Infinitive verbs have the word *to* before them.

Main verb: In a sentence or clause, the word that shows the action or links the subject to the rest of the sentence or clause.

Helping verb: A verb form used with the main verb to show tense.

Regular verb: One of a group of verbs that add *-ed* to show past tense and *-s* when used with third-person subjects.

Irregular verb: A verb that does not follow a particular form when marking past tense or when used with a helping verb.

Present participle: The form of a verb ending in *-ing* used with a helping verb when functioning as the main verb in a sentence.

Past participle: The form of a verb ending in *-ed* in regular verbs and taking various forms in irregular verbs.

Verb tense: The time marked by the main verb in a sentence or clause, marked either by the ending of regular verbs, by the form of irregular verbs, or by helping verbs.

Present tense: The forms of verbs used to show action going on at the time of the writing, habitual action, or a general truth. In regular verbs, formed with the base form from the infinitive, except the third-person singular form, which adds an *-s*.

Past tense: Forms locating action in the past and ending in *-ed* in regular verbs and in various forms in irregular verbs.

Future tense: The form of the verb used to locate action in the future, formed with the addition of the helping verb *will* to the base form of the infinitive.

Perfect tenses: Formed by adding the helping verbs *has, have,* or *had* to verbs in past, present, or future tenses. Perfect tenses show more-complex relationships of time and action.

Number: A condition of subjects and verbs according to whether the subject is singular or plural.

First person: The subjects *I* and *we*.

Second person: The subject *you* (singular and plural).

Third person: The subjects *he, she, it, they,* or any singular or plural subject being discussed between the writer and audience.

chapter sixteen
Editing Pronoun Problems

Pronouns are some of the most commonly used words in the language. Before we look at a full definition of pronouns, remember that pronouns substitute for nouns. Thus, they help us avoid having to repeat the same words over and over. You use pronouns in daily conversation to refer to yourself, to others, and to activities, objects, or ideas. Yet pronouns are often misused by beginning writers. In fact, a recent study of student errors ranked pronoun errors as the second most common, behind misspelled words. Learning to use standard-English pronouns correctly can reduce distracting errors a great deal.

As you may remember from the discussion in Chapter 7, the repetition and variation of key words help give a paragraph coherence. Study the following paragraph on former President Jimmy Carter, noticing the connections of the varied references to the "new President." Also notice how other pronouns refer to nouns:

> The new President . . . was an ambitious and intelligent politician. *He* had a rare gift for sensing what people wanted and appearing to give it to *them*. Liberals thought *he* clearly stood with *them;* conservatives were equally convinced that *he* was on *their* side. *He* was especially adept at using symbols. *He* emerged from airplanes carrying *his* own garment bag; after *his* inauguration, *he* walked up Pennsylvania Avenue hand-in-hand with *his* wife, Rosalyn, and daughter, Amy.
>
> Robert A. Divine et al., America, Past and Present

These uses of *he* and *his* show how pronouns are used to refer to the noun *President*. The pronouns *them* and *their* refer to different groups: *people, liberals,* and *conservatives*. You may remember the definitions of nouns and pronouns from earlier schooling, but let's review them:

Noun: A person, place, thing, feeling, or condition. Nouns can be singular, plural, or possessive—for example, president, presidents, president's.

Pronouns: Words that take the places of nouns. Pronouns can be singular, plural, or possessive, and they show whether the noun is masculine, feminine, or neuter (having no sex). Like subjects and verb forms, pronouns also show the concept of person. When using *I* or *we,* we are using first-person pronouns because we are referring to ourselves. When using *you,* singular or plural form, we are using second-person pronouns because we are addressing a second party. When using *he, she, it,* or *they,* we are using third-person pronouns because we are referring to a third party.

Without pronouns, writing would become so repetitious that readers would quickly become bored. For example, read the paragraph on President Carter, rewritten without pronouns:

The new President . . . was an ambitious and intelligent politician. The President had a rare gift for sensing what people wanted and appearing to give what people wanted to people. Liberals thought the President clearly stood with liberals; conservatives were equally convinced that the President was on the conservatives' side. The President was especially adept at using symbols. The President emerged from airplanes carrying the President's garment bag; after the President's inauguration, the President walked up Pennsylvania Avenue hand-in-hand with the President's wife, Rosalyn, and daughter, Amy.

As you can see, without the pronouns this paragraph not only sounds ridiculous but is confusing to read.

Exercise 16.1

In the following paragraph, all the pronouns are used correctly. Circle each pronoun and draw a line connecting it with the noun it refers to.

Writing is necessary for many jobs. It is particularly important in business. Executives have to write letters even if they have secretaries to do the typing. Memos are the life's blood of office communications. They are written to people above and below the executive. When a memo is well written, it will get the executive's point across no matter who the audience is.

In good writing, pronouns help create coherence, but if the writer does not use them correctly, they can confuse and distract readers.

Common Types of Pronouns

There are several different types of pronouns, and they can be classified by the way in which they function in sentences. You have seen relative pronouns in earlier chapters. Other common types are **subject pronouns, object pronouns, possessive pronouns,** and **reflexive pronouns.** Their names state their function, with subject pronouns used as subjects, object pronouns used as objects, possessive pronouns used to show possession, and reflexive pronouns used to reflect back on a noun. These types of pronouns also take different forms depending on whether they refer to the first, second, or third person:

Subject Pronouns

	Singular	*Plural*
First person:	I	we
Second person:	you	you
Third person:	he, she, it	they

Object Pronouns

	Singular	*Plural*
First person:	me	us
Second person:	you	you
Third person:	him, her, it	them

Possessive Pronouns

	Singular	*Plural*
First person:	my, mine	our, ours
Second person:	your, yours	your, yours
Third person:	his, her, hers, its	their, theirs

Reflexive Pronouns

	Singular	*Plural*
First person:	myself	ourselves
Second person:	yourself	yourselves
Third person:	himself, herself, itself	themselves

Editing Nonstandard Uses of Pronouns

Because there are so many pronouns, it is easy to mix them up. In conversation, people mix up pronouns all the time, even speakers who generally use standard English. Unlike writing, conversation usually enables the listener to know what the speaker means even when the speaker is misusing pronouns. In writing, however, pronoun usage that is not standard English can distract and confuse readers. Some problems that can arise with pronoun usage are **faulty reference, faulty agreement, shifts of person,** and **misused pronoun case.**

Editing Faulty Reference

As we said in the definition, pronouns take the place of nouns. That means a pronoun must have a noun to take the place of, or refer to. For example, in the sentence *Jim knew he passed the exam,* the pronoun *he* refers to Jim. The noun that the pronoun refers to is called its **antecedent.**

When writers use pronouns without having a noun to refer to, readers can get confused. Read the following sentences, and play close attention to the underlined pronouns:

> City services are becoming worse every day, but *they* are not doing anything to solve the problem. *They* need to find funding to fix the roads, to provide more police protection, and to improve public transportation. *It* gets worse all the time, and *they* need to raise money to improve *services.*

Who are *they*? City council members? The people who perform city services? And what is *it* that gets worse all the time? Police protection? Public transportation? Or the problems in general? Compare a rewritten version:

> City services are becoming worse every day, but *city politicians* are not doing anything to solve the problem. *They* need to find funding to fix the roads, to provide more police protection, and to improve public transportation. *These services* get worse all the time, and *the city* needs to raise money to improve *them.*

In the rewritten version, the pronoun *they* now refers back to the noun *city politicians,* making clear whom the writer means. Replacing the pronoun *it* with the noun *these services* makes clear that the writer is referring to all the problems. The pronoun *they* in the last sentence has been replaced by *the city,* and the pronoun *them* added at the end of the paragraph refers back to *these services.*

Exercise 16.2

The following short paragraphs contain faulty pronoun references. To make the paragraphs more coherent, correct any faulty reference by adding a noun where needed.

1. The Concorde is a supersonic jetliner built by France and England. It takes them across the Atlantic Ocean to America in only three hours. I would like to do it, but it costs around $1500.
2. "Jeopardy" is my favorite TV game show. It takes intelligence on "Jeopardy." They have to answer some tough questions, but they win a lot of money. They are on all different subjects, and they cannot always answer them.
3. I enjoy boats. My father bought it used, but it is good for fishing, waterskiing, or just cruising. We go out in it on weekends and enjoy the sunshine, fresh air, and water. Dad usually lets me drive it.

Editing Faulty Agreement

When a pronoun refers to a noun, the pronoun must agree with the noun in number (singular or plural) and gender (masculine, feminine, or neuter). Almost no one has a problem with gender agreement. You would not write, for instance, "*Alonzo* was proud because *it* earned an A in math."

However, faulty agreement in number is a common error. Examine the underlined words in these sentences:

Faulty agreement

Every time a *father* has to punish *their* children, *they* feel as bad as the kids do. (The sentence mentions a singular father but uses the plural pronouns *their* and *they* to refer to him.)

Correct Agreement

Every time <u>fathers</u> have to punish <u>their</u> children, <u>they</u> feel as bad as the kids do. (This sentence makes the noun <u>father</u> plural so that it agrees with the plural pronouns.)

Every time a <u>father</u> has to punish <u>his</u> children, <u>he</u> feels as bad as the kids do. (This sentences uses the singular pronouns <u>his</u> and <u>he</u> to refer to the singular noun <u>father.</u>)

The most common type of pronoun agreement error occurs in the type of sentences we just examined. Notice in the first sentence that a *father* means any father. In other words, we are using an example of one to refer to all fathers. Compare this sentence:

A student can usually get financial aid if it is needed.

Here the one student is eligible for financial aid. We use this form often in speech, and very few people notice a nonstandard usage if we say, "A *student* can get financial aid if *they* need it." In writing, however, this usage can confuse readers because when they begin reading the sentence, it refers to one person, but by the end, the sentence is talking about more than one person. The best way to correct this type of error is to change the noun to the plural form:

Students can get financial aid if *they* are eligible.

If you keep the singular noun, you have to write, "A student can get financial aid if he or she is eligible." This sounds a bit awkward, so when you are referring to groups, use plural forms for the noun and pronouns as often as possible.

Exercise 16.3

Correct pronoun-agreement errors in these sentences. If a sentence contains no errors, put a C next to it.

1. A person will not have many friends if they always talk about themselves.
2. In my math class, a student must do all of their homework problems on time, or they risk failing the course.
3. A Major League batter must be able to hit a curveball if they are going to be any good.

4. A parent has an obligation to make sure their child behaves well in school and does their homework.
5. A voter should know the issues before they vote for a candidate.
6. People should have a good knowledge of the issues before they vote.
7. If a teacher finds that most students are doing poorly, he or she should look for new methods of teaching.
8. Although a marine must be brave in combat, they cannot be foolhardy.
9. A woman should get a good education so that they will never have to depend on others for financial support.
10. A mail carrier must wear comfortable shoes unless he or she wants sore feet.

Exercise 16.4

The following short paragraphs have pronoun agreement problems. Make all pronouns agree with nouns to add to the coherence of the paragraphs.

1. Most police officers carry guns. It is usually a .38 caliber pistol. Every time a police officer shoots their gun, they must file a report telling why and how the weapon was used.
2. American automobiles look more like foreign cars these days. It is usually small and square. The engine has four cylinders, and they get good gas mileage and need little service.
3. A counter worker in a fast-food restaurant has a difficult job. They have to deal with a customer and put up with all their complaints. Even if the customers are pleasant, the counter workers have to write down the order correctly, but most of all he or she is responsible for all the money in the cash register.

Editing Unnecessary Shifts of Person

As we saw in the definition, pronouns show whether a first, second, or third person or group is being written to or about. Thus, these words can be classified as first-, second-, or third-person pronouns:

	Singular	*Plural*
First person:	I	we
Second person:	you	you
Third person:	he, she, it	they

When you are writing an essay, you need to be as consistent as possible in using first-, second-, or third-person pronouns. For example, read this short paragraph in which the subject pronouns are in italics:

> Many people do not vote because *they* do not believe that their vote makes a difference. *They* think all politicians are the same and it does not matter who wins, so *you* just don't bother to vote.

In reading this paragraph, you probably noticed that the first two pronouns are in the third-person form, *they*. This form is the best choice because the writer is speaking to the reader about a third party—people who do not vote. But with the last pronoun, the writer shifts to the second-person form, *you*. Thus, the writer has gone from speaking about others to speaking directly to the reader. This shift can cause confusion. Does the writer mean other people or the reader?

The second-person form, *you*, should be used only when you mean the reader him- or herself. For example, I have often used *you* in this book because I am talking to you as an individual student reading the book. Other times, I might use the third-person pronoun *they* when talking about beginning writers as a whole group of people, of which you are one member.

Most shifts of person occur when writers change to the second person *you* but are not addressing the reader directly. For instance, if you were writing to your fellow college students about English requirements in your high school, you should not say, "In my high school, you had to take senior English." The second-person *you* would not work because few, if any, members of your audience went to your high school. As you edit your papers, be sure to use second-person forms only when you are addressing your audience directly.

Exercise 16.5

Change any pronoun forms that create an unnecessary shift of person. If a sentence is correct, put a C at the end of it.

1. Samantha really enjoys running because it challenges you to be disciplined.
2. Before teachers can be licensed, you have to pass the National Teacher Examination.
3. To change a flat tire, you must first have a jack, a lug wrench, and a spare tire.
4. If people try fad diets, you should check with your doctor before dieting.
5. Auto repairs are expensive, but you can save money by doing them yourself if you purchase a good book on auto repair.
6. We were playing well against the best team in the conference, but you never knew when they would get hot and crush you.
7. Would you like to win $10,000?
8. Plumbing is a good trade because most plumbers work for themselves, and you earn high wages.
9. When class began, you had to be in your seat and ready to begin.
10. Recycling aluminum products can help you earn extra money.

Exercise 16.6

Edit unnecessary shifts of person in this paragraph.

Throughout the country, many small cities and towns have community theater groups that draw on local talent to present live plays. Community members do the acting, they build stage sets, they operate lighting, or they sell tickets. Citizens can work for a community theater if you have the time and interest. If people cannot work for a community theater group, you should buy tickets and attend the plays to support the work of those who do.

Editing Misuses of Pronoun Case

When we speak of the case of a pronoun, we are asking whether the pronoun is being used as a subject, an object, reflexive, or possessive. The following list reviews the different forms:

Subject Pronouns	Object Pronouns	Possessive Pronouns	Reflexive Pronouns
I	me	my, mine	myself
you	you	your, yours	yourself
he	him	his	himself
she	her	her, hers	herself
it	it	its	itself
we	us	our, ours	ourselves
they	them	their, theirs	themselves

Misusing Subject and Object Pronouns.   When you write sentences, it is sometimes easy to confuse these pronouns and use one that is not a subject when you need one that is, or vice versa. The following italicized pronouns are nonstandard because they are all object pronouns used as subjects:

> *Her* and her husband are planning a trip to Europe.
> Jim and *me* study math every Thursday.
> *Us* and the Jones family went on a picnic.
> *Me* wants some candy.

In the last sentence of these four, you probably recognize the language of a very young child. Here the error is obvious, and as an adult you would never use *me* in this way. In the other sentences, however, the errors are not so clear, because each sentence has two subjects: *her* and *her husband*, *me* and *Jim*, *us* and *the teachers*. When there is only one subject, you probably have very little trouble choosing the right pronoun. For instance, you would not say, "*Her* is planning a trip to Europe," or "*Us* went on a picnic." But the second subject can easily throw you off because *her and her husband* does not sound too bad. If we correct the sentences above, they would read like this:

> *She* and her husband are planning a trip to Europe.
> Jim and *I* study math every Thursday.
> *We* and the Jones family went on a picnic.
> *I* want some candy.

Some of these sentences may sound a little strange to you if you are not used to using these forms in your speech, but they are the forms used in standard English, especially in writing.

Exercise 16.7

In the following sentences, cross out any pronoun that does not follow the standard-English form for subject pronouns. Then replace the pronoun you crossed out with the subject form.

1. Nick, Constance, and me went swimming yesterday.
2. Leonard and me made some new friends this week, and tomorrow us and them are meeting for lunch.
3. Linda, Ramon, and me were sorry to miss your party.
4. As the train left, us and Sonya waved to Mike.
5. Ellen loves to smoke cigarettes, but she knows them are not good for her health.
6. Her and her kids clean the house every week.
7. The children decorated the Christmas tree with their father, and after they went to bed, him and their mother put presents under the tree.
8. Him and John worked construction together last summer.
9. Because him and his brother enjoy deep-sea fishing, another fellow and them bought a cabin at the seashore.
10. Erica, Jill, and me hate brussel sprouts, but it seems as if them and carrots are on the cafeteria menu almost every day.

Just as object pronouns can be confused for subject pronouns, subject pronouns can end up in places where object pronouns should be. Object pronouns often receive the action of the verb directly or indirectly. In the following sentences, the subject pronouns are in places where object pronouns should be:

The police officer's attitude angered *she* and Lois.
The teacher gave *we* students a difficult assignment.
Mr. Washington took his son and *I* out to dinner.

The pronouns in these sentences all function as the objects of verbs (*angered/ she, gave/we, took/I*), but they are in the subjective case when they should be object pronouns:

The police officer's attitude angered *her* and Lois.
The teacher gave *us* students a difficult assignment.
Mr. Washington took his son and *me* out to dinner.

As you may remember from Chapter 9, words that follow prepositions are also considered objects. When a pronoun follows a preposition, it should be in the objective form. Compare these sentences:

Nonstandard

Between you and *I*, the new manager seems incompetent.
We bought presents for *she* and her children.
Larry gave his money to *he* and Mike.

Standard English

Between you and *me*, the new manager seems incompetent.
We bought presents for *her* and her children.
Larry gave his money to *him* and Mike.

Exercise 16.8

Replace misused subject pronouns with object pronouns.

1. Shirley made lunch for she and I.
2. Classical music can be appreciated by we teenagers.
3. Carol's daughter is a brat, but let's keep my feelings between you and I.
4. Dawn hurt he and Chuck when she said she did not want to be seen with they.
5. Marilyn went to a party at the Jordans' house but did not like they or their friends.
6. Grammar is difficult for other students and I, but we are catching on.
7. The teacher gave we students a lot of praise so that we would gain confidence in our ability.
8. Please do not leave because of Sheila and I.
9. Between we two, the Boyers' new furniture is really ugly.
10. Because Pam is a good singer, the preacher asked she and her husband to join the church choir.

Exercise 16.9

In the following sentences, correct misuses of both subject and object pronouns. If a sentence contains no errors, place a C next to it.

1. Him and Vicki tried to call us last night, but our phone was busy.
2. The rainstorm drenched he and Bette before they could run for shelter.
3. Them and their friends did not invite us to join them for dinner.
4. George baked a birthday cake for she and her twin sister.
5. Give the message to Susan and them.
6. The children wanted Milky Way bars; them and Snickers were their favorites.
7. When Matt lost his job, him and his family went on a strict budget.
8. Jessie's progress on the trumpet pleased he and his teacher.
9. Leslie and I will be happy to visit you for the holidays.
10. Us students face as much stress as people who work in the "real" world.

Misuse of Reflexive Pronouns. One use of reflexive pronouns is to show people and things acting for themselves or on themselves. Another use is to add emphasis to the word they refer to. Reflexive pronouns always have antecedents—nouns or subject pronouns that they refer to:

Acting for Self
Mrs. Barratt bought *herself* a new car. (The pronoun makes clear that the action was done by the subject for the subject.)

Acting on Self
Not realizing the gun was loaded, *Howard* shot *himself* in the foot. (The subject performs and receives the action.)

Emphasizing the Subject
Much hoopla precedes every Super Bowl, but the *game itself* is often rather dull. (The pronoun emphasizes the game to separate it from the pregame publicity.)

Sportswriters evaluate and criticize the performance of professional athletes although few *writers* have played professionally *themselves*. (The pronoun emphasizes that the writers have not played, in contrast to the athletes.)

Nonstandard uses of reflexive pronouns do not occur as often as other pronoun errors, but they can cause problems. Some beginners use forms of reflexive pronouns that come from dialects. Compare the dialect forms to the standard-English forms:

Dialect	Standard
me/meself	myself
hisself	himself
ourselfs	ourselves
theirselves	themselves
theyself	themselves
themselfs	themselves

If you use one or more of the dialect forms, you will have to memorize the correct forms if you want to use standard English. With the plural forms—*ourselves* and *themselves*—always remember that they end in *-ves*, not *-fs*.

More and more we hear people using reflexive pronouns as subjects and objects. Even educated people, such as politicians speaking on television, do it. This may mean that standard English is changing, that eventually reflexive forms will become acceptable as subjects and objects. However, such changes take many years, so you should stick to using reflexives only to show a subject acting for or on itself or to emphasize the subject. In standard English, the use of reflexive pronouns as subjects and objects is still considered an error by many people, especially in writing:

Reflexive misused as subject: Donald and *myself* completed a science project together.
Standard: Donald and *I* completed a science project together.
Reflexive misused as object of verb: Eddie asked Rob and *myself* if we would help him move on Saturday.
Standard: Eddie asked Rob and *me* if we would help him move on Saturday.

Exercise 16.10

Correct any misuses of reflexive pronouns in the following sentences. If a reflexive pronoun is standard, place a C above it.

1. The angry parent would not talk to the teacher but asked to see Mr. Pelkowski, the principal himself.
2. The Johnsons decided to paint their house theyself rather than hire a contractor.

3. In general, the film itself was entertaining even though the acting was not top quality.
4. Martha and yourself are the best friends I have.
5. The little boy crossed the street all by hisself.
6. Lonnie and Rick are part owners of a bar, but they theirselves do not drink.
7. I bought me a new suit for my job interview.
8. Jennifer was angry at Vanita and myself, but she herself was to blame for her problem.
9. After his brother and hisself graduated, they moved to different states.
10. The message should reach yourself by tonight.

Misuse of Possessive Pronouns. Possessive pronouns, as their name indicates, show ownership: *my* car, *your* coat, *its* price, *her* idea, *his* friend, *our* house, *their* class. Some nonstandard uses of possessive pronouns are rare, but they occur in certain dialects; other nonstandard uses occur more frequently when writers add apostrophes to possessive pronouns. Though nouns add an apostrophe and an *s* or just an apostrophe to show possession, possessive pronouns never take apostrophes. The following list compares standard and nonstandard forms of possessive pronouns:

Standard	*Nonstandard*
my	me
mine	mines
your	you
hers	her's
his	he's
its	it's
their	they

The most common misuse occurs when writers use *it's* (*it is*) for *its*. You will eliminate this error by remembering that pronouns never use apostrophes to show possession. The same is true for *hers*. The other misuses are dialect forms, so if you recognize them as part of your dialect, you will have to memorize the standard forms and use them in situations requiring standard English.

Exercise 16.11

Correct all misuses of possessive pronouns. Place a C above any possessive pronoun used correctly.

1. Mr. and Mrs. Bevins take they children to church every Sunday.
2. The black-and-white dog is mines, but where is your dog?
3. Cecily would rather drive her father's car than her's.
4. Gerald likes the coat because of it's styling, but its color does not suit him.
5. Where are me keys?
6. The large one on the left is they house; the smaller yellow one on the right is mines.
7. Don't forget to bring you book to class because I cannot lend you mines today.
8. We liked the house, and it's size was perfect for our family.
9. This stereo was not very expensive, but the quality of it's sound is excellent.
10. When you finish your dinner, call David and Liz and tell them we will meet them at their house.

Exercise 16.12

The following short narrative essay contains a variety of pronoun errors. Edit the essay so that all pronouns are in standard English.

One time when I was in high school back in Amityville, Long Island, a couple of friends and me decided to cut school and drive into New York. I had just got my driver's license and bought an old Pontiac. With it's rusty fenders and faded blue paint, the car was not much to look at, but it was mines. Driving to New York that day, I never realized that I was in for one of the greatest thrills of me young life.

When we first got to the city, my friends and me spent a couple of hours walking around Times Square looking in all the stores. Then we went to Greenwich Village. We didn't have much money with us, but a teenager can still have fun in New York if they just want to watch the people and goof around. We were having a good time, but when it came time to leave and we walked back to the car, it was gone.

We found a police officer and told him we thought the car had been stolen. Us and the police officer walked to where the car had been parked. When we got there, the officer laughed and pointed to a sign saying, "No Parking, Tow-Away Zone." He told us we would have to go to the city garage at West 28th Street, where they kept impounded cars, and we would have to pay the ticket to get our car back. Between my friends and myself, we had about twenty dollars, so we walked to the garage, thinking we could pay the ticket, and they would return our car. Little did we know about New York ticket prices and towing charges.

When we arrived at the garage, we saw a lot of people going in and out to get they cars. When I approached the desk and gave them my license number, I was handed a ticket and they directed me toward the cashier. I was stunned to see that the fine was fifty dollars, plus twenty-five more for towing it.

My friends and me were really worried. In another two hours, our parents would be expecting us home from school. We decided to try to panhandle for money there in front of the garage because a lot of people were coming in and out. But usually when we asked a person for some change or a dollar, they just gave us a dirty look and walked on. After nearly an hour, we had only another six dollars. We began to panic. One of my friends suggested that we use our money to take the bus home and have my father come back for the car. "No way!" I said. I told them that they could leave theirselves, but I was going to keep trying.

Just then a young couple and another man, all well dressed, walked up to us, and the man asked why we were arguing. He looked very familiar, but I could not think where I had seen he or his friends. We told our story and asked for two dollars. The man reached for my ticket, took it from myself, and went inside. As we waited, the young couple asked if we knew who the man was. They then told us amazed teenagers that he was Mel Brooks, the producer and actor, and that they were production assistants helping him scout a movie location.

Neither my two friends nor myself knew what to say. We were all fans of his movies. In fact, I had seen *Young Frankenstein* three times. When Mel Brooks came out of the garage, he handed me a receipt for a paid-up ticket and tow charge and told me to go in and get my car. We all started thanking him and asked for his address so we could send him back the money, but he just laughed and told us that seeing his next movie would be thanks enough. He then talked to us for a few minutes, making jokes about how in New York they always rip you off. When he left, he smiled and wished us luck that we would get home on time.

Driving back to Long Island, we could not stop talking about our experience and how surprised we were. I couldn't believe that even if a person is famous, they can really be nice. Who would ever think that a celebrity would bail three goofy teenagers like us out of a jam. When I got home, I wanted to tell my parents about my adventure, but of course I could not. When my mon asked me how my day had gone, I just said, "Oh, same old thing."

Exercise 16.13

Examine a paper you have written and edit any misused pronouns to conform to standard English.

Pronoun errors are hard to eliminate completely because the many forms of pronouns are easy to confuse. As you draft, revise, and edit your papers, pay close attention to the pronouns. They add coherence to your writing, but when misused, they can confuse your reader. If you find that you misuse pronouns, work hard at reducing your errors; your effort will pay off in clearer, more coherent writing.

Key Terms

Noun: Any word that refers to a person, place, thing, quality, or condition. Nouns have singular, plural, and possessive forms.

Pronoun: Any word that takes the place of a noun. Pronouns have singular, plural, and possessive forms and also show gender: masculine, feminine, or neuter.

Antecedent: The noun a pronoun refers to.

Faulty reference: An error that occurs when a pronoun does not have an antecedent noun to refer back to, or when the reader cannot tell what the antecedent is.

Faulty agreement: An error that occurs when the pronoun differs in number or gender from the noun it refers to.

Subject pronouns: Pronouns that function as subjects in sentences and clauses.

Object pronouns: Pronouns that receive the action of a verb or follow a preposition.

Reflexive pronouns: Pronouns that emphasize a noun or another pronoun or show a subject acting for or on itself.

Possessive pronouns: Pronouns that express ownership.

chapter seventeen
Editing Misused Words

Without words, of course, there could be no writing and probably no thought. Individual words can communicate some meaning. For example, everyone responds somehow when hearing words such as *love, war, cancer.* Also, single words can communicate strongly in commands—*Stop! Help! Listen!* Single words, though they have meaning, mean much more when combined to make sentences. Because words depend on one another in a sentence, an error in the use of one word can distract the reader from the meaning of the whole sentence.

Most word errors occur when the writer is unfamiliar with some grammatical principle. For example, you have learned that regular verb forms in the past tense end in *-ed.* If a writer leaves the *-ed* off such a verb, it is in the present tense. This error does not result because the writer does not know a word form but because he or she is unfamiliar with the standard-English rules for past tense. Likewise, if a writer uses the wrong pronoun, the error results from not knowing the rules for pronouns. Other errors result, however, when the writer does not know standard-English rules regarding individual words. Perhaps the most common of such errors, besides outright misspellings, occur when beginning writers must add suffixes to words.

Adding Suffixes

We have defined suffixes earlier in this book, but let's review the definition. A *suffix* is one or more letters added to the end of a word to change its function. There are numerous suffixes. We will cover those that trouble beginning writers most.

Adding Suffixes to Form Plural Nouns

Nouns, as you remember, are words that refer to a person place, thing, condition, idea, or activity. Most singular nouns become plural by adding suffixes.

Adding -s to Nouns.   Most nouns form the plural by simply adding an -s, and undoubtedly you are familiar with such words:

books, cars, desks, miles, schools

Plurals formed by simply adding -s generally end in consonants. As you know, consonants are all letters of the alphabet except *a, e, i, o, u*. These five letters are vowels. Most nouns ending in consonants add -s to form plurals, but in some dialects the -s is left off:

I read three *book* last summer.
It is about twenty *mile* from here to Durham.
Marcus went to three different *school* before finding one he liked.

Although we can understand that these words are plural without the -s, they are nonstandard forms and should not be used in college writing. If you are aware that such forms are common in your dialect, you need to edit very carefully to make sure you add the -s required on plural nouns in standard English.

Exercise 17.1

Add -s to any nouns that need to be plural in the following sentences.

1. Coach Locke suspended four player this week for violating team policy.
2. The child was sent to the store to get three bar of soap.
3. We live just two block from the railroad track.
4. Most bird fly south for the winter.
5. Although winter would soon arrive, there were many bird still on our campus.
6. I want to get to know the student from other countries.

Adding -es to Nouns.   Adding -s is the most common way to form plurals, but when nouns end in -s, -x, -z, -ch, or -sh, you must add -es.

pass	+	es	=	passes
fox	+	es	=	foxes
buzz	+	es	=	buzzes
brush	+	es	=	brushes
couch	+	es	=	couches

Having looked over the examples, read them aloud, listening carefully to the *-es* sound. It sounds like *-ez*. If you hear the sound in speaking and listening, you will be less likely to forget to add *-es* when writing.

Exercise 17.2

Fill in each blank with the plural form of the noun in parentheses. Some nouns will merely take *-s*; others will require *-es*.

1. (kite) With the breeze blowing steadily, the children knew they could fly their _____ .
2. (box) Jessica received three _____ of candy for Valentine's Day.
3. (bunch; flower) She was hoping for _____ of _____ .
4. (mass) St. Vincent's church schedules two _____ Saturday evening and three Sunday morning.
5. (beach) Hawaii is known for its many beautiful _____ .
6. (class) Yesterday's _____ were cancelled because of the snowstorm.
7. (cathedral; church) _____ are larger than _____ .
8. (loss) The company needed to increase sales to make up for last month's _____ .
9. (leash) All dogs must be kept on _____ in Fowler Park.
10. (month) I will see you again in six _____ .

Adding Suffixes to Nouns Ending in -y. Nouns ending in *-y* are perhaps the trickiest when it comes to forming plurals because some of them simply add *-s* while others require that you change *-y* to *-i* and then add *-es*. If a vowel comes before the *-y*, simply add *-s*; if a consonant comes before the *-y*, you must change *-y* to *-i* and add *-es*.

Nouns Ending in -y

Preceded by a Vowel		Preceded by a Consonant	
Singular	*Plural*	*Singular*	*Plural*
alley	alleys	ally	all*ies*
boy	boys	battery	batter*ies*
day	days	city	cit*ies*
essay	essays	lady	lad*ies*
key	keys	minority	minorit*ies*
play	plays	party	part*ies*
toy	toys	treaty	treat*ies*

Exercise 17.3

Fill in the plural forms of the nouns in parentheses.

1. (country) Malcolm and Denise visited six _____ on their tour of South America.
2. (replay) In the National Football League, referees can use_____ to review controversial calls.
3. (entry) All _____ must be received by July 10 to be eligible to win the contest.
4. (deity) Most modern religions worship one god, but ancient religions had many _____ .
5. (ray) Certain _____ of the sun are harmless; others can damage the skin.
6. (anxiety) Students must learn to manage their _____ about writing papers and taking tests.
7. (decoy) Duck hunters often use _____ .
8. (memory) Our _____ of last summer are very pleasant.
9. (diary) Some years ago, a German magazine published excerpts from the _____ of Hitler, but they turned out to be counterfeit.
10. (alloy) These bolts are made of steel-and-zinc _____ .

Forming Irregular Noun Plurals.   Unfortunately, some nouns do not form plurals using the rules above. Thus, they are considered irregular. Because there are no rules for these nouns, you have to memorize the plural forms, or check a dictionary when you are not sure. You probably know most irregular plurals already from speaking and hearing them, but look for the ones that give you trouble and be sure to memorize them.

Nouns ending in *-f* or *-fe* that form plurals with *-ves:*

Singular	*Plural*
calf	cal*ves*
half	hal*ves*
hoof	hoo*ves*
knife	kni*ves*
leaf	lea*ves*
life	li*ves*
loaf	loa*ves*
self	sel*ves*
shelf	shel*ves*
thief	thie*ves*
wharf	whar*ves*
wife	wi*ves*

Nouns changing in the middle or with highly irregular endings:

Singular	*Plural*
child	children
foot	feet
goose	geese
man	men
mouse	mice
ox	oxen
woman	women

Nouns not changing in plural (note that all are animals or fish):

bass	bass
carp	carp
deer	deer
fish	fish
moose	moose
sheep	sheep
shrimp	shrimp

Many irregular plurals are very common words—for example, children, men, people, women. However, beginners sometimes make errors when they add -*s* to words that are already plural:

Nonstandard: The men*s* went fishing and caught six carp*s*.
Standard: The men went fishing and caught six carp.
Nonstandard: Some people*s* are always trying to be better than others.
Standard: Some people are always trying to be better than others.
Nonstandard: After running around all day, the children*s* said their feet*s* hurt.
Standard: After running around all day, the children said their feet hurt.
Nonstandard: Two moose*s* and three deer*s* ran across the pasture, scaring the sheep*s*.
Standard: Two moose and three deer ran across the pasture, scaring the sheep.

Exercise 17.4

Correct any nonstandard plurals in these sentences. If a plural is correct, put a C above it.

1. The mens were arrested for carrying knifes.
2. Not all womens want to be wives.
3. While camping on a mountainside one night, we heard the heavy hooves of mooses crossing the field below.
4. Use these knives to cut those loafs of bread, and make sure all the childrens get slices with butter and jam.
5. Some peoples do not remember that they were once children.
6. The mouses ran out the door.
7. Our culture teaches women to believe that small feet are a sign of femininity.
8. The men made a rustling sound as they walked through the fallen leafs.
9. It is said that cats have nine lifes, but many fishermen believe fishes have nine lives too.
10. In the nineteenth century, few persons lived in homes with indoor plumbing.

Adding Suffixes to Verbs

If you have studied Chapter 16, you know that regular verbs add the suffix -s in the third-person form of the present tense and the suffix -ed in the past tense and past participle:

Third-person present: he plays, she plays, it plays
Past tense: I played, you played, we played, they played
Past participle: she has played, they have played

While most verbs form these tenses this way, some do not, and to avoid erroneous forms or misspellings, you must follow rules similar to those you followed when forming plural nouns.

Adding -es to Verbs in Third-Person Present.   When verbs end in -s, -x, -z, -ch, or -sh, you must add -es.

bless	+	es	=	blesses
box	+	es	=	boxes
buzz	+	es	=	buzzes
touch	+	es	=	touches
crush	+	es	=	crushes

As you did with noun plurals, read these examples aloud, listening carefully to the -es sound. Try to hear the sound in speaking and listening so that you won't forget to add -es when using this form of the verb.

Exercise 17.5

Fill in the blanks with the third-person present form of the verb in parentheses.

1. (quench) Lemonade _____ thirst on a hot day.
2. (reach) Even the *average* car in the Indianapolis 500 _____ speeds of over 200 miles an hour.
3. (kiss) Though the Linders are in their seventies, Mr. Linder_____ his wife goodbye each time he leaves the house.

4. (crush) The large machine at the junkyard _____ cars down to the size of a mattress.
5. (sass) If a high school student continually _____ teachers, he or she can be suspended.
6. (touch) The little boy's nose barely _____ the window sill as he peeks out at his friends.
7. (box; punch) A lightweight fighter generally _____ while a heavyweight _____ .
8. (push) Professor Thorpe _____ students to do their best.
9. (buzz) A bumble bee _____ louder than a fly.
10. (reach; plunge) The roller coaster slowly _____ the top of the first hill and then _____ furiously down the other side.

Adding Suffixes to Verbs Ending in -y. Some verbs that end in -y simply add -s to form the third-person present and -ed to form the past and past participle. In these verbs, the -y is preceded by a vowel (a, e, i, o, u). But if a consonant comes before the -y in a verb, to form the third-person present you change the -y to -i and add -es. To form the past and past participle, you change the -y to -i and add -ed.

Verbs Ending in -y

	Preceded by a Vowel		Preceded by a Consonant	
Base	*Third-Person Present*	*Base*	*Third-Person Present*	*Past and Past Participle*
bray	brays	cry	cries	cried
delay	delays	dry	dries	dried
obey	obeys	defy	defies	defied
play	plays	fry	fries	fried
pray	prays	pry	pries	pried
stay	stays	try	tries	tried

Of course, this rule works only for regular verbs ending in -y. Irregular verbs will take different forms:

Base	*Third-Person Present*	*Past*	*Past Participle*
buy	buys	bought	bought
fly	flies	flew	flown
pay	pays	paid	paid
say	says	said	said

If you are not sure whether a verb ending in -*y* is regular or irregular, refer to a dictionary and check the section on irregular verbs in Chapter 15.

Exercise 17.6

Fill in the standard forms for the verbs in parentheses. All verbs are regular.

1. (deny) Charles Manson _____ all charges brought against him in the murder of Sharon Tate.
2. (replay) A VCR records and _____ movies and television programs.
3. (supply) Wanaque Reservoir _____ northern New Jersey with much of its water.
4. (stay; rely) Gus _____ away from casual acquaintances and _____ on only a few close friends.
5. (defray) Scholarships have _____ high tuition costs for deserving students.
6. (horrify) Child abuse _____ any humane person.
7. (display) Last night Leon _____ his immaturity.
8. (allay) An A on the midterm _____ any fears Jerome had about doing poorly in chemistry.
9. (parlay) Jesse _____ an outgoing personality and a fierce determination into fame and fortune.
10. (ply) Jack _____ his sister with compliments before asking to borrow her car.

Editing Faulty Comparisons

Words can easily be misused when a sentence is making a comparison. Comparisons are made with adjectives and adverbs, which function as modifiers. Adjectives modify nouns and other adjectives by describing them. For example, in the phrase *a bright red coat*, both *bright* and *red* are adjectives, with *red* describing the noun *coat* and *bright* describing the adjective *red*. Adverbs can modify verbs, other adverbs, adjectives, or even whole groups of words. As a native speaker of English, you use adjectives and adverbs all the time without thinking about them. And most of the time you probably use the standard-

English forms, so you need not worry about how to define them or how they function. However, beginning writers sometimes misuse them when making comparisons.

Adverbs and adjectives often show comparisons when they end in *-er* and *-est:*

Adjective (each modifying the noun *student*):
Lance is a *good* student.
Meredith is a *better* student.
Maria is the *best* student.

Adverb (each modifying the verb *reads*):
Lance reads *fast.*
Meredith reads *faster.*
Maria reads *fastest.*

Making comparisons with *-er* and *-est* endings is not usually difficult, but you need to remember to use the *-er* form to compare two things and the *-est* form only to compare more than two:

Nonstandard: Lyle is the young*est* of the two brothers.
Standard: Lyle is the young*er* of the two brothers.

You can remember this rule by thinking how you would make the comparison using *than.* Compare these sentences:

Nonstandard: Kyle is youngest than his brother.
Standard: Kyle is younger than his brother.

Adjectives and adverbs can also be compared by using the words *more/most* and *less/least:*

Adjective
Mike is *active* in student government.
Rita is *more active* in student government.
Heather is *the most active* in student government.

Adverb
Kevin dances *gracefully.*
Kim dances *less gracefully* than Kevin.
Isaac dances *least gracefully* of the three.

You may wonder when you should use *-er* and *-est* endings to show a comparison, and when you should use *more/most* or *less/least*.
Adverbs ending in *-ly* are compared with *more/most* and *less/least:*

bravely	more bravely	most bravely
deadly	more deadly	most deadly
loudly	more loudly	most loudly
poorly	more poorly	most poorly
quietly	more quietly	most quietly

As for adjectives, if they are one syllable, they are always compared by adding *-er* and *-est:*

bright	brighter	brightest
drunk	drunker	drunkest
fine	finer	finest
great	greater	greatest
poor	poorer	poorest
rich	richer	richest

Two-syllable adjectives ending in *-y* also can form comparisons using *-er* and *-est*, but notice that the *-y* is changed to *-i*. Two-syllable adjectives ending in *-le* add *-r* and *-st.*

able	abler	ablest
easy	easier	easiest
funny	funnier	funniest
happy	happier	happiest
mighty	mightier	mightiest
nimble	nimbler	nimblest
simple	simpler	simplest
tiny	tinier	tiniest

Any two-syllable adjectives not ending in *-y* or *-le* and any adjectives with more than two syllables form comparisons by using *more/most* and *less/least:*

active	more active	most active
beautiful	more beautiful	most beautiful
effective	more effective	most effective
famous	more famous	most famous
grateful	more grateful	most grateful
magnificent	more magnificent	most magnificent

outrageous	more outrageous	most outrageous
passive	more passive	most passive
tolerant	more tolerant	most tolerant

Notice that aside from being longer words, these adjectives end in *-ive, -ful, -nt,* or *-ous.*

Nonstandard comparisons occur when writers misuse the means of comparisons:

Nonstandard: Not many people are *more rich* than Donald Trump.
Standard: Not many people are *richer* than Donald Trump.
Nonstandard: Louise is the *attractivist* girl in the class, but her sister is even *beautifuller.*
Standard: Louise is the *most attractive* girl in the class, but her sister is even *more beautiful.*

Your familiarity with English should tell you that these comparisons simply do not sound right, but if you are not used to writing or do not edit carefully, you can slip into making faulty comparisons.

Another type of faulty comparison occurs when the writer uses an *-er* or *-est* ending along with *more/most* or *less/least:*

Nonstandard: Alex's brother is *more bigger* than he is.
Standard: Alex's brother is *bigger* than he is.
Nonstandard: That joke was the *least funniest* I have ever heard.
Standard: That joke was the *least funny* I have ever heard.

Exercise 17.7

For each adjective and adverb, write the comparative forms:

courageous	_____	_____
feisty	_____	_____
surely	_____	_____
stingy	_____	_____
gray	_____	_____
supple	_____	_____
awful	_____	_____
angry	_____	_____

small	_____	_____
light	_____	_____
efficient	_____	_____
truly	_____	_____
wise	_____	_____
wisely	_____	_____
tiny	_____	_____
subtle	_____	_____

Exercise 17.8

Correct any faulty comparisons. If a comparative form is correct, place a C above it.

1. Mexican food is more spicier than Italian food.
2. *Huckleberry Finn* is the best of the two books.
3. This movie is less duller than that one.
4. Both Henry and Tommy Aaron played major league baseball, but Henry played better and longest.
5. Lana is the hardest-working person I know.
6. A Corvette is expensiver than a Camaro, and it also looks more sportier.
7. Time passed quicklier than we expected.
8. Liz is seriouser about her studies than Faye is, but Faye still earns the best grades.
9. Richard wanted to find a better apartment than the one he lived in.
10. Natalie is always the noisiest person at the party.

Exercise 17.9

Write five sentences of your own in which you use adjectives or adverbs in comparisons.

Using the Dictionary

Many word errors can be edited by using a dictionary. If you do not already own a good dictionary, buy one to use throughout college. Avoid pocket-size dictionaries, which usually do not contain all the information a good dictionary should. Your instructor may require a particular dictionary for class. If not, here are a few of the many to choose from. Each is available in paperback:

American Heritage Dictionary of the English Language
Merriam Webster's Collegiate Dictionary
Random House Dictionary of the English Language
Webster's New World Dictionary

Though you will most often use the dictionary to find the meaning of words, dictionary entries can tell you much more. Below is a definition from the *American Heritage Dictionary of the English Language*.

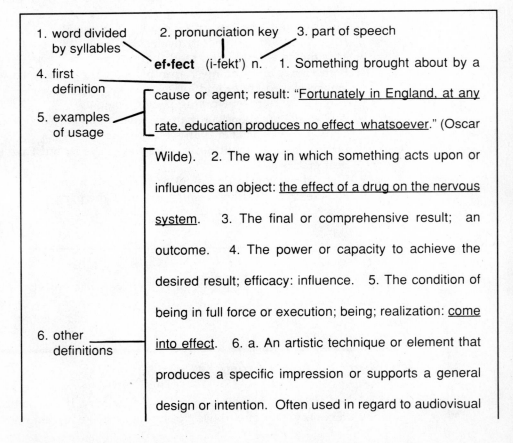

1. word divided by syllables   2. pronunciation key   3. part of speech

ef·fect (i-fekt') n.   1. Something brought about by a cause or agent; result: "Fortunately in England, at any rate, education produces no effect whatsoever." (Oscar Wilde).   2. The way in which something acts upon or influences an object: the effect of a drug on the nervous system.   3. The final or comprehensive result; an outcome.   4. The power or capacity to achieve the desired result; efficacy: influence.   5. The condition of being in full force or execution; being; realization: come into effect.   6. a. An artistic technique or element that produces a specific impression or supports a general design or intention. Often used in regard to audiovisual

4. first definition

5. examples of usage

6. other definitions

7. Idiomatic usage and definitions

techniques: <u>The effectiveness of the animated cartoon depends on special effects</u>.   b. The impression produced by an artifice or manner of presentation.   7. The basic meaning or tendency of something said or written; purport: <u>He said something to that effect</u>.   **—in effect**. 1. In fact; actually. 2. In essence; virtually. 3. In active force; in operation. **—take effect**. To become opera-

8. Second part of speech and definitions

tive; gain active force. **—**<u>tr. v.</u> 1. **effected, -fecting, fects.**   1. To produce as a result; cause to occur; bring about: <u>"If he is taught to fear and tremble, enough has been effected</u>." (De Quincey).   2. To execute; to make: <u>"important change of ancient custom can only be effected by act of Parliament</u>" (Winston Churchill).

9. Cross references

—See Synonyms at **perform**.   **—**See usage note at **affect**. [Middle English, from Old French, from Latin

10. Etymology

<u>effectus</u>, past participle of <u>efficere</u>, to accomplish, perform, work out: <u>ex-</u>, out + <u>facere</u>, to do (see dhe-[1] in and suffixes Appendix*] **—ef fect' er** <u>n</u>. **—ef fect' ible** <u>adj</u>.

11. Other forms and suffixes

12. Synonyms and explanations of different meanings	**Synonyms:** <u>effect, consequence, result, and outcome, upshot, sequel, consummation</u>. These nouns denote occurrences, situations, or conditions that are traceable to something antecedent. An <u>effect</u> is that which is produced by the action of an agent or cause and follows it in time immediately or shortly. A <u>consequence</u> also follows the action of an agent and is traceable to it, but the relationship between them is less sharply definable and less immediate that that between a cause and its effect. A <u>result</u> is . . .

As you can see from this example, dictionary definitions can tell us a lot. And they can seem complicated! However, all the parts of a definition, and the way parts are presented, are explained in the introduction at the front of the dictionary. The explanation of the parts of this definition will help you get an idea of how dictionaries work.

1. Word divided by syllables: The entry for each word in a dictionary breaks the word into parts (syllables) according to the way the word is pronounced. Syllables are separated by dots. Paying attention to the syllables can help you spell the word.
2. Pronunciation key: In parentheses, you have the phonetic spelling of the word. That is, the word is spelled and marked according to the way it is pronounced. Some of the symbols may seem confusing. To find out how to pronounce them, check the chart in the front of the dictionary or look at the bottom of the page. Beginning at the bottom of the left-hand page and running across to the bottom of the right page is a list that uses common words to give examples of

the sounds. For instance, *ar/care* means the *ar* in a word is pronounced like the *ar* in *care,* rather than like the *ar* in *bar* or *carry.*

3. Part of speech: In the example, *n.* stands for *noun—effect* is defined first as a noun. Other abbreviations are *v.* for *verb, adv.* for *adverb, adj.* for *adjective,* and so on. A complete list of abbreviations is available in the front of your dictionary.

4. First definition: The front of your dictionary will tell you what the order of definitions means. It is important to know because some dictionaries list the definitions by beginning with the one most widely used and then moving to the one used least. Other dictionaries arrange the definitions historically, beginning with the way the word was first used and then moving to the more modern uses. In this type, definitions in use today will come last, and the first couple of definitions might not be in use anymore.

5. Example of usage: Sometimes, but not always, the definition will show how the word is used in a phrase or sentence. Sometimes the sentence in the example comes from a famous writer, whose name then appears in parentheses.

6. Other definitions: Often a word has more than one definition. Good dictionaries list most or all meanings. Poor dictionaries might only give you a couple, and you may not find the meaning you need.

7. Idiomatic usage and definitions: When a word is used in an idiom, it is used in a way particular to the language. It also is used in combination with another word or other words. For instance, if you ask a friend to *come over* for dinner, the phrase *come over* is an idiom because those words are used together that way only in the English language. Most languages have idioms of their own. A few common ones in English are *take up, carry on, turn off, sleep in, stay up, wait out.* If a word is used in idioms, a good dictionary will define the idioms. See *in effect,* for example.

8. Second part of speech and definitions: Often a word can be used as more than one part of speech. The dictionary will usually give definitions first for the part of speech in which the word is most often used. The definition of *effect* first gives definitions of the word as a noun because it is used most frequently as a noun. Then *effect* is defined as a transitive verb (*tr. v.*). Notice that the definitions start again

at number one after the word is defined as a different part of speech.

9. Cross references: Cross references begin with the word *see* and direct you to another part of the dictionary for more information. In the definition of *effect*, one cross reference tells you to "See usage note at **affect**." People often confuse the words *effect* and *affect*, so the usage note with the definition of *affect* would help them to avoid that error. Another cross reference tells you to see the appendix, a section at the back of the dictionary that tells more about the words.

10. Etymology: The etymology of a word is its history, from its first use to its most recent use. The etymology tells what languages the word came from before it came into English. Unless you become a language historian, you might not find etymology very useful, but it can be fascinating at times to know where words come from. For instance, the word *sandwich* comes from the Fourth Earl of Sandwich, the eighteenth-century Englishman who invented that way of eating so that he would not have to leave the gambling table to eat his meals.

11. Other forms and suffixes: As you know, suffixes can change the functions of words. Often dictionary definitions will contain suffixes. If the word is a verb, most likely the definition will provide suffixes to show the different forms of the verb, as in walk, walk*s*, walk*ed*, walk*ing*. Definitions often provide the plural forms of nouns and the comparative forms of adjectives.

12. Synonyms: Words that have similar definitions are called *synonyms*. For some words in the dictionary, you will find lists of synonyms, as is the case with our example. Then each word will be defined and small differences in meaning explained.

13. Labels: The sample definition of *effect* has no labels, but labels are worth knowing about. There are two types of labels. The first type notes specialized uses of a word: the way it's used in a certain field or activity. For example, under the word *down*, one definition reads, "*Football*. Any of a series of four plays during which a team must advance at least ten yards to retain possession of the ball." This first type of label often refers to areas of study, from architecture to zoology, and tells us how people in a given field use the

word. This can be helpful because your textbooks often use words in a specialized way. The second type of label tells if a meaning is nonstandard, slang, informal, vulgar, poetic (used only in poems), regional (used only in a certain geographic area), obsolete, and so on.

As you can see from this discussion of the *American Heritage* definition of *effect*, a dictionary can provide much information about a word. You probably will use the dictionary most to find the spellings and meanings of words, but becoming familiar with the parts of dictionary definitions can teach you much more.

Exercise 17.10

Use your dictionary to answer the following questions. If you have trouble, refer to the introduction at the front of your dictionary for help.

1. How is the word *exemplify* divided into syllables?
2. What languages are listed under the etymology of *oil* in your dictionary?
3. List and translate the abbreviations for the parts of speech under your dictionary's definition of *sack*.
4. What symbols represent the two a's in *paradise*?
5. Write a word that has an *a* sound like the second *a* in *paradise* and circle the letter that represents the sound.
6. What is the label for the definition of *ain't?*
7. List the suffix forms given in the definition of *reflect*.
8. Give one label referring to a field in the definition of the word *plea*.
9. Find a word in your dictionary that lists synonyms. Choose one of the synonyms and explain how it is different from the word you have chosen.
10. Does your dictionary list definitions historically from the first usage to the latest? Or does it list them according to how frequently they are used?

While the dictionary can tell you much about words, often you will use it to find the correct spellings of words. Perhaps you have had teachers tell you to use the dictionary to check your spelling. Students often wonder how they can find a word in the dictionary if they cannot spell it. That's a good question.

When you misspell a word, you are usually off by only one or two letters, and almost never will you miss the first letter. As a result, you have a place to start in the dictionary. For instance, suppose you write *discribe,* and your teacher marks the word wrong. Begin in the dictionary under the letter *d,* but do not, of course, look at all the words. Start with words beginning with *di.* If you do not find the word there—and you won't—ask yourself what other letter might follow the *d.* Use vowels—*a, e, i, o, u*—first. If you try *a,* you will probably recognize quickly that it does not fit, because you will know that *da* will not produce the sound *disk* in *discribe.* So you try *e.* It seems possible, and when you look under *de* in the dictionary, you will find *describe,* properly spelled with an *e.* Like everything else, using the dictionary to find correct spellings takes practice, so let's practice a bit.

Exercise 17.11

Using your dictionary, find the correct spelling for each of the following misspelled words.

1. artical	7. benifit
2. defenite	8. atitude
3. calander	9. impatients
4. enevelop	10. preformance
5. occured	11. mistery
6. analize	12. fullfil

Editing Easily Confused Words

Many English words sound the same—or almost the same—as other words when spoken, yet they are spelled differently and have different meanings. When you write, it is easy to confuse such words because you do not hear the difference even when you read the writing aloud. For example, in a draft, you might write, "A four-bedroom house is probably to large for a single person." If you noticed that the word *to* does not seem right, you have caught me confusing *to* with *too*. Although there are many such confusing words, you probably have trouble with only a few of them.

The following list explains the meanings and differences between words that can easily be confused. If you find yourself having trouble with any of these words, consult the list as you edit your draft and after your teacher has returned your paper. Confusing words take time and patience to eliminate, but if you find out which words give you the most trouble, the list will help you eliminate your errors.

a/an When we refer to most things in English, we use *a*: a boat, a boy, a school, a computer, a house. *A* appears more often than *an* because *a* is used before words beginning with most consonants, and there are twenty-one consonants in the alphabet as opposed to only five vowels. *An* is used with almost all words that start with the vowels *a,e,i,o,* and *u*, if the *u* is pronounced to sound like *uh*. For example: an umbrella, an ulcer, an uncle, an upset, an unfortunate person. If a word begins with a *u* or any sound that is pronounced like *you*, use *a*. For example: a unicorn, a university, a useful tool, a eulogy, a European. To simplify the rules, remember that *an* is used before all vowel sounds except those that sound like *you*; otherwise, use *a*. Study the following lists:

a	*an*
a bus	an apple
a eunuch	an envelope
a home run	an honor (the *h* is silent)
a kite	an improvement
a miracle	an octopus
a useless plan	an urgent message

are/our When you confuse these two words, you are mixing up a verb, *are*, with a word that shows possession, *our*. Compare these words in the following sentences:

Jim and Mike *are* coming to *our* house tonight.
Our tomato plants *are* growing tall.
They *are* rooting against *our* team.
Are you coming to *our* party this weekend?
Where *are our* books?

do/due *Do* is a verb, as in the following sentence: "I *do* my homework late in the evening." *Due* means something must be done by a certain time: "My car payment is *due* the first week of each month." Or *due* can be used in place of *because*: "The picnic was cancelled *due* to the rain." Compare these words in the following sentences:

> *Do* you know when our term papers are *due*?
> *Due* to the holiday, your paper will not be *due* until next week. Thus, you will have time to *do* other assignments.
> We always *do* our income taxes the day before they are *due*.

ever/every *Ever* is an adverb that refers to time: "Do you *ever* go to the opera?" *Every* is an adjective that means *each:* "*Every* student must work hard to learn to write well." Compare these words in the following sentences:

> If I *ever* win the lottery, I will travel to *every* country in the world.
> *Every* payday, Jim wondered if he would *ever* get all his bills paid.

feel/fill You *feel* good or bad, or you *feel* something with your hands. You *fill* a glass, a bowl, or any other container:

> I always *feel* better when I *fill* my gas tank.
> The boss *feels* we should *fill* the large storage room with the old merchandise.
> If you *fill* your stomach with junk food, you won't *feel* like having dinner.

have/of Rarely does anyone confuse these two words, except when using *of* for *have* as part of a verb form. For example, you might mistakenly write, "I should *of* done better on the test." Using *of* as a verb is nonstandard. It happens because we often make contractions of verb forms that include *have: Could have* becomes *could've; would have* becomes *would've;* and *should have* becomes *should've.* But when someone says *could've,* for instance, we hear instead *could of,* which is not a standard-English form. Compare the sentences below. Which ones use standard forms?

> We *could have* danced all night.
> We *could've* danced all night.
> We *could of* danced all night.

hear/here *Hear* is what you do with your ear. This meaning is not hard to remember because the word *ear* is in *hear. Here* refers to a place:

> Come *here* so that I can *hear* you better.
> Did I *hear* you say you won't be *here* tomorrow?
> When he gets *here,* we will have to *hear* all about his trip.

it's/its *It's* is a contraction of *it is:* "*It's* raining today." *Its* is the possessive form of *it:* "We liked the car because of *its* shiny paint job." You would never say or write: "We liked the car because of *it is* shiny paint job," but it is easy to write "*it's* paint job" because we associate apostrophes with possession and often think that all words with apostrophes are possessive (see discussion of apostrophes in Chapter 18). However, the apostrophe is never used with personal pronouns to show possession. *Its* is a pronoun and thus never uses an apostrophe to show possession. Compare *it's* and *its* in these sentences:

> Our dog hides when *it's* time for *its* bath.
> We assumed the computer was broken when *its* screen went blank, but *it's* working now.

knew/new *Knew,* like the word *know,* comes from the word *knowledge.* Notice that all three start with *kn. New* means fresh, unused:

> Herschel bought *new* shoes. Tammy has a *new* haircut.
> Anton *knew* that soon he would have to make *new* friends.
> The *new* coach *knew* she would have to win her players' confidence.
> The experienced soldiers *knew* that the *new* recruits were not ready for combat.

know/no Like *knew, know* comes from *knowledge. No* is a negative answer or a word used to mean *not any* or *hardly any:*

> *No,* we can't go with you to the show; we *know* you will forgive us.
> I *know* I will have *no* chance to pass Chemistry I unless I study.
> Linda *knows* the course will pose *no* problems for her because she got an A in advanced chemistry in high school.
> Did you *know* that *no* one is going to Vic's party?

passed/past *Passed* is the past-tense form of the verb *to pass:*

> Driving through Washington, D.C., we *passed* the White House.
> I *passed* her the ketchup.
> Anna *passed* the test.

In contrast, *past* can be a noun, adjective, or adverb, but it is never a verb:

> The *past* can come back to haunt us.
> She is *past* president of the city council.
> We walked *past* the ice cream shop.

Compare the use of *passed* and *past:*

> In *past* seasons, the Bears' quarterback *passed* much more effectively than he did this year.
> The word *passed* is the *past* tense of the verb *pass.*
> She was not a good student in the *past*, but this semester she has *passed* all her tests and is earning high grades.

right/write When you *write*, you do what this book has been trying to teach you to do. When you are *right*, you are not wrong. Also you have a *right* to vote, and you know *right* from *left*. Note the differences as these words are used below:

> All American citizens have the *right* to speak or *write* their opinions freely.
> Next time, I will *write* down the directions to your house, for I got lost when I made a *right* instead of a left at the corner.
> Your plan for increasing sales seems *right*, but *write* a report so the sales force will know what you are trying to do.

than/then These words are very confusing in writing because many people pronounce them the same way when speaking. *Than* is used when you are comparing: "Her chili is spicier *than* mine." *Then* marks time, signifying that one thing came after another: "Keith set the table; *then* we all sat down for dinner." If you confuse these words, be careful to edit them by sight as you read your draft. Listening for the difference between them won't help unless you pronounce them differently. Compare their use in these sentences:

> If you would rather buy a German car *than* an American car, *then* you probably will have to spend more money.
> *Then* Jośe said that the Cubs are a better team *than* the Cardinals.
> Typewriters made writing easier *than* it had been when writers used only pen and paper; *then* computers came along, making writing even easier.

their/they're/there These words may be confused more often than any others, so you need to edit carefully if you have trouble using them. *Their* is a pronoun that shows possession: "All the farmers are harvesting *their* crops." *They're* is a contraction of *they are:* "*They're (They are)* harvesting their crops." *There* refers to a place or is used with a verb to point to something: "I like New York, but I have not been *there* in years. *There* is the Statute of Liberty!" Compare the way the words are used in sentences:

They're going to Disneyland for *their* vacation even though they have been *there* six times before.
In the Rocky Mountains, *there* are some of the tallest peaks in the world. *They're* as much as 14,000 feet above sea level.

threw/through *Threw* is the past form of the verb *throw:* "The pitcher *threw* his fastball." *Through* is not a verb: "Are you *through* watching television? I would not want to sit *through* that movie again." Note the differences:

Merle was galloping *through* the woods when her horse *threw* her.
After making a crucial error, Lenny *threw* down his mitt and decided he was *through* with baseball.
When Michelle was *through* reading the newspaper, she *threw* it away.

to/too/two *Two* is the word for the number 2. It is rarely confused with the others, but *to* and *too* are not as easy to keep straight. *To* is a preposition indicating motion toward: *to* the store. Or it is part of the infinitive form of a verb: *to* have, *to* be, *to* run. Students rarely use *too* when they mean *to*, but very often when they mean *too*—as in *too* large, too tired—they leave off the second *o*. To remember when to use *too*, think of it as having *too* many *o*'s. Compare the usages in these sentences:

We stayed up late *to* watch a Dracula film festival on cable, but after seeing *two* movies, we were *too* tired to see anymore.
Too many students want *to* major in business without knowing *too* much about it.
Two drinks can be *too* much if you are driving.

weather/whether *Weather* refers to climate conditions—rain, snow, wind, sunshine: "The *weather* should be clear today." *Whether* can substitute for *if:* "Phil does not know *whether* he wants to major in aviation." Note the different uses of these words:

The team did not know *whether* the game would be cancelled because of bad *weather*.
The *weather* report was unclear about *whether* it would rain.
Whether you live in a warm or cold climate, there will always be days when the *weather* is not to your liking.

who's/whose *Who's* is a contraction of *who is:* "*Who's* (Who is) at the door? *Whose* is a possessive pronoun and thus never uses an apostrophe to show possession. Comparing *who's* and *whose* in these sentences should help you see the difference:

Who's the person *whose* car is parked in the driveway?
Who's having a party at *whose* house?

you're/your *You're* is a contraction of *you are. Your* is a possessive pronoun and therefore has no apostrophe: *your* parents, *your* children, *your* book, *your* grades. Compare *you're* and *your* in the following sentences:

You're doing well in this course, and *your* grades reflect *your* effort.
Your friends and relatives are proud that *you're* attending college.
If *you're* working hard, *you're* getting closer to attaining *your* goals.

Exercise 17.12

Circle the form of the words that should be used in each sentence.

1. How (do/due) you (feel/fill) about this cold (whether/weather)?
2. (Its/It's) supposed to warm up tomorrow, but I'm not (to/too/two) sure it will.
3. I (know/no) that the (whether/weather) reports can't be trusted (ever/every) time.
4. In the (past/passed), my grades were low, but now that I have learned to (write/right), I am improving in all of my work.
5. I (should've/should of) done better last semester, but (its/it's) (too/to) late (to/too) worry about that now.
6. I (knew/new) I wasn't a good student (then/than), but this semester I am studying more effectively, and I (know/no) I will earn higher grades (than/then) I did last semester.
7. (Who's/Whose) writing course are you taking?
8. Excuse me, I didn't (hear/here) you.
9. (Who's/Whose) (your/you're) writing teacher?
10. Dr. Gaston is (knew/new) (here/hear) this year.
11. I (should've/should of) signed up for her class (too/to/two) because I need to get (through/threw) my English requirements.
12. Writing courses are not something you should just get (through/threw).

13. I (know/no), but at times (their/they're/there) really tough for me; I barely (passed/past) my first one.
14. Maybe you (should've/should of) given your teacher (a/an) apple. Or better yet, you (should've/should of) handed in (you're/your) papers when they were (do/due).
15. (Write/Right)!

Exercise 17.13

Correct any words that are misused in these sentences.

1. Many of the varsity athletes our doing well academically.
2. But their are some people who believe athletes are not serious about there education.
3. These people don't know how hard athletes have too work during the season.
4. Their expected to practice four hours a day and do not have to much time to study.
5. A athlete also must miss some classes when he or she goes on road trips with the team.
6. Some of the athletes try to due there homework while riding on the team bus.
7. Still, its common to here some students and teachers stereotype ever athlete as a dumb jock.
8. There not aware that at many schools the GPA of the athletes is higher then the GPA of the student body as an whole.
9. Granted, some athletes do not have good grades, but then their are many nonathletes who's grades aren't to good either.
10. Weather there athletes or not, all students are do respect, and know one has the write to stereotype them.

Exercise 17.14

Correct misused words in the following paragraphs.

Its sometimes common to believe that large cities such as New York and Los Angeles are the best places to live for people who enjoy a urban lifestyle. But smaller, Midwestern cities have much too offer. St. Louis, for example, with it's renovated waterfront and numerous restaurants and theaters, is a charming city. Indianapolis, do to much recent development, will soon be known for more then the Indy 500. Cincinnati boasts major league sports teams, some excellent restaurants, and a wonderful music hall, while maintaining the fill of a small town in it's ethnic neighborhoods. Even Minneapolis, despite the cold whether, is more cosmopolitan then most people no. So if your looking to settle in a city, don't overlook the cities of the Midwest.

Their has been much controversy about "colorized" films. Ted Turner, owner of cable stations WTBS and TNT, has purchased the rights too many of the great black-and-white film classics of the passed. Turner has had many of these films colorized, much too the displeasure of many directors, actors, producers, and fans. They argue that its wrong to change the way the original filmmakers conceived these films. A adventure film, such as *Captain Blood* with Errol Flynn, almost seems to benefit from colorization, but theirs something lost when *The Maltese Falcon,* with it's shadowy scenes and dark plot, is made to look as bright as ever situation comedy. Legally, Turner has the write to due what he wants with the films, but weather colorization is morally or artistically ethical is not to easy to say.

Exercise 17.15

Read over a short piece of your writing. Circle easily confused words that you have used correctly. Change any that you have used incorrectly.

Key Terms

Suffix: a letter or letters added to the end of a word to change its meaning or function.
Vowel: One of the letters *a, e, i, o, u.*
Consonant: Any letter except *a, e, i, o, u.*
Adjective: Modifying word used to describe nouns and other adjectives.
Adverb: Word that modifies verbs, adjectives, other adverbs, or whole groups of words.

chapter eighteen
Editing Punctuation and Capital Letters

As you have been developing your writing skills, you probably have had questions about punctuation, which can be troublesome. Many teachers have heard the story about the student who always left commas out. He became so frustrated that he put a line full of them at the end of his paper and then wrote his teacher a note saying she could put them in anywhere she wanted. This story may not be true, but it is funny and it shows the frustration writers sometimes feel when they do not have control of punctuation. Punctuation can be tricky, but actually there are not as many rules as you think. And the use of capital letters is not governed by as many rules as punctuation. But using a small (lowercase) letter when you need a capital can distract your reader just as any other error can. As with all other errors, you need to learn which points of punctuation give you trouble and then study the rules governing them.

End Punctuation

As you know, all sentences end with some mark of punctuation. The most common mark, of course, is the **period**. Other marks of end punctuation are the **question mark** and the **exclamation point**. Each has a purpose and affects meaning. Periods end declarative statements, question marks follow questions, and exclamation points express emotion:

> Declarative statement: The United States entered World War II in 1941.
> Question: Do you know how long World War II had been going on when the United States entered?
> Emotion: Hitler's concentration camps killed over five million people!

End punctuation is not too difficult to manage even for beginning writers because you can usually tell when you are simply making statements and when you are asking questions. Exclamation points can get a little trickier because in using one you assume that the reader will feel the same emotion as you do about the statement you are making. In most cases, the reader does. Some beginners, however, tend to overuse exclamation points. When there are too many in an essay, they no longer create the emphasis they are designed for. So reserve exclamation points for the strongest of statements.

Though used primarily as end punctuation, periods are also used in many abbreviations. Many words can be abbreviated, but the most common abbreviations refer to places, titles, time, and measurements. Can you identify the following abbreviations:

Places: St., Ave., N.Y., L.A., Fla.
Titles: Mr., Mrs., Dr., Maj., Pres.
Time: A.M., P.M., Feb., Dec.
Measurements: oz., qt., yd., lb., tsp.

Exercise 18.1

Supply the correct end punctuation and periods in abbreviations in the following sentences.

1. Can you believe that Mike added two tbsp of sugar to the recipe
2. The faculty will meet at 3:00 PM to discuss the new curriculum guide
3. The firefighter escaped from the building seconds before it collapsed
4. Kill the umpire
5. Leland asked Tonya for a date
6. A Mrs Cora Delano of St Johnsbury, Vt won over a million dollars in the Irish Sweepstakes
7. Have you ever walked down Sunset Blvd in Hollywood
8. The movie lasted four hours
9. Alex asked the waiter for more bread
10. Can I have more bread

Using the Comma

The comma is the mark of punctuation used most often. Some people say they can punctuate with commas by listening for pauses when they read sentences aloud. This method works sometimes, but not always, and it can cause you to add unnecessary commas. While it is good to use your ear as you punctuate, you cannot rely on it alone. There are five rules that can help you use commas effectively.

Rule 1: Commas Come Before Coordinating Conjunctions

Chapter 14 discussed the use of coordinating conjunctions as a way to fix comma splices and run-on sentences. You may also remember the coordinating conjunctions from Chapters 9 and 14: *but, and, for, nor, or, so, yet*. These chapters discussed how together the first letter of each conjunction spells *BAFNOSY*, a nonsense word that can help you remember the conjunctions. The rule governing commas used with coordinating conjunctions (or BAFNOSY words) is:

Put a comma before the conjunction when the conjunction joins two complete sentences. Remember that a sentence must have at least one subject and one verb. Note the examples:

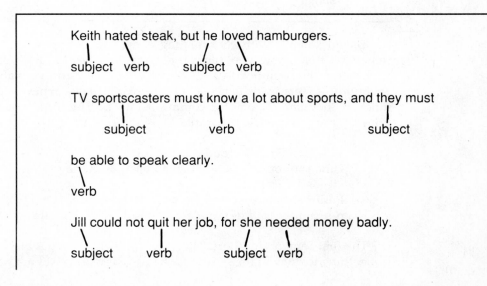

Keith hated steak, but he loved hamburgers.
subject verb   subject verb

TV sportscasters must know a lot about sports, and they must
subject   verb   subject

be able to speak clearly.
verb

Jill could not quit her job, for she needed money badly.
subject   verb   subject verb

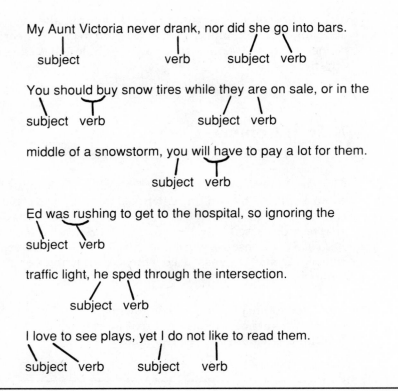

My Aunt Victoria never drank, nor did she go into bars.
subject   verb   subject verb

You should buy snow tires while they are on sale, or in the
subject verb   subject verb

middle of a snowstorm, you will have to pay a lot for them.
subject verb

Ed was rushing to get to the hospital, so ignoring the
subject verb

traffic light, he sped through the intersection.
subject verb

I love to see plays, yet I do not like to read them.
subject verb   subject   verb

Using commas with coordinating conjunctions is not too difficult if you remember that before you add the comma, you need at least one subject and verb before the conjunction and at least one subject and verb after. Sometimes beginning writers learn half the rule, thinking that whenever they use a conjunction they should place a comma before it. This notion leads to a lot of unnecessary commas. For example:

Vito is poor, *but* proud.

Gina cannot decide whether to use her money to buy a new car, *or* to save it for a vacation.

I must save money now because in the summer I am buying new dining room furniture, *and* in the fall a new sofa for the living room.

The first sentence is short. Thus, the comma seems out of place. But length has nothing to do with the punctuation. The comma should not be there because there is no subject and verb after the conjunction *but*. In contrast, the third sentence is quite long—twenty-seven words, in fact. When beginners see a sentence this long, they panic, thinking a sentence of twenty-seven words must need a comma somewhere. But if you look at the ten words following the conjunction *and*, you will not find a subject and verb. Thus, the comma isn't needed.

Exercise 18.2

Add any commas needed before conjunctions, and cross out any that are not needed. If a comma is used correctly with a conjunction, place a C above it.

1. Jody is an excellent swimmer but he is afraid to try scuba diving, or water skiing.
2. After becoming the first person to fly across the Atlantic, Charles Lindbergh became an international hero, and he was invited to many different countries.
3. Calvert Country Club has a short, but difficult golf course.
4. Last year's president of the student government ran again this year, but she lost by four hundred votes.
5. The movie was, so long and boring.
6. The novel *Mutiny on the Bounty* has been made into a film many times yet no version is as good as the one with Clark Gable and Charles Laughton.
7. Would you rather paint the house this summer, or wait for the cool weather in the fall?
8. Louise enjoys living in the city because she can go downtown to shop and see films or out to the parks to jog.
9. Angelo eats neither porkchops, nor veal cutlets yet he claims to love meat.
10. The university planned a reception, for the new freshmen from Japan.

Exercise 18.3

Add and cross out commas to correct the punctuation of this paragraph. Circle any commas used correctly.

Charles Darwin's theory of evolution shocked the world in the nineteenth century, and still causes controversy today. Through the study of plants, and animals, Darwin theorized that humans had evolved from animals. Scientists were fascinated by Darwin's work yet they worried that it questioned the teachings of the Bible. Thus, Darwin had many enemies in the scientific community but also many friends who defended him. The British philosopher Thomas Huxley believed strongly in Darwin's theory, so he wrote essays, and gave speeches in Darwin's defense. Today most scientists accept Darwin's theory of evolution but many religious people question it. People can believe in Darwin's theory, or in the biblical story of creation, but the origin of the human race remains a controversial topic.

Review a paper you have written, adding and removing commas used with coordinating conjunctions.

Rule 2: Commas Follow Sentence Openers

All sentences, as you know, must have at least one independent clause. But very often, sentences do not start with an independent clause. Instead, a sentence may open with a word, a phrase, or a dependent clause:

Words:	*Yesterday,* the Electro Power Company announced that it may build two nuclear power plants.
	However, the plants will be much smaller than those now operating in the United States.
Phrases:	*In 1979,* a near-meltdown in the nuclear reactor at Three Mile Island, Pennsylvania, led to new safety regulations for nuclear power plants.
	Despite the near tragedy at Three Mile Island, the Electro Company believes nuclear plants are safe.
	Before Electro builds the reactors, its plans must be approved by the federal government.
	After the construction begins next May, federal inspectors will visit the plants periodically to ensure regulations are followed.

Rule 2 is not as difficult to remember as some others. In most cases, you can trust your ear to help you punctuate because you pause after you have read the sentence beginning and before you read the independent clause. This is not always true for one-word beginnings, but for the others, listening for the pause can help you hear where to put the comma.

Exercise 18.4

Put commas where needed after the sentence openers.

1. On the fourteenth of July the French celebrate Bastille Day.
2. Just as the Fourth of July celebrates America's freedom Bastille Day celebrates freedom for the French.
3. In many countries there is one national holiday that is as significant to the people as July Fourth is to Americans.
4. For example the English celebrate Guy Fawlkes Day.
5. Despite its name this holiday does not honor Fawlkes.
6. As a member of a revolutionary group Fawlkes devised a plan to blow up Parliament, the building that houses British lawmakers.
7. Before Fawlkes could carry out his plan he was caught.
8. As a result he was hanged for treason.
9. On the first day of May the U.S.S.R. celebrates the anniversary of the Communist Revolution of 1917.
10. Though many Americans do not think Communism is something to celebrate May Day is the most important holiday in the Soviet Union.

Exercise 18.5

Add commas after sentence openers in this paragraph.

Although workers today take medical insurance for granted it is only in the last fifty years that companies began to provide benefits for workers who fall ill or are injured on the job. In nineteenth-century industrial America medical benefits were unheard of. If workers were hospitalized they had to pay their own bills. Even when injured on the job a worker would not receive any compensation from the company. In contrast a worker injured in a job-related accident today would have all bills paid by the company and might even receive an additional sum if the injury occurred as a result of the company's negligence.

Review a paper you have written, circling the commas you have used after sentence openers. If you find any commas missing, add them.

Rule 3: Commas Follow Each Item in a Series

When you have a series of three or more words, phrases or clauses, separate them with commas:

Words:	Ricardo bought *a hat, a sweater, and a coat.*
Phrases:	Brian takes a walk *in the morning, just after lunch, and early in the evening.*
	Althea has won awards for *singing in a church choir, working with disadvantaged children, and protecting the rights of animals.*
Clauses:	Now is not a good time to apply for a mortgage *because not much property is available, prices are high, and interest rates are rising.*

Exercise 18.6

Add commas to separate items in a series.

1. The prisoner's dinner consisted of a piece of stale bread a bowl of soup and a cup of water.
2. He tore at the bread with his teeth gulped up the soup and washed them down with the water.
3. Bananas mangos coconuts and pineapples are all tropical fruits.
4. Washington Jefferson Lincoln Roosevelt Truman and Kennedy are very famous Presidents, but who remembers Fillmore Pierce Hayes Taft or Cleveland?
5. To become a good carpenter, you must learn to use tools to identify different types of wood and to make careful measurements.
6. The band stopped playing the dancers stopped dancing and the lights dimmed.

7. When you go to the store, pick up milk bread and eggs.
8. John Mike and Sarah are all baseball fans, but John likes the Red Sox Mike likes the Yankees and Sarah likes the Cubs.
9. Looking straight ahead balancing herself gracefully and stepping carefully forward, the tightrope walker began her performance.
10. The Studebaker the De Soto and the Nash were once popular cars, but they are no longer manufactured.

Rule 4: Commas Set off Sentence Interrupters

Sometimes a word or phrase interrupts the flow of a sentence. This does not mean that there is something wrong with the sentence. The interrupter adds information, although the sentence could be understood without it. Interrupters can be one word, a phrase, or even a clause. Use a comma both before and after the interrupter.

Words:	The drinks are expensive. The food, *however,* is priced reasonably and is very tasty.
	The restaurant, *consequently,* attracts customers who care more about food than drinks.
Phrases:	We will, *of course,* come to the wedding.
	Most everyone, *at one time or another,* falls in love.
Clauses:	Writing an essay, *as you know,* takes planning and time.
	Siamese cats, *though they can be mean,* are very popular pets.

Sentence interrupters, like sentence openers, can often be punctuated by ear. If you read the example sentences aloud, you will notice a pause before and after the interrupter. Put commas where you pause. Most beginning writers have little trouble with the comma before the interrupter, but they tend to forget the comma after it. Remember to put commas both *before* and *after* sentence interrupters.

Exercise 18.7

Add commas where needed with sentence interrupters. If a comma is correctly used, circle it.

1. Walt Whitman, according to F. O. Mathiessen is America's greatest poet.
2. Other American poets of course have written great poems.
3. Emily Dickinson along with Whitman is considered one of the greatest American poets of the nineteenth century.
4. In the twentieth century, T. S. Eliot wrote "The Wasteland," and it, of course, ranks among the best poems ever written.
5. Eliot as a result earned respect and fame worldwide.
6. Eliot's poems however are difficult to read.
7. Many Americans, consequently, have not read "The Wasteland" or any other Eliot poems.
8. Poetry, as we know has never been very popular in America.
9. Walt Whitman nevertheless tried to write poems that would be read by common people.
10. Eliot unlike Whitman, wrote poems that only highly educated people can understand.

Exercise 18.8

Where needed, add commas to set off sentence interrupters. Circle any commas used correctly to punctuate interrupters.

Painting a room is not that difficult if you follow the right procedures. You will, however have to have the proper equipment: paint rollers, a roller pan, drop cloths, a brush for the trim, masking tape, and of course enough paint. Before painting, you must prepare the walls by filling in all cracks and holes with spackling compound and by washing the walls thoroughly. The preparation though time consuming will ensure a good paint job. Once you have prepared the walls, place masking tape on the edges of the woodwork. Then, spread your drop cloths on the floor. Next, using the brush, paint about a two-inch border around the woodwork. Now, fill the roller pan with paint. Using the roller begin painting the walls. Painting with a roller unlike painting with a brush, takes very little time. Use even strokes to cover the walls thoroughly. Before you know it, your room will look fresh and clean. And as a result of doing the job yourself you will save money.

Review an essay of your own, circling commas used correctly with interrupters and adding commas where needed.

Rule 5: Commas Set off Nonessential Phrases and Clauses

Nonessential phrases and clauses add information to a sentence, but without them, the sentence would still make its main point. Nonessential phrases and clauses often appear in the middle of sentences, as in these examples:

Phrases:	Enrico Fermi, *a University of Chicago professor,* was a pioneer in the development of nuclear power.
	The furnace, *installed in 1970,* no longer works efficiently.
	Isaiah Williams, *running at his best,* won the marathon.
Clauses:	Enrico Fermi, *who was a University of Chicago professor,* was a pioneer in the development of nuclear power.
	Sicilian pizza, *because it has a thick crust,* is more filling than other types of pizza.

Nonessential phrases and clauses also can appear at the end of a sentence. When they do, a comma comes before them and a period after.

Phrases:	The boy fell off his tricycle, *scraping his knee.*
	Mrs. Phelps wanted a Pekingese, *a dog originally bred in China.*
Clauses:	The workers at the nursing home were doing a wonderful job, *though no one except the patients knew it.*
	Sabina rode a Vincent's Black Shadow, *which is a rare motorcycle no longer manufactured.*

In all of these sentences, we could take out the words between the commas or after the comma and before the period, and we would still get the main point of the sentence. Of course, we would not have as much information, but the main point would not change. Like sentence interrupters, nonessential phrases and clauses can sometimes be punctuated by ear. But remember: If the nonessential part is in the middle of the sentence, put the comma *before and after* it.

Exercise 18.9

Add commas needed to punctuate nonessential phrases and clauses. Circle commas used correctly with a nonessential phrase or clause.

1. Alejandro Varges a doctor from Brazil recently moved to California and opened a clinic.
2. Mexico which is the name of a country, is also the name of a small town in Missouri.
3. We are reading *Billy Budd* Herman Melville's last book.
4. The draft of *Billy Budd*, which was unfinished when Melville died, was edited by scholars and published in the 1920s, nearly forty years after it was written.
5. Buzz Aldrin who was one of the first humans on the moon had a difficult life in the years immediately after he retired from NASA, but he overcame his problems including depression.
6. Willi Kwong a senior from Malaysia was offered a job by the bank of Hong Kong which is one of the most prestigious banks in the world.
7. A Rolls-Royce Silver Cloud which costs over $100,000 is guaranteed for life.
8. The Silver Cloud once had a sealed hood, which prevented anyone but a certified Rolls-Royce mechanic from working on the car.
9. Boston Celtics' star Larry Bird played college basketball at Indiana State University which is often mistaken for Indiana University known for its great teams coached by Bobby Knight.
10. Bird who was a freshmen at Indiana University transferred to Indiana State because he wanted to attend a smaller school.

Exercise 18.10

In the following paragraph, add commas needed to punctuate nonessential phrases and clauses. Circle any comma used correctly with a nonessential phrase or clause.

Shopping at home which was unheard of just a few years ago is now a billion-dollar business. With cable TV reaching millions of homes, TV has become a live catalogue, and buyers with major credit cards can pick up the phone and make a purchase choosing items from jewelry to barbecue grills. The various items, which are supposedly priced low appear on the screen for about five minutes with their price and a phone number. An enthusiastic announcer describes the item making it sound like the bargain of a lifetime. Though TV shopping is growing, most people wanting to see exactly what they are buying still shop in stores.

When you punctuate a sentence having nonessential phrases and clauses, make sure they are nonessential. Sometimes a phrase or clause is necessary to tell what or whom you are talking about. In this case, you do not set it off in commas:

Phrases:	The woman *sitting in the third row* is George's mother. (Without the phrase, we would not know which woman was George's mother.)
	William Shakespeare's play *Timon of Athens* is often considered his weakest work. (Without the phrase giving us the title, we would not know which of Shakespeare's plays was being discussed.)
Clause:	I do not enjoy interacting with people **who are not courteous**. (Here the clause is necessary to identify the kind of people the subject does not like.)

You would not set off the phrases and clauses in these sentences because they essential to the reader's understanding of the sentences.

Exercise 18.11

Add and remove commas where necessary in the following sentences.

1. Students who study, will earn better grades.
2. Mark Twain's novel, *Huckleberry Finn,* can be enjoyed by young and old alike.
3. My roommate who is from Georgia attended private schools all her life.
4. Tim burst into the room screaming that Martians were chasing him.

5. Several of the friends, that Leon made in college, still keep in touch with him.
6. *The Rocky Horror Picture Show* which was originally a play, was made into a film that has become a cult classic with college students around the nation.
7. The car, in the left lane, swerved in front of me as I pulled onto the highway.
8. The American team boycotted the 1980 Olympics in Moscow when Russia invaded Afghanistan an act that angered President Carter.
9. Some, of the Olympians, were not in favor of the boycott which was designed to protest the invasion.
10. The Apple Computer Company which was founded by Steve Jobs progressed from a tiny operation to an international corporation in less than twenty years.

Review an essay of your own, correcting any comma errors in the use of nonessential clauses and phrases.

Using Semicolons

The semicolon has two uses. One is rare; the other is common. The rare use requires a semicolon between items in a series when there are commas within each item. This sounds confusing, but the following paragraph will illustrate the rule:

The favorites to win the state basketball tournament are the Greenville Tigers, whose star players are Hall, Marx, and O'Keefe; the West Park Braves, who rely on Palmero, Van Bibber, and Cruz; and the South Central Titans, who boast the strongest frontline in the league with McGee, Washington, and Nix.

The three main items in a series in this sentence are the teams: the Tigers, the Braves, and the Titans. But for each team a list of players is mentioned. Each list forms a series by itself, so the players' names must be set off in commas. To avoid confusion, the main items in the sentence—the names of the teams—are separated by semicolons. This kind of sentence is rare, but if you want to know more about it, consult a handbook of grammar.

The second use of the semicolon is quite common. As you may remember from the discussion in Chapter 14, semicolons can help you to fix comma splices and run-on sentences. Simply stated, the rule is:

Use a semicolon when you join two sentences without a coordinating conjunction (BAFNOSY).
    The sun was going down; people were leaving the beach.
    My new suit fit well; my new shoes were too tight.
    Writing is fun; however, grammar can be boring.
    Some people think studying grammar is fun; others hate it.
    Although the Corvair was a poorly engineered car, it is now a classic; consequently, collectors will pay a high price for a Corvair in good condition.

Notice that each pair of sentences could also be joined with a coordinating conjunction and a comma. Notice also that some sentences use conjunctive adverbs, such as *however* and *consequently*. But because these connectors are not coordinating conjunctions, you need to use the semicolon with them. Compare the sentences above with these, which use a comma and a coordinating conjunction:

    The sun was going down, *and* people were leaving the beach.
    My new suit fit well, *but* my new shoes were too tight.
    Writing is fun, *yet* grammar can be boring.
    Some people think studying grammar is fun, *but* others hate it.
    Although the Corvair was a poorly engineered car, it is now a classic, *so* collectors will pay a high price for a Corvair in good condition.

Whether you choose to join sentences with a comma and coordinating conjunction or with a semicolon depends on the effect you want to create. A semicolon usually draws a tighter relationship between the sentences and can be especially effective if both sentences are short: "Edmund moved to Chicago; he stayed there the rest of his life." Also, you should vary the way you connect sentences to create sentence variety.

The semicolon is an easy way to join two sentences, but be sure that when you use it, both sentences you join are complete. A common error is to begin a sentence with a dependent clause (not a complete sentence), follow it with a semicolon, and then end with an independent clause. That is nonstandard because the dependent clause should be followed by a comma. Compare these sentences:

Nonstandard: Because many people rent movies to watch at home on a VCR; attendance is down at cinemas.
Standard: Because many people rent movies to watch at home on a VCR, attendance is down at cinemas.

Another common error is to join two sentences with a comma and a connector that is *not* a coordinating conjunction (*consequently, however, moreover, nevertheless, then, thus, therefore,* etc.).

Nonstandard: The lights in the theater dimmed, *then*, the curtain went up.
Standard: The lights in the theater dimmed; *then*, the curtain went up.

Exercise 18.12

Add semicolons where needed in these sentences. Replace an incorrectly used semicolon with a comma. If a sentence is punctuated correctly, put a C next to it.

1. Orange juice is sweet grapefruit juice is sour.
2. When the orange crop is threatened by an early frost; the price of oranges rises.
3. The winter will be over soon then, the weather will get warmer.
4. Although we were tired, we went to the opera; after all, we had paid a lot of money for the tickets, so we couldn't waste them.
5. Your paper was excellent it earned an A.
6. Because knights wore heavy armor; they were not very agile in a fight, but they were well protected.
7. Disposable lighters first became popular in the late 1960s now they are more common than matches.
8. Broken bones were once set in casts made of plaster; today, casts are made of fiberglass.
9. Because fiberglass casts are lighter; patients on crutches have an easier time getting around.
10. Beginning writers often confuse semicolons and commas, therefore, it is good to know the rules for using them.

Exercise 18.13

In the following paragraph, correct any errors in the use of semicolons and commas.

We take plastic bags for granted, however, the process by which they are made is interesting and complex. Plastic pellets are put into a machine called an extruder. It melts them down and forces them through a long, steel tube, then a plastic film comes out of the other end in a bubble. The machine, in other words, works like a child's bubble pipe. The plastic bubble is then blown full of air until it is the right size for the bags being made. This bubble is then stretched into a tube and inserted into a set of rollers. The plastic tube passes through the rollers, and it is flattened and cooled. At the end of the rollers, there is a cutting and sealing device it cuts a certain length of the tube and seals the bottom end to make a bag. Though this process is complex; an extruder is capable of producing thousands of bags a day.

Using Apostrophes

You are very familiar with apostrophes used in contractions: *couldn't, don't, doesn't, he'll, I'm, I'll, she'd, we're, they're,* and so on. You also know that apostrophes are used to show possession, but beginning writers often have trouble with the rules for using apostrophes to show possession. Before we discuss the rules, try the following exercise.

Exercise 18.14

Underline the name of the author in each sentence. Remember that the titles of the author's work are either in quotation marks or in italics.

1. The stories in Doris Lessing's *The Grass Is Singing* are based on her experiences as a young British woman living in Africa.
2. Ken Purdy's essay "The Honest Repairman—A Vanishing American" is unfair to those repairmen who do honest work.
3. In Don Yago's "Symbols of Mankind," there are many instances of striking or catchy language.
4. "Letter from Birmingham Jail" is one of Martin Luther King's most powerful essays.
5. I like Shakespeare's plays more than modern plays; for example, I find Eugene O'Neill's plays depressing.

6. Shakespeare's *As You Like It* is my favorite comedy, but I think *King Lear*, which is one of Shakespeare's tragedies, is my favorite play of all.
7. In our political science class, we are reading Nicolò Machiavelli's *The Prince*, a book written in the Renaissance but relevant to politics today.
8. Kurt Vonnegut's novels have been very popular with college students over the last twenty years, but many literary critics believe that only Vonnegut's *Slaughterhouse Five* is a truly accomplished novel.
9. In the last ten years, Mina Shaughnessy's *Errors and Expectations* has had an impact on methods of teaching beginners to write.
10. Richard Altick's *Victorian People and Ideas* offers valuable historical background for the student of Victorian literature.

Now that you have underlined the names of each author, compare them. What do they all have in common? If you answered that each has an apostrophe and *-s* added to the end, you are right. The added apostrophe and *-s* show that the author is the "owner" of the work that follows, for example: Shakespeare's *King Lear,* Lessing's *The Grass Is Singing,* O'Neill's plays, King's most powerful essays.

You use the apostrophe and *s* to show possession when you are writing about someone's work, whether Shakespeare's *Othello* or your friend Mary's essay. But you also need to show possession when you are writing about other types of ownership as well. For example, if you were writing about a car belonging to your father, you would write, "my father's car." Here are some additional examples: Professor Klein's class, Wally's sister, Lisa's grades. Washington's victories, the car's engine, Monday night's television schedule, the book's pages, and so on.

These last two examples may seem a bit confusing. You may wonder how a night of the week can own anything. But if you think about it, the television schedule *belongs* to Monday night rather than to another night of the week, just as the pages belong to the book you are talking about rather than to some other book. Here are some additional examples: today's world, yesterday's news, the machine's controls, the rocket's flight, the essay's thesis. In each of these examples, the word following the apostrophe and *s* belongs to the word that has the apostrophe and *s* on the end of it.

The only possessive words that do not contain apostrophes are pronouns (see Chapter 16). When a pronoun contains an apostrophe, it is a contraction. Compare these lists of pronouns:

Contractions	Possessives
it's = it is	its
who's = who is	whose
he's = he is	his
she's = she is	her, hers
we're = we are	our, ours
you're = you are	your, yours
they're = they are	their, theirs

Exercise 18.15

Add apostrophes where needed in the following sentences.

1. People admired Alans dog for its thick, shiny coat.
2. Sunbathers will be very happy with tomorrows weather forecast.
3. The writers job is to make the readers job as easy as possible.
4. Few young people today have seen any of Charlie Chaplins films.
5. Of all of Phillip Roths novels, *Portnoys Complaint* probably was the most successful with the general public because of its controversial sexual content.
6. Eves car is older than yours.
7. All seasons have their beauty, but nothing compares with autumns brightly colored leaves.
8. Though Doug did poorly on last weeks exam, he earned an A on this weeks.
9. The mayor was opposed to the city councils call for higher taxes.
10. Many of E. L. Doctorows novels use historical persons as fictional characters.

Exercise 18.16

In the following paragraphs, add apostrophes where needed. The possessive words already have the -s added, so all you need to do is add the apostrophe before the -s.

1. Last weekend, my friend Bills car broke down in the middle of the night as he was driving back to campus after attending his former high schools homecoming game. So he called me at 3:00 A.M. to come out to

help him. He told me he had his tools with him, but Bills mechanical ability leaves much to be desired, so he needed my help. When I got there, the cars trunk was stuck, so we couldn't get to Bills tools. He ended up calling a tow truck, which he could have done in the first place. Needless to say, I wasn't too happy.

2. Englands theatrical tradition may be the greatest in the world. While there were plays written before the English Renaissance, the Renaissance represents the beginning of greatness on the British stage. Thomas Kyds *The Spanish Tragedy* is one of the important plays of this period because it probably influenced Shakespeares *Hamlet*. Christopher Marlowes *Edward II* and *Dr. Faustus* certainly rank among the great plays of the English Rennaissance, and, of course, Shakespeares *Hamlet*, *King Lear*, and *Macbeth* may be the most powerful tragedies ever written.

In the previous exercises, the possessive words were singular. To show possession when a word is plural, there are two rules to follow:

1. If the plural word ends in *s*, just add an apostrophe, for example: the birds' flight south, the Smiths' home, the Yankees' position in the standings, the companies' hiring policies, the three boys' parents.
2. If the word is plural but does not already end in *s*, then add the apostrophe and *s*: the women's opinions, the men's opinions, the children's favorite stories.

Exercise 18.17

Add apostrophes where needed in the following sentences. Be careful to consider both singular and plural words.

1. The Presidents speech praised the Northeastern states success in reducing unemployment.
2. The childrens school clothes cost more than their parents new coats.
3. Three cars tires were slashed yesterday on Ninth Street.
4. Outside the deans office, marchers and signs proclaimed the unfairness of the tuition hikes, but the students protest turned out to be futile when tuition was raised for the next semester.

5. The doctors fee for setting Peters broken leg was more than reasonable.
6. Did you receive this months *Time* magazine in todays mail?
7. Carlos worked so quickly that he earned a days pay in a half a days time.
8. Kenny got a job selling womens shoes.
9. The child ruined the tables finish when he tried to clean it with cleanser.
10. The Larsons new home is located on Poplar Street.

Exercise 18.18

Add apostrophes where needed in this paragraph.

By twelve o'clock, nearly a hundred men lined up outside the citys only soup kitchen. When the doors opened, they filed in. Tables lined the long hall. The mens lunch was a bowl of soup, a slice of buttered bread, and a cup of coffee. Tired and hungry, they were thankful for anything to eat. When they finished the meal, they knew they would be back on the streets, facing unemployment and peoples indifference.

Using Other Marks of Punctuation

Less commonly used marks of punctuation are the **colon, dash,** and **quotation marks.** Though you may not use these marks often, you should know the rules governing them.

The Colon

The colon is formed with two dots (:), like a period above a period. The colon has two uses that beginning writers should know:

To divide hours and minutes in reference to time:
It is now 9:56 A.M.

The accident occurred at 2:15 P.M. at Center Avenue and Main Street.
To introduce a list following a complete statement:
Valerie earned letters in three sports: volleyball, basketball, and field
hockey.
Tyrone is taking four courses this semester: basic writing, world civ-
ilization, short fiction, and computer science.

Using the colon to separate hours and minutes is not difficult. Using the
colon to introduce a list can be tricky. Notice that in each example a complete
statement comes before the list. The statement must make sense without the list.
Thus, you do not use a colon after a verb that introduces a list. Compare these
sentences:

Incorrect: Valerie's favorite sports are: volleyball, basketball, and field
hockey.
Correct: Valerie's favorite sports are volleyball, basketball, and field
hockey.
Correct: Valerie has three favorite sports: volleyball, basketball, and field
hockey.

The first sentence is incorrect because without the list it would not make sense
by itself. You could not just write, "Valerie's favorite sports are," for the reader
would not know what you meant. Introduce the list with a colon only when the
statement before it can make sense without the list.

Exercise 18.19

Add colons where needed, cross out unneeded colons, and circle colons used
correctly.

1. Eileen has begun a strict exercise program that includes: jogging,
   weightlifting, and aerobics.
2. Though the South lost the Civil War, the Confederate Army boasted
   three great generals Robert E. Lee, Stonewall Jackson, and James
   Longstreet.
3. Barbara subscribes to five magazines: *Time, Newsweek, Life, Discover,*
   and *Fortune.*

4. Dr. Rentz had only three appointments available next week 3 15 on Monday, 11 30 on Tuesday, and 2 45 on Friday.
5. Kevin's favorite teachers are: Brennan, Jones, Hoffman, and Kleiner.
6. Kevin is in Kleiner's history class, which meets a 1 45 P.M.
7. We thought we would travel light to Europe, but we ended up taking: four suitcases, two garment bags, and two carry-on bags.
8. Elaine did not care what she got for Christmas, but her brother wanted: a Nintendo game, a new bicycle, hockey skates, and a pair of Air Jordans.
9. Three factors can affect a student's performance on a test: lack of preparation, fatigue, and unfair questions.
10. Three of the factors that can affect a student's performance on a test are: lack of preparation, fatigue, and unfair questions.

The Dash

The dash is a mark of punctuation that creates emphasis. On a typewriter or computer keyboard, you make a dash by typing two hyphens with no space in between. Though you should use dashes sparingly, they can come in handy when you want to draw attention to something. You can use dashes for the following:

To set off items in the middle of a sentence for emphasis:
Sandy Koufax—perhaps the greatest pitcher of the 1960s—refused to pitch on Jewish holidays because of his strong religious beliefs.
The Scandinavian countries—Denmark, Norway, Sweden, and Finland— are among the least warlike of nations.
To set off a list at the end of a sentence (in this use, the dash is an informal substitute for the more formal colon):
Returning from the carnival sick, the boy confessed to stuffing himself with all kinds of junk food—cotton candy, corn dogs, pizza, popcorn, elephant ears, and ice cream.
On Halloween, the Capitol Cinema will present an all-night show of the some of the scariest horror films ever made—*The Exorcist, Night of the Living Dead, Halloween,* and *Nightmare on Elm Street.*

To indicate an abrupt shift in the content of a sentence:
> Mrs. Wright, an eighty-year-old widow, drove only once a week—to church in a bright red Corvette.
> Dave dressed himself in his Sunday best—a pair of torn jeans and an old flannel shirt.

Remember to reserve the dash only for situations when you really want to add emphasis. Too many dashes will not create emphasis and will distract your reader.

Exercise 18.20

Write two sentences of your own for each use of the dash.

Quotation Marks

You use quotation marks primarily to indicate that you are using someone else's exact words. If you have translated someone else's words into your own words, you *do not* use quotation marks. Compare the following sentences:

> Exact words with quotation marks:
> John F. Kennedy said, "Ask not what your country can do for you, ask what you can do for your country."
> Lena asked, "Will you be going to Puerto Rico this summer?"
> Exact words translated with no quotation marks:
> John F. Kennedy said that we should not ask what our country can do for us, but we should ask what we can do for our country.
> Lena asked if I am going to Puerto Rico this summer.

In the second set of sentences, without the quotation marks, the words are the writer's, not the speaker's. Lena did not say, "if I am going to Puerto Rico this summer." Therefore, her words are not quoted.

Quotation marks are also used to indicate titles of songs, essays, stories, poems, chapter titles, and articles in magazines and newspapers:

Song: "I Want to Hold Your Hand," by the Beatles
Essay: "The American Scholar," by Ralph Waldo Emerson
Story: "The Lottery," by Shirley Jackson
Poem: "The Raven," by Edgar Allan Poe
Chapter title: "The Nature of Consciousness," in *Psychology and Life,* by Phillip G. Zimbardo
Magazine article: "Inquest on Intelligence," in *Newsweek*

Exercise 18.21

Add quotation marks where needed, cross out unneeded quotation marks, and circle any quotation marks used correctly.

1. Shakespeare wrote, Neither a borrower nor a lender be.
2. When Martin Luther King said "he had a dream," he inspired millions of struggling blacks.
3. Lynn said that her favorite song was Satisfaction by the Rolling Stones.
4. As Yogi Berra once said, "It ain't over 'til it's over."
5. The Bible says that "we should honor our parents."
6. Rita said that she is reading Hawthorne's short story "Young Goodman Brown" in her literature class.
7. I'll see you later, said Phil.
8. Lana is helping Tim edit his essay, Coping with Student Stress.
9. Did you say "you would come with us on vacation"?
10. In grade school, we learned to sing "The Star-Spangled Banner."

Quotation marks can also be used as a substitute for *so-called.* Often the word is used in jest. For instance, if someone who was supposed to be your friend treated you badly, you might write:

My "friend" Glen borrowed my car and then used it to take out my girl-friend.

Here Glen's actions no longer allow us to take the word *friend* seriously, so although Glen is called a friend, the writer does not really mean it.

Using Capital Letters

Writers use capital letters for many different purposes. Some are very common, and you probably know them already. Other uses are not as common, and you will need to edit carefully to ensure that you have capitalized all the necessary words. Let's look at nine of the most common uses of capital letters.

1. The first word of every sentence is capitalized. Though you may have learned this rule in grade school, don't forget it:

   Transistor radios first became popular in the 1950s.

2. The pronoun *I* is always capitalized. This is another common rule you should never forget:

   When the storm began, **I** quickly ran for cover because **I** was wearing a new suede jacket.

3. People's names are always capitalized, another common rule:

   Cliff and **Linda North** moved in next door to the **Johnsons**.

4. Specific titles are capitalized:

   Secretary of Education William Bennett advocated a core curriculum to standardize education in America.
   Dr. Andrea Lee was named **Chief Surgeon** at **Union Hospital**.
   Note: Do not capitalize titles used in a general way: The **president** of my fraternity resigned last week.

5. The names of races, religions, nationalities, places, and languages are capitalized whether they are used as nouns or adjectives:

Nouns	*Adjectives*
Italy	Italian food
English (the people or the language)	English customs
Judaism	Jewish holidays
Islam	Islamic faith

6. Capitalize names of historical periods, events, and documents:

History 101 includes coverage of the **Bronze Age.**
The British surrendered to the American colonists at the **Battle of Yorktown** in 1781.
In grade school, we memorized Lincoln's **Gettysburg Address.**

7. Capitalize names of organizations, businesses, and government departments and agencies:

Terri is pledging **Alpha Omicron Pi.**
After earning a degree in electronics, Susan went to work for **Zenith.**
The **Department of Education** was created during Carter's first term.

8. Capitalize the names of schools, departments in schools, specific courses, and degrees:

Mona earned a **Master of Business Administration** degree at **Temple University.**
Eric works in the offices of the **Department of English.**
The **Chemistry Department** supplies tutors for students taking **Chemistry 110.**
Note: Capitalize only *specific* courses: Usually, Vince hates history courses, but he is enjoying **History 240: History of India.**

9. Capitalize the names of days, months, and holidays:

Thanksgiving is celebrated on the third **Thursday** of **November.**
The first **Monday** in **September** is **Labor Day.**

Exercise 18.22

Add capital letters where needed, cross out unneeded capitals, and circle any capital letters used correctly.

1. Every October, jews celebrate rosh hoshanah, a holiday signifying the new year on the hebrew calendar.
2. Rufus Johnson, a former medical doctor, retired in florida.

3. professor Annette cook teaches Sociology at Sparks College.
4. If i cannot go bowling with you tomorrow, maybe we can go on saturday.
5. In 1776, the founders of America signed the declaration of independence, and today the signing is celebrated on the fourth of july.
6. i enjoy Mexican food because I like hot dishes.
7. The U.S senate consists of two members from each state.
8. Do you plan to take a Speech course this semester?
9. Yes, I have signed up for speech 105.
10. Several reporters interviewed lord Bacon of the british parliament.

Key Terms

Period: End punctuation that looks like a dot and that marks the end of declarative sentences and abbreviations.

Question mark: End punctuation that looks like a hook above a dot and that signifies that a sentence is a question.

Exclamation point: End punctuation that looks like a vertical line above a dot and that signifies emphasis or emotion.

Sentence opener: Any word, phrase, or dependent clause that comes before the first independent clause in a sentence. A comma is usually placed after a sentence opener.

Items in a series: Any of three or more words, phrases, or clauses that occur in a row. Commas separate items in a series.

Sentence interrupter: A word, phrase, or dependent clause that interrupts the flow of an independent clause. Interrupters are punctuated with commas before and after them.

Nonessential phrase or clause: A phrase or clause that occurs after or in the middle of an independent clause. It adds information, but the point of the sentence could be understood without it. It is set off from the independent clause with commas.

Semicolon: A mark of punctuation that looks like a period above a comma and that has two uses, one rare and one common. The rare use sets off items in a series that already have commas within them. The common use joins independent clauses without a coordinating conjunction or with connecting words such as *consequently, however, thus, then, therefore,* and so on.

Apostrophe: A mark of punctuation indicating where letters have been taken out in a contraction (*they're, he's, it's, couldn't*) or used with an *s* to show pos-

session (*Milt's gloves, Elaine's children*). If a word already ends in *s*, the apostrophe follows it (*the Tigers' coach, the houses' owners, the students' favorite hangout*).
Colon: The colon is a mark of punctuation that looks like one period placed above another and that is used to separate hours from minutes in time references or to introduce a list after a complete statement.
Quotation marks: Marks of punctuation placed around the exact words of a speaker or writer when repeated by another writer.

unit five

Essays for Reading

These essays all discuss aspects of standard English and attitudes toward correctness. In her essay "Grammar: I Survived It, So Can You," student Lori Floyd offers other students advice and encouragement as she tells of her own frustrations and accomplishments learning to use standard English in her writing. Rachel Jones wrote "What's Wrong with Black English?" when she was a sophomore at Southern Illinois University. The essay was then published in *Newsweek* and has since been reprinted many times in writing textbooks. Jones examines the problems dialect speakers—in her case, black dialect—face when they are in situations requiring standard English. "Speech Communities," by the late Paul Roberts, comes from his book *Understanding English*. Roberts, a former English professor and professional writer, argues that correctness in language depends upon the place in which speakers find themselves and the social groups to which they belong.

Grammar: I Survived It, So Can You
Lori Floyd (junior)

The word *grammar* evokes images that cause most people to cringe. It represents a field of knowledge that can make us feel inferior, uneasy, and frustrated. However, grammar can become interesting when you work to learn and understand it. I will admit that grasping grammatical concepts takes a long time; I feel ill when I think of all the exercises I have completed with limited success. However, I finally "got it" when I was a freshman in college and began applying grammar to writing. The long process of learning standard-English grammar takes a lot of practice and patience.

Grammar is difficult because as little children we learn sentence structure, verb forms, and so on from our parents, friends, and others around us. These basic "rules" seem adequate to guide us into our adult lives, but often we have picked up nonstandard usages. When we use standard English, our grammar must become more and more refined, and even though we feel learning grammar is difficult, we must try to perfect our use of standard English. Why? The best incentive I have found is money. Money and grammar may seem unconnected; however, we will not advance in our jobs, or even get a good job, if we cannot use standard English (particularly in writing) to communicate. This situation may not seem fair, but it is truly something to consider.

After I entered college and began to realize the connection between mastery of standard English and job opportunities, I panicked. I remembered completing all of those parts-of-speech exercises, fragment exercises, punctuation exercises, and so on, but I could not apply what I was supposed to be learning to my writing. It seemed as if these worksheets were first assigned in the primary grades and continued through high school and into college with only the subject matter changing. The first ones talked about a dog named Spot, and the last ones described sports, dances, or historical events. Now in college, I needed to know what comma splices were not just to complete an exercise but to eliminate them in my writing.

For me, writing became a way to understand the mechanics of standard English as well as a way to express myself. In my freshman composition class, I wrote (and wrote and wrote!) until I could see the framework of my sentences. Looking at the various parts of my own sentences, I could begin to see how they fit together into a whole working piece. It was like baking a cake. I knew what the individual ingredients of the exercises tasted like, but until I learned how to put them together, I didn't know what the finished product tasted like. After beginning to see the various ways to write and edit sentences, I began to try mixing these "ingredients" of standard English in different ways—adding a little spice, so to speak.

With variety comes mistakes, though, so being careful is a must because few people can achieve the best structure the first time through. It was hard for me to realize the importance of editing because after writing a sentence I did not want to cut half of it out or have to rearrange it. It is hard to be your own critic, but editing is the icing on the writing cake. After you have written and edited your own sentences several times, you will better understand those nasty "rules" that when violated cause low grades and lower self-esteem.

When you head for your 8:00 A.M. English class, remember that your feelings toward grammar are not isolated. Many people feel the same as you. It really helps to write and edit your own sentences as well as other people's. As you put forth the effort, think of the improved academic success and job opportunities, and be patient. Learning standard English takes time. When you learn to avoid an error, be proud of your accomplishment. When you learn how to fix a comma splice or correct a verb error, teach a friend; knowledge is more fun when it is shared, and standard English is something we can all share.

Questions for Study and Discussion

1. How did Floyd finally come to understand standard-English grammar?
2. How does Floyd say we first learn grammar? Why can our first lessons be inadequate?

3. What motivated Floyd to learn and apply standard English? Does her motivation make sense?

4. Why was Floyd unable to learn grammar by just doing exercises?

5. How did she finally apply what she learned in exercises to her own writing?

6. Why was it hard for Floyd to realize that she could not always achieve standard sentence structure "the first time through"?

7. When Floyd began to grasp grammatical principles, what did she do in her sentences? With what results?

8. What is Floyd's purpose, and who is her audience?

9. Why does Floyd suggest teaching a point of grammar to another student? Can you think of another benefit of teaching someone else?

10. Write a brief paragraph discussing how Floyd's experience with grammar is similar to or different from your own.

What's Wrong With Black English?
Rachel Jones

William Labov, a noted linguist, once said about the use of black English, "It is the goal of most black Americans to acquire full control of the standard language without giving up their own culture." He also suggested that there are certain advantages to having two ways to express one's feelings. I wonder if the good doctor might also consider the goals of those black Americans who have full control of standard English but who are every now and then troubled by that colorful, grammar-to-the-winds patois that is black English. Case in point—me.

I'm a 21-year old black born to a family that would probably be considered lower middle class—which in my mind is a polite way of describing a condition only slightly better than poverty. Let's just say we rarely if ever did the winter-vacation thing in the Caribbean. I've often had to defend my humble beginnings to a most unlikely group of people for an even less likely reason. Because of the way I talk, some of my black peers look at me sideways and ask, "Why do you talk like you're white?"

The first time it happened to me, I was nine years old. Cornered in the school bathroom by the class bully and her sidekick, I was offered the opportunity to swallow a few of my teeth unless I satisfactorily explained why I always got good grades, why I talked "proper" or "white." I had no ready answer for her, save the fact that my mother had from the time I was old enough to talk stressed the importance of reading and learning, or that L. Frank Baum and Ray Bradbury were my closest companions. I read all my older brothers' and sisters' literature textbooks more faithfully than they did, and even lightweights like the Bobbsey Twins and Trixie Belden were allowed into my bookish inner circle. I don't remember exactly what I told those girls, but I somehow talked my way out of a beating.

'White pipes'. I was reminded once again of my "white pipes" problem while apartment hunting in Evanston, Illinois, last winter. I doggedly made out lists of available places and called all around. I would immediately be invited over—and immediately turned down. The thinly concealed looks of shock when the front door opened clued me in, along with the flustered instances of "just got off the phone with the girl who was ahead of you and she wants the rooms." When I finally found a place to live, my roommate stirred up old memories when she remarked a few months later, "You know, I was surprised when I first saw you. You sounded white over the phone." Tell me another one, sister.

I should've asked her a question I've wanted an answer to for years: How does one "talk white"? The silly side of me pictures a rabid white foam spewing forth when I speak. I don't use Valley Girl jargon, so that's not what's meant in my case. Actually, I've pretty much deduced what people mean when they say that to me, and the implications are really frightening.

It means that I'm articulate and well versed. It means that I can talk as freely about John Steinbeck as I can about Rick James. It means that "ain't" and "he be" are not staples of my vocabulary and are only used around family and friends. (It is almost Jekyll and Hyde-ish the way I can slip out of academic abstractions into a long, lean, double-negative-filled dialogue, but I've come to terms with that aspect of my personality.) As a child, I found it hard to believe that's what people meant by "talking proper"; that would've meant that good grades and standard English were equated with white skin, and that went against everything I'd ever been taught. Running into the same type of mentality as an adult has confirmed the depressing reality that for many blacks, standard English is not only unfamiliar, it is socially unacceptable.

James Baldwin once defended black English by saying it had added "vitality to the language," and even went so far as to label it a language in its own right, saying, "Language [i.e., black English] is a political instrument" and a "vivid and crucial key to identity." But did Malcolm X urge blacks to take power in this country "any way y'all can"? Did Martin Luther King, Jr., say to blacks, "I has been to the mountaintop, and I done seed the Promised Land"? Toni Morrison, Alice Walker, and James Baldwin did not achieve their eloquence, grace, and stature by using only black English in their writing. Andrew Young, Tom Bradley, and Barbara Jordan did not acquire political power by saying, "Y'all crazy if you ain't gon vote for me." They all have full command of standard English, and I don't think that knowledge takes away from their blackness or commitment to black people.

Soulful. I know from experience that it's important for black people, stripped of culture and heritage, to have something they can point to and say,

"This is ours, *we* can comprehend it, *we* alone can speak it with a soulful flourish." I'd be lying if I said that the rhythms of my people caught up in "some serious rap" don't sound natural and right to me sometimes. But how heartwarming is it for those same brothers when they hit the pavement searching for employment? Studies have proven that the use of ethnic dialects decreases power in the marketplace. "I be" is acceptable on the corner but not with the boss.

Am I letting capitalistic, European-oriented thinking fog the issue? Am I selling out blacks to an ideal of assimilating, being as much like white as possible? I have not formed a personal political ideology, but I do know this: It hurts me to hear black children use black English, knowing that they will be at yet another disadvantage in an educational system already full of stumbling blocks. It hurts me to sit in lecture halls and hear fellow black students complain that the professor "be tripping dem out using big words dey can't understand." And what hurts most is to be stripped of my own blackness simply because I know my way around the English language.

I would have to disagree with Labov in one respect. My goal is not so much to acquire full control of both standard and black English, but to one day see more black people less dependent on a dialect that excludes them from full participation in the world we live in. I don't think I talk white, I think I talk right.

Questions for Study and Discussion

1. According to William Labov, what is the goal of most black Americans regarding language?
2. How did Jones learn to speak standard English?
3. Why did Jones have trouble with bullies in school?
4. What other problems did she have as a result of her speech?
5. Why does Jones think it is dangerous to believe that speaking in standard English is "talking white"?
6. Jones quotes James Baldwin, a great black writer. What did Baldwin mean when he said, "Language is a political instrument" and "a key to identity"?
7. What examples does Jones give that show language as a political instrument?
8. Jones mentions several black politicians and writers, arguing that they used standard English to gain power. Can you think of times these people might use black English?
9. Jones seems to contradict herself when she says she often enjoys speaking black English with friends and family, but then says she talks "right" when

speaking standard English. Is one language right and the other wrong? Are there times when black English would be right?

10. Write a brief paragraph discussing your exposure to dialect, your own or that of others. Consider how dialects can be necessary to personal identity and a hindrance to social mobility.

Speech Communities
Paul Roberts (professional)

Speech communities are formed by many features: age, geography, education, occupation, social position. Young people speak differently from old people, Kansans differently from Virginians, Yale graduates differently from Dannemora graduates. Now let us pose a delicate question: Aren't some of these speech communities better than others? That is, isn't better language heard in some than in others?

Well, yes, of course. One speech community is always better than all the rest. This is the group in which one happens to find oneself. The writer would answer unhesitatingly that the noblest, loveliest, purest English is that heard in the Men's Faculty Club of San Jose State College, San Jose, California. He would admit, of course, that the speech of some of the younger members leaves something to be desired; that certain recent immigrants from Harvard, Michigan, and other foreign parts need to work on the laughable oddities lingering in their speech; and that members of certain departments tend to introduce a lot of queer terms that can only be described as jargon. But in general, the English of the Faculty Club is ennobling and sweet.

As a practical matter, good English is whatever English is spoken by the group in which one moves contentedly and at ease. To the bum on Main Street in Los Angeles, good English is the language of other L.A. bums. Should he wander onto the campus of UCLA, he would find the talk there unpleasant, confusing, and comical. He might agree, if pressed, that the college man speaks "correctly" and he doesn't. But in his heart, he knows better. He wouldn't talk like them college jerks if you paid him.

If you admire the language of other speech communities more than you do your own, the reasonable hypothesis is that you are dissatisfied with the community itself. It is not precisely other speech that attracts you but the people who use the speech. Conversely, if some language strikes you as unpleasant or foolish or rough, it is presumably because the speakers themselves seem so.

To many people, the sentence "Where is he at?" sounds bad. It is bad, they would say, in and of itself. The sounds are bad. But this is very hard to prove. If "Where is he at?" is bad because it had bad sound combinations, then presumably "Where is the cat?" or "Where is my hat?" are just as bad, yet no one thinks them so. Well, then, "Where is he at?" is bad because it uses too many words. One gets the same meaning from "Where is he?" so why add the *at*? True. Then "He going with us?" is a better sentence than "Is he going with us?" You don't really need the *is*, so why put it in?

Certainly there are some features of language to which we can apply the terms *good* and *bad*, *better* and *worse*. Clarity is usually better than obscurity; precision is better than vagueness. But these are not often what we have in mind when we speak of good and bad English. If we like the speech of upper-class Englishmen, the presumption is that we admire upper-class Englishmen—their characters, culture, habits of mind. Their sounds and words simply come to connote the people themselves and become admirable therefore. If we knew the same sounds and words from people who were distasteful to us, we would find the speech ugly.

This is not to say that correctness and incorrectness do not exist in speech. They obviously do, but they are relative to the speech community—or communities—in which one operates. As a practical matter, correct speech is that which sounds normal or natural to one's comrades. Incorrect speech is that which evokes in them discomfort or hostility or disdain.

Questions for Study and Discussion

1. What does Roberts mean when he says the best speech community "is the group in which one happens to find oneself"?

2. How serious is Roberts when he says that the best English is found in the Men's Faculty Club of San Jose State College?

3. Why wouldn't L.A. bum "talk like them college jerks if you paid him"?

4. Why do people, according to Roberts, admire some versions of English more than others? Does his argument apply to Rachel Jones's admiration of standard English?

5. What point is Roberts trying to make in the paragraph where he says that "He going with us?" is a better sentence than "Is he going with us?"

6. To what "features of language can we apply the terms *good* and *bad*, *better* and *worse*"?

7. Do you agree with Roberts's point that language connotes the people who speak it? Why or why not?

8. Roberts says most people see speech as incorrect when it makes them feel uncomfortable or hostile toward the speaker. Relate this argument to Jones's problem with her peers.

9. Rachel Jones argues that standard English is "right." Roberts argues that correctness is "relative to the speech community." What do you think?

10. Roberts says "correct speech is that which sounds normal or natural to one's comrades." Write a brief paragraph explaining to what extent you agree or disagree.

Index